On the Penitentiary System in the United States, and Its Application in France

ON THE

PENITENTIARY SYSTEM

IN

THE UNITED STATES,

AND

ITS APPLICATION IN FRANCE;

WITH AN APPENDIX

ON PENAL COLONIES,

AND ALSO,

STATISTICAL NOTES.

BY

G. DE BEAUMONT AND A. DE TOQUEVILLE,

COUNSELLORS IN THE ROYAL COURT OF PARIS, AND MEMBERS OF THE HISTORI-
CAL SOCIETY OF PENNSYLVANIA.

TRANSLATED FROM THE FRENCH,

WITH AN INTRODUCTION, NOTES AND ADDITIONS.

By FRANCIS LIEBER.

PHILADELPHIA:
CAREY, LEA & BLANCHARD.
1833.

PRINTED BY LYDIA R. BAILEY.

TO

EDWARD LIVINGSTON,

LATE SECRETARY OF STATE OF THE UNITED STATES,

ROBERTS VAUX, Esq.,

OF PHILADELPHIA,

AND

C. J. A. MITTERMAIER,

PROFESSOR OF CRIMINAL LAW IN THE UNIVERSITY OF HEIDELBERG,

THIS VOLUME

IS MOST RESPECTFULLY INSCRIBED,

BY

FRANCIS LIEBER.

PREFACE AND INTRODUCTION

OF THE TRANSLATOR.

———

MM. de Beaumont and de Tocqueville had the kindness to send me, a few months ago, their work on the Penitentiary System in the United States, before it had issued from the press in Paris, requesting me, at the same time, to translate it, if possible, for the American public. My time was, at that period, and is still so much occupied by previous engagements, that I doubted at first whether I should be able to comply with the wishes of my friends, though my personal regard for them would not have allowed me to hesitate for a moment. The great importance of the subject, however, soon induced me to undertake the task, trusting that the public would excuse, in a work of this kind, the value of which essentially depends upon statements of facts, and upon statistical numbers, a want of that accuracy and precision of language, without which, in the ordinary course, no work ought to appear before its reader. The authors themselves seem to have considered the facts and observations which they had to communicate, of an importance greatly superior to the manner of conveying them to the public; but may I not hope for the reader's indulgence for yet another reason? A man may adopt a foreign country as his own, and be devoted to its institutions with his whole soul, because they are what he always wished and strove for; he may physically and morally acclimatize himself, yet his language will prove the most difficult in accommodating itself to the change. In my case I feel it sensibly: The heart is much more willing than the tongue. If the reader, however, will excuse some peculiarities, and a want of ease and pliability of style, my translation will be found, I hope, at least clear and intelligible, I know it to be faithful. A few of the statements of the authors I have thought to be erroneous, and I have not omitted to add in a note what I hold to be correct. In most cases, however, the reader will find that they investigated the subject, for the inquiry of which they were sent by their government to this country, with faithful zeal, intelligence, and that readiness to see and state the truth, which we do not find too often in visiters of our country. It is always of great service to hear the observations upon one's own country, made by a foreigner who has a discerning eye and an honest heart. What intelligent German has not read with profit some parts of Madame de Staël's work on his country? Even if such observers are mistaken, which they cannot possibly always avoid being, provided they are intelligent and sincere, their remarks will always be useful and welcome to those who truly love their country. But sickened as the Americans naturally are by the smattering observations of hasty travellers, whose arrogance generally is in an inverse ratio to the length of time which they spent in this country, the chief interest of which consists in the beauty of its nature, and the character of its institutions, it will be a peculiar satisfaction to the reader to find in the following pages an important institution of his country once carefully inquired into. Institutions must be studied, their history as well as their operation cannot be understood by a superficial glance, and hence there is good reason why we find so little of them in the descriptions of a six weeks', three months', eight months' residence, or at most in that of a year and a half in the United States. In the work of which I offer a translation, the authors give the result of their minute inquiry into an institution, which, besides its importance to all mankind, has for Americans the additional interest of having originated with them, and been brought to a high degree of perfection. Whether they praise or censure, is in itself of little interest, compared with the fact that they studied their subject earnestly, and state their result frankly. Truth appears to have been their sole object, and no pains were spared to arrive at this noble end, or to give an accurate statement of the various investigations—a care which shows itself even in the correct writing and printing of the many names of persons and places occurring in the work, which, though apparently an insignificant matter, will appear in a different light to all who are acquainted with the general and great neglect of the orthography of foreign names in French works.

I have added numerous notes, sometimes when I differed in opinion with the authors, sometimes further to elucidate their statements, but they do not form a regular series of comments, partly because I had not sufficient leisure for this work, and partly because I should have been obliged to touch upon subjects which it was impossible for me to treat of with any satisfaction to myself in a note, having made them for a long time already objects of study and inquiry, and being desirous to give the result in a more connected form, when I hope to treat of the constitutional progress of the European nations, and their descendants, in all its branches—a task which I ardently desire to perform, but which requires means not altogether under my own control. I have also added some documents to the Appendix, and in several cases I have brought down the statistical statements of the original to the present date, according to the latest reports. Notes and appendixes are not unfrequently treated with some neglect, and I would therefore take the liberty of suggesting to the reader disposed to dismiss the work after a perusal of the first half of it, containing the general account by the authors, that if the two great divisions of this publication differ at all in the degree of their importance, the higher will probably be assigned to the latter half, in which the authors give a number of statistical and comparative tables, and a variety of statements of peculiar interest; but both parts, though different in form, are not only closely connected with each other, but one is the necessary complement to the other.

An article on the Pennsylvania penitentiary system will be found at the end of the volume It was originally written by the translator for the *Encyclopædia Americana*, who appended it, with some additions, to this work, called upon to do so by some gentlemen, to whose knowledge in matters of prison discipline he owes great deference. The circumstance that the writer of the article speaks upon some subjects connected with solitary confinement from personal experience,* so unusual with those who are called upon to discuss a subject of this nature publicly, had undoubtedly influenced their partial request.

Prisons have been called hospitals for patients labouring under moral diseases, but until recently, they have been in all countries where any existed, and unfortunately continue still to be in most countries, of a kind that they ought to be compared rather to the plague-houses in the East, in which every person afflicted with that mortal disorder is sure to perish, and he who is sent there without yet being attacked, is sure to have it. The awful inscription which the mighty bard of Florence tells us he read over the gates of the infernal regions,† would have found a fit place over the entrance of these moral lazarettos, intended for punishment and for the prevention of crime, but in reality, generating it and effecting the total ruin and corruption of their unhappy inmates. In some countries no prisons have been

---

* He was imprisoned in a period of political excitement.

    † Through me you pass into the city of wo
    Through me you pass into eternal pain :
    · Through me among the people lost for aye.
    * * * * * *
    All hope abandon ye who enter here.
             Dante, Inferno, Canto III., trans. by Carey.
These lines, it ought to be observed, are by no means a fair specimen either of Mr. Carey's translation, or of the grand original, in which this inscription is majestic and awful.

erected as yet. Thus we learn from Mr. Burkhardt's report on houses of correction and punishment in Switzerland, Zürich, 1827, that in the canton of Uri, no prison for punishment exists; and corporal punishment, the pillory, branding and placing the culprit in foreign military service, are used as substitutes. In Appencell-Outer-Road, imprisonment is inflicted for lighter offences only.*

The progress of mankind from physical force to the substitution of moral power in the art and science of government in general, is but very slow, but in none of its branches has this progress, which alone affords the standard by which we can judge of the civil development of a society, been more retarded than in the organization and discipline of prisons, probably for the simple reason that those for whom the prisons are established, are at the mercy of society, and therefore no mutual effort at amelioration, or struggle of different parties, can take place. At length the beginning has been made, and it is a matter of pride to every American, that the new penitentiary system has been first established and successfully practised in his country. That community which first conceived the idea of abandoning the principle of mere physical force even in respect to prisons, and of treating their inmates as redeemable beings, who are subject to the same principles of action with the rest of mankind, though impelled by vitiated appetites and perverted desires; that community, which after a variety of unsuccessful trials, would nevertheless not give up the principle, but persevered in this novel experiment, until success has crowned its perseverance, must occupy an elevated place in the scale of political or social civilization. The American penitentiary system must be regarded as a new victory of mind over matter—the great and constant task of man. Though of more vital interest to the whole civilized world, it exhibits the same progress of society, which is indicated by the abolition of the *laths*† in the Prussian army, and

---

* See Mittermaier's Comment on the *Compte général de l'Administration de la Justice criminelle pendant l'année* 1827, Berlin, 1829, page 34.

† When, in 1807, stripes were abolished in the Prussian army, it was believed necessary to substitute the *laths* (in German *Latten*) for the punishment of running the gauntlet. They consisted of triangular prismatic laths, nailed on the floor of a low and small prison, in such a way that one of the sharp edges of each lath was turned up, and that these edges formed, with other small pieces of wood corresponding in form on the surface, a number of small squares of sharp edges, on which the prisoner was obliged to lie or sit, no kind of furniture being allowed, nor was the prison high enough for the prisoner to stand in an erect position. It was so severe a punishment, that the prisoner could endure it but for a few hours at a time, after a proportionate rest he was reconducted to this place of torment. The severest punishment of this kind lasted three days. It was inflicted for heavy offences, and in consequence of a sentence by a court-martial only. In 1832, the king issued an order declaring that the moral state of the army was of a kind no longer to require this hard disciplinary measure. In the Austrian and Russian armies, and probably in some of the

of corporal punishment for most offences in the army of Great Britain. At least it is fervently hoped, that the house of lords

Italian states, corporal punishment continues to be made use of in the old style, but the period we hope is not distant, when even Austria will be obliged to follow the general progress of improvement —My expression that the American penitentiary system is a new victory of mind over matter, requires, perhaps, some explanation. I do not except the Auburn system, applied in so remarkable a way, in Sing-Sing, to nearly one thousand prisoners The Auburn system, as is well known, is mainly founded on the principle of silence, which isolates the prisoner in a moral respect This silence, however, it will be objected, is supported by the whip, which, it must be allowed, is not a very intellectual or moral means of discipline. But, without speaking of those penitentiaries on the Auburn plan, in which corporal punishment is resorted to but in cases of extremity or not at all, and considering for a moment the question whether the Auburn principle can be applied consistently and effectually without the whip, as decided in favour of the Sing-Sing discipline, I yet maintain that the principle on which this system is founded, partakes much more of a moral than physical character. The whip is the physical means to enforce the principle of silence, and, besides, it is not so much the actual pain inflicted upon the convict, which induces him to keep silence, as the knowledge of an *inevitable* and *immediate* punishment for any contravention of the rule, it is the thorough conviction which the prisoner acquires of the necessity of complying with the order of the prison, which makes it possible that from thirty to thirty-five persons are actually capable of superintending, of guiding, and watching nearly a thousand convicts, and in a manner altogether unknown in any of the old prisons where galley-slaves in dresses of two contrasting colours—a repulsive uniform of fools and villains—drag their heavy chains in yards, surrounded by high and thick walls and fortifications, and nevertheless, continual escapes take place, whilst they are a thing nearly unknown in Sing-Sing (two or three escapes only excepted, during the time of the cholera, which carried off a great number in that prison) though many convicts work in the open field There are, at present, in actual service at a time, six guards near the prison, eight guards distributed in the quarries, and twenty keepers, who watch the prisoners, and superintend and direct at the same time their labour. Thirty-four individuals, therefore, keep in order from eight hundred to a thousand convicts, and enforce the laws of silence and constant labour. There were at one time, one thousand and eighteen prisoners at Sing-Sing, and the above number of guards and keepers was found sufficient. The locality, I allow, favours somewhat the watching over their attempts to escape, yet the whole remains a surprising phenomenon which could not possibly be produced except by the aid of moral power If the whip is mentioned as a disciplinary measure, we must also mention labour as such, and if I mistake not it contributes much more to maintain order than the whip That labour has a powerful disciplinary effect with criminals (it is the same with all men) the reader will find asserted by a high authority in the course of this book ; it has, as Mr Dumont, the translator and editor of Jeremy Bentham's works, expresses it with a word derived from medicine, a *sedative* effect, it calms and assuages the mind of the irritated convict. To the authority, indicated above, I would add Mr Vasselot's, who was for a long time director of a *maison centrale* in France. He was twice in great danger of losing his life by the revolted convicts under his charge They were idle , all disturbances, plots, &c ceased, as soon as they were employed He adds, "In order to live in safety in the midst of many hundred prisoners, it is better to love than to fear them " It appeared to me, in visiting the American penitentiaries, that the salutary effect of labour, shows itself strongly also in the expression of the faces of the convicts They do not only look healthy, but I could discover none of those features, expressive of brooding revenge or deep hatred subdued only for the moment by physical force—in short, none of those criminal faces with which you always will meet in any of the old prisons, containing a large number of convicts. To repeat it then, sp-

2 *

will not thwart the endeavours of the commons to remedy an
evil, in respect of which the discipline of English troops has re-

lence is the fundamental principle, and this, as well as order in general, is maintained on the one hand, by continual employment, on the other hand, by the
convict's perfect conviction that he must comply with the rules of the establishment, he may infringe them, he may break the rules, but he must suffer
the consequences, and sooner or later—and generally it is soon—he comes to
the thorough conviction, that he must yield, that the order of the penitentiary
will be maintained, and that he is the only sufferer if he tries to contravene it.
This conviction, however, is very different from a mere physical prevention of
escape by walls, fosses, chains, bars between the feet, balls, clogs, iron horns,
collars, manacles, bells fastened to the head, &c. But how are the convicts
brought to this perfect conviction? How is it that we see at Sing-Sing criminals
who have been in Botany-Bay, have escaped from different prisons and never
have been kept in obedience except by powerful physical means, patiently
submit here to the established order (even in cases of the greatest excitement,
such as at the time of the cholera) and obey so hard a law as that of constant
silence must be to every human being? If we answer "all this is effected by
the whip," the assertion is liable to serious misunderstanding. It is true that
the whip is used, it is true that the stripes inflicted with it smart acutely Since
this small instrument produces so great results, I was anxious to know its exact
effect, I devised a means to obtain this personal knowledge in a way which satisfies me that I experienced the effects of this disciplinary instrument in as
great a degree as the refractory convict does. I do not deny that the pain inflicted by this whip, made much like the scourge used in former times for flagel-
lations, is very acute, and without causing injury seems in a peculiar way painfully to affect the nerves, owing no doubt to its consisting of six thin cords, yet
criminals have defied punishments much more severe than this, have often
braved cruel tortures, and, in my opinion, stripes alone as they are inflicted in
Sing Sing, would not be sufficient to produce such results, particularly if we
consider that there is, comparatively speaking, seldom occasion to resort to
them The principle, however, upon which this punishment produces effects
so great, is this, active in all men, that the present evil is always the greatest,
which remains true, though extended and modified, if we say, "the nearer
evil or pain is feared more than the distant, though greater" Ten smart stripes,
certain to be inflicted the very next moment after an infringement of order, are
feared more than a hundred stripes to be suffered after the lapse of a year, the
certain drawing of a tooth is feared more for the moment, than even death,
which every one considers distant If, then, punishment is *certain* of falling
immediately upon the offender, it has the greatest effect This, and the otherwise humane treatment of the criminals which does not brutalize them as other
prisons do, the calm deportment of the keepers, who probably find no inconsid-
erable means of safety in resorting to corporal punishment only, if there is
ground for it, are the causes of so unique a phenomenon as that exhibited at
Sing-Sing The criminals are prevented from plotting or from any combination
of their strength or thoughts, otherwise than in the prescribed way, by silence
imposed upon them, and by a strict compliance with the rules of the establishment, silence and order are maintained by labour and the thorough conviction of
the unavoidable necessity of obedience, conviction of necessary obedience is
produced by the threat of corporal punishment, corporal punishment is rendered
effectual by its certainty and instantaneousness I admit, that so many criminals
can be kept in perfect submission by so few officers and guards only in a country in which the government is considered by the people as entirely their own,
acting solely for their interest, and to which they therefore give all their moral
support, as is the case with us The same cannot take place in countries in
which government and people form two different bodies Yet the principles of
silence, labour, and immediate punishment, will produce proportionately the
same effect everywhere.—The study of a diseased or disordered state of our

mained so long behind that of the land forces of the most civilized nations on the European continent

Though the penitentiaries are monuments of a charitable disposition of the honest members of society toward their fallen and unfortunate brethren, and of a penetrating practical sense, we must not forget that little more than the mere beginning has as yet been accomplished, and it cannot be impressed too much upon the mind of the public how necessary is a reformation of all prisons, how impossible it is to think of a *penitentiary system*, without its principle being carried through in all branches. It is praiseworthy, indeed, that the state prisons have been changed into penitentiaries, and that houses of refuge for juvenile offenders have been established, but there remain yet, almost every where in our country, all the other prisons to be refashioned in the same spirit As long as this is not done, as long as there shall not exist *houses of detention*, in which persons arrested under the presumption of guilt, indicted individuals and witnesses, as urgent circumstances sometimes require their detention, are separated from each other, as well as from prisoners who have been convicted and sentenced, our system will be like the calling for medical assistance after all the gradual stages of the disease have been neglected, when aid would have been easy and cheap, and the disorder shows itself with alarming violence, or has become a settled and incurable disease ; or like paying attention only to dykes and embankments when the flood rushes

body, of the mind, or of political society, has led to the most important knowledge respecting their healthy state, and the nature of their organization. We frequently see in such a state, one faculty, organ, power, &c., developed at the expense of the others, which causes the disease by disturbing the necessary equilibrium, but at the same time offers a peculiar opportunity for observation The prison of Sing-Sing affords in a similar way a variety of most interesting observations, and among other things the all-important principle that crimes and offences are not checked by the severity of the law, but by the certainty and rapidity of punishment, is most strikingly exhibited If it were possible to devise a system of administering justice which would *infallibly* punish *immediately* after the offence had been committed, many hideous crimes might be prevented by the threat of very trifling punishments. This is impossible, the necessity of protecting innocence, though suspected, brings with it the possibility of impunity, on which the criminal calculates when he commits a premeditated crime, as every man grasps at the most favourable hope, but the problem remains to arrive at least as near perfection as possible, and if we consider it already a necessary evil that many criminals escape punishment, how much more afflicting an evil must the abuse of the pardoning power appear to us, which has been carried to a degree that the criminal is perfectly right in counting it among the chances (sometimes the probabilities) of impunity. But we shall speak more on this subject —For the rest, I have on various occasions stated, that I consider the Pennsylvania penitentiary system much more philosophical in its principle, more radical and thorough in its operation, more practical and easy in its application, more charitable in its whole spirit than the Auburn system, wherever the means can be obtained to erect the necessary buildings, which often will be difficult, and in such cases the Auburn system remains, so far, the next preferable

in, after having looked with indolence upon the injury when it was time yet for efficient repair. He who neglects repeated colds, must not be surprised when consumption shows its first and fearful symptoms; he who does not diligently inspect his dykes, and quickly repair whatever injury he finds, must be prepared for disastrous inundations. But it is not only unwise that we have, in most cases, confined our attention to the state prisons; it is contrary to justice and religion,—the first, because we expose those who have not yet been tried, and others who have been found guilty of slight offences only, to the poisonous infection of aggravated and confirmed crime; the latter, because we occupy ourselves with the convict, who suffers for grave crimes, whilst we neglect him whose first offences are perhaps but the fruits of bad seeds, which a vicious education laid deeply in his soul, or the effects of weakness, rashness, or oppressive want. Our vanity is flattered more by our exertions to redeem a hardened criminal, than by kindly preventing many from becoming such; but a gardener who loves his garden, roots out the weeds as early as he can, and does not allow them to shoot up and scatter their destroying seeds before he concludes to rid his beds of them. If it is noble to reclaim fallen virtue, it is much better still to prevent the fall.

So many gifted authors have spoken upon this important point, that I fear I should trespass on the reader's patience, were I to dwell any longer upon it; I shall only point out one of them, who has exhibited the magnitude of its importance in his accustomed lucid manner—Mr. Edward Livingston. His just and eloquent remarks on this subject, as well as on many others* connected with prison discipline, will be found in this work. The erection of the Blackwell's Island penitentiary, and the appointment of a committee by the legislature of Massachusetts, to inspect all prisons, and report on a general plan, which shall embrace the prison system of the whole state, show that this want of a general penitentiary system is felt in the community at large, and begins to have its practical effects.† But the necessity for reforming all prisons in a state according to the same

* They are chiefly taken from Mr. E Livingston's letter to Mr. Roberts Vaux, and from his Introductory Report to the Code of Prison Discipline, &c.

† The House of Representatives of Massachusetts recently appointed Joseph Tuckerman and Louis Dwight, of Boston, and John W Lincoln, of Worcester, commissioners to make personal inspection of all the jails and houses of correction in the state, with a view to devise or obtain plans and descriptions of such houses, better calculated to subserve the important design of their institution; to prepare a tabular form of annual returns, to examine the several statutes for the regulation of the existing institutions, and report thereupon at the next session, with such suggestions of change or modification, as in their judgment may conduce to their improvement in security, economy, health, or moral benefit.— Papers of April, 1833,

principle, is not any more urgent than that for the erection of houses of arrest or detention, as I have indicated above, destined for the reception of detained but not yet imprisoned persons. Humanity, justice, even a spirit of decency require it. *

There is one point, however, connected with this special topic, to which I should invite the reader's attention for a few moments longer—the imprisonment of women. It is a branch of administration of penal justice, much and unfortunately neglected in our country.

In all countries women commit less crimes than men, but in none is the disproportion of criminals of the two sexes so great as in ours. The authors of the present work have given some interesting comparative tables on this subject, and I have stated my views on some of the causes of this fact. Unhappily, the small number of crimes committed in our country by women, has caused a comparative neglect of female criminals. Public attention has hardly turned itself toward this subject, and yet none claims it in a higher degree †

The influence of women, as wives and mothers, upon their family, and also, if they stand single in society, upon those who are in some connexion with them, is, generally speaking, greater than that of men, as husbands, fathers, or single, upon the morals of those who surround or are connected with them. The influence of woman upon manners in society, is not greater than that which she may exercise on morals, and even upon crimes, in those classes whose wants expose them more to commit offences than

---

* I render a much greater service to the reader if I recommend him to read what Mr. Livingston says on the necessity of these houses of detention, in the above quoted Introductory Report, Philadelphia, 1827, from page 31 to 38, should he be unacquainted with this work, than by stating my views, coinciding with those of the learned jurist, in my own words

† " The attention of the legislature has often been called to this subject, and the necessity of a separate prison for female convicts urged with great force. The inspectors of this prison repeat the recommendation to the legislature, to provide for this unfortunate and criminal class of the community, a different place of confinement ; a place which, by the discipline established, shall tend to reform, and not, as in their present condition, lead to inevitable ruin.

" No doubt is entertained, but the same discipline which now controls and subdues the male convict, may be made equally serviceable with the females Under the charge of a judicious matron, we cannot believe but great moral reformation may be produced. This consideration alone calls with great force for a change in the mode of punishing female convicts. It is also worthy of consideration, to inquire whether the expense to the state would not be diminished by such change. The state now pays one hundred dollars a year for each female convict kept at Bellevue. They are not employed at any thing except cooking, washing, making and mending clothes for themselves, and this occupies but a small part of their time. The law is imperative as to the place where these convicts must be confined, and such sum must be paid as the corporation of New York choose to demand, whether that sum be a fair compensation, or beyond the value of the services rendered "—Report of the Inspectors of the Mount-Pleasant (Sing-Sing) State Prison, January, 1833.

others. A prudent and moral mother, may, in a great degree, counteract in her family the unhappy consequences of her husband's intemperate or dissolute life, much more than it is possible for an honest and industrious husband to counteract the melancholy effects of the bad conduct of an immoral wife. The wife's sphere is supremely that of domestic life ; there is the circle of activity for which she is destined, and there, consequently, she has the greatest influence ; and the lower we descend in the scale of society, the greater the influence of woman in her family. If she is unprincipled, the whole house is lost, whilst, if she walks on the path of virtue and religion, she is the safest support of a son, thrown upon the agitated sea of life, or of a husband, oppressed by misfortune or misery, and beset by a thousand temptations. That tender age, in which the very seeds of morality must be sown and fostered in the youthful soul, is much more dependant upon the mother's care, than upon that of the father—in all working classes it is almost solely dependant upon the former. A woman given to intemperance, and, what is generally connected with it, to violence and immoral conduct in most other respects, is sure to bring up as many vagabonds and prostitutes as she has male and female children ; and I believe I am right in stating, that the injury done to society by a criminal woman, is in most cases much greater than that suffered from a male criminal. Around one female criminal flock a number of the other sex, and ask any police officer what incalculable mischief is done by a single woman who harbours thieves and receives stolen goods, called in the slang of criminals *a fence.* I have taken pains to ascertain the history of a number of convicts, and though my inquiry has been but limited, yet, as far as it goes, it shows me that there is, almost without an exception, some unprincipled or abandoned woman, who plays a prominent part in the life of every convict, be it a worthless mother, who poisons by her corrupt example the soul of her children, or a slothful and intemperate wife, who disgusts her husband with his home, a prostitute, whose wants must be satisfied by theft, or a receiver of plunder and spy of opportunities for robberies. It might be said, that man and woman being destined for each other's company, some woman will be found to play a prominent part in the life of every man, and nothing more natural, therefore, than that we find the same to be the case with criminals. This is true, and would only corroborate what I say, that the influence of woman is great ; but in addition, I maintain that I found that most criminals have been led on to crime, in a considerable degree, by the unhappy influence of some corrupted female.

To all this must be added the fact, known to all criminalists, that a woman once renouncing honesty and virtue, passes over to the most hideous crimes which women commit, with greater ease than a man proceeds from his first offence to the blackest crimes committed by his sex. There is a shorter distance between a theft committed by a woman and her readiness to commit murder by poison, or arson, from jealousy or hatred, than between forgery or theft committed by a man, and murder or piracy. A male criminal may be a thief for a long series of years, and yet as unwilling to steep his hands in the blood of a fellow man, as many honest men ; a person may commit depredation upon public property for his whole life, and yet shudder at the idea of highway robbery. With women this is not often the case. It seems, moreover, that the majority of those characters in the annals of crimes at which we shudder most, have been females. That crime, the most revolting to human nature—poisoning, has found its blackest and foulest adepts among the women. I only need remind the reader of the society of female poisoners under the direction of Hieronyma Spara, of the Marchioness de Brinvilliers, and of the woman Gottfried,* who, in 1831, was executed in Bremen for having poisoned more than thirty persons, among whom were her parents, children, husbands, lovers, friends, and servants.†

This rapid and precipitous moral fall of women, can be sufficiently accounted for. The two sexes have been destined by the Creator for different spheres of activity, and have received different powers to fulfil their destiny. The woman destined for domestic life, and that sphere in which attachment and affection are the most active agents, has been endowed with more lively feeling and acuter sensibility : she feels; man reasons. Her morality has its roots more in her feelings than in her understanding or reasoning faculty, and if she has once lost that delicate bloom of moral bashfulness, if she has lost the acuteness of her moral feelings, if she has stepped further and committed an offence against the laws, the almost only ground on which her moral actions depended is shaken, if she once gives up the retired activity of her domestic sphere, she is led into an element for which she is but rarely calculated. This seems to be also the reason why, with all nations and at all times, the loss of chastity has been considered with women so much more grave and dangerous an offence than with men. They felt that the former lose more of their moral nature by it than the latter.‡

* A shocking contrast between her name, which means *Peace in God,* and her deeds!

† See her Life described, (in German,) by her Difensor, (Legal Counsellor,) Bremen, 1832; and Beckmann's History of Inventions, &c, translated from the German by Johnston, Vol I, Division *Secret Poison.*

‡ Delicacy is one of the most active principles in female life—in respect to morals as well as manners, language, dress, taste, feelings, and thoughts It is the same principle which causes women all over the globe to wear wider garments (if their tribe or nation dress at all) than men, induces the men to court

It is otherwise with man   The Creator destined him for an agitated life. He has to make his way, to break new paths; he must, as Schiller says, "win and dare," and has to decide between opposed interests, and, not unfrequently, between conflicting duties   He, therefore, has been endowed with feelings less acute and prompt, stronger reasoning powers, and calmer judgment.   If he loses the delicacy of his feelings, great as the loss may be, his judgment will yet supplant it in a degree; his moral guide does not yet, for this reason, entirely fail him. Hence it often happens that men, committing acts which are considered by all others immoral, perhaps criminal, make themselves what the French call *des raisons,* false excuses indeed, yet they prevent them not unfrequently from going further. The manifold scenes of life, politics, the varieties of business make him acquainted with many impure actions, with which a woman is not brought into contact , it accustoms his mind to see acts which do not agree with the strict laws of morality, and if he himself commits a similar one, he need not have sunk so deep as a woman if she commits the same, and he retains yet a considerable part of that power which always regulated his moral conduct. Besides, crimes which, according to the state of our civil society, may be easily committed by women, are mostly of a kind requiring great baseness.

It appears, then, from the preceding observations, that a woman, when she commits a crime, acts more in contradiction to her whole moral organization, i. e. must be more depraved, must have sunk already deeper than a man. She abandons shame as much as a man, who commits the same; but shame is of still greater moral importance to her than to him.

I have thought I found in these arguments also, the reasons why, in all countries, girls, in houses of refuge for juvenile offenders, are so much more difficult to be reclaimed than boys; and that it is almost impossible to reclaim them, if they have been prostitutes, as the reader will find in a note added to the chapter on houses of refuge.

We should be wrong in concluding from the small number of crimes committed by women, compared with those committed by men, that there is a greater moral capacity in women in general; and thence again, that penitentiaries for females are comparatively unimportant. Women commit fewer crimes from three causes chiefly: 1. because they are, according to their destiny and the consequent place they occupy in civil society, less

the women, and not the women the men, and which, in short, makes coarseness, want of taste, deficiency in neatness, boldness, &c in women so shocking and disagreeable to every feeling person, and—to repeat—on account of which, an indelicate woman has deviated much more from the character, destined for her by the Creator, than a man who offends against delicacy.

exposed to temptation or to inducement to crime; their ambition is not so much excited, and they are naturally more satisfied with a dependant situation;* 2. they have not the courage or strength necessary to commit a number of crimes which largely swell the lists of male convicts, such as burglary, robbery, and forcible murder; 3. according to their position in society they cannot easily commit certain crimes, such as bigamy, forgery, false arrest, abuse of official power, revolt, &c. There are some crimes they cannot commit at all, such as rape; but there are on the other hand, crimes which men cannot commit, as abortion; or to which they are not so easily induced, as infanticide. According to the *Compte général de l'Administration de la Justice criminelle* (in France) for 1826 and 1827, we find that in 1826, 5712 men, and 1276 women were accused of crimes, and 126,089 men, and 33,651 women of offences judged by "correctional tribunals" In 1827, 5657 men, and 1272 women were accused of crimes, and 133,936 men, and 37,210 women of offences Of these were accused in 1827

For counterfeiting, no women at all.

For killing,	11 women and	277 men.
For murder,	32 "	236 "
For maiming,	22 "	353 "
For highway robbery,	10 "	183 "

But this proportion, so favourable to the female sex, changes immediately in respect to parricide and poisoning Of 23 parricides, 16 were men, and 7 women, 12 women, and 22 men were accused of poisoning; 25 women, and 61 men of arson. In 1826, 12 women, and 14 men had been accused of poisoning So in 1826, there were 427 women, and 745 men accused of domestic theft (*vol domestique*), in 1827, 343 women, and 554 men; whilst for common theft, 2563 men, and 531 women were accused.

Are we then justifiable, after all these considerations, in not providing more effectually for the correction of female convicts? The only remaining question can be, are separate penitentiaries for females required? I believe they are, if the Pennsylvania penitentiary system is not adopted, and with that system a matron at least will be necessary for the special superintendence of the female prisoners; she is quite indispensable if the Auburn system is applied to women as well as men, she alone can enforce the order of this system, whilst it is nearly impossible for male keepers. The whole spirit of opposition in womankind is raised against him. Besides, the moral management of female convicts must differ from that of male criminals, and even their labour re-

---

* There are some crimes to which their dependant situation induces them, sooner than men, but they are comparatively few in number.
3 *

quires a total separation   Separate houses might be easily built, and proper committees appointed to superintend them   In Wethersfield and Auburn, women are subjected to the penitentiary system, which takes its name from the latter; matrons superintend them. If it should be found impossible to make the labour of female convicts as profitable as that of men, we must not allow ourselves to be retarded by a financial consideration in providing for them, since we have seen how important their proper treatment is.

The penitentiary system has not escaped the common fate of all questions of vital interest to society; many of its opponents as well as its advocates, have run into extremes; the former, judging by vague impressions derived from superficial knowledge, both of the character of convicts and the penitentiary system, assert not unfrequently, with a kind of levity, that criminals ought to suffer severely for their crimes, and should not be treated with tenderness, the latter, carried away by a pious zeal, often believe that an individual who has from early childhood received bad impressions, imbibed vicious principles, and has allowed himself to be governed during his whole life by unchecked desires and unbridled appetites, who has, in fact, contracted bad habits deeply rooted in his whole character, may be influenced by the same religious means which affect honest persons, and suddenly become a contrite sinner, and, soon after, change into a saint.

It ought always to be borne in mind, that a convict is neither a brute nor a saint, and to treat him as either, is equally injurious to himself and to society.

Though opposition to the penitentiary system has greatly abated, and entirely ceased to take an active part in many states of our Union, there are, nevertheless, many individuals who believe that too much pains are taken with convicts; and, as I have heard it myself not unfrequently expressed, say that "they ought to be punished." Were they to inquire but slightly into the matter, they would soon find that as long as a convict remains unchanged in mind, a penitentiary with its constant labour and strict order, its silence, its solitude during night, or, if we speak of the Pennsylvania system, its uninterrupted solitude day and night, is a punishment to him whose element has been disorder and idleness, (as is the case with most criminals) a hundred times greater than a prison, the inmates of which, though loaded with chains and oppressed with filth, and unhealthy diet, yet can freely communicate with each other.   It is a fact that criminals fear penitentiaries much more than prisons on the old plan ; yet they know that they live, physically, much better in the former, and are aware of the torturing misery of the latter. But what they are afraid of is, the order, obedience, and silence imposed upon them ; they shun, consciously, or instinctively, that moral character which pervades the whole system, so odious to criminal people; they shun, by a vague presentiment, perhaps, the being corrected and reformed in spite of themselves, and the contemplation of their unhappy life, spent and lost in evil deeds. It is this, the same instinct which causes so often the wicked to fear moral society, the same feeling which makes a criminal so afraid of his own lucid intervals, and leads him on to new perverted activity, to quiet, for the moment, his unhappy soul.

Were those opponents but to inquire into prisons, the statistics of crimes, and the history of criminals, they soon would find that charity, our own interest, and justice, equally require their most active support of the penitentiary system—charity requires it, because, though crime necessarily must be punished, yet the history of by far the greatest majority of criminals, shows the afflicting fact, that they were led to crime by the bad example of their parents, loose education, hard masters, or a gradual progress in vice, for which society often offers but too many temptations. Ask those conversant with the lives of criminals, how many of them are led to the prison by the lottery alone! Interest requires it, because the old prisons were an enormous burthen to society, whilst the penitentiaries cost little, and often yield a revenue. Even Sing-Sing, which had to contend with many unusual and great difficulties, will, as I have been assured from the best authority, defray all its expenses during the next year. Justice requires it, because society has a right to punish, but not to brutalize, to deprive of liberty, but not to expose to filth and corruption ; and if it is obstinately insisted upon that government, as such, has no obligation to correct the morals of convicts, it is, at all events, its sacred duty not to lead them to certain ruin, and society takes upon itself an awful responsibility, by exposing a criminal to such moral contagion, that, according to the necessary course of things, he cannot escape its effects Besides, is it not the *interest* of society to try all means at its disposal to reclaim a criminal?

However, we are happy to say, that, in this country, there are few, if any, who pretend that the question of morality should not enter at all into the discussion of this topic

Those, on the other hand, who try to attract great attention to a few cases, in which, according to their opinion, criminals have become most pious men, ought to remember that there is no greater contradiction in itself, than noisy piety or showy devotion, especially with a convict If an individual, who has greatly sinned against divine and human laws, make a sincere effort to return to the path of virtue, what honest man would not rejoice at it with all his heart? But direct not public attention to such cases, because nothing but long experience can show

the truth or deception of the case, and, if in truth a convict have
morally recovered, he must sincerely wish to remain in quiet
and unobserved communion with his Maker, and not to attract
public attention now by his devotion, as formerly by his crime.
If the success of the penitentiary system depended upon these
few cases, it would be founded upon no firm ground, they always must remain but few in number, and have those few cases
answered the pious expectation of those who directed public attention to them? Many former convicts are now honestly gain-
ing their livelihood, but among them are few of those who gave
surprising signs of sudden conversion. If those convicts who
suddenly became devout, were sincere at the time they showed
those symptoms of piety, it must have been an excitement of
feeling, which has subsided as soon as the exciting causes ceased, and which is not sufficient to prevent a relapse into former
vices, when former temptations re-appear. To correct a criminal
radically, more is required than an excitement of feeling; his
habits must be *broken* · his mind must be *trained* Society
cannot be expected, and has not even the right to do any thing,
except it is directly or indirectly for the general interest. Penitentiaries cannot be erected, in order to bring out of many
thousand criminals, a few to a state of great and therefore uncommon piety, but it is its interest to establish them, if according to the organization of the human soul, and the principles of our actions, it can be fairly supposed that many of these
convicts will contract better habits, more correct views of
society, and of themselves, and come to a better knowledge
of their obligations toward God, and society, and especially
if experience shows the success of these praiseworthy endeavours All who are well acquainted with the penitentiary system, know that re-committals decrease, and, probably, would
become rare, if released convicts could be prevented from returning to large cities The re-committals of those convicts,
who go into the country after the expiration of their imprisonment, are comparatively few.* In all countries, the population of large cities produces proportionally more crimes than
the rest of the nation, and again the cities and towns more than
the villages, &c It is so in France, in all states of Germany, in
England; it is so with ourselves There is in large cities a
greater and more variegated activity, and, therefore, more opportunity for crimes than elsewhere; wants are greater, temptations more frequent and powerful, inducements to pleasure and
idleness more alluring and diversified; life is more unobserved,

* I have it from the best authority, that, in Sing-Sing, the proportion of recommitted convicts, who had gone to live in the country, to those who had
gone to the city of New York, is, in all probability, not more than one to
twenty

and as the concourse of people in general is greater, so also that of criminals, who soon meet with each other in corrupting company, which, for a former convict, is peculiarly dangerous. In several countries, therefore, the government has thought it necessary to prevent released convicts from going to the capital and its vicinity, for a series of years, after the expiration of their imprisonment. A French galley-slave, leaving the bagne, is not allowed to go to Paris. Our large cities are, if not equally dangerous to released convicts, sufficiently so to authorize us to adopt some similar measures, but none in so high a degree as New York, owing to its peculiar situation, and unequalled activity, the many emigrants who resort to it, and several other reasons, unnecessary to be mentioned here, but which, if I remember right, cause the greater number of convicts, released from Auburn or Sing-Sing, soon to be re-committed, if they go to the city of New York. The legislature of the state of New York, therefore, ought to consider the propriety of passing a law, which would make the prohibition of going to the city of New York, for a number of years, proportionate to the duration of imprisonment, after its expiration, inherent in each sentence. The justice of such a law cannot be doubted; its expediency would be evident. If the penitentiary system is a truly salutary one, if it attempts the moral, or at least the civil restoration of an individual, nothing can be more natural than to prohibit a person, whom the law considers convalescent, to expose himself to an atmosphere dangerous to his feeble state. On general grounds, such a measure could not possibly be found unjust, provided the prohibition is included in the sentence; and the objection that it would be assuming arbitrary power over citizens restored to all their rights, would be sufficiently refuted by the consideration, that, in case such measure should be adopted, the law would not consider the individual as yet entirely restored to all the rights of a citizen. Such a law would have no characteristic trait of a police measure; the prohibition would be legally awarded as a sentence. There are, moreover, in several of our states, New York included, laws which disqualify a former convict for certain civil functions. It remains only to inquire whether the advantage of a greater opportunity which a released convict finds in New York, for the practice of the trade which he has learned in Sing-Sing or Auburn, and consequently the greater chance of leading an honest life, does not overbalance the disadvantage of moral exposure. This question of mere expediency can be decided only by the examination of facts. If most convicts, proceeding to New York after the expiration of their sentence, are re-committed, and most of those who go into the country do not return, or if a proportionately greater number of the former are re-committed, it is of course expedient to pass the law.* The inhabitants of New York could not, in such case, be considered as favoured at the expense of the other citizens, for two reasons, 1. Even after such a law should be passed, they will remain nevertheless more exposed to the depredations of foreign criminals, and those brought up in our country, attracted as they all are by the largest city in the country, which everywhere operates as a kind of drain of bad subjects. The whole state of New York profits by the activity of the city of New York, but the people are not proportionately as exposed to criminals as the inhabitants of the city; 2. Most of the released convicts are supposed to lead an honest life if they go into the country, or the law would not be passed.

It is with such a law, that, in my opinion, the penitentiary system would show itself to its greatest advantage, because it would rapidly decrease that criminal population which forms a kind of society for itself; and though it never can prevent crime, because desires, temptations, and opportunities, do not lie in its reach, it would lead back to honest life many individuals, by teaching them how to support themselves honestly, and by guarding them, during the time of imprisonment, against further corruption, and thus prevent the propagation of crime by the released convicts, who, it is well known, are the most dangerous and most numerous members of that criminal community, just alluded to. If the penitentiary system have once succeeded in breaking up or greatly diminishing this corrupted and rapidly corrupting community, for which the Pennsylvania system is so eminently qualified; if it have once succeeded in reducing most crimes to individual acts, produced by degenerated appetites, or want of principles, indeed, but not by long confirmed corruption, which makes a profession of crime—its greatest and surest victory will be gained Most criminals then will enter the prison less hardened, they will be more susceptible to the influence of the penitentiary system, and, after the expiration of their imprisonment, it will be easier for them to live honestly, because they have not become the initiated members of a corrupted society, which now entangles those who sincerely resolve to reform with a thousand difficulties. There are few men, indeed, who having been imprisoned for the first time, and suffered a severe but not brutalizing, infamous, or still more corrupting punishment, are not disposed to attempt a life more congenial to the laws of their

---

* In writing this, I am well aware of the fact that some master workmen in the city of New York have taken, from their own accord, convicts of Sing-Sing, whose term had expired, because they have great confidence in their new habits, their industry and skill. The law therefore might provide for those cases, and allow a convict to return to New York, provided the agent is satisfied that the master who wishes to have him is a worthy person I should think it however preferable to exclude them from New York altogether

country. They find out, if no better reason influences them, that an honest life is after all more comfortable than a dishonest one, and every person, after he has attained his thirtieth year, wishes more or less some kind of solid comfort. The roving disposition loses much of its activity after this period, and it is well known that most crimes are committed between the ages of twenty and thirty. Let a former convict but acquire habits of honesty, and he will also gradually acquire honest views and feelings. Let him obey the just laws of our country, and he will soon love them.

From the recommittals of convicts who go to live in the country, and small towns, and not in the most populous cities, after the expiration of their punishment, it would, perhaps, be the fairest to judge of the efficacy of the penitentiary system, because it ought to be supported and assisted by all necessary laws which justice permits, and because in several countries, perhaps in most, in which the old prison system exists, such laws are actually existing. We would then only make the comparison on even ground. But even if the criminals recommitted from the largest cities must be taken into account, it is by the recommittals, not by the sum total of criminals, that we must judge of the efficacy of a prison discipline. Yet not even by the recommittals alone can we be guided.

The prevention of first crimes depends much more upon the certainty of punishment, and, therefore, upon the excellence of laws and the administration of justice, than upon the manner of punishment. As long as we see an overwhelming number of commitments and indictments compared to convictions, we may safely conclude either that the law is deficient, in allowing, by not being sufficiently accurate, too easily of accusation or acquittal, or in the prescribed procedure and form of trial. There are some exceptions to this rule, for instance, in our times, the numerous accusations in France for offences of the press against government, and the almost universal acquittals. I only speak of common crimes, and a state of society not excited by some peculiar causes. The opposite, that few acquittals always indicate sound laws, and a wise administration of justice, is by no means equally true. The Turkish cadis acquit rarely; and in many countries, (e. g. in most, I believe in all states of Germany,) exists the absolving *ab instantia*, which neither finds guilty nor acquits, but leaves the trial suspended—a measure which is in most cases extremely hard, and altogether repulsive to our ideas of justice. We find in the year 1826–7, that 3594 persons were tried in the kingdom of Bavaria, for crimes and offences; of these, were

Found guilty of crimes, - - 644
Do.   do.   offences,   -   1141
Absolved *ab instantia* for crimes,   396

Absolved *ab instantia* for offences, 609
'Absolved for crimes,   -   .-   328
Do.   - offences,   -   -   453
Declared innocent of crimes, -   7!
Do.   do.   offences,   16!

I hope that what the authors and myself have said on the insufficiency of judging of the efficacy of the penitentiary system
by the increase or decrease of crimes in general, will contribute
to dissipate so great and injurious an error.   The number of
crimes, or to speak more accurately, of trials and convictions,
because they are the only known crimes, proves, without further
consideration, actually nothing ; so much so, that in some cases
the increase of trials and convictions may indicate the decrease
of crimes. If the *compte général* of criminal justice in France,
shows that in 1825 there were only thirty-three criminal trials
for adultery, in 1827 only fifty-seven trials of this kind, are we
to conclude that the thirty-one millions of people with whom so
few trials for adultery occur, are uncommonly chaste, or that on
the contrary, if domestic manners should improve with them,
adultery would be more often punished? I believe the latter.
There are several nations, for instance the Spanish and Portuguese, with whom murder is very often but negligently prosecuted, because the people do not feel the same indignation or
horror at a murder committed under certain circumstances, which
the crime produces with other nations.   In Italy every one of
the lower classes assists a criminal in escaping the arms of justice; with us every citizen assists government as much as it
is in his power, and a comparison between murders and other
violent crimes tried in Italy, and those tried in this country,
without making allowance for this difference, would lead to erroneous results.

A minute knowledge of all co-operating circumstances is nowhere more indispensable, in order to arrive at just conclusions,
than in the statistics of crimes   There are certain laws which
experience teaches us, and if we disregard them we shall continually be liable to draw false conclusions; for instance, that
certain causes, as an unusually cold winter, famine, stagnation of
business, and poverty, caused by war, &c , never fail to effect a
rapid increase of crimes, whilst the ceasing of these causes by
no means effects a proportionally rapid decrease of crime These
considerations respecting the increase or decrease of crime, are
not only important in regard to prison discipline, but also as to
the progress of morality, or the demoralization of mankind in
general.

Civilization certainly increases the number of tried crimes and
offences, for two very simple reasons : 1. because it increases the
opportunity of crime, since it increases the variety of pursuits

and mutual relations between men ; every progress in industry offers naturally to the wicked a new opportunity for abusing this industry, or the new relations which it creates between men ; civilization, moreover, increases our wants and our ambition ; 2. because it increases at the same time the means and opportunities for prosecutions of crime. It sounds paradoxical, when Pangloss, shipwrecked on the coast of Portugal, drew the inference from seeing men in chains that he was in a civilized country; yet he was right considering his time, and it may be safely said, that a community of any magnitude, within which no crime is committed, cannot be far advanced in civilization. There is a latent criminality in such communities, which shows itself whenever opportunity offers If the wants of men are reduced to the simplest food which the field offers, and to clothing which is provided by their own flocks, they are easily satisfied, and hardly an opportunity exists for the numerous crimes and offences committed against property in a civilized and active society. There is or may be an absence of crime, but between this and positive morality there is yet a vast difference. Mankind are destined for civilization, and the great problem is to arrive through civilization at morality. I have spoken here of mankind only as it has shown itself so far. That same power which operated such great changes in the dispositions of men—which has taught them that there is greater security in living close together, in towns and villages, than isolated in fastnesses, depending on mere physical security; that taught them that free labour is more productive than the labour of compelled serfs ; that governments, supported by moral power, stand firmer than states founded on brutal strength ; that nations may serve their own interest much more efficiently by treating their neighbours liberally, than by injuring or paralyzing them ; that diplomatic frauds lead to no good in their mutual intercourse; or which has already rendered the more brutal crimes rarer, that same power may also, at some future period, diminish the number of crimes in general Mankind may not grow better, but a more correct knowledge of their true interest may become diffused among them, and may by degrees largely influence their general feeling, as in fact has been the case already in some other respects. Some more remarks on this subject may be found in a note of mine added to a passage of this work, in which the authors speak of the influence of knowledge on crimes.

In respect to the moral state of a nation, I would not attach so much importance to the fact, that crimes against persons decrease in proportion to crimes against property, with the progress of civilization, as of late several writers, and particularly Mr. Lucas, have been inclined to do.

It is impossible for me to enter here into a discussion on the question, so often put, whether civilization renders nations

4*

more moral or not * It would be necessary previously to agree
upon the accurate meaning of a number of expressions, generally as freely used as they are indistinctly applied ; my wish is
merely to show here that this division of crimes alone, though
very interesting and useful for various inquiries, does not authorize us as yet to draw any definite conclusion respecting the
moral state of nations.   First, the line dividing crimes against
persons from those against property, is not so distinct as it may
appear at first glance.   False testimony, perjury, escape of prisoners, are enumerated among the crimes against persons, but a
witness who gives false testimony, actuated so to do by compas-
sion for the prisoner, does not necessarily injure the rights of
persons, though he acts contrary to his duty as a citizen.   Even
rebellion, ranked among crimes against persons, is not necessarily such, and at all events it indicates very often a less degree
of demoralization than a number of crimes against property; on
the other hand, a number of crimes against property partake
much of the character of crimes against persons, for instance,
arson from vengeance, or exchanging of infants Secondly, I do
not believe that this division separates at the same time the more
heinous crimes from the less immoral ones.   Society punishes,
in general, crimes against persons with greater severity than
those against property, because they are more dangerous to the
general peace, and more injurious to the suffering party, but if
we wish to judge of the degree of demoralization requisite for
committing this species of crime, we ought not to forget that the
greater part of crimes against persons are acts committed in
rashness, whilst those committed against property are nearly all
premeditated crimes, and often require a baseness not necessarily
to be supposed in the authors of crimes against persons.   It is
this consideration which explains, why the laws of ancient Ger-
manic tribes punished theft with death, whilst they required
compositio (fine) only for killing and maiming. Whoever is
acquainted with criminal justice, will remember numerous crimes
which have been committed rashly, and necessarily punished by
the law with a heavy penalty, but which nevertheless left no
doubt but that their authors were morally better than numerous
convicts, again and again recommitted for petty larceny.   How
often is the very principle of honour, or the feeling of being un-
worthily treated, the cause of a passion which leads an individual
to crime—feelings which never disturb the baseness of others,
who commit crimes against property.

* After the work had gone to press, I became acquainted, through the reviews, with several passages of Mr Guerry's *Essai sur la Statisque Morale de la
France, avec Cartes,* I have not yet been able to procure the work itself.   To
judge from those passages, the author coincides with my views respecting the
influence of civilization on crimes, as I have stated them in the notes.

Moreover, the moral state of a society cannot be judged merely by the number of committed crimes, cognizable by the law, perhaps not even chiefly. To do this, we must inquire into a number of other subjects. Suppose we apply the rule by which Mr. Lucas judges, to the various classes of society. There was never, perhaps, a more demoralized class of men than the highest classes in France, under the regency of the Duke of Orleans, or Louis XV., or the court of Charles II.; yet, were we in possession of statistical accounts of those times, we should in all probability find that most crimes, of which the law takes cognizance, were committed amongst the lowest and middling classes, that, nevertheless, had not arrived at that state of demoralization in which their fellow-subjects of the highest nobility revelled. The comparison of the immorality of man to a state of disease, is applicable also to the point in question. The climate of some places renders the greater number of their inhabitants more or less sickly, though violent diseases affecting a great number at the same time may be there rare, and other places may now and then suffer much from disorders of this kind, and yet be on the whole more generally healthy.

I trust the reader does not misunderstand me; I am far from intimating that those countries in which few crimes against property are committed, and many against persons, are probably more moral than those countries in which the contrary takes place. My previous remarks must show that I am no admirer of that state of ignorance which guards a whole nation against many crimes, only by leaving it without wants, but which nourishes revenge, and leaves passions unbridled. My object is to show, that so far, this division of crimes allows us only to conclude, that civilization renders people calmer, i. e more civilized.

Among many other considerations, which ought to guide us, if we are desirous of drawing conclusions respecting the morality of a people from the list of crimes, a division into premeditated and unpremeditated crimes, will be found necessary. Still more we ought to judge from the motives, to which the admirable and already often quoted *Comptes généraux de l'Administration de la Justice criminelle*, annually published by the keeper of the seals of France, assign a separate table. And having mentioned these important and instructive documents, I cannot refrain from expressing my belief, that few more important services could be rendered to the well-being of our people, than the passing of laws which should enjoin the proper authorities, the clerks of the courts, and agents of the penitentiaries, in particular, to keep accurate and complete statistical tables, according to prescribed forms, to be laid annually before the legislatures. We have an excellent model in the above *comptes généraux*, which already have led to several inquiries of vital inte-

rest to the French nation; and the influence of which, if continued as we hope, must be incalculable. Statistical accounts, if
judiciously used, are the very charts of legislators; legislation
without them, is, in most cases, but a groping in the dark They
often dispel prejudices, though for centuries cherished, by irresistible facts, and again direct our attention to points, where we
least expected the roots of a long known evil. At the same time,
the trouble of collecting those at least of which I speak here in
particular, is very little compared with the magnitude of their
importance. The clerks of the courts, and the agents of the penitentiaries, have but faithfully to fill the blanks of prescribed sche-
dules, from which a competent committee may make its annual
reports. The politician, the moralist, the public economist, the
criminalist, the divine, the promoter of prison discipline—all
who have the welfare of their nation at heart, are equally interested in this measure What important consequences would
result from such accurate and extensive statistical accounts, if
but Maryland, Pennsylvania, New York, Connecticut, Massachusetts, &c. would resolve to keep them, especially if they were
so kept, that they should agree in their chief features, which, by
an easy understanding, might be effected without any difficulty.
I sincerely hope that the statistical part of this work will support the expression of this wish. I am well aware that much has
been done already by the annual reports of the agents of several
penitentiaries; but the statistical part of them may yet be much
improved.

It is among other things important to know the sex, age, and
education of the convict, whether the latter was bad, common,
good, or polite, his trade, colour, the trade of his parents, whether he lost them, and at what age, in what month the crime
was committed, (*whether it is a first, second, third, &c. crime,*)
from what motive, (from want, revenge, dissipation, &c.) whether
the crime was premeditated or not, the causes of the convict's
bad habits, (intemperance, lottery, women, gambling, &c. bad example of parents or masters,)—if the convict is a female, whether
a prostitute, (which is generally the case,) if they are emigrants,
how long in this country; whether married or not, whether he or
she has children, how many, when and where convicted, nature
of the crime, sentence, how long imprisoned before the trial;
how long after the crime was committed the trial took place, &c.;
general state of health; what religion, or, at least, in which educated; whether the term expired, or was abbreviated by pardon
or death, behaviour in prison, &c. It is farther of the greatest
importance to know how many indictments, and for what offences, took place; how many acquittals, and for what the in-
dictment was; how many recommendations by the court, or
court and jury to mercy, how many crimes were committed by

a single individual or more; how many pleaded guilty; how many criminal cases were finished by the court during one term, &c. I believe that a single glance at the tables of which the French *comptes-généraux* consist, will satisfy every body of their great utility That similar statistical accounts of civil cases would be of great importance to the legislator, I have no doubt; but it does not fall within the province of this work to treat of them.

I have now come to the last topic of my preface, with which I have, perhaps, detained the reader already too long—the power of pardoning. So much has been written on this point, so urgently has been the abolition of the abuse of pardon, asked for by writers full of eloquence and energy, that it might appear to many of my readers superfluous to touch again upon this subject, especially in this place, since the work itself exposes the abuse in strong colours; but the defect appears to me of such magnitude, and of so vital an interest to our society, that I may be allowed to add a few general observations.

Two things seem very certain:

1. That as long as the pardoning power shall be abused in the way that now but too frequently happens, the effect of penitentiaries, as well as of criminal justice, can be but limited It is the certainty of the punishment, not its cruelty, which prevents crime The criminal, yet at large, calculates on pardon as one of his chances of impunity, and the imprisoned convict, having a chance of being pardoned any day, is deprived of that calm resignation, which the certainty of his punishment alone can produce, and which must precede any salutary reflection on his past life, and earnest resolution to become a better member of society.

2. That as long as one individual in a state is invested with the pardoning power, it will be often abused to the injury of society.

It seems to me, that wherever the pardoning power is intrusted to a single person, this person does not withstand, in many cases, the vehement solicitations and personal prayers which have the opportunity of reaching him. But the difference is, that, in monarchies, few individuals of those personally interested in the fate of convicts, have an opportunity to accost the monarch, or, if so, to state their whole case; whilst the governor of a republican state, as our commonwealths are, is, and by right ought to be, accessible to the people. He therefore will yield sometimes to the urgent prayers of the distressed, or to the recommendations of people well disposed but weak, when, according to justice, he ought not to make use of that privilege which the constitutions of most of our states bestow upon the chief magistrates. Yet does this comport with the spirit which pervades our whole political government? We boast, that the law is our only master, and here an individual defeats their effect at his pleasure. The constitution, indeed, bestows this privilege upon him, but can a constitution, which emanated from one moral person only, and is no compromise between conflicting parties, possibly contain any provision which intentionally defeats the operation of other provisions of the law? Can such a constitution contain any other provision but such as was at least supposed would give effect to the law, and promote the welfare of the people? Certainly not; and the only interpretation which can be given to the provision investing the governor with the privilege of pardoning, is, that he shall use it for the still more effective operation of the law. If a law, owing to the imperfection of human language, foresight, or any other deficiency, operates against its own spirit, its own intention, as cases of this kind will happen, a governor may conscientiously make use of his privilege. If the innocence of a convicted person is proved, or rendered highly probable, the laws of the land which established the trial, court, and the law by which sentence was passed, operated against their spirit, which is to protect innocence, and a governor ought to pardon. If a number of peculiar circumstances, which the law, owing to its generality, without which it would not be a law, could not contemplate, contribute to excuse an individual who, nevertheless, according to its strict letter is guilty, the governor may, or ought to use his privilege. Such a peculiar case happened quite recently in one of the Atlantic states. But the case of a mother of many children, suffering great poverty, because the arm of stern justice took their protector away from them, to be punished in a prison: or a respectable family, known in the best society, distressed by the shame brought upon them by the crime of a worthless son, and a number of other cases, hard and cruel as they are for the sufferers, do not entitle the individual in question to a pardon, because the legislators well knew, when they passed the law, that it would strike fathers of poor families, and sons of respected parents, as well as other individuals; and, if its free course is interrupted, the sway of the law has ceased What would be thought of a society who erected, with great expense, dykes against the inroads of the hostile element, but invested one individual with the peculiar privilege of boring holes in these dykes at his own pleasure, and allowing the flood to rush in and to destroy their property? It would be a strange privilege, and yet nothing more than the privilege of pardoning, as it is now abused by some chief magistrates of our states. We make laws with great expense; we enforce them at great expense, by paying judges, juries, witnesses, the police, &c.; and by rewards for arresting criminals, and a single individual, after all, defeats their operation. Are those who thus return a convict upon society, before the-expiration of the time of imprisonment which it has thought proper to fix for a given crime, prepared to be responsible for the new injuries inflicted upon society, by these imperfectly punished criminals, and, before all, for the injury done by themselves, by thus rendering the operation of the law still more uncertain than it unfortunately always must be, according to the imperfection of human institutions? Yet, who will say, that, placed in the same situation, besieged by the same prayers, and importuned by the same recommendations, and endowed with the same power to grant the relief so pressingly asked for, they would never yield? Now and then, an individual may be placed at the head of our state governments, who, gifted with peculiar energy, may resist with the calm conviction of duty: but, according to the common character of man, this can be but rarely the case; and, as it is in general one of the noblest tasks of man to make reason triumph over chance, it is peculiarly so in the province of law and justice Besides, the pardoning power, where it is vested in a single individual, has come to us somewhat in a traditional form, and probably not been established by unbiassed reflection. In European monarchies, the pardoning privilege rose out of the power, not legally bestowed, but physically exercised, to interfere with justice; and, at the same time, from a vague feeling of the necessity that somewhere a power ought to exist, which might sometimes modify the literal application of the law, particularly when the latter is cruel Having originated in times in which all the branches and operations of government were but illy defined, this power gradually rose into a distinct privilege, cherished by as many rulers, probably, for its great political importance, as for its merciful character, so grateful to a paternal monarch It agreed well with the religious-political character, given to the exalted station of the crowned and anointed sovereign, poetry compared it to divine mercy. The privilege existed when we separated from our mother country; it was necessary to invest somebody with it, or to abrogate it. It was, naturally enough, given to the chief magistrates. But it is time to inquire whether it agrees with our institutions, which are rendered as little as possible dependant upon the individuality of a single person. In monarchies, one of the fundamental principles of which is to reconcile abstract law with the individuality of a single person, this interference of an individual with the free and unchecked operation of the law, has nothing contrary to their characteristic spirit; with us, it is out of place Let us then try to remedy the evil.

It is evident, that the privilege of pardoning, or as it would be called with much more propriety, the *responsibility*, ought to be vested in a body of men, not in an individual. If you divide the responsibility for any act, it is much easier to bear it. Some of our states have conferred the power of pardoning on the legislature. I think they ought not to be imitated. Legislatures are chosen for political purposes, are,too much occupied with legislative business, and above all, are much too numerous to be able to investigate a petition for pardon with that patience, care, and nicety which a question, the very character of which is, to deviate from the law, necessarily requires. The most advisable, therefore, would seem to be, to establish a committee or chamber of pardon, consisting of seven or nine members, some of whom ought to be judges, perhaps under the presidency of the chief justice, which might convene twice a year to recommend for pardon those prisoners to the governor, who have been judged by them to be fit subjects for it, after hearing a deliberate report on each case by one of their members, because it would be improper to leave this important act dependent upon indefinite and vague feelings. But as it is injurious to leave in matters of law any thing indefinite which need not be so, and as it would operate injuriously upon the penitentiary system, to allow the hope of pardon to be any longer the cause of excitement to the prisoners, it would be proper perhaps to adopt a law similar to that of the republic of Geneva, where the penitentiary system has been introduced, i. e. that every prisoner has a right to petition the *commission de recours*—a committee consisting of nine members for judging of the fitness for pardon—after two-thirds of the imprisonment, for which he has been sentenced, have elapsed. Sentence for life is considered in this case equal to thirty years. The court and jury alone, who have felt themselves bound by facts and law to award a certain judgment, but feel, nevertheless, that it is a case in which the law falls too hard upon the convict, should have the right to recommend a case to the consideration of the committee of pardon, previously to the lapse of two-thirds of the imprisonment, and the governor, or any other authority, yet definitely invested with this privilege, might have the power to charge the committee to consider a case at any time, and to report thereon respecting the propriety of making use of the pardoning power. But in no case ought the governor or any other authority to have the right of pardoning without a previous investigation of the case.by the committee of pardon. It may be objected that a rogue, in order to obtain pardon after the expiration of two-thirds of his term, to which a similar law would give him a kind of right, may behave apparently well, without truly reforming; but let a man who has been sentenced for ten years, behave apparently well for six years and a half, and nine times out of ten it will have a salutary influence Besides, is hypocrisy not much more excited at present when pardon may be granted at any time?

Mr. Dumont is so convinced of the necessity of eliminating uncertainty from all matters of law and punishment as much as possible, that he uses the following words in his report to the representative council of Geneva, January 5, 1825, in consequence of which the above-mentioned law of that republic was adopted: "It may be laid down as an incontestable principle, that in matters of penal justice, I was going to say, in penal pharmacy, every thing which diminishes the certainty of punishment is an evil; every punishment which is not fixed, which floats between fear and hope, is a punishment badly contrived. The causes of uncertainty between the law and its operation, are already but too numerous, if this is an inevitable evil, it ought to be reduced to its narrowest limits, but what shall we think of a law, the object of which is to render the punishment uncertain! and this is nevertheless the result of a tribunal of pardon, open to the petitions of the prisoner during the whole term of his imprisonment. We should know man very imperfectly were we not aware of the readiness with which he takes his wishes for hopes, and his hopes for probabilities. I agree, that a convict wishing for pardon, will take care not to create himself difficulties by acts of insubordination or violence, I allow that he will pay attention to his words and behaviour but it is a fact, that this idea, always present to his mind, causing a disturbed feeling of anxiety and expectation, will absorb and prevent him from being resigned to his situation, and following his labour with reflection and calmness. He feels like an indigent person, who having taken a lottery ticket, has his imagination absorbed by dreams of success, and fears of misfortune. It has been observed that prisoners, after having been unsuccessful in their petitions for pardon, became more calm and resigned to their situation and duties as soon as their fate was fixed. I owe this interesting observation to our jailor. Thus far the double end of increasing the certainty of punishment and of making it more subservient to moral correction, this indefinite recourse to pardon ought to be abolished, and a fixed character be given to it."*

The committee of pardon of Geneva consists of nine members, most of whom are judges.

Such, or a similar limitation of the pardoning power, would require in some states, the modification of certain laws, which seem to continue in their severity only, because it is understood that the governor shortens the imprisonment of all those, whose sentence (by the law) seems to be hard according to our present views. It is peculiar, but it is nevertheless true, that, comparatively speaking, criminal law has been little attended to in

* Page 26 of Dumont's *Rapport sur le projet de loi pour le régime intérieur des prisons,* printed, together with his report relative to the establishment of a penitentiary (delivered 1822) in Geneva, 1825.

5 *

England, or in the United States, whilst in two countries, in which the citizen is by far less protected in his rights—Germany and Italy—criminal law has been made the subject of the deepest study by many of their first jurists. Beccaria, Filangieri, Feuerbach, Mittermaier, may be mentioned out of a host. The reason may be, that in a free and well regulated country, the criminal trial forms but a very limited part of that whole system which guaranties to the citizen his rights and privileges, so that little interest is attached to it by the nation at large, whilst in absolute monarchies the penal trial is one of the very few cases in which the individual and the government meet as parties, and, as it were, on even ground, (which at least is the case where the court does not accuse, inquire, try, defend, and sentence). It is the criminal trial in many countries, the only case in which the citizen, or rather the subject, appears under the ægis of distinct and acknowledged rights and privileges, and it cannot surprise us therefore, if we find some authors treating criminal law as if they were treating of constitutional law. However this may be, it is very desirable that criminal law should be made in our country a subject of more general and deeper study; because this is the only preparation for such laws which finally will entirely accord with the penitentiary system. A chair for criminal law is indispensable, and let us never forget that the Germans and Italians have attended most to criminal law, the French and English least; to the literature of the former, particularly to the first, we must direct our attention.

In France, pardon is reduced in some degree to certainty, by Article 463 of the *Code Pénal,* according to which the judges have the right to award in certain cases, a punishment under the *minimum* of punishment mentioned by the code. In the year 1827, use was made of this provision in 10,493 cases. But it must be remembered that this provision has reference to *correctional cases* only, in which no jury exists Of late a law was issued in France, according to which pardon was held out as a reward for good behaviour in prison; at first it had an admirable effect, but soon it created the reverse, by disappointing some prisoners, exciting others, &c.

The authors have only treated of our prisons and those of France I intended at first, to extend my notes to the consideration of prisons in all other countries of the civilized world, as far as the materials in my possession would enable me, but I soon found, that this vast subject could not conveniently be treated in the form of notes or an appendix. It would be an ample subject for a work of itself.

Several times I have had occasion to refer, in the course of this work, to the *Encyclopædia Americana.* For the English readers of this work, I would remark, that the British Cyclopædia, now publishing in England, contains an almost literal reprint of all articles of general interest in the *Americana*, to judge from those numbers which have reached this country, though the British Cyclopædia calls itself in the title page, only founded "on the celebrated German Conversation-Lexicon." As the *Americana* is also called "on the basis of the Conversations-Lexicon," the English editor probably supposed the articles were but translations of the German work

By some accident, the latest report on the Sing-Sing prison, sent to me, whilst the present work was in progress, miscarried. This alone is the reason why the reader will find in the statistical accounts and tables, statements of the last report on the Auburn prison, but not on that of Sing-Sing   When I received the report, the work had already gone to press *

* The translator received information from Paris on the day when this introduction went to press, that a second edition of the original was preparing

After the whole of the present work, the above preface not excepted, was in type, I received the Extracts from the Information obtained by his Majesty's Commissioners, as to the Administration and Operation of the Poor Laws, published by Authority, London, 1833. It is a work of the highest interest, uncovering as it does, a dangerous evil, in the very vitals of the community, which nevertheless grew out of laws, enacted with the best intentions, and, as the frailty of human nature establishes but too near a connexion between pauperism and crime, work-houses and prisons, the one being so often the cause of the other, I seize upon this opportunity to recommend its perusal to all interested in penal matters, and the administration of paupers. It is a work full of most instructive matter.

Manhattanville, City of New York, May, 1833.

TABLE OF CONTENTS.

ERRATA.

Page 40, line 6 from the foot of the page, insert · *i. e ethical,* after the word *moral.*

Page 64, line 9, read *Quételet's* instead of *Quéteset's.*

Page 88, line 2 from the foot of the page, add *generally* after *and.*

Page 187, line 16, read *Quételet* instead of *Ouételet.*

Page 200, line 11 from the foot of the page, read *ought not* instead of *ought;* and in the next following line, read *the warden of a prison,* instead of *him.*

LIST OF JUSTIFICATORY DOCUMENTS.*

The authors have, on their return from America, deposited in the office of the Minister of Commerce and Public Works, six volumes in folio, containing the following documents :

Vol. I.

Massachusetts.

1. Report for the year 1820, on the Charlestown prison, near Boston.
2. Report for the year 1821.
3.   "   "   1822.
4.   "   "   1823.
5.   "   "   1824.
6.   "   "   1825.
7.   "   "   1826.
8.   "   "   1827.
9.   "   "   1828.
10. Report of the inspectors of the new penitentiary for the year 1829.
11. Report for 1830.
12. Laws of the State of Massachusetts, respecting the penitentiary, and rules of the prison.
13. Some statistical documents on the prison, and a manuscript of the superintendent, who gave it to us.
14. Regulations of the old prison (1823).

Connecticut.

15. Report of the committee appointed to inspect the old Newgate Prison, for 1825.
16. Report of the committee appointed to inspect the old Newgate Prison, for 1826.
17. Report of the committee appointed to construct a new prison, for 1827.

* We give this list, because it will be agreeable to those interested in the work, and in prisons in general, to know from what sources the authors derived their information, besides personal inspection.—TRANS.

18. Report of the inspectors of the Wethersfield Prison for 1828.
19.   "   .   "   .   "   "   1829.
20.   "   "   "   "   1830.
21.   "   "   "   "   · 1831.

22. Law of Connecticut respecting the penitentiary system, 1827.

23. Statistical table of crimes and offences, from 1790 to 1831.·

24. Letter to us by Mr Barrett, chaplain of Wethersfield, on the penitentiary system, October 7th, 1831

25 Copy of a contract between the superintendent of Wethersfield and a contractor.

26. Manuscript notice by Mr. Barrett, on the discipline of Wethersfield, October, 1831.

Vol. II.

New York.—Ancient Newgate Prison.

1. Original document by Mr. Flagg, secretary of state, to us, containing a report on Newgate, of December 31, 1817; another of December 31, 1818, and a third, of January 20, 1819.

2. Report of the comptroller of the State of New York on Newgate, March 2, 1819.

3. Report of the inspectors of Newgate, January 21, 1820
4.   "   "   "   of 1824 and 1827.
      "   "   "   of 1823 and 1826.

5 Statistical tables, showing the number and nature of crimes in the state of New York, copied by us from the registers of Newgate

6. Statistical table, showing the number of prisoners pardoned, escaped, and of those who died; also, the expenses of the old Newgate Prison from 1797 to 1819.

Penitentiary of Sing-Sing.

7. Report of the inspectors to the legislature for 1825
8.   "   "   "   of 1827 for 1826.
9.   "   "   "   of 1828 for 1827.
10   "   "   "   of 1829 for 1828.
11.   "   "   "   of Jan'y 6, 1830
12   "   "   "   of Jan'y. 5, 1831.
13   "   "   "   of Jan'y.12,1832.

14. Report of Mr. Hopkins on Mr. Elam Lynds, March 19, 1831.

15. Manuscript memorandum on the discipline of Sing-Sing, given to us by Mr Wiltse, superintendent of this prison.

16. Plan of Sing-Sing, and memorandum of Mr. Cartwright, containing a plan and estimate of the expenses of this prison.

Penitentiary of Auburn.

17. Manuscript report of the commissioners appointed to inspect Auburn, March 16, 1818.

18. Report of the inspectors of the Auburn Prison, of February 1, 1819.

19. Report of the inspectors of the Auburn Prison, for the year 1820.

20. Report of the inspectors of the Auburn Prison, of January 1, 1824, for 1823

21. Report of the inspectors of the Auburn Prison, of January 26, 1825, for 1824.

22. Report of the inspectors of the Auburn Prison, of February 2, 1826, for 1825 _

23. Report of the inspectors of the Auburn Prison, of January 8, 1827, for 1826.

24. Report of the inspectors of the Auburn Prison, of January 5, 1828, for 1827.

25. Report of the inspectors of the Auburn Prison, of January 1, 1829, for 1828.

Vol. III.

Continuation of Auburn.

1. Report of the inspectors of the Auburn Prison, of January 18, 1830, for 1829.

2. Report of the inspectors of the Auburn Prison, of January 24, 1831, for 1830.

3. Report of the inspectors of the Auburn Prison, of January 30, 1832, for 1831.

4. On the construction and discipline of Auburn, by Gershom Powers, 1826.

5. Report of Gershom Powers on Auburn Prison, 1828.

6. Letter of Gershom Powers, in answer to Edward Livingston, 1829.

7. Report of Messrs. Hopkins and Tibbits on the Auburn Prison, January 13, 1827.

8. Remarks of Gershom Powers on disciplinary punishments, 1828.

9. Inquiry into the Auburn discipline, and on the system of contract.

10. Manuscript given to us by the clerk of Auburn, respecting the order and discipline of that prison.

11. Conversation which we had with Mr. Smith, chaplain of the Auburn Prison.

Vol. IV.

Maryland.—Old Prison, and New Penitentiary of Baltimore.

1 Legislative documents respecting the Maryland Penitentiary, 1819.

2 Regulations of the new penitentiary, December 22, 1828.

3. Report of the directors of the penitentiary, December 23, 1828.

4. Report of the directors of the penitentiary, December 21, 1829.

5 Report of the directors of the penitentiary, December 20, 1830.

6 Observations of Mr. Niles on the penitentiary, December 22, 1829.

7. Letter of Mr. MacEvoy on the same, December 4, 1831.

8. Table of executions in Maryland, from 1786 to this day.

Pennsylvania.—Walnut Street and Pittsburg Prisons, and Penitentiary of Cherry Hill.

9. Report to the legislature on the penitentiary system, January 27, 1821.

10. Notice of Roberts Vaux on the penitentiary system in Pennsylvania, 1826.

11. Letter of Roberts Vaux to William Roscoe on the same subject, 1827.

12. Letter of Edward Livingston to Roberts Vaux on the same subject.

13. Observations on the same subject by Dr. Bache, 1829.

14 Description of the new penitentiary, 1829.

15. Constitution of the Prison Society of Philadelphia

16 First and second reports on the new penitentiary, 1831.

17. Acts of the legislature, containing the new penal laws connected with the new penitentiary system. Regulations of the prison.

18. Letter of Dr. Bache on the new penitentiary system, contained in a number of the Journal of Law.

19. Three numbers of Hazard's Register, containing statistical documents on the penitentiary system of Pennsylvania.

20. Letter of Samuel Wood on the penitentiary system, 1831.

21. Report of the commissioners appointed for the revision of the Penal Code of Pennsylvania, December 24, 1827.

22. Of the penitentiary system in Pennsylvania, by Mease, 1828.

Vol. V.

*General documents on the Penitentiary System, or indirectly
connected with it.*

1. Six reports of the Boston Prison Discipline Society, from 1826 to 1832.

2. Report of Mr. Gray respecting the erection of workshops for delivered prisoners.

3. Introductory Report to the Code of Prison Discipline, prepared for the state of Louisiana by Edward Livingston, 1827.

4. On the abolition of capital punishment, by the same.

5. Reflections on the Penitentiary System, by Mr M Carey, of Philadelphia, 1831.

6 Essay on the Penal Code of Pennsylvania, by Tyson.

7. Report of 1831 on the Temperance Society of New York.

8 " " " " of Pennsylvania.

9. Medical Statistics of Philadelphia, by Emerson, 1831.

10. Report on primary schools of Pennsylvania, 1831.

11. Laws respecting schools in Pennsylvania.

12. Three statistical tables on the sanatory state of Baltimore.

13. Report on the school fund in Connecticut

14 Letter directed by Mr. Elam Lynds to ourselves, on the penitentiary system, October 10, 1831.

15 Opinion of Mr Elam Lynds on the penitentiary system. (Manuscript sent by him to ourselves, July 8, 1831)

16 Statistical table on the number of crimes in Ohio.

17 Another table on the number of crimes since 1815.

18. Letter of Mr. M'Lean, Judge of the Supreme Court of the United States, on the penitentiary system.

19. Statistical table of convictions pronounced in the city of New York, by the Court of Oyer and Terminer, from 1785 to 1795

20. Statistical table of convictions pronounced by the Supreme Court.

21. Statistical table of convictions from 1800 to 1810, and from 1820 to 1830.

22. General table of convictions pronounced in the state of New York during the year 1830, for crimes, offences, &c (with the exception of judgments pronounced by police magistrates)

23. Manuscript of Judge Wells (at Wethersfield), containing his opinion on the penitentiary system, the plan of a prison for 500 prisoners, and the estimate of expenses of their support.

24. Copy of a letter addressed to Dr Hosack of New York, by William Roscoe.

Vol. VI.

House of Refuge.—(New York.)

1. Discourse on the opening of the House of Refuge of New York, 1826.

2. Report of 1827 on the House of Refuge.

3.	"	1828	"	"	"
4.	"	1829	"	"	"
5.	"	1830	"	"	"
6	"	1831	"	"	"
7.	"	1832	"	"	"

8. Regulations of the House of Refuge of New York, and appeal to the inhabitants of New York, by the committee on prisons, in order to obtain their support.

Philadelphia and Boston, &c.

9. Appeal of the directors of the House of Refuge of Philadelphia, in order to obtain funds, 1826.

10. Discourse pronounced by Mr. J. Sergeant, on the opening of the House of Refuge of Philadelphia.

11. Another appeal of the directors of the House of Refuge to their fellow citizens, 1828

12. First report on the House of Refuge of Philadelphia, 1829.

13. Second " " " " 1830.

14. Third " " " " 1831.

15. Regulations of the House of Reformation of Boston, 1830.

16. Report of the committee for the establishment of a House of Refuge in Baltimore

17. Form of an indenture for individuals leaving the House of Refuge of Philadelphia

18. Inquiry into the House of Refuge of New York.

19. Various documents, seven in number, on the House of Refuge of New York.

The whole, composing one hundred and twenty-seven pieces, arranged in the way indicated above, in six volumes folio, have been deposited by the Minister of Commerce and Public Works, in the archives of his office

The *maître des requêtes*, secretary-general of the office of the Minister* of Commerce and Public Works, acknowledges to have received from Messrs de Beaumont and de Toqueville the volumes above mentioned, which have been deposited in the archives of the "ministry," section of the library.

The *maître des requêtes*, secretary-general,

(Signed)   EDMOND BLANC.

---

* There is no word in English for the French *ministère*, which is used in the original in this place, or for the German *ministerium*, because, in fact, the thing itself does not exist in England or the United States, it belongs essentially to *bureaucracy*.

PREFACE.

SOCIETY, in our days, is in a state of disquiet, owing, in our opinion, to two causes:*

The first is of an entirely moral character; there is in the minds of men an activity which knows not where to find an object; an energy deprived of its proper element; and which consumes society for want of other prey.

The other is of an entirely material character; it is the unhappy condition of the working classes who are in want of labour and bread; and whose corruption, beginning in misery, is completed in the prison.

The first evil is owing to the progress of intellectual improvement; the second, to the misery of the poor.

How is the first of these evils to be obviated? Its remedy

---

* We live, every one will admit, in an agitated period—one of those epochs (in the opinion of the translator) which are characterized in history by the conflict of new principles with old, and whose agitation can cease only when the former acquire a decided ascendency over the latter We must be careful, however, that the Present does not appear to us in those magnified dimensions, with which it never fails to impress itself on our minds, if we do not view the Past and the Present with conscientious impartiality, and examine both with unprejudiced scrutiny—in many cases the most difficult task of the historian The present evil always appears the greatest, but if we allow ourselves to be thus biassed, we shall be liable to mistake the real aim after which we ought to strive, and the means by which we endeavour to arrive at it, and unconsciously will lend assistance to those who, more than any others, raise in our age the cry at our disturbed times—the advocates of crumbling institutions They ought to be aware, that few times were more peacefully disposed than that in which we live, and which they are so anxious to represent as deprived of all solid foundation If we examine century by century, from the seventeenth up to the beginning of the common era, where and when do we find peace ? We meet every where with war, turmoil and party strife, contests often originating in frivolous cabinet intrigues, or kindled by religious fanaticism, or by interest and ambition hiding themselves under the pretence of defending sacred rights, inherent in individuals, for the purpose of obtaining sway over nations The sober student of history must admit, that there never was a period possessing more powerful elements of peace, than our own, since the interests which determine the condition of society have become more and more expanded, are of a general and national, not of a limited, individual, and therefore, arbitrary character These observations are by no means directed against the writers of the present work, but merely intended as a general remark on what we conceive to be a misconception very common in our time, and particularly against those who, taking for granted that the time we live in is more unsettled and disturbed, and that society is in a more feverish state than heretofore, are opposed to salutary and necessary reforms, extolling former times as those of happy ease.—TRANS.

seems to depend more upon circumstances, than upon human provisions. As to the second, more than one effort has already been made to free mankind from it; but it is not yet known whether success is possible.

Such is the insufficiency of human institutions, that we see melancholy effects resulting from establishments which in theory promise none but happy results

In England it has been believed that the springs of crime and misery may be dried up by giving work and money to the unfortunate; but we see the number of paupers and criminals every day increasing in that country.

There is not one philanthropic institution, the abuse of which does not border closely on its usefulness.

Alms, however well distributed, tend to produce poverty: and assistance afforded to a forsaken child causes others to be abandoned. The more we contemplate the melancholy spectacle presented by public benevolence, struggling without success against human sufferings, the more we are obliged to acknowledge, that there exist evils, against which it is generous to strive, but of which our old societies seem incapable to rid themselves

Yet the wound exists, open to every eye. There are in France two millions of paupers, and forty thousand liberated convicts, who have gone forth from the bagnes or other prisons. *

Alarmed by so formidable an evil, public opinion asks a remedy from government, which does not cure it, perhaps, because it considers it incurable

But notwithstanding it may be true that this vicious state of society cannot be cured altogether, it seems equally certain that there are circumstances which tend to aggravate it, and institutions whose influence renders it less fatal.

Various voices are raised in our time to indicate to government the path which is best to be pursued

Some ask for the establishment of agricultural colonies in those parts of the French soil which have as yet been left uncultivated, and where the labour of convicts and paupers might be made useful and productive.

This system, which has met with great success in Belgium and Holland, is worthy of the particular attention of statesmen.†

Others are particularly struck with the danger to which society is exposed from liberated convicts, whose corruption has been increased in prison. These believe that the evil would be

* See *Des Colonies Agricoles*, by Mr. Huerne de Pommeuse statistical tables at the end of this volume.
† See the work cited in the preceding note, [and an article on *Pauper Colonies* in that on *Colonies* in the *Encyclopædia Americana.*—TRANS.]

remedied in a great degree, if the criminals were subjected during the time of their imprisonment to a penitentiary system, which, instead of further depraving them, made them better.

Some writers (one of whom has just received a prize from the French academy) being persuaded that the moral reformation of the criminal is impossible, and that his restoration to society cannot take place without imminent danger, think that it would be better if all convicts were transported out of France.*

In the midst of these clashing opinions, some of which however are not irreconcilable, it appeared to us that it would be of use to introduce into this discussion some authentic documents on one of the important points in dispute.

Such has been the origin of the travels we have undertaken under the auspices of the French government.

Having been commissioned to examine into the theory and practice of the penitentiary system in the United States, we have accomplished this task; government has received our report,† and we now owe it to our country to give an account of our labours.

If the results of our investigations shall be deemed valuable, it is chiefly owing to the generous hospitality with which we were received in the United States. Every where in that country, establishments of all kinds were thrown open to us, and all necessary materials were furnished with a readiness which awakened in us the liveliest feeling of gratitude.

The importance of our mission was understood in America, and the public functionaries of the highest order, as well as private gentlemen, vied with each other in facilitating its execution

We have had no means of manifesting our sense of so much kindness. But if this book should find its way to America, we are happy to think that the inhabitants of the United States will find here a feeble expression of our heartfelt gratitude.

* M Ernest de Blosseville, author of the *Histoire des Colonies pénales dans l'Australie*, Paris, 1831   The system of transportation, to which public opinion in France seems pretty *generally* favourable, appears to us surrounded with dangers and difficulties.   See the Appendix on Penal Colonies

† This report has been handed in to the Minister of Commerce and Public Works. Count d'Argout has received it with an interest which we ought to acknowledge with gratitude.

PART I.

CHAPTER I.

Historical Outline of the Penitentiary System.

Origin of the Penitentiary System in 1786.—Influence of the Quakers —Walnut Street Prison in Philadelphia, its faults and its advantages —The Duke of La Rochefoucault-Liancourt.—Discipline of Walnut Street adopted by several states, its evil effects —Origin of Auburn —Pittsburg —Cherry-Hill. —Fatal experience of absolute solitary confinement it is succeeded by the Auburn system, founded upon isolation and silence : success of this system in several states of the Union.—Wethersfield foundation of Sing-Sing by Mr. Elam Lynds.—Institution of houses of refuge in the State of New York — Pennsylvania abandons the system of absolute solitude without labour new discipline of imprisonment combined with new penal laws —States which have not yet made any reform in their prisons, in what this reform is incomplete in those states in which it exists.—Barbarity of some criminal laws in the United States.—Recapitulation.

THOUGH the penitentiary system in the United States is a new institution, its origin must be traced back to times already long gone by. The first idea of a reform in the American prisons, belongs to a religious sect in Pennsylvania. The Quakers, who abhor all shedding of blood, had always protested against the barbarous laws which the colonies inherited from their mother country. In 1786, their voice succeeded in finding due attention, and from this period, punishment of death, mutilation and the whip were successively abolished in almost all cases by the Legislature of Pennsylvania.* A less cruel fate awaited the convicts from this period. The punishment of imprisonment was substituted for corporeal punishment, and the law authorized the courts to inflict solitary confinement in a cell during day and night, upon those guilty of capital crimes. It was then that the Walnut Street prison was established in Philadelphia. Here the convicts were classed according to the nature of their

---

* At present, punishment of death is pronounced by the Code of Pennsylvania, for murder in the first degree only. [It may not be amiss to refer the reader to an article on the Revised Code of Pennsylvania, in No. XXV, of the American Quarterly Review, which contains valuable information.]—TRANS.

1

crimes, and separate cells were constructed for those whom the courts of justice had sentenced to absolute isolation : these cells also served to curb the resistance of individuals, unwilling to submit to the discipline of the prison.   The solitary prisoners did not work.*

This innovation was good but incomplete.

The impossibility of subjecting criminals to a useful classification, has since been acknowledged; and solitary confinement without labour has been condemned by experience.   It is nevertheless just to say, that the trial of this theory has not been made long enough to be decisive.   The authority given to the judges of Pennsylvania, by the law of April 5, 1790, and of March 22, to send criminals to the prison in Walnut Street, who formerly would have been sent to the different county jails, soon produced in this prison such a crowd of convicts, that the difficulty of classification increased in the same degree as the cells became insufficient.†

To say the truth there did not yet exist a penitentiary system in the United States.

If it be asked why this name was given to the system of imprisonment which had been established, we would answer, that then as well as now, the abolition of the punishment of death was confounded in America, with the penitentiary system. People said—*instead of killing the guilty, our laws put them in prison; hence we have a penitentiary system*

The conclusion was not correct   It is very true that the punishment of death applied to the greater part of crimes, is irreconcilable with a system of imprisonment; but this punishment abolished, the penitentiary system does not yet necessarily exist; it is further necessary, that the criminal whose life has been spared, be placed in a prison, whose discipline renders him better.   Because, if the system, instead of reforming, should only tend to corrupt him still more, this would not be any longer a *penitentiary system*, but only a *bad system of imprisonment.*

This mistake of the Americans has for a long time been shared in France.   In 1794, the Duke de la Rochefoucauld-Liancourt, published an interesting notice on the prison of Philadelphia: he declared that this city had an excellent prison system, and all the world repeated it.‡

However, the Walnut Street prison could produce none of the

---

* These cells were or are still thirty in number, in the Walnut Street prison.

† See letter from Samuel Wood to Thomas Kittera, Philadelphia, 1831. See Notices of the original and successive efforts to improve the Discipline of the Prison at Philadelphia, and to reform the Criminal Code of Pennsylvania, by Roberts Vaux.

‡ See *Des Prisons de Philadelphie par un Européen, (La Rochefoucauld-Liancourt,) l'an IV., de la République.* Paris.

effects which are expected from this system. It had two principal faults: it corrupted by contamination those who worked together. It corrupted by indolence, the individuals who were plunged into solitude.

The true merit of its founders was the abolition of the sanguinary laws of Pennsylvania, and by introducing a new system of imprisonment, the direction of public attention to this important point. Unfortunately that which in this innovation deserved praise, was not immediately distinguished from that which was untenable.

Solitude applied to the criminal, in order to conduct him to reformation by reflection, rests upon a philosophical and true conception. But the authors of this theory had not yet founded its application upon those means which alone could render it practical and salutary. Yet their mistake was not immediately perceived; and the success of Walnut Street prison boasted of in the United States still more than in Europe, biassed public opinion in favour of its faults, as well as its advantages.

The first state which showed itself zealous to imitate Pennsylvania, was that of New York, which in 1797, adopted both new penal laws and a new prison system.

Solitary confinement without labour, was admitted here as in Philadelphia; but, as in Walnut Street, it was reserved for those who especially were sentenced to undergo it by the courts of justice, and for those who opposed the established order of the prison. Solitary confinement, therefore, was not the ordinary system of the establishment; it awaited only those great criminals who, before the reform of the penal laws, would have been condemned to death. Those who were guilty of less offences were put indiscriminately together in the prison. They, different from the inmates of the solitary cells, had to work during the day; and the only disciplinary punishment which their keeper had a right to inflict, in case of breach of the order of the prison, was solitary confinement, with bread and water.

The Walnut Street prison was imitated by others. Maryland, Massachusetts, Maine, New Jersey, Virginia, &c., adopted successively, the principle of solitary confinement, applied only to a certain class of criminals (a) in each of these states; the reform of criminal laws preceded that of the prisons.

Nowhere was this system of imprisonment crowned with the hoped-for success. In general it was ruinous to the public treasury; it never effected the reformation of the prisoners,[*] every

* See the statistical tables at the end of the work, division on finances.
See Report to the Legislature by the Comptroller of the State of New York, March 2, 1819.
See Fifth Report of the Boston Prison Discipline Society, pages 412, 423 & 451
See also Report on the Prisons of Connecticut and Massachusetts.

year the legislature of each state voted considerable funds towards the support of the penitentiaries, and the continued return of the same individuals into the prisons, proved the inefficiency of the system to which they were submitted.*

Such results seem to prove the insufficiency of the whole system; however, instead of accusing the theory itself, its execution was attacked. It was believed that the whole evil resulted
from the paucity of cells, and the crowding of the prisoners;
and that the system, such as it was established, would be fertile
in happy results, if some new buildings were added to the prisons already existing. New expenses therefore, and new efforts
were made.

Such was the origin of the Auburn prison, [1816.]

This prison, which has become so celebrated since, was at
first founded upon a plan essentially erroneous; it limited itself
to some classifications, and each of these cells was destined to
receive two convicts:† it was of all combinations the most unfortunate; it would have been better to throw together fifty criminals in the same room, than to separate them two by two.
This inconvenience was soon felt, and in 1819 the Legislature
of the State of New York, ordered the erection of a new building at Auburn, (the northern wing) in order to increase the
number of solitary cells However, it must be observed, that
no idea as yet existed of the system which has prevailed since.
It was not intended to subject all the convicts to the system of
cells; but its application was only to be made to a greater number. At the same time the same theories produced the same
trials in Philadelphia, where the little success of the Walnut
Street prison would have convinced the inhabitants of Pennsylvania of its inefficiency, if the latter, like the citizens of the
State of New York, had not been led to seek in the faults of execution, a motive for allowing the principle to be correct.

In 1817, the Legislature of Pennsylvania decreed the erection
of the penitentiary at Pittsburg, for the western counties; and
in 1821, that of the penitentiary of Cherry-Hill, for the city of
Philadelphia and the eastern counties.‡

---

* See our statistical observations on the various States of the Union, No. 17,
Comparative Table of re-committals.

"It is a melancholy truth, that the greater part of the convicts do not reform
during their imprisonment, but on the contrary, harden still more in their wickedness, and are, after they are delivered, more vicious and consummate criminals, than they were before "—RE TRANSLATION.

(Report of January 20, 1819, to the Legislature of New York.)

† The Auburn Prison, i. e. the southern wing, built in 1816, 1817, and 1818,
contained sixty-one cells, and twenty-eight rooms, each of which afforded room
for from eight to twelve convicts

‡ Cherry-Hill is the New Penitentiary of Philadelphia, put into operation in
1829.

The principles to be followed in the construction of these two establishments were, however, not entirely the same as those on which the Walnut Street prison had been erected. In the latter, classification formed the predominant system, to which solitary confinement was but secondary. In the new prisons the classifications were abandoned, and a solitary cell was to be prepared for each convict The criminal was not to leave his cell day or night, and all labour was denied to him in his solitude. Thus absolute solitary confinement, which in Walnut Street was but accidental, was now to become the foundation of the system adopted for Pittsburg and Cherry-Hill.

The experiment which was to be made, promised to be decisive: no expense was spared to contruct these new establishments worthy of their object, and the edifices which were elevated, resembled prisons less than palaces.

In the meantime, before even the laws which ordered their erection, were executed, the Auburn prison had been tried in the State of New York. Lively debates ensued on this occasion, in the legislature; and the public was impatient to know the result of the new trials, which had just been made.

The northern wing having been nearly finished in 1821, eighty prisoners were placed there, and a separate cell was given to each. This trial, from which so happy a result had been anticipated, was fatal to the greater part of the convicts : in order to reform them, they had been submitted to complete isolation ; but this absolute solitude, if nothing interrupt it, is beyond the strength of man; it destroys the criminal without intermission and without pity ; it does not reform, it kills (*b*)

The unfortunates, on whom this experiment was made, fell into a state of depression, so manifest, that their keepers were struck with it; their lives seemed in danger, if they remained longer in this situation; five of them, had already succumbed during a single year ;(*c*) their moral state was not less alarming ; one of them had become insane; another, in a fit of despair, had embraced the opportunity when the keeper brought him something, to precipitate himself from his cell, running the almost certain chance of a mortal fall.

Upon similar effects the system was finally judged. The Governor of the State of New York pardoned twenty-six of those in solitary confinement; the others to whom this favour was not extended, were allowed to leave the cells during day, and to work in the common work-shops of the prison. From this period, (1823) the system of unmodified isolation ceased entirely to be practised at Auburn : proofs were soon afforded that this system, fatal to the health of the criminals, was likewise inefficient in producing their reform. Of twenty-six con-

victs, pardoned by the governor, fourteen returned a short time
after into the prison, in consequence of new offences *

This experiment, so fatal to those who were selected to undergo it, was of a nature to endanger the success of the penitentiary
system altogether.   After the melancholy effects of isolation, it
was to be feared that the whole principle would be rejected: it
would have been a natural re-action. The Americans were wiser:
the idea was not given up, that the solitude, which causes the
criminal to reflect, exercises a beneficial influence; and the problem was, to find the means by which the evil effect of total solitude could be avoided without giving up its advantages.   It
was believed that this end could be attained, by leaving the convicts in their cells during night, and by making them work during the day, in the common work-shops, obliging them at the
same time to observe absolute silence.

Messrs Allen, Hopkins, and Tibbits, who, in 1824, were
directed by the Legislature of New York to inspect the Auburn
prison, found this new discipline established in that prison. They
praised it much in their report, and the Legislature sanctioned
this new system by its formal approbation.

Here an obscurity exists which it has not been in our power
to dissipate.   We see the renowned Auburn system suddenly
spring up, and proceed from the ingenious combination of two
elements, which seem at first glance incompatible, isolation and
re-union.   But that which we do not clearly see, is the creator
of this system, of which nevertheless some one must necessarily
have formed the first idea.   *   *   *

Does the State of New York owe it to Governor Clinton,
whose name in the United States is connected with so many
useful and beneficial enterprises?

Does the honour belong to Mr. Cray, one of the directors of
Auburn, to whom Judge Powers, who himself was at the head
of that establishment, seems to attribute the merit?

Lastly, Mr. Elam Lynds, who has contributed so much to
put the new system into practice, does the glory also of the in-
vention belong to him?†

We shall not attempt to solve this question, interesting to
the persons whom we have mentioned, and the country to which
they belong, but of little importance to us.

* See Report by Gershom Powers, 1828, and the manuscript note by Elam
Lynds.

† Public opinion in the United States attributes almost universally to Mr
Elam Lynds the creation of the system, finally adopted in the Auburn prison.
This opinion is also that of Messrs. Hopkins and Tibbits, charged, in 1826,
to inspect the Auburn prison, see page 23, and of Mr Livingston, see his
Introductory Report to the Code of Prison Discipline, page 10, Philadelphia
edition, 1827.   We have found this opinion contested only in a letter addressed
by Mr. Powers to Mr. Livingston in 1829.   See this letter page 5, and sequel.

In fine, does not experience teach us that there are innovations, the honour of which belongs to nobody in particular, because they are the effects of simultaneous efforts, and of the progress of time?

The establishment of Auburn has, since its commencement, obtained extraordinary success. It soon excited public attention in the highest degree. A remarkable revolution took place at that time in the opinions of many; the direction of a prison, formerly confided to obscure keepers, was now sought for by persons of high standing; and Mr. Elam Lynds, formerly a Captain in the army of the United States, and Judge Powers, a magistrate of rare merit, were seen, with honour to themselves, filling the office of directors of Auburn.

However, the adoption of the system of cells for all convicts in the state of New York, rendered the Auburn prison insufficient, as it contained but five hundred and fifty cells after all the successive additions which it had received;* the want of a new prison, therefore, was felt. It was then that the plan of Sing-Sing was resolved upon by the legislature (in 1825,) and the way in which it was executed, is of a kind that deserves to be reported.

Mr. Elam Lynds, who had made his trials at Auburn, of which he was the superintendent, left this establishment, took one hundred convicts, accustomed to obey, with him, led them to the place where the projected prison was to be erected; and there, encamped on the bank of the Hudson, without a place to receive, and without walls to lock up his dangerous companions; he sets them to work, making of every one a mason or a carpenter, and having no other means to keep them in obedience, than the firmness of his character and the energy of his will.

During several years, the convicts, whose number was gradually increased, were at work in building their own prison; and at present the penitentiary of Sing-Sing contains one thousand cells, all of which have been built by their criminal inmates †
At the same time (in 1825,) an establishment of another nature was reared in the city of New York, but which occupies not a less important place among the improvements, the history of which we attempt to trace. We mean the house of refuge, founded for juvenile offenders.

* In 1823, there were in Auburn but three hundred and eighty cells On April 12th, 1824, the Legislature ordered the construction of sixty-two more cells

† The manner in which Mr Elam Lynds has built Sing-Sing, would undoubtedly meet with little credit, were it not a recent fact, known by every one in the United States In order to understand it, it is necessary to know all the resources which an energetic mind may find in the new discipline of American prisons. If the reader is desirous of forming an idea of the character of Mr. Elam Lynds, and of his opinion on the penitentiary system, he has only to read the Conversation which we had with him, and which we felt obliged to give at length. See No 11.

There exists no establishment, the usefulness of which, experience has warranted in a higher degree. It is well known that
most of those individuals on whom the criminal law inflicts punishments, have been unfortunate before they became guilty.
Misfortune is particularly dangerous for those whom it befalls in
a tender age; and it is very rare that an orphan without inheri-
tance and without friends, or a child abandoned by its parents,
avoids the snares laid for his inexperience, and does not pass
within a short time from misery to crime. Affected by the fate
of juvenile delinquents, several charitable individuals of the city
of New York* conceived the plan of a house of refuge, destined
to serve as an asylum, and to procure for them an education and
the means of existence, which fortune had refused. Thirty thousand dollars were the produce of a first subscription; thus by the
sole power of a charitable association, an establishment eminently useful, was founded, which, perhaps, is still more important
than the penitentiaries, because the latter punish crime, whilst
the house of refuge tends to prevent it.

The experiment made at Auburn in the state of New York,
(the fatal effects of isolation without labour,) did not prevent
Pennsylvania from continuing the trial of solitary confinement;
and in the year 1827, the penitentiary of Pittsburg began to receive prisoners. Each one was shut up, day and night, in a
cell, in which no labour was allowed to him. This solitude,
which in principle was to be absolute, was not such in fact. The
construction of this penitentiary is so defective, that it is very
easy to hear in one cell what is going on in another, so that each
prisoner found in the communication with his neighbour a daily
recreation, i e. an opportunity of inevitable corruption; and as
these criminals did not work, we may say that their sole occupation consisted in mutual corruption. This prison, therefore, was
worse than even that of Walnut street; because, owing to the
communication with each other, the prisoners at Pittsburg were
as little occupied with their reformation, as those at Walnut
Street; and whilst the latter indemnified society in a degree by
the produce of their labour, the others spent their whole time in
idleness, injurious to themselves, and burthensome to the public
treasury. (*d*)

The bad success of this establishment proved nothing against
the system which had called it into existence, because defects in
the construction of the prison, rendered the execution of the sys-

* I shall show, in a note further on, that houses of refuge were first established in Germany, at least in modern times. But the founders of the New
York house of refuge, it is nevertheless true, were unacquainted with their existence in Germany, and were led to this re-invention by the imperious wants of
their own community.

tem impossible: nevertheless, the advocates of the theories on which it was founded, began to grow cool. This impression became still more general in Pennsylvania, when the melancholy effects caused by solitude without labour in the Auburn prison, became known, as well as the happy success of the new discipline, founded on isolation by night, with common labour during the day.*

Warned by such striking results, Pennsylvania was fearful she had pursued a dangerous course; she felt the necessity of submitting to a new investigation the question of solitary imprisonment without labour, practised at Pittsburg, and introduced into the penitentiary of Cherry-Hill, the construction of which was already much advanced.

The legislature of this state, therefore, appointed a committee in order to examine which was the better system of imprisonment. Messrs. Charles Shaler, Edward King, and T. I. Wharton, commissioners charged with this mission, have exhibited, in a very remarkable report, the different systems then in practice, (December 20, 1827,) and they conclude the discussion by recommending the new Auburn discipline, which they pronounce the best.†

The authority of this inquiry had a powerful effect on public opinion, it however met with powerful opposition: Roberts Vaux, in Pennsylvania, Edward Livingston, in Louisiana, continued to support the system of complete solitude for criminals The latter, whose writings are imbued with so elevated a philosophy, had prepared a criminal code, and a code of Prison Discipline for Louisiana, his native state ‡ His profound theories, little understood by those for whom they were destined, had more suc-

* Not only in the Auburn prison, solitary confinement without labour, produced fatal effects on the mind and body of the prisoners The prisons of Maryland, Maine, Virginia, and New Jersey, did not obtain happier results, in the latter prison, ten individuals are mentioned as having been killed by solitary confinement See the Fifth Report of the Boston Prison Discipline Society, page 422. In Virginia, when the governor ceased to pardon convicts, it was never the case that any one of them survived an attack of disease.
(See Report of the Commissioners for revising the Penal Code of Pennsylvania, page 30)
So far the authors. Without the least intention to advocate solitary confinement without labour, we cannot help expressing some surprise at these results, as it has been, from times immemorial, not uncommon on the continent of Europe, to condemn certain prisoners, i e. high offenders against the government, suspected of peculiar talent for intrigue, to perpetual solitary confinement· and of how many are we not told that lived for a long series of years in this wretched state !—Trans

† This report is one of the most important legislative documents in existence on the American prisons It has been, in Europe, the subject of a special and thorough study of certain publicists

‡ This is a great mistake, not only because Mr Livingston is a native of the State of New York, where he received his education, formed his mind, and spent many years of his riper age, but also because Mr Livingston's writings, and we

2

cess in Pennsylvania, for which they had not been intended. In this superior work, Mr. Livingston admitted, for most cases, the principle of *labour of the convicts:* and, altogether, he showed himself less the advocate of the Pittsburg prison, than the adversary of the Auburn system; he acknowledged the good discipline of the latter, but powerfully opposed himself to corporal punishment used to maintain it. Mr. Livingston, and those who supported the same doctrines, had to combat a powerful fact: this was the uncertainty of their theories, not yet tested, and the proven success of the system they attacked. Auburn went on prospering: every where its wonderful effects were praised, and they were found traced each year with great spirit, in a work justly celebrated in America, and which has essentially co-operated to bring public opinion in the United States, on the penitentiary system, to that point where it now is: we mean the annual publications of the Prison Discipline Society at Boston. These annual reports—the work of Mr. Louis Dwight, give a decided preference to the Auburn system. (*e*)

All the states of the Union were attentive witnesses of the controversy respecting the two systems.

In this fortunate country, which has neither troublesome neighbours, who disturb it from without, nor internal dissensions which distract it within, nothing more is necessary, in order to excite public attention in the highest degree, than an essay on some principle of social economy. As the existence of society is not put in jeopardy, the question is not how to live, but how to improve.

Pennsylvania was, perhaps, more than any other state, interested in the controversy: the rival of New York, it was natural she should show herself jealous to retain, in every respect, the rank to which her advanced civilization entitles her among the most enlightened states of the Union.

She adopted a system which at once agreed with the austerity of her manners, and her philanthropical sensibility; she rejected solitude without labour, the fatal effects of which experience had proved every where, and she retained the absolute separation of the prisoners—a severe punishment, which, in order to be inflicted, needs not the support of corporal chastisement.

The penitentiary of Cherry-Hill, founded on these principles, is therefore a combination of Pittsburg and Auburn. Isolation during night and day, has been retained from the Pittsburg system: and, into the solitary cell, the labour of Auburn has been introduced. (*f*)

This revolution in the prison discipline of Pennsylvania, was

may say his whole philosophy of law are of a decided Anglo-American character, though his residence in Louisiana must have aided his penetrating mind in taking a still more extensive view of the subjects of his inquiry.—Trans.

immediately followed by a general reform of her criminal laws. All punishments were made milder; the severity of solitary imprisonment permitted an abridgment of its duration; capital punishment was abolished in all cases, except that of premeditated murder. (*g*)

Whilst the states of New York and Pennsylvania made important reforms in their laws, and each adopted a different system of imprisonment, the other states of the Union did not remain inactive, in presence of the grand spectacle before them.

Since the year 1825, the plan of a new prison on the Auburn model, has been adopted by the legislature of Connecticut; and the penitentiary at Wethersfield has succeeded the old prison of Newgate.

In spite of the weight which Pennsylvania threw into the balance, in favour of absolute solitude with labour, the Auburn system, i. e. common labour during the day, with isolation during night, continued to obtain a preference; Massachusetts, Maryland, Tennessee, Kentucky, Maine, and Vermont, have gradually adopted the Auburn plan, and have taken the Auburn prison as a model for those which they have caused to be erected.* (*h*)

Several states have not stopped here, but have also founded houses of refuge for juvenile offenders, as an addition, in some measure, to the penitentiary system, in imitation of New York. These latter establishments have been founded in Boston in 1826, and in Philadelphia in 1828. There is every indication that Baltimore also, will soon have its house of refuge.

It is easy to foresee, that the impulse of reform given by New York and Pennsylvania, will not remain confined to the states mentioned above.

From the happy rivalship which exists among all the states of the Union, each state follows the reforms which have been effected by the others, and shows itself impatient to imitate them.

It would be wrong to judge all the United States by the picture which we have presented of the improvements adopted by some of them.

Accustomed as we are to see our central government attract every thing, and propel in the various provinces all the parts of the administration in a uniform direction, we sometimes suppose that the same is the case in other countries; and comparing the centralization of government at Washington with that at Paris, the different states of the Union to our departments, we are tempted to believe that innovations made in one state, take, of

---

* Since Messrs Beaumont and Toqueville visited our country, the legislature of New Jersey has made provisions for the erection of a state-prison on the Pennsylvania principle, which the reader is requested to bear in mind, in perusing several subsequent passages of this work.—TRANS

necessity, place in the others.* There is, however, nothing like
it in the United States.†

These states, united by a federal tie into one family, are in respect to every thing which concerns their common interests,
subjected to one single authority.‡ But besides these general
interests, they preserve their entire individual independence,
and each of them is sovereign master to rule itself according to
its own pleasure.   We have spoken of nine states which have
adopted a new system of prisons; there are fifteen more which
have made as yet no change §

In these latter, the ancient system prevails in its whole force;
the crowding of prisoners, confusion of crimes, ages, and sometimes sexes, mixture of indicted and convicted prisoners, of criminals and debtors, guilty persons and witnesses;‖ considerable
mortality; frequent escapes; absence of all discipline; no silence
which leads the criminals to reflection; no labour which accustoms them to an honest mode of subsistence; insalubrity of the
place which destroys health; ignism of the conversations which
corrupt, idleness that depraves; the assemblage, in one word,
of all vices and all immoralities—such is the picture offered by
the prisons which have not yet entered into the way of reform. (i)

By the side of one state, the penitentiaries of which might
serve as a model, we find another, whose jails present the ex-

* Mr. Charles Lucas, who has published a much esteemed work on the penitentiary system, has fallen into the mistake here mentioned.
   " Two systems," he says, " present themselves, one belonging exclusively to
the old world, the other to the new.   The former is the system of transportation
pursued by Great Britain and Russia, the second is the penitentiary system established in *all the states of the Union.*"
   " • • • • • •   The penitentiary system," he says, in another passage,
"which Caleb Lownes created in 1791 in Pennsylvania, whence it extended al-
most simultaneously in all the states of the Union " • • • •
   See *Du système pénal et du système répressif en général par M. Charles Lucas.
Introduction,* pages 58, 59, and 60
   † The political system of the United States is so entirely unique in history, that
we do not remember ever having met with a correct, or even a fair view of it in
works whose authors have not had their knowledge from personal observation,
for few of those who visit this country, penetrate the whole machinery, with its
manifold limitations and connexions of a variety of powers, which though in some
cases impeding a rapid progress toward a desired end, constitute the very
safeguard and protection of most improvements in our country.   Our penitentiary
system never would have risen and been carried through in a large country with
a concentrated government   If the United States excite so great an interest in
Europe, as to judge from the periodical press of that part of the world, we should
believe, it is surprising that we meet constantly with such gross ignorance respecting American institutions even in a nation speaking the same language with
us.   But lately South Carolina was called a province in one of the most respectable English papers.—Trans
   ‡ That of Congress.
   § In Ohio, New Hampshire, and some other states, there is, indeed, a system
of imprisonment; but it is a bad system, and no PENITENTIARY SYSTEM.
   ‖ Provision has lately been made for the erection of a prison on the Auburn
plan at Concord, New Hampshire.—Trans.

ample of every thing which ought to be avoided. Thus the
State of New York is without contradiction one of the most
advanced in the path of reform, while New Jersey, which is
separated from it but by a river, has retained all the vices of the
ancient system *

Ohio, which possesses a penal code remarkable for the mildness and humanity of its provisions, has barbarous prisons We
have deeply sighed when at Cincinnati, visiting the prison, we
found half of the imprisoned charged with irons, and the rest
plunged into an infected dungeon ; and are unable to describe
the painful impression which we experienced, when, examining
the prison of New Orleans, we found men together with hogs,
in the midst of all odours and nuisances † In locking up the
criminals, nobody thinks of rendering them better, but only of
taming their malice ; they are put in chains like ferocious beasts ;
and instead of being corrected, they are rendered brutal ‡

If it is true that the penitentiary system is entirely unknown
in that part which we mentioned, it is equally true that this system is incomplete in those states even where it is in vigour.§
Thus at New York, at Philadelphia, and Boston, there are new
prisons for convicts, whose punishment exceeds one or two years'
imprisonment ; but establishments of a similar nature do not exist
to receive individuals who are sentenced for a shorter time,
or who are indicted only.‖ In respect to the latter, nothing has
been changed ; disorder, confusion, mixture of different ages and

---

* Since the above was written, a society has been formed in that state, which
proves that it will not remain without efficient improvements in its prisons, and
what is more important, the legislature provided in 1833 for the erection of a
state-prison on the Pennsylvania principle —Trans.

† The place for convicted criminals in New Orleans cannot be called a prison
it is a horrid sink, in which they are thronged together, and which is fit only
for those dirty animals found here together with the prisoners it must be observed that those who are detained here are not slaves it is the prison for persons
free in the ordinary course of life. It seems, however, that the necessity of a reform
in the prisons is felt in Louisiana, the governor of that state said to us, that he
would not cease to ask the legislature for funds for this object It seems equally
certain that the system of imprisonment in Ohio is about to be entirely changed

‡ In general the Southern states are in respect to prisons as well as to all other
things, far behind those of the North In some of them, the reform of prison discipline is by no means asked for by public opinion , quite recently the penitentiary system has been abolished in Georgia, after having been established a year
before.

§ As soon as the law of March 30, 1831, shall be executed in Pennsylvania,
this state will have the most complete system of imprisonment which ever existed in the United States This law orders the erection of a prison on the plan
of solitary confinement, destined for indicted persons, debtors, witnesses, and
prisoners, convicted for a short term of imprisonment. See Acts of the general
assembly, relating to the eastern penitentiary and to the new prisons of the city
and county of Philadelphia, page 21.

‖ The prison of Blackwell's Island near New York, recently erected, is the only
one which has been built for prisoners convicted of small offences.

moral characters, all vices of the old system still exist for them: we have seen in the house of arrest in New York (Bridewell) more than fifty indicted persons in one room.* These arrested persons are precisely those for whom well regulated prisons ought to have been built. It is easy in fact to conceive, that he who has not yet been pronounced guilty, and he who has committed but a crime or misdemeanor comparatively slight, ought to be surrounded by much greater protection than such as are more advanced in crime, and whose guilt has been acknowledged.

Arrested persons are sometimes innocent and always supposed to be so. How is it that we should suffer them to find in the prison a corruption which they did not bring with them?

If they are guilty, why place them first in a house of arrest, fitted to corrupt them still more, except to reform them afterwards in a penitentiary, to which they will be sent after their conviction? (*j*)

There is evidently a deficiency in a prison system which offers anomalies of this kind.

These shocking contradictions proceed chiefly from the want of unison in the various parts of government in the United States.

The larger prisons (state-prisons) corresponding to our *maisons centrales*, belong to the state, which directs them; after these follow the county jails, directed by the county; and at last the prisons of the city, superintended by the city itself.

The various branches of government in the United States being almost as independent of each other, as the states themselves, it results that they hardly ever act uniformly and simultaneously. Whilst one makes a useful reform in the circle of its powers, the other remains inactive, and attached to ancient abuses.

We shall see below, how this independence of the individual parts, which is injurious to the uniform action of all their powers, has nevertheless a beneficial influence, by giving to each a more prompt and energetic progress in the direction which it follows freely and uncompelled.†

---

* In this prison, intended only for indicted persons, no regard is paid to the different crimes with which they stand charged, to the youth of the one or the old corruption of the other. None of these individuals has a bed, a chair, nor even a board, to lie upon. They have no yard to catch the fresh air. A short distance from it is a prison in perfect order, in which *convicted* criminals are detained. The best and the most vicious prisons are found in the United States — So far the authors. They ought to have said " the best and some of the most vicious prisons are found in the United States," because the worst American prisons are not worse, we are sorry to say, than many in several countries of the European continent. What descriptions might be given!—TRANS.

† As the authors refer the reader to a subsequent passage in this work, the Translator also will refer for his remarks to a note to the same passage.

We shall say nothing more of the defective parts in the prison system in the United States: if at some future period France shall imitate the penitentiaries of America, the most important thing for her will be to know those which may serve as models. The new establishments then, will form the only object of our further inquiry.

We have seen, in the preceding remarks, that few states have as yet changed entirely their system of imprisonment; the number of those which have modified their penal laws is still less. Several among them yet possess part of the barbarous laws which they have received from England.*

We shall not speak of the Southern states, where slavery still exists; in every place where one half of the community is cruelly oppressed by the other, we must expect to find in the law of the oppressor, a weapon always ready to strike nature which revolts or humanity that complains. Punishment of death and stripes —these form the whole penal code for the slaves † ‡ But if we throw a glance at those states even which have abolished slavery, and which are most advanced in civilization, we shall see this civilization uniting itself, in some, with penal laws full of mildness, and in others, with all the rigour of a code of Draco.

---

* That England has many barbarous laws, and that some of them have escaped the many modifications and changes, to which the British laws have been subjected in the various states of the Union, is not denied   But in speaking of barbarity in this respect, we ought never to omit to consider two things—the laws and the administration of justice. Thus the French code is in general milder than the English, though much severer than the Prussian; but now it is very different, if we consider the whole machinery of the administration of French justice, civil and criminal, so thoroughly and soundly exhibited in Mr. Von Feuerbach's work, on the Administration of Justice in France, Giessen, 1825—a work of uncommon merit. Certainly, it is but simple truth if we call the administration of justice in France, barbarous in many instances. Where are so many people convicted, who at a subsequent period, are proved to be innocent ? Where does the heavy weight or cunning skill of prosecution oppress an indicted person so much, and in a way so opposed to true justice, as in France ? Where is the oppression by lawyers greater than by the French *avoués* —TRANS.

† There are no prisons to shut up slaves imprisonment would cost too much! Death, the whips, exile, cost nothing ! Moreover, in order to exile slaves, they are sold, which yields profit   See Statistical Notes on the State of Maryland.

‡ On this unfortunate subject, the reader is referred to Mr Stroud's Sketch of the Laws relating to Slavery, &c. Philadelphia, 1827, a work which corroborates the above statement.   Two circumstances probably have contributed more than others, to render the laws for slaves in the Southern states of the Union so severe, and in many cases much severer than corresponding laws with other nations' 1. The circumstance that those states are republics without standing armies, and in general without the power of a concentrated government, so that the severity of laws must supply the strength of government so as to meet the danger with which slave population always is pregnant.   2. The circumstance that in the Southern states the owners of the slaves are the law-makers and government themselves, whilst in monarchies government stands more between the two parties, and the slave has, in it, in many cases, a powerful protector.—TRANS.

Let us but compare the laws of Pennsylvania with those of New England, which is, perhaps, the most enlightened part of the American Union. In Massachusetts, there are ten different crimes punished by death—among others, rape and burglary.* Maine, Rhode Island, and Connecticut, count the same number of capital crimes † Among these laws, some contain the most degrading punishments, such as the pillory; others revolting cruelties, as branding and mutilation ‡ There are also some which order fines equal to confiscations § Whilst we find these remains of barbarism in some states, with an old population, there are others, which, risen since yesterday, have banished from their laws all cruel punishments not called for by the interest of society. Thus, Ohio, which certainly is not as enlightened as New England, has a penal code much more humane than those of Massachusetts or Connecticut.

Close by a state where the reform of the penal laws seems to have arrived at its summit, we find another, the criminal laws of which are stamped with all the brutalities of the ancient system. It is thus that the States of Delaware and New Jersey, so far behind in the path of improvement, border on Pennsylvania, which, in this respect, marches at the head of all others.‖

* We comprise in this number, the crimes against the Federal government, that of treason against the Union, piracy, and robbing the mail.

† The laws of the latter state also pronounce imprisonment for life in seven different cases

‡ A law of Connecticut orders a mother's hiding the death of her infant, to be punished with public exhibition of the mother with a cord round her neck.

A law of Massachusetts punishes fornication with a fine, and adds that if the convicted individual shall not pay the fine within twenty-four hours after conviction, ten stripes with the whip, shall be inflicted upon him Blasphemy, according to the laws of the same state, is punished with pillory and stripes For-gery in Rhode Island is punished with the pillory. During this exhibition, a piece of each ear of the convict is to be cut off, and he is to be branded with a C. (counterfeiting) After all this, he undergoes an imprisonment not exceed-ing six years So far the authors That such laws have fallen into disuse we need not mention —TRANS

§ For instance, a law of the State of Delaware orders for a single crime the fine of 10,000 dollars

‖ The laws of Delaware pronounce death against six different crimes, (capi-tal crimes against the United States not included) They punish forgery thus. the convict is sentenced to a fine, the pillory, and three months solitary confine-ment, at the expiration of this punishment he wears on his back, for not less than two, and not more than five years, the letter F (forgery) in scarlet colour, on his dress, this letter must be six inches long, and two inches wide.

Poisoning is thus punished...

The convict may be sentenced to a fine of 10,000 dollars, one hour's exhibi tion at the pillory, and to be publicly whipped, he must receive sixty stripes, "well laid on," he then goes for four years into prison, after which, he is sold as a slave, for a time not exceeding fourteen years

Another heavy punishment pronounced for an offence comparatively slight is, twenty-one stripes for a pretended sorcerer or magician In New Jersey, every person re convicted for murder, rape, arson, theft, forgery, and sodomy, is punished with death. * * * * *

We should forget the object of our report were we to dwell any longer on this point. We were obliged to present a sketch of the penal legislation of the United States, because it exercises a necessary influence on the question before us.

In fact it is easy to conceive to what point the punishments which degrade the guilty, are incompatible with a penitentiary system, the object of which is to reform them. How can we hope to awaken the moral sense of an individual who carries on his body the indelible sign of infamy, when the mutilation of his limbs reminds others incessantly of his crime, or the sign imprinted on his forehead, perpetuates its memory?*

Must we not ardently wish, that the last traces of such barbarism should disappear from all the United States, and particularly from those which have adopted the penitentiary system, with which they are irreconcilable, and whose existence renders them still more shocking?†

Besides, let us not blame these people for advancing slowly on the path of innovation. Ought not similar changes to be the work of time, and of public opinion? There are in the United States a certain number of philosophical minds, who, full of theories and systems, are impatient to put them into practice; and if they had the power themselves to make the law of the land, they would efface with one dash, all the old customs, and supplant them by the creations of their genius, and the decrees of their wisdom. Whether right or wrong the people do not move so quick. They consent to changes, but they wish to see them progressive and partial. (*k*) This prudent and reserved reform, effected by a whole nation, all of whose customs are practical, is, perhaps, more beneficial than the precipitated trials which would result, had the enthusiasm of ardent minds and enticing theories free play ‡

* The brand is placed in the United States, generally on the forehead • • • In the month of June, 1829, prisoners, who had been re-committed, were yet marked on the arm, when their imprisonment expired, the words " Massachusetts State Prison," were tattooed on the arm   June 12, 1829, this custom was abolished

† We do not deny to society the right to punish with death We believe even that this punishment is, in certain cases, indispensable to the support of social order.   But we believe that as soon as the law punishes with death without absolute necessity, it becomes useless cruelty, and an obstacle to the penitentiary system, the object of which is, to reform those whose life society spares

‡ Among the philosophers of the United States, who call for the abolition of capital punishment, Mr Edward Livingston must be distinguished   He does not dispute the right of society to take away the life of certain of its members; he only maintains that this fearful punishment, which, without remedy, may strike an innocent person, does in general not produce the expected effect, and that it can be efficiently supplanted by punishments less rigorous, which produce less violent, but more durable impressions   Put upon this ground, the question is not solved, but brought to its true point   See remarks on the expediency of abolishing the punishment of death   By Edward Livingston Philadelphia, 1831.

3

Whatever may be the difficulties yet to be overcome, we do not·hesitate to declare that the cause of reform and of progress in the United States, seem to us certain and safe.

Slavery, the shame of a free nation, is expelled every day from some districts over which it held its sway; and those persons themselves who possess most slaves, are convinced that slavery will not last much longer.

Every day punishments which wound humanity, become supplanted by milder ones; and in the most civilized states of the north, where these punishments continue in the written laws, their application has become so rare that they are to be considered as fallen into disuse.

The impulse of improvement is given. Those states which have as yet done nothing, are conscious of their deficiency; they envy those which have preceded them in this career, and are impatient to imitate them. *

Finally, it is a fact worth remarking, that the modification of the penal laws and that of prison discipline, are two reforms intimately associated with each other, and never separated in the United States.

Our special task is not to enlarge on the first; the second alone shall fix our attention.

The various states in which we have found a penitentiary system, pursue all the same end: the amelioration of the prison discipline. But they employ different means to arrive at their object. These different means have formed the subject of our inquiry.

---

* Since the authors visited our country, New Jersey has made provisions for a State prison, on the Pennsylvania principle, and New Hampshire for another at Concord, on the Auburn principle.—Trans.

CHAPTER II.

Discussion —Object of the Penitentiary System —First section —what are the fundamental principles of this system ?—Two distinct systems, Auburn and Philadelphia.—Examination of the two systems.—In what they agree in what they differ.

The penitentiary system in the proper acceptation of the word, relates only to individuals condemned and subjected to the punishment of imprisonment for the expiation of their crime.

In a less confined sense, it may be extended to all arrested persons, whether their arrest precedes or follows the judgment: that is to say, whether these persons are arrested as suspected or indicted for a crime, or as condemned for having committed it; in this wider acceptation, the penitentiary system comprehends prisons of all kinds, state and other prisons, houses of arrest and refuge, &c., &c.

In this latter sense we shall use it.

We have already said that in the United States those prisons which correspond to our houses of arrest, (*maisons d'arrêt*) that is to say, those which are destined for persons provisionally arrested, and for individuals sentenced to a short imprisonment, have undergone no reform as yet. Consequently, we shall not speak of them. We should be able to present in this respect but a theory; and it is practical observations with which we have, above all, to occupy ourselves.

We shall therefore, immediately direct our attention to the penitentiaries, properly so called, which contain in the United States, those convicts, who, according to our laws, would be sent to the "central houses of correction," of "detention," and to the "bagnes."

The punishment of imprisonment in the different states in which it is pronounced, is not varied as by our laws. With us a distinction is made between simple imprisonment, "*reclusion,*" detention, and hard labour, each of these punishments has certain traits which are peculiar to it, imprisonment in the United States has a uniform character; it differs only in its duration.

It is divided into two principal classes: 1. Imprisonment from one month to one or two years, applied to breaches of the laws of the police, and to lighter offences (*délits*); 2. Imprison-

ment from two years to twenty or for life, which serves to punish crimes of a graver character. It is for the convicts suffering
the second class of punishment, that in the United States a penitentiary system exists:*

1. In what consists this system, and what are its fundamental principles?

2. How is it put into practice?

3. By what disciplinary means is it maintained?

4. What results have been obtained in respect to reformation
of the prisoners?

5. What have been its effects in a financial respect?

6. What information can we obtain from this system for the
amelioration of our prisoners?

These are the principal questions respecting which we shall
give a summary of our observations and inquiries.

Having accomplished this task, we shall conclude our report
by an examination of the houses of refuge for juvenile offenders:
these establishments are rather schools than prisons, but they
form, nevertheless, an essential part of the penitentiary system,
since the regulations to which these young prisoners are subjected, have for their object, to punish those who have been
declared guilty, and aim at the reformation of all.

SECTION I.

In what consists the Penitentiary System, and what are its fundamental principles?

WE find in the United States two distinctly separate systems:
the system of Auburn and that of Philadelphia.

Sing-Sing, in the State of New York, Wethersfield, in Connecticut; Boston, in Massachusetts; Baltimore, in Maryland;
have followed the model of Auburn.†

On the other side, Pennsylvania stands quite alone.

The two systems opposed to each other on important points,
have, however, a common basis, without which no penitentiary
system is possible; this basis is the *isolation* of the prisoners. (*l*)

* We shall treat of the penitentiary system in the United States exclusively,
because it formed the sole object of our inquiry. The reader who wishes for
documents and statements respecting European prisons, is referred to the remarkable works of Messrs Julius, Lagarmitte, and Mittermaier. So far the authors. We have often had occasion to mention Dr. Julius' Lectures on Prisons,
and his periodical on Knowledge of Prisons, a work of great merit. The reader
is referred for further information to the article, *Statistics of Crime,* in the Encyclopædia Americana —TRANS.

† Kentucky, Tennessee, Maine, Vermont, have also adopted this system, but
so recently, that they cannot yet afford useful information.

Whoever has studied the interior of prisons and the moral state of their inmates, has become convinced that communication between these persons renders their moral reformation impossible, and becomes even for them the inevitable cause of an alarming corruption This observation, justified by the experience of every day, has become in the United States an almost popular truth ; and the publicists who disagree most respecting the way of putting the penitentiary system into practice, fully agree upon this point, that no salutary system can possibly exist without the separation of the criminals.*

For a long time it was believed that, in order to remedy the evil caused by the intercourse of prisoners with each other, it would be sufficient to establish in the prison, a certain number of classifications But after having tried this plan, its insufficiency has been acknowledged. There are similar punishments and crimes called by the same name, but there are no two beings equal in regard to their morals; and every time that convicts are put together, there exists necessarily a fatal influence of some upon others, because, in the association of the wicked, it is not the less guilty who act upon the more criminal, but the more depraved who influence those who are less so †

---

* See the Report of the Commissioners to revise the Pennsylvania Code, 1828, page 16, and particularly page 22. See letter of Roberts Vaux to Mr Roscoe, 1827, page 9. See the report of the Committee of the Penitentiary at Baltimore, to Governor Kent, December 23, 1828 See Introductory Report to the Code of Prison Discipline, by Edward Livingston, page 31, and the letter of the same to Roberts Vaux, 1828. See Report of John Spencer to the Legislature of New York.

Solitary confinement in the United States met with many opponents. Among its most distinguished adversaries were William Roscoe of Liverpool and General Lafayette the former gave up his opinion as soon as he knew that labour was admitted into the solitary cells in Philadelphia (See his letter to Dr Hosack of New York, dated July 13, 1830, shortly before his death) As to General Lafayette, he has always been strongly opposed to the punishment of solitude — "This punishment," he says, "does not reform the guilty. I have passed several years in solitude in Olmutz, where I was detained for having made a revolution, and in my prison I dreamed but of new revolutions "

General Lafayette has perhaps, also modified his opinion, after having learned that the solitary confinement as first established in Pennsylvania, has undergone important changes.

The new revolutions of which General Lafayette dreamed, prove nothing, because a person, imprisoned for political offences, does not merely consider his offence no crime, but generally a praiseworthy action. It is very different with theft, assault, burglary—crimes and offences which present themselves as such to the weakest intellect —Trans.

† This is consistent with the common law, that, when a number of individuals having received a common impulse, are applying their activity toward a common aim, he who distinguishes himself most in this direction, exercises the greatest influence—the most learned among scholars, the most daring among soldiers, the most resigned among martyrs, the most virtuous among the virtuous, the most inspired among artists, the most wicked among criminals Each propels his society further and quicker on its chosen path —Trans.

We must therefore, impossible as it is to classify prisoners, come to a separation of all. (*m*)

This separation, which prevents the wicked from injuring others, is also favourable to himself.

Thrown into solitude he reflects. Placed alone, in view of his crime, he learns to hate it; and if his soul be not yet surfeited with crime, and thus have lost all taste for any thing better, it is in solitude, where remorse will come to assail him.

Solitude is a severe punishment, but such a punishment is merited by the guilty. Mr. Livingston justly remarks, that a prison, destined to punish, would soon cease to be a fearful object, if the convicts in it could entertain at their pleasure those social relations in which they delighted, before their entry into the prison.*

Yet, whatever may be the crime of the guilty prisoner, no one has the right to take life from him, if society decree merely to deprive him of his liberty. Such, however, would be the result of absolute solitude, if no alleviation of its rigours were offered.†

This is the reason why labour is introduced into the prison. Far from being an aggravation of the punishment, it is a real benefit to the prisoner.

But even if the criminal did not find in it a relief from his sufferings, it nevertheless would be necessary to force him to it. It is idleness which has led him to crime; with employment he will learn how to live honestly.

Labour of the criminals is necessary still under another point of view: their detention, expensive for society if they remain idle, becomes less burthensome if they labour.

The prisons of Auburn, Sing-Sing, Wethersfield, Boston, and Philadelphia, rest then upon these two united principles, solitude and labour. These principles, in order to be salutary, ought not to be separated: the one is inefficient without the other.‡

In the ancient prison of Auburn, isolation without labour has been tried, and those prisoners who have not become insane or did not die of despair, have returned to society only to commit new crimes.

In Baltimore, the system of labour without isolation is trying at this moment, and seems not to promise happy results.

* See his Introductory Report to the Code of Prison Discipline.
† We have stated our opinion upon this point already, in a previous note.— Trans
‡ They are these two principles upon which Mr. Livingston founds his Prison Discipline. And upon this point as well as several others to be touched upon in the sequel of this work, I must recommend the perusal of Mr Livingston's Introductory Report, to those readers, who have deprived themselves as yet of the great satisfaction of becoming acquainted with a valuable work.—Trans

Though admitting one-half of the principle of solitude, the other half is rejected; the penitentiary of this city contains a number of cells equal to that of the prisoners who are locked up at night; but during day, they are permitted to communicate freely with each other. Certainly separation during night is the most important; but it is not sufficient. The intercourse of criminals is necessarily of a corrupting nature; and this intercourse must be prevented if we wish to protect the prisoners from mutual contagion. (n)

Thoroughly convinced of these truths, the founders of the new penitentiary at Philadelphia, thought it necessary that each prisoner should be secluded in a separate cell during day as well as night.

They have thought that absolute separation of the criminals can alone protect them from mutual pollution, and they have adopted the principle of separation in all its rigour. According to this system, the convict, once thrown into his cell, remains there without interruption, until the expiration of his punishment: he is separated from the whole world; and the penitentiaries, full of malefactors like himself, but every one of them entirely isolated, do not present to him even a society in the prison; if it is true that in establishments of this nature, all evil originates from the intercourse of the prisoners among themselves, we are obliged to acknowledge that nowhere is this vice avoided with greater safety than at Philadelphia, where the prisoners find themselves utterly unable to communicate with each other; and it is incontestable that this perfect isolation secures the prisoner from all fatal contamination. *

As solitude is in no other prison more complete than in Philadelphia, nowhere, also, is the necessity of labour more urgent. At the same time, it would be inaccurate to say, that in the Philadelphia penitentiary labour is imposed; we may say with more justice that the favour of labour is granted. When we visited this penitentiary, we successively conversed with all its inmates. (o) There was not a single one among them who did not speak of labour with a kind of gratitude, and who did not express the idea that without the relief of constant occupation, life would be insufferable.†

What would become, during the long hours of solitude, without this relief, of the prisoner, given up to himself, a prey to the remorses of his soul and the terrors of his imagination? Labour gives to the solitary cell an interest; it fatigues the body and relieves the soul.

* See our Inquiry into the Philadelphia penitentiary, Appendix No 10.
† All said to us that Sunday, the day of rest, was to them much longer than the whole week together.

It is highly remarkable, that these men, the greater part of whom have been led to crime by indolence and idleness, should be constrained by the torments of solitude, to find in labour their only comfort: by detesting idleness, they accustom themselves to hate the primary cause of their misfortune, and labour, by comforting them, makes them love the only means, which when again free, will enable them to gain honestly their livelihood.

The founders of the Auburn prison acknowledged also the necessity of separating the prisoners, to prevent all intercourse among themselves, and to subject them to the obligation of labour; but they follow a different course in order to arrive at the same end.

In this prison, as well as in those founded upon the same model, the prisoners are locked up in their solitary cells at night only. During day they work together in common workshops, and as they are subjected to the law of rigorous silence, though united, they are yet in fact isolated. Labour in common and in silence forms then the characteristic trait which distinguishes the Auburn system from that of Philadelphia.

Owing to the silence to which the prisoners are condemned, this union of the prisoners, it is asserted, offers no inconvenience, and presents many advantages.

They are united, but no moral connexion exists among them. They see without knowing each other. They are in society without any intercourse; there exists among them neither aversion nor sympathy The criminal, who contemplates a project of escape, or an attempt against the life of his keepers, does not know in which of his companions he may expect to find assistance. Their union is strictly material, or, to speak more exactly, their bodies are together, but their souls are separated; and it is not the solitude of the body which is important, but that of the mind. At Pittsburg, the prisoners, though separated, are not alone, since there exist moral communications among them. At Auburn, they are really isolated, though no wall separates them. *

Their union in the work-shops has, therefore, nothing dangerous: it has, on the contrary, it is said, an advantage peculiar to it, that of accustoming the prisoners to obedience.

What is the principal object of punishment in relation to him who suffers it? It is to give him the habits of society, and first to teach him to obey. The Auburn prison has, on this point, its advocates say, a manifest advantage over that of Philadelphia.

Perpetual seclusion in a cell, is an irresistible fact which curbs

* Our opinion respecting this isolation and some other points connected with the Auburn prison is given in the article on the Pennsylvania penitentiary system, appended to this work.—TRANS.

the prisoner without a struggle, and thus deprives altogether his submission of a moral character; locked up in this narrow space, he has not, properly speaking, to observe a discipline; if he works, it is in order to escape the weariness which overwhelms him : in short, he obeys much less the established discipline than the physical impossibility of acting otherwise.

At Auburn, on the contrary, labour instead of being a comfort to the prisoners, is, in their eyes, a painful task, which they would be glad to get rid of. In observing silence, they are incessantly tempted to violate its law. They have some merit in obeying, because their obedience is no actual *necessity.* It is thus that the Auburn discipline gives to the prisoners the habits of society which they do not obtain in the prisons of Philadelphia * (*p*)

We see that silence is the principal basis of the Auburn system; it is this silence which establishes that moral separation between all prisoners, that deprives them of all dangerous communications, and only leaves to them those social relations which are inoffensive.

But here we meet with another grave objection against this system; the advocates of the Philadelphia system say, that to pretend to reduce a great number of collected malefactors to absolute silence, is a real chimera; and that this impossibility ruins from its basis, the system of which silence is the only foundation.†

We believe that this reproach is much exaggerated. Certainly we cannot admit the existence of a discipline carried to such a degree of perfection, that it guaranties rigorous observation of silence among a great number of assembled individuals, whom their interest and their passions excite to communicate with each other. We may say, however, that if in the prisons of Auburn, Sing-Sing, Boston, and Wethersfield, silence is not always strictly observed, the cases of infraction are so rare that they are of little danger. Admitted as we have been into the interior of these various establishments, and going there at every hour of the day, without being accompanied by any body, visiting by turns the cells, the work-shops, the chapel and the yards, we have never been able to surprise a prisoner uttering a single

---

* Our opinion is directly the reverse The prisoner in Philadelphia is calmed, the prisoner in Auburn irritated —Trans.

† See Letter of E Livingston to Roberts Vaux, 1828, pp 7 and 8   There are undoubtedly, some instances which prove the infraction of silence in some cases, this is so true that in each of the prisons, with the inquiry of which we are occupied, some convicts have been punished for it, and a certain number of infractions remains always undiscovered. But the question is not whether there are some cases of contravention, the point to be examined is, whether these infractions of silence are of a nature to destroy the order of the establishment, and to prevent the reformation of the prisoners.

4

word, and yet we have sometimes spent whole weeks in observing the same prison.

In Auburn, the building facilitates in a peculiar way the discovery of all contraventions of discipline. Each work-shop where the prisoners work, is surrounded by a gallery, from which they may be observed, though the observer remains unseen. We have often espied from this gallery the conduct of the prisoners, whom we did not detect a single time in a breach of discipline. There is moreover a fact which proves better than any other, how strictly silence is observed in these establishments; it is that which takes place at Sing-Sing.* The prisoners are there occupied in breaking stones from the quarries, situated without the penitentiary ; so that nine hundred criminals, watched by thirty keepers, work free in the midst of an open field, without a chain fettering their feet or hands. It is evident that the life of the keepers would be at the mercy of the prisoners, if material force were sufficient for the latter ; but they want moral force. And why are these nine hundred collected malefactors less strong than the thirty individuals who command them? Because the keepers communicate freely with each other, act in concert, and have all the power of association, whilst the convicts separated from each other, by silence, have, in spite of their numerical force, all the weakness of isolation. Suppose for an instant, that the prisoners obtain the least facility of communication ; the order is immediately the reverse ; the union of their intellects effected by the spoken word, has taught them the secret of their strength ; and the first infraction of the law of silence, destroys the whole discipline † The admirable order which prevails at Sing-Sing, and which silence alone is capable of maintaining, proves then that silence there is preserved. (q)

We have thus shown the general principle upon which the systems of Auburn and of Philadelphia rest : how are these prin-

* Respecting the safety in keeping the prisoners on the Auburn plan, see our last note added to No XIII of No 17, Statistical Notes, and respecting the enforcement of silence, see our note appended to the article Pennsylvania Penitentiary System at the end of the volume —Trans

† The question, so often made, why does history exhibit so many instances of whole nations allowing themselves to be tyrannized over by a few, to whom they sacrifice their dearest interests, and whom they serve with daily suffering, cannot be answered in a clearer way, than by the above statement—because the rulers have the "power of association," and the oppressed are "isolated " Separate the interest of the officers of your government from that of the people, establish easy and rapid communications between the former, and destroy as much as possible free intercourse among the latter, deprive them of all opportunities of association, and you may rule with an iron sceptre as long as you can maintain this order of things If this remark is irrelevant, I nevertheless trust to be excused for having directed the reader's attention to this point, as nothing is more frequent than to see nations, bearing silently their yoke, accused of being unworthy of a better fate, and to find this very silence exhibited as a proof of content with their present lot.—Trans.

ciples put into action? How and by whom are the penitentiary establishments administered? What is the order of the interior, and what is the regulation of each day? This shall form the subject of the following section.

SECTION II.

Administration.

Administration —Superintendents —Clerk —Inspectors —By whom appointed. —Their privileges.—Their salary.—Importance of their choice —Influence of public opinion —Regulation of every day.—Rising; going to sleep, labour; meals —Nourishment.—No tippling-houses —No reward for good conduct.— No unproductive labour —Difficulty of labour in the solitary cells of Philadelphia —Contract in what it differs from the system established in France. —Absence of all individual earning, except at Baltimore.

THE administration of the prison is intrusted every where to a superintendent,* whose authority is more or less extensive. He employs a clerk, charged with the financial business of the establishment.

Superior to the superintendent, are three inspectors, charged with the general direction and moral surveillance of the prison,† and under him is a number more or less considerable of inferior jailors.

At Auburn, Sing-Sing, Philadelphia, and Wethersfield, the superintendent is appointed by the inspectors, in Boston, the governor appoints him, in Connecticut, the inspectors are chosen by the legislature; in Massachusetts, by the governor, and in Pennsylvania, by the supreme court. Every where the power which appoints the superintendent, has the right to discharge him at pleasure.

The reader sees that the election of those persons who direct the penitentiary establishments, belongs to important authorities.

The nomination of the jailors belongs, in the prisons of Sing-Sing, Wethersfield, Boston, and Philadelphia, to the superintendent himself; at Auburn they are chosen by the inspectors. The

---

* He is indifferently called *warder, keeper, agent* or *superintendent.*

† It is generally thought that it is advantageous that the inspectors should not change too often, and that they should not be all renewed at the same time. (See Report of December 20, 1830, or the penitentiary of Maryland) In Boston, they are appointed for four years (See the law of March 11, 1828) In Philadelphia, the inspectors of the penitentiary are exempt from the militia service, from being jurymen, overseers of the poor, &c. (See Regulations of the prison) Until the year 1820, there were five inspectors of the Auburn prison this number was found to be too large, and it was reduced from that time to three (See Report of 1820, by Mr Spencer)

superintendents of all the prisons, with the single exception of
that of Philadelphia, are bound to give sufficient security for
their good behaviour. * At Philadelphia and at Wethersfield, the
office of inspector is without any compensation, and in the other
prisons it is very trifling. The sum which they receive in Massachusetts is hardly equal to the expense incurred by visiting
the prison.† They are always chosen from among the inhabitants of the place.‡ Persons distinguished by their standing in
society, are desirous of filling this place; it is thus that we see in
Philadelphia, among the inspectors of the penitentiary, Mr.
Richards, mayor of the city, and in Boston, Mr. Grey, senator
of Massachusetts.

Though the inspectors are not the immediate agents of the
administration, they nevertheless direct it   They make the regulations, which the superintendent is charged to execute, and
they constantly watch over this execution; they have even the
power to modify them at their pleasure, according to the exi-
gency of circumstances   In no case do they take part in the acts
of the actual administration of the prison; the superintendent
alone directs it; because he alone is answerable for it.   They
have every where the same legal authority; yet they do not exercise it in the same way, in all the prisons of which we treat.
Thus at Sing-Sing, the superintendence of the inspectors appeared to us superficial, whilst at Auburn and at Wethersfield
they took a much more active part in the affairs of the prison.

On the whole we may say, that the privileges of the inspectors
are much more extended in law than in reality; whilst the superintendent, whose written authority is not very great, is yet
the soul of the administration.

The most important place then in the prison, is without a
doubt, that of the superintendent.   Generally it is intrusted in
the penitentiaries of the United States, to honourable men, entitled by their talent to functions of this nature.   It is thus that
the Auburn prison has had for directors men like Mr. Elam
Lynds, a former captain of the army, and Mr. Gershom Powers,
a Judge of the State of New York. At Wethersfield, Mr. Pillsbury; at Sing-Sing, Mr. Robert Wiltze; at Boston, Mr. Austin,
a captain in the navy, are all men distinguished by their knowledge and their capacity.   To great probity and a deep sense of
their duty they add much experience, and that perfect know-

* At Auburn, the security is 25,000 dollars. See Report of 1832. The same
at Sing-Sing.
    † Each inspector receives 100 dollars. In Baltimore, the committee of super-
intendence receive annually, 1,144 dollars   See Report of 1830
    ‡ The report of the inspectors of Wethersfield states, that little reliance can
be placed on any system of regulations, if there is not a committee who assures
itself of the execution of the rules by frequent personal inspection.

ledge of men so necessary in their position   Among the superintendents of the American penitentiaries, we have especially to
mention Mr. Samuel Wood, director of the new Philadelphia
prison—a man of superior mind, who, influenced by religious
sentiments, has abandoned his former career, in order to devote
himself entirely to the success of an establishment so useful to
his community.

The inferior agents, the under-wardens, are not so distinguished either for their standing in society or for talent.   They
are, however, in general, intelligent and honest men.   Charged
with superintending the labour in the work-shops, they have almost always a special and technical knowledge of the mechanical
arts with which the prisoners occupy themselves. (*r*)

The salary of the various officers, without being exorbitant, is
nevertheless sufficient to furnish an honourable support to the
superintendents, and to the others, all the necessaries of life.*

Besides, we must not judge of the merit of the prison officers by the amount of their salary   In Virginia, the superintendent of the Richmond prison receives annually 2000 dollars.
Yet he is the director of one of the bad prisons in the United
States; whilst the superintendent of Wethersfield, which is one
of the good prisons, if it is not the best, receives but 1200 dollars.† We may make the same observation by comparing the good
prisons among each other; thus in Connecticut, the whole sum
paid for the various salaries of the officers at Wethersfield, does
not amount to more than 3713 dollars 33 cents for one hundred
and seventy-four prisoners; whilst in that of Boston, the corresponding expenditure for two hundred and seventy-six prisoners,
amounts to 13,171 dollars 55 cents; so that at Boston, where
the number of the prisoners is not double those at Wethersfield,
the expenses of the officers amount to three times and a half
more than in the latter prison ‡

In investigating the organization of the new establishments,
we have been struck with the importance which is attached to
the choice of the individuals who direct them.   As soon as the
penitentiary system was adopted in the United States, the *per-
sonnel* changed its nature.   For jailor of a *prison*, vulgar people only could be found; the most distinguished persons offer-

* Though the salaries of the officers of American prisons are pretty high, they
are much less than they at first appear   The various arts and occupations in that
country are so profitable, that every individual endowed with some capacity, finds
easily a more profitable career, than that offered by the administration of prisons.
And men like Mr Samuel Wood would not be found at the head of American
penitentiaries, were they not influenced by a nobler sentiment than that of pecuniary interest

† See Report on the prison of Connecticut, of 1830, p 11
‡ See Statistical Tables, financial division, salary of the officers, No. 19.

ed themselves to administer a *penitentiary* where a moral direction exists

We have seen how the superintendents, however elevated their
character and position may be, are subject to the control of a superior authority—the inspectors of the penitentiary. But above
both, there is an authority stronger than all others, not written in
the laws, but all-powerful in a free country; that of public opinion. The improvements in these matters having excited general attention, public opinion directed itself entirely toward this
point, and it exercises without obstruction its vast influence.

There are countries in which public establishments are considered by the government as its own personal affair, so that it
admits persons to them only according to its pleasure, just as
a proprietor refuses at his pleasure admission into his house;
they are a sort of administrative sanctuaries, into which no profane person can penetrate. These establishments, on the contrary, in the United States, are considered as belonging to all.
The prisons are open to every one who chooses to inspect them,
and every visiter may inform himself of the order which regulates the interior. There is no exception to this liberty but in
the penitentiary at Philadelphia. Yet, if one wish, he may see
the buildings and the interior of the establishment. It is only not
permitted to see the prisoners, because the visits of the public
would be in direct contradiction to the principle of absolute solitude, which forms the foundation of the system.*

Instead of avoiding the inspection of the public, the superintendents and inspectors of the prisons ask for the examination
and attention of all.† Each year the inspectors give an account,
either to the legislature or to the governor, of the financial situation of the prison, as well as of its moral state; they indicate
existing abuses and improvements to be made. Their reports,
printed by order of the legislatures, are immediately handed over
to publicity and controversy; the papers, the number of which
in that country is immense, republish them faithfully. Thus
there is not a citizen of the United States who does not know

---

* Admission to this penitentiary is readily granted if inquiry and not curiosity
be the motive for desiring it, as the instance of our author shows.—TRANS.

† "It is very desirable that citizens of the state, and especially gentlemen honoured with the power of making and administering the laws, should frequently
visit this prison." (See Report of Mr Niles, 1829.)

The modern penitentiaries attract many curious persons. According to the
law, the superintendent would have the right to refuse admission, but he never
makes use of this right, and all desirous to visit the prison are allowed to enter
on the payment of 25 cents. These visits thus become a source of revenue,
and the administrator of the prison, keeps account of it. During the year 1830,
the Auburn penitentiary received in this way 1,524 dollars 87 cents. (See Revised Statutes of the State of New York, sec. 64, art. 2, chap. 3, tit. 2, fourth
division, Vol II.)

how the prisons of his country are governed, and who is not able to contribute to their improvement, either by his opinion or by his fortune. The general interest being thus excited, in each town, particular societies form themselves for the progress of prison discipline : all public establishments are carefully examined, all abuses are discovered and pointed out. If it is necessary to construct new prisons, individuals add their contributions to the funds furnished by the state, to meet the expenses. This general attention, a source of perpetual vigilance, produces with the officers of the prisons, an extraordinary zeal and extreme circumspection, which they would not be possessed of, were they placed in the shade This surveillance of public opinion which constrains them in some respects, produces also its compensation, because it is this public opinion which elevates their functions, and makes them honourable, low and obscure as they formerly were.

We have seen the elements of which the prison is composed. Let us now examine how its organization operates.   When the convict arrives in the prison, a physician verifies the state of his health. He is washed : his hair is cut, and a new dress, according to the uniform of the prison is given to him.   In Philadelphia, he is conducted to his solitary cell, which he never leaves, there he works, eats, and rests, and the construction of this cell is so complete, that there is no necessity whatever to leave it.*

At Auburn, at Wethersfield, and in the other prisons of the same nature, the prisoner is first plunged into the same solitude, but it is only for a few days, after which he leaves it, in order to occupy himself in the work-shops † With day-break, a bell gives the sign of rising; the jailors open the doors.   The prisoners range themselves in a line, under the command of their respective jailors, and go first into the yard, where they wash their hands and faces, and from thence into the work-shops, where they go directly to work.   Their labour is not interrupted until the hour of taking food.   There is not a single instant given to recreation ‡

At Auburn, when the hours of breakfast or of dinner have arrived, labour is suspended, and all the convicts meet in the large refectory.   At Sing-Sing, and in all other penitentiaries, they retire into their cells, and take their meals separately.

---

* Each cell is ventilated by a proper contrivance, and contains a *fosse d'aisance*, which by its construction is perfectly odourless It is necessary to have seen these cells of the Philadelphia prison, and to have passed whole days in it, in order to form an exact idea of their cleanliness and the purity of the air which one breathes there

† The cells at Auburn are much smaller than those at Philadelphia , they are seven feet long and three and a half wide   A ventilator keeps the air pure

‡ For much stronger reasons, every game at hazard is prohibited the regulations are uniform on this point and faithfully executed.

This latter regulation appeared to us preferable to that at Auburn. It is not without inconvenience and even danger, that so large a number of criminals can be collected in the same room, their union renders the discipline much more difficult.

In the evening, at the setting of the sun, labour ceases, and the convicts leave the work-shops to retire into their cells. Upon rising, going to sleep, eating, leaving the cells and going back to them, every thing passes in the most profound silence, and nothing is heard in the whole prison but the steps of those who march, or sounds proceeding from the work-shops. But when the day is finished, and the prisoners have retired to their cells, the silence within these vast walls, which contain so many prisoners, is that of death. We have often trod during night those monotonous and dumb galleries, where a lamp is always burning: we felt as if we traversed catacombs; there were a thousand living beings, and yet it was a desert solitude.

The order of one day is that of the whole year. Thus one hour of the convict follows with overwhelming uniformity the other, from the moment of his entry into the prison to the expiration of his punishment. Labour fills the whole day. The whole night is given to rest. As the labour is hard, long hours of rest are necessary; it is not denied to the prisoner between the moment of going to rest and that of rising And before his sleep as after it, he has time to think of his solitude, his crime and his misery.

All penitentiaries it is true have not the same regulations; but all the convicts of a prison are treated in the same way. There is even more equality in the prison than in society.[*]

All have the same dress, and eat the same bread. All work; there exists in this respect, no other distinction than that which results from a greater natural skill for one art than for another. On no condition is labour to be interrupted. The inconvenience of giving a task, after which the prisoner is at liberty to do nothing, has been acknowledged. It is essential for the convict as for the order of the prison, that he should labour without interruption; for him, because idleness is fatal to him; for the prison, because according to the observation of Judge Powers, fifty individuals who work, are more easily watched than ten convicts doing nothing.[†]

Their food is wholesome, abundant, but coarse;[‡] it has to sup-

---

[*] Is this intended as a gentle cut?—Trans

[†] See Report of Mr G Powers, 1828, p 14.

[‡] See Revised Statutes of the State of New York, Vol. II. p 707, § 57. If the reader wishes to know in detail of what the food consists at Auburn, we refer him to Judge Powers' Report of 1828, page 43, and the manuscript note of the Clerk of Auburn. Respecting the food at Wethersfield, see report on this prison in 1828, page 19. For the food at Boston, see the law of March 11, 1828. Respecting Baltimore, see Rules and Regulations page 6, 1829.

port their strength, but ought not to afford them any of those gratifications of the appetite, which are agreeable merely.

None can follow a diet different from that of the prison. Every kind of fermented liquor is prohibited; water alone is drunk here.* The convict who might be possessed of treasures, would nevertheless live like the poorest among them; and we do not find in the American prisons, those eating houses which are found in ours, and in which the convict may buy every thing to gratify his appetite The abuse of wine is there unknown, because the use of it is interdicted †

This discipline is at the same time moral and just. The place which society has assigned for repentance, ought to present no scenes of pleasure and debauch. And it is iniquitous to allow the opulent criminal, whose very riches increase his criminality, to enjoy himself in his prison by the side of the poor wretch whose misery extenuates his fault ‡

Application to labour and good conduct in prison, do not procure the prisoner any alleviation Experience shows that the criminal who, whilst in society, has committed the most expert and audacious crimes, is often the least refractory in prison. He is more docile than the others, because he is more intelligent; and he knows how to submit to necessity when he finds himself without power to revolt. Generally he is more skilful and more active, particularly if an enjoyment, at no great distance, awaits him as the reward of his efforts; so that if we accord to the prisoners privileges resulting from their conduct in the prison, we run the risk of alleviating the rigour of imprisonment to that

---

* See Report on the Wethersfield prison, 1828, page 19

† A picture of these as well as many other most revolting abuses in French prisons, is given in the Memoirs of Vidocq, who was himself a convict in the bagnes, and at a later period principal agent of the French police. A translation of this work appeared in 1829, in London Though these Memoirs contain in some parts fictitious representations of facts, yet the latter are mostly sufficiently warranted, and there can be no doubt but that the work is "true in itself," as the Germans appropriately term it We seize upon this opportunity to recommend M. Vidocq's Memoirs to the perusal of every gentleman who takes a lively interest in the important subject of prison discipline, though the author may not always treat his subject in a manner which the reader less familiarized with these pests of society might desire —TRANS

‡ We only indicate here the most important points of which the order, discipline, and government of the penitentiaries are composed. In order to know the details of the established rules in the new prisons, the division of the day, the nature of the labour, the duties of the officers and of the prisoners, the nature of the authorized punishments, the obligations imposed upon the contractors, &c., &c, we refer to the regulations of the Connecticut prison given in the Appendix as No. 13, also to the regulations drawn up by Mr. Austin, January 1, 1831, for the Massachusetts prison; also the two reports of Mr. Powers on the Auburn prison in 1826 and 1828, and lastly to the regulations of the new penitentiary at Philadelphia. We have also consulted, on this point, the manuscript notes given to us by the clerk of the Auburn prison, and by the superintendent of Sing-Sing, (Mr. Wiltse).

5

criminal who most deserves them, and of depriving of all favours those who merit them most.

Perhaps it would be impossible, in the actual state of our prisons, to manage them without the assistance of rewards granted for the zeal, activity, and talent of the prisoners. But in America, where prison discipline operates supported by the fear of chastisement, a moral influence can be dispensed with in respect to their management.

The interest of the prisoner requires that he should never be idle; that of society demands that he should labour in the most useful way. In the new penitentiaries none of those machines are found, which, in England, the prisoners set in motion without intelligence, and which occupy them merely in a mechanical way.

Labour is not only salutary because it is the opposite of idleness; but it is also contemplated that the convict, whilst he is at work, shall learn a business which may support him when he leaves the prison.

The prisoners therefore, are taught useful trades only; and among these, care is taken to choose such as are the most profitable, and the produce of which finds the easiest sale. (*s*)

The Philadelphia system has often been reproached with rendering labour by the prisoners impossible. It is certainly more economical and advantageous to make a certain number of workmen labour together in a common workshop, than to give each of them employment in a separate place It is moreover true, that a great many arts cannot be pursued with advantage by a single workman in a narrow place; yet the penitentiary of Philadelphia shows that the various occupations which can be pursued by isolated men, are sufficiently numerous to occupy them usefully.* The same difficulty is not met with in those prisons in which the convicts work in company. At Auburn and at Baltimore, a very great variety of arts is pursued. These two prisons offer the sight of vast manufactories which combine all useful occupations. At Boston and Sing-Sing the occupation of the convicts has, so far, been more uniform. In these two prisons, the greater part of the criminals are employed in cutting stones. Wethersfield offers, on a small scale, the same spectacle as Auburn.

In general, the labour of the prisoners is hired to a contractor, who gives a certain price for each day, and receives every thing manufactured by the convict.

---

* The arts pursued in the Philadelphia penitentiary, are weaving, shoemaking, tailoring, joiner's work, &c. See the annual reports on that penitentiary. [Respecting the productiveness of labour in solitary confinement, see our note added to PENNSYLVANIA SYSTEM, paragraph 2 of Section ii. of No. 19, *Financial Division.*—TRANS.]

There is an essential difference between this system and that which is practised in our prisons. With us the same person contracts for the food, clothing, labour, and sanitary department of the convicts—a system equally injurious to the convict and the discipline of the prison;* to the convict, because the contractor, who sees nothing but a money affair in such a bargain, speculates upon the victuals as he does on the labour; if he loses upon the clothing, he indemnifies himself upon the food; and if the labour is less productive than he calculated upon, he tries to balance his loss by spending less for the support of the convicts, with which he is equally charged. This system is alike fatal to the good order of the prison. The contractor, regarding the convict as a labouring machine, thinks only how he can use him to the greatest advantage for himself; every thing appears allowable, in order to excite the zeal of the prisoner, and he cares little if the expenses of the convict are made to the injury of good order. The extent of his privileges, moreover, gives him an importance in the prison, which he ought not to have; it is therefore advisable to separate him as much as possible from the penitentiary, and to counteract his influence, if it cannot be neutralized entirely. (*t*)

It appeared to us, that the evil which we have thus pointed out, has been generally avoided in the new penitentiaries in the United States. In these establishments, neither the system of entire domestic management, nor that by contract, have been exclusively adopted.

The clothing and bedding of the convicts are generally furnished by the superintendent, who himself makes all the contracts relative to these subjects; he avoids many purchases, by causing the prisoners themselves to make the materials necessary for their clothing. At Auburn, Sing-Sing, and Boston, the prisoners are fed by contract, but this contract is not allowed to be made for more than one year. At Wethersfield, the prison itself provides this article. The contractor who, at Auburn, is charged with the food of the prisoners, is not the same who makes them work.

There exists also a different contractor for each branch of industry; the contracts thus being multiplied, the contractor cannot obtain in the prison more than a limited and passing influence. At Wethersfield, the government of the prison not only nourishes and maintains the convicts without the assistance of contract, but it also realizes the value of the greater part of the labour.†

* In the *maison centrale de détention* at Melun, a considerable library exists for the use of the convicts. It belongs to the contractor, who lets the books for a certain sum. The reader may judge from this fact, of the nature of the books.
† See art. 4, of section i. of the regulations of the Connecticut prison, No. 13.

In all these establishments, the contractor cannot, under any pretext, interfere with the internal discipline of the prison, nor influence in the least degree its regulations. He cannot hold any conversation with the prisoners, except in order to teach them that art, with which he is charged to instruct them; and can only do this in the presence and with the consent of one of the jailors. *

In spite of these precautions, the presence of the contractor or his agents in the prisons has been found to be not without its inconvenience. Formerly the Auburn prison managed itself all its affairs;† and when the principle of contract was introduced, Mr. Elam Lynds, then its superintendent, did not allow the contractor to approach the convicts The contractor engaged to give the stipulated price for the articles manufactured by the prisoners, and these articles were delivered to him, without his having directed their manufacture Much was gained in point of discipline by this order of things ; if it were advantageous to limit the intercourse between the contractor and the convicts, it was still better to prevent it entirely. However, such a system of administration was found both difficult and expensive.

The contractors, being deprived of the right of inspecting the labour, imposed disadvantageous conditions upon the prison ; on the other hand, their exclusion from the workshops, made it requisite that the jailors should be capable of instructing the prisoners in the respective arts; and such persons, possessing the necessary skill and technical knowledge, were not easily found. Finally, the sale of the articles was less easy and productive for the superintendent, than for the contractors, exclusively occupied with commercial operations. The result therefore, has been the adoption of a system of contract such as we have described ; this system, surrounded by the guaranties which accompany it, possesses advantages which seem much to outweigh its inconveniences. However, Mr. Elam Lynds seems constantly to fear that the presence of the contractors in the prison, will lead sooner or later to the total ruin of the discipline.

We shall soon see, when we have occasion to treat of the expenses and income, that the labour of the prisoners is in general very productive. Visiting these various establishments, we have been surprised by the order, and sometimes the talent, with which the convicts work, and what makes their zeal quite surprising, is, that they work without any interest in its produce. In our prisons, as well as in those of the greater part of Europe, a part of the produce of their labour belongs to the prisoners. This por-

---

* See G. Powers' report, 1828, page 42. Resp. Boston, see regulations, Jan. 1, 1831.
† See Report of G. Powers, page 41, 1828.

tion, called the *pécule*,* is more or less in various countries; in the United States it does not exist. There the principle is adopted, that the criminal owes all his labour to society, in order to indemnify it for the expenses of his detention. Thus, during the whole time of their punishment, the convicts work without receiving the slightest remuneration; and if they leave the prison, no account is given to them of what they have done. They merely receive a certain portion of money, in order to carry them to the place which they propose to make their new residence.†

This system appears to us excessively severe. We do not dispute the right of society to indemnify itself by the labour of the convict for the expenses he causes, it is an incontestable right; moreover we do not know in what degree a considerable *pécule* or earning is useful to the convict, who, when he leaves the prison, generally sees in the money earned by him, but a means to satisfy passions, the more excited as they have been the longer repressed. But where would be the inconvenience in giving a slight stimulus to the zeal of the convict, by a small reward to his activity? Why should we not give him in his solitude, and in the midst of his sufferings, an interest in a gain however small, yet to him of immense value?‡ Moreover, is it not necessa-

---

* The *pécule* is now always called in America, *over-stint* —Trans.

† The law of the State of New York does not permit the superintendent to give more than three dollars to the convict at the time of his leaving the prison, but he must give him clothes, which must not cost more than ten dollars. See Rev. Stat. of N. Y., 4th divis chap iii, tit. 2, art 2, § 62 At Philadelphia the superintendent may give four dollars to the liberated criminal. See art. 8 of the regulations. See report of 1831 At Boston he is authorized to give five dollars and a " decent suit of clothes" worth about twenty dollars The inspectors of the Massachusetts prison seem to regret that so much is given to the convicts whose terms have expired. See their report of 1830, page 4. Resp Wethersfield, see the report of 1828, on the Connecticut prison.

‡ The first question is, does it interfere with the whole penitentiary system or not, that a convict should be allowed to have his *pécule* or over-stint? It is the opinion of Judge Welles of Wethersfield, that a reasonable over-stint may be allowed with advantage If it is considered injurious, no further question is necessary, because the disposal of the labour of the convict is as lawful as that of his person. But, it might be said, the state may oblige the convict to produce what he costs and no more. This is unfounded, for two reasons 1. The labour certainly must be at his disposal, at whose the whole person is 2 If the matter is considered in a financial point of view, the convict owes to society a far greater debt than that of his support Does he not oblige society to establish courts for him, to pay juries, to have a police, and to incur numerous other expenses? Has he refunded all the injury he has done? The best application of a surplus arising from prison labour, would be, perhaps, to the support of schools, if ever it should amount to a considerable sum. As for the necessity of some pecuniary means for a liberated convict, in order to re-establish him in society, the great difficulty always remains, that those means which by some would be properly used, would with the unreformed but serve for the gratification of vicious habits, so long repressed, and become rather an inducement to plunge once more into crime, than the means of beginning an honest livelihood. Something effectual might perhaps be done by allowing the prisoners to save a *pécule* after they had

ry that on the day when he re-enters society, he should have, if
not a considerable sum at his disposal, at least some means of
support whilst he is in search of labour?* Why not adopt the
system of the Baltimore prison, where, though the principle of
the other American penitentiaries has been acknowledged, yet
its rigour has been alleviated? In that prison every prisoner has
his fixed task for the day : when that is finished, he does not
cease to work, but he begins to work for himself, all that he does
after his task, forms his *pécule;* and as he does not receive his
earning before he leaves the prison, it is certain that it cannot
become injurious to its discipline. There was a time when the
prisoners at Baltimore could spend their earnings immediately
for eatables. Their labour was then much more productive; but
the inconvenience of such indulgence has been acknowledged to
be destructive of good discipline; and at present their *pécule* remains untouched until the moment of their leaving the prison.†

Such is the order established in the American penitentiaries.
We have said that this discipline is applied to all prisoners in
the state prison; however, the women have so far not yet been
subjected to it, except in Connecticut. Generally they are found
together in the American prisons as with us; and in that country, as with us, they are exposed to all the vices growing out of
contaminated intercourse.

Some persons believe that it would be extremely difficult to
apply to women a system, the basis of which is silence : yet the

been for a certain time in prison and behaved well, which, however, should not
be at their free disposal, when they leave the prison (and never at their disposal
before,) but might be paid to them in small portions when it appeared that they
wanted the money actually for good purposes So it might also perhaps be proper to allow such prisoners as have families, to save something to be paid for the
support of their wives and children This would be a moral stimulus. Here we
must mention that the penitentiary system, to be perfect, requires in our opinion,
societies who occupy themselves with devising means to aid delivered convicts
to re-establish themselves in society, a matter which, according to the most natural course of things, is of such extreme difficulty for any convict, however firm
his resolution may be to begin an honest life. We are truly happy therefore to
find, that by the unwearied exertions of Mr. Louis Dwight, a farm is soon to be
established in Massachusetts, where liberated convicts can find labour, and what
is equally important, re-accustom themselves to society , because if penitentiaries
ought to be the moral hospitals of society, the patients should gradually be accustomed to the free air, and to the temptations and clashing interests of society.
We hope to be able to give an accurate account of this novel and important institution, at the end of this work.—TRANS.

* Generally speaking, the most dangerous moment for a delivered convict, is
that when he leaves the prison Not unfrequently they spend their whole *pécule*
within the first twenty-four hours of their liberty In Geneva, to redress this
evil, the whole *pécule* is not delivered to the convict when he leaves the jail. It
is sent to him to the place of his new residence. The same is now done in France
with the convicts who leave the bagnes and *maisons centrales.* This is a wise measure, which it is important to preserve.

† See Report on the Penitentiary of Maryland of December 23, 1828, to Governor Kent ; and the Report on the same of 1830.

experiment made at Wethersfield, where the women are, like the rest of the prisoners, subject to isolation in cells during night, and absolute silence during day, proves that the difficulty is not insurmountable * Again, it is not the difficulty of execution in this point which has prevented reform in the prisons of the United States. If, in the application of the new penitentiary system, the women have been omitted, this fact must be ascribed above all, to the small number of crimes committed by them in that country, it is because they occupy little space in the prison, that they have been neglected † It is the same with most evils of society, a remedy for which is ardently sought if they are important; if they are not alarming they are overlooked.

SECTION III.

Disciplinary Means.

The necessity of distinguishing the Philadelphia system from that of Auburn —
The first much easier to be put in practice, and to be maintained —That
of Auburn has for an auxiliary corporal punishment —Moderate discipline at
Wethersfield —Discretionary power of the superintendents —Aversion to
corporal punishments.—What is their influence upon the state of health of
the prisoners?

LET us now examine by what disciplinary means the order of things which we have explained above, is established and maintained.

How is silence so rigorously maintained among a number of assembled criminals? How are they made to work without any interest of their own?

Here also we have to distinguish between the Auburn and Philadelphia systems.

In Philadelphia, the discipline is as simple as the system itself. The only critical moment is that when the prisoner enters the prison. The solitary cell of the criminal is for some days full of terrible phantoms. Agitated and tormented by a thousand fears, he accuses society of injustice and cruelty, and in such a disposition of mind, it sometimes will happen that he disregards

---

* The difficulty is doubled,—
1. It is generally thought that women submit much more reluctantly to absolute silence, than the men.
2. A coercive method, used with men, is wanting in regard to women. The laws of the United States, which authorize corporal punishment in respect to male prisoners, prohibit the same from being applied to women

† See Statistical Observations, No. 17, § 4 Proportion of crimes committed by women to those committed by men.—So far the authors. The reason of this great difference is known to every body who is acquainted with the different stations women occupy in the United States from that in most countries of Europe.—TRANS.

the orders, and repels the consolations offered to him. The only chastisement which the regulations of the prison permits, is imprisonment in a dark cell with reduction of food. It is rare that more than two days of such discipline are required, to curb the most refractory prisoner. When the convict has overcome the first impressions of solitude; when he has triumphed over the terrors which almost surrendered him to insanity or despair;* when, in his solitary cell, in the midst of the pains of a stinging conscience, and the agitations of his soul, he has fallen into a dejection of mind, and has sought in labour a relief from his griefs; from that moment he is tamed, and for ever submissive to the rules of the prison. What breach of order is it possible to commit in solitude? The entire discipline consists in the isolation of the prisoners, and the impossibility of their violating the established rule. In the other prisons, disciplinary punishments are inflicted on the prisoners who break the law of silence, or refuse to work. But silence is easy for him who is alone; and labour is not refused by those whose only consolation it forms.†
We have pointed out the inconvenience of absolute solitude, the deficiency of which is, that it deprives the prisoner's submission of its moral character,‡ but we must at the same time acknowledge its advantages in respect to discipline; and the facility of ruling an establishment of this nature, without the application of severe and repeated punishment, is certainly a very great advantage. There are some persons who consider the order established at Philadelphia complicated, organized with difficulty, and maintained with trouble. They are, in our opinion, greatly mistaken. The Philadelphia system is expensive, but not difficult to be established; and once established, it maintains itself. It is this very system, the discipline of which offers the least embarrassment; each cell is a prison in itself, and the convicts who are

* Though a guilty conscience never stings with keener pain, or smites the soul with greater grief than when we are alone and "only in presence of our crime," and though the Philadelphia system is founded on this very truth, yet we believe that the greater part of the cases the authors have depicted here in too lively colours —Trans

† The convict would be willing enough to work as much as is necessary in order to *désennuyer* himself, and to exercise his body, and to remain idle when he felt himself fatigued But this is not allowed, and justly so; he must always work or not at all. If he refuses to work in a line he has begun, he is placed in a dark cell. He has therefore the choice between constant leisure in darkness, or uninterrupted labour in his cell His choice is never long in suspense, and he always prefers labour.—See Reports on the Philadelphia prison in 1831.

‡ I confess freely that I was unable to understand the authors here, or in other passages on the same point To attribute a moral character to a submission which is produced only by the threat of instant corporal punishment in the moment of infraction, seems to me a solecism. The prisoner's moral exertion certainly is not more proved by submitting to silence because he would be severely punished were he to break it, than by the material impossibility of breaking it; and whilst the former means irritate, the latter lead to contemplation.—Trans

detained there cannot render themselves guilty of offences which can only be possibly committed in company with others. There is no punishment, because there is no infraction.

The discipline at Auburn, Sing-Sing, Boston, Wethersfield, and Baltimore, could not have the same character of simplicity : these various establishments themselves, follow, in this respect, different courses.

At Sing-Sing, the only punishment for those who infringe the established order, is that of the whip. The application of this disciplinary means is there very frequent ; and the least fault is punished with its application For various reasons this punishment is preferred to all others. It effects the immediate submission of the delinquent ; his labour is not interrupted a single instant ; the chastisement is painful, but not injurious to health ; finally, it is believed that no other punishment would produce the same effects * The same principle is admitted at Auburn, but in its application is extremely rare. The penitentiaries of Boston and Baltimore, a little more severe than that at Auburn, are nevertheless much less so than Sing-Sing : Wethersfield differs from all others by its extreme mildness. (v)

In this latter prison stripes are not altogether objected to ; but their application is as much as possible avoided : Mr. Pillsbury, superintendent of the establishment, has assured us, that for three years he has but one single time been obliged to inflict stripes. It is a severity to which recourse is had only if it is well ascertained that every other and milder way has been tried without effect : before resorting to stripes, absolute solitude day and night without labour is tried . if we believe the officers of the prison, nothing is rarer than to see a prisoner resist this first trial ; he has been scarcely subjected to the rigour of absolute isolation, than he solicits the favour of again taking his place in the common workshop, and submits willingly to all that discipline requires. However, if he is not curbed at the first moment, greater severity is added to his solitude, such as entire privation of light, and diminution of food ; sometimes also his bed is taken from him, &c , &c., &c. If the prisoner still obstinately resists, then, and then only, the whip is used, as the still more effective means of submission. The directors of this establishment seem to have a decided aversion to corporal chastisement ; yet they would regret it much if they were not invested

---

* No register is kept of disciplinary punishments. We have been told that about five or six whippings (among one thousand prisoners,) take place every day at Sing-Sing. At Auburn, though very frequent in the beginning, they are now very rare One of the officers of this prison said to us I remember having seen, at the beginning, nineteen prisoners whipped in less than an hour. Since the discipline was well established, I once had no occasion to resort to the whip a single time for four months and a half —(See our inquiry in MS. into the Auburn discipline.)

with the right to inflict it. They reject the application of cruel pain; but they find a powerful means of acting upon the criminals, in their authority to order it.

The tempered discipline of Wethersfield seems to suffice for the success of the establishment. Yet in the other prisons it is thought that the management of the whole would be impossible without the assistance of the whip. This is the opinion of all practical men whom we have seen in the United States, particularly of Mr. Elam Lynds, whom we have mentioned above.[*] The legislatures of New York, Massachusetts, Connecticut, and Maryland, have had the same conviction, since they have formally authorized the infliction of corporal punishment. These chastisements have also received the sanction of judicial authority; and the country, through the organ of her jury, has given several verdicts in favour of jailors who acknowledged having beaten the prisoners. (*x*)

We have noticed the remarkable differences which exist in the disciplinary order of the various establishments; all, however, admit the principle of corporal punishment; and it is just to say, that there exist in the particular situation of each of the prisons, certain circumstances, which tend to explain the mildness or severity of its discipline.

If we remember the nature of the labours executed at Sing-Sing, and the order established in that prison, we easily understand the insurmountable obstacles with which disciplinary order would meet in this prison, were it not supported by the most energetic measures of repression. Auburn does not require so much severity, because the same dangers do not threaten the order of the establishment. Wethersfield is, in this respect, in a still more favourable position; it contains less than two hundred criminals, whilst Auburn has six hundred and fifty, and Sing-Sing more than nine hundred. It is evident, that the number, more or less considerable, of criminals, and the nature of the labour, render the penitentiary more or less easy of government.

Now, could these various penitentiaries dispense with corporal chastisement? This is a question which we dare not solve. We are merely able to say, that, deprived of this assistance, prison discipline would meet with difficulties very difficult to be overcome. Its embarrassments would be so much the greater, as it is founded on an unique basis, that of absolute silence; and should it ever be deprived of this foundation, the whole fabric must inevitably crumble to pieces; now, how is it possible to maintain absolute silence among criminals, if they are not continually overawed by the fear of a prompt and rigorous chastisement? In the American prisons, this discipline, founded upon

---

[*] See our conversation with Mr. Elam Lynds, at the end of the volume.

stripes, is so much more powerful, as it is practised more arbitrarily.* At Sing-Sing, and at Auburn, there are no written regulations: the superintendents of these prisons, have only, in their government, to conform themselves to the verbal prescriptions which they receive from the inspectors, and to a few principles expressed in the law; these principles are: solitary imprisonment of the convicts during night, and labour in silence during day. For the rest, they enjoy, as to all acts of execution, a discretionary power.(*y*) At Sing-Sing, the superintendent has even the right to delegate this discretionary power to all his inferior agents; and in fact he has transmitted his power to thirty jailors, who are invested like himself with the power of chastising the convicts. At Auburn, the superintendent alone has the power to punish, yet the same authority belongs to the inferior keepers, in all cases of urgent and absolute necessity. The same is the case in Boston. In Wethersfield, the regulations of the prison are in writing;† the subaltern officers can in no case exercise the right of punishing, with which the superintendent alone is invested, and which he uses with so much moderation. Important debates have taken place in the state of New York, on the question whether the presence of an inspector ought to be required when inflicting stripes upon a prisoner: according to the letter of the law, this guaranty was indispensable; but the obligation of the inspectors to be present at such punishments, was so frequently inconvenient, and caused them such painful feelings, that they asked immediately to be absolved from this duty; and at present the right of the officers to inflict stripes without these official witnesses is acknowledged ‡ The inspectors have nevertheless a great influence on the application of disciplinary chastisement. Sing-Sing is the only prison where their superintendence has appeared to us superficial upon this point. The administration of this vast penitentiary is so difficult, that

---

* We will mention here a remarkable fact, which proves the efficiency of this discipline. On the 23d of October a fire broke out in the Auburn prison; it consumed a part of the buildings belonging to the prison. As it became dangerous even to the lives of the prisoners, the latter were let out of their cells, but the order was not disturbed for a moment, all assisted zealously to extinguish the fire, and not one of them attempted to profit by this circumstance to escape. (See Report of 1829 of the Inspectors of Auburn)

† In Boston the regulations are likewise in writing, and the duties of the officers are traced in it. However, these provisions are directory only the superintendent and the sub director are invested not the less with a discretionary power. —Regulations of the New Prison, page 100. So far the authors. This is one of the many instances which show that an officer of a government entirely dependent upon public opinion, may often be clothed with much more power than a similar officer in a more arbitrary government, for the very reason that he remains always under the inspection and influence of the public —TRANS.

‡ See Report of the Inspectors of Auburn, January 26, 1825.

there seems to be no disposition to dispute the least part of the absolute power of the keepers.

We shall not investigate here whether society has the right to punish, with corporal chastisement, the convict who refuses to submit to the obligation of labour, or to the other exigencies of penitentiary discipline.

Such theoretical questions are rarely discussed, to the interest of truth and human society.

We believe that society has the right to do every thing necessary for its conservation, and for the order established within it; and we understand perfectly well, that an assemblage of criminals, all of whom have infringed the laws of the land, and all of whose inclinations are corrupted, and appetites vicious, cannot be governed in prison according to the same principles, and with the same means, as free persons, whose desires are correct, and whose actions are conformable to the laws. We also conceive perfectly well, that a convict who will not labour, ought to be constrained to do so, and that severity ought to be used in order to reduce him to silence, who will not observe it; the right of society seems to us, on this point, beyond all doubt, if it cannot arrive at the same end by milder means, but in our opinion that is not the question.

To what point are corporal chastisements reconcilable with the object of the penitentiary system itself, which is the reformation of the guilty? If this pain be ignominious, does it not go directly against the end which we propose to obtain, viz. to awaken the morality of an individual, fallen in his own opinion?

This question seems to us to be the only one to be examined; but we do not believe that it ought to be solved in an arbitrary manner. It would seem that much depends upon the light in which public opinion, and that of the prisoners, consider bodily punishment.

The discretionary power, by virtue of which, the lowest keeper at Auburn, and even the turnkeys at Sing-Sing, lash the prisoners, is little contested in the United States

" The right of the keepers over the persons of the prisoners, it is said, is that of a father over his children, of the teacher over his pupils, of the master over his apprentice, and of a sea-captain over his crew."*

The punishment of stripes is in use in the American navy, with no idea of infamy attached to it. In the beginning, the whip was not admitted as a disciplinary means in the penitentiary system. When it was introduced as an auxiliary to the regulations, some voices were raised against it; but this opposi-

---

* Report of Mr. G, Powers, page 11, 1827,

tion was much more a dispute of philosophy than one of repugnance to national customs.*

Pennsylvania is, perhaps, the only state in the Union which continues to protest against corporal punishment, and which excluded it from the regulations of her prisons. The quakers cease not to protest against the inhumanity of this punishment, and their philanthropic protestations are joined by the eloquent voice of Edward Livingston, who also rejects this means of discipline from his code. It is chiefly on account of corporal punishment, made use of at Auburn, that he declares himself the adversary of the system which is in practice in that prison.†

But their words find few corresponding voices in most parts of the Union, and, at present, all new penitentiaries, that of Philadelphia only excepted, make use of the whip; the laws of the country authorize the discipline which they have adopted, and these laws have the sanction of public opinion.

There is certainly much exaggeration in the reproaches made against the Auburn discipline. First, stripes are not so frequent as is believed; necessary, as they are, to establish silence in a newly founded prison, they are seldom made use of in order to maintain this regulation if once established.

Now, is the whole system of these prisons, as is asserted, injurious to health, and are the rigours of solitude and the cruelties of the discipline, fatal to the life of the imprisoned? We are able to furnish positive documents upon this point.

All prisoners, whom we have seen in the penitentiaries of the

* We believe that the authors speak here in terms much too general. If no idea of peculiar infamy is attached to stripes inflicted upon a prisoner, they are at all events much against the feeling of a great part of the community, who especially object to the arbitrary power of the officers to inflict them. It is with them a matter of humanity, not of philosophy —Trans

† Mr. Livingston says, in his letter to Mr Roberts Vaux, 1828, page 11, that the question is whether the whip is the most efficient means to instil religious and moral sentiments, the love of labour and knowledge into the soul of the convict, and whether a man would relish labour better for being constrained by stripes, or the fear of them, to do every day his task Mr Gershom Powers, director of the Auburn prison, the discipline of which Mr. Livingston thus attacked, answered "It is understood that (at Philadelphia) stripes are not to be tolerated under any circumstances, and that diet is to be the principal, if not only means of enforcing discipline; or in other words, the convicts are, from motives of humanity, to be starved into submission." See his Report of 1828, page 97. [Every candid reader will see how far the spirit of controversy misled the deceased and highly meritorious author of the above report. There is, besides, in most cases, a very great difference in punishments which consist of privations, and those which are composed of actual inflictions. The latter irritate our feelings much more, and lead to hatred and vengeance, whilst the former curb with more calmness. Skilful tyrants never forget this rule, founded upon general principles of the human mind —Trans]

Mr. Elam Lynds, with whom we have had numerous conversations on this point, has often told us, that when the prisoners at Auburn were in constant solitary confinement, a great number of them passed more than half of their time in the hospital.

United States, had the appearance of strength and health; and if we compare the number of those who die there with the mortality in the old prisons, we shall see that the new penitentiaries, in spite of their severe regulations and barbarous discipline, are much more favourable to the life of the imprisoned. Mr. Edward Livingston wishes to see solitary confinement during night and day, without labour, and reduction of food substituted for the whip, as a disciplinary measure; it does not seem that at Wethersfield this punishment, which as we have seen, is preferred to stripes, has produced bad effects. However, ten individuals are mentioned as having died in consequence of this kind of punishment in the prison of Lamberton in New Jersey, whilst there is no case yet on record of a prisoner having become the victim of corporal whipping.*

In the old Walnut street prison, there was formerly, during each year, one death out of sixteen prisoners, and in that of New York (Newgate,) one out of nineteen. In both these prisons, the criminals were neither in solitary confinement, nor obliged to be wholly silent, nor subjected to corporal punishment.†

In the new penitentiaries, founded upon the principles of silence and isolation supported by the discipline of stripes, death takes place in an infinitely smaller proportion.

At Sing-Sing, one prisoner died out of thirty-seven; at Wethersfield one of forty-four; at Baltimore one of forty-nine; at Auburn one of fifty-six; and at Boston one of fifty-eight.

Still more: if we compare the mortality of the prisoners to that of persons enjoying liberty and society, we shall yet arrive at a result favourable to the penitentiaries. There dies, in fact, in Pennsylvania, every year, one out of thirty-nine persons, and in Maryland one out of forty-seven. Again, in the old prisons where free communication existed, and where the discipline was mild, one half more died than in society generally; and in the new penitentiaries, subject to the austere system of isolation, silence, and stripes, deaths are less numerous.‡

These cyphers are better answers than all possible arguments, to the objections which have been raised.

We have said nothing on the sanitary state of the new Phila-

---

* See Fifth Report of Prison Disc. Society at Boston, page 92.

† See Statistical Observations, No. 17. At Auburn the prisoners are treated much more severely: in Philadelphia they are much more unhappy. In Auburn, where they are whipped, they die less frequently than in Philadelphia, where, for humanity's sake, they are put in a solitary and sombre cell. The superintendent of Walnut street prison, where the disciplinary punishments are mild, told us, that he had incessantly to punish the prisoners for infractions of discipline. So that the disciplinary punishments at Walnut street, milder than those at Auburn, are also more often repeated and more fatal to the lives of the prisoners, than the severe chastisements used in this latter prison.

‡ See Statistical Tables of the States of New York, Pennsylvania, Connecticut, Maryland, and Massachusetts, at the end of the Vol., No. 17.

delphia prison, which has been in existence for too short a time to judge fully of its effects. We have every reason to believe that the system of perpetual and absolute seclusion, established there in full vigour, will prove less favourable to the health of the prisoners than the Auburn system. Yet the physician of that establishment believes himself able already to declare that the mortality will be less there than in the ancient prison of Walnut street. *

To sum up the whole on this point, it must be acknowleged that the penitentiary system in America is severe. Whilst society in the United States gives the example of the most extended liberty, the prisons of the same country offer the spectacle of the most complete despotism.† The citizens subject to the law are protected by it; they only cease to be free when they become wicked.

* See Report on the Philadelphia Penitentiary 1831, and Observations of Mr. Bache, physician to the prison. So far the authors. We would refer also to the inquiry made into the Philadelphia Penitentiary by the authors, and given by the authors in the appendix to the work, also to Mr Wood's last statement on the prison, and our own article on the Pennsylvania Penitentiary System at the end of the vol —TRANS

† I have preferred translating literally, even passages which on account of their lively expression, so natural to the nation to which our authors belong, appear very different in English, to which the reader is accustomed to give its full and positive meaning, and think it would be unnecessary to dwell upon the impropriety of calling a system despotic, which mainly grew out of the feeling of humanity, and continues to be kept up by it—a system which, at the most, can appear despotic only at the first glance, but which is truly merciful if compared to the former systems of prisons—or, to speak more correctly, total want of any system.—TRANS.

CHAPTER III.

. Reform.

Illusions of some philanthropists respecting the penitentiary system.—In what consist its real advantages —Prisoners cannot corrupt each other.—Means employed to effect their moral reform —Primary and religious instruction —Advantages and disadvantages of the Philadelphia system on this point —The Auburn system, less philosophical, depends more for its success upon individuals charged with its execution —Influence of religious persons on reformations —Their reformation, is it obtained ?—Distinction between radical and external reformation.

SECTION I.

THERE are in America as well as in Europe, estimable men whose minds feed upon philosophical reveries, and whose extreme sensibility feels the want of some illusion. These men, for whom philanthropy has become a matter of necessity, find in the penitentiary system a nourishment for this generous passion. Starting from abstractions which deviate more or less from reality, they consider man, however far advanced in crime, as still susceptible of being brought back to virtue. They think that the most infamous being may yet recover the sentiment of honour; and pursuing consistently this opinion, they hope for an epoch when all criminals may be radically reformed, the prisons be entirely empty, and justice find no crimes to punish. (z)

Others, perhaps without so profound a conviction, pursue nevertheless the same course; they occupy themselves continually with prisons; it is the subject to which all the labours of their life bear reference. Philanthropy has become for them a kind of profession; and they have caught the *monomanie* of the penitentiary system, which to them seems the remedy for all the evils of society.

We believe that both overrate the good to be expected from this institution, of which the real benefit can be acknowledged without attributing to it imaginary effects.

There is, first, an incontestable advantage inherent in a penitentiary system of which isolation forms the principal basis. It is that the criminals do not become worse in the prison than they were when they entered it. On this point this system differs essentially from that pursued in our prisons, which not only render the prisoner no better, but corrupt him still more. With us all great crimes have been planned in some measure in a prison, and been deliberated upon in the midst of assembled malefactors. Such is the fatal influence of the wicked upon each other, that one finished rogue in a prison suffices as a model for all who see and hear him, to fashion their vices and immorality upon his. (*aa*)

Nothing, certainly, is more fatal to society than this course of mutual evil instruction in prisons; and it is well ascertained that we owe to this dangerous contagion a peculiar population of malefactors, which every day becomes more numerous and more alarming. It is an evil which the penitentiary system of the United States cures completely.*

It is evident that all moral contagion among the imprisoned is impossible, particularly in Philadelphia, where thick walls separate the prisoners day and night. This first result is important; and we must take good care not to underrate its importance. The theories on the reform of the prisoners are vague and uncertain.† It is not yet known to what degree the wicked may be regenerated, and by what means this regeneration may be obtained: but if the efficiency of the prison in correcting the prisoners is yet doubtful, its power of depraving them still more *is* known, because experience proves it. The new penitentiaries, in which this contagious influence is avoided, have therefore gained a signal advantage; and as long as that prison has not yet been found whose discipline is completely regenerating in its effects, perhaps we may be permitted to say that the best prison is that which does not corrupt.

It is nevertheless clear, that this result, however weighty, does not satisfy the authors of the system; and it is natural that having preserved the prisoner from the corruption with which he was threatened, they aspire at reforming him. Let us see by what means they endeavour to arrive at this end. We shall then also examine the success of their efforts.

Moral and religious instruction forms, in this respect, the whole basis of the system. In all penitentiary systems, those who have not learned to read are instructed in it. These schools

* Respecting the frightful contamination in prisons of the old kind, and the deplorable effects of the false shame of appearing less familiar with crime and immorality than others, we again refer the reader to Vidocq's Memoirs, cited above.

† "* * * But from a closer and more intimate view of the subject, I have rather abandoned a hope I once entertained, of the *general reformation of offenders* through the penitentiary system. I now think that its chief good is in the prevention of crime by the confinement of criminals." (Mr. Niles, former commissioner of the Penitentiary of Maryland, December 22, 1829.)

7

are voluntary. Though no convict is obliged to join them, they consider it as a favour to be admitted: and if it is impossible to receive all who offer themselves, those among the prisoners are selected who are most in need of the benefit of instruction.* The free choice left to the prisoners to join or not the school, makes those who enter it thus voluntarily, much more zealous and docile. This school is kept every Sunday. It precedes the morning service. The minister who administers this service, accompanies it almost always with a sermon, in which he abstains from every dogmatical discussion, and treats only of religious morals; so that the instruction of the minister is as fit for the Catholic as for the Protestant, for the Unitarian as for the Presbyterian. The meals of the prisoners are always preceded by a prayer, offered up by the chaplain of the establishment; each of them has a Bible, given by the state, in his cell, in which he may read the whole time that he is not engaged in labour.

This order exists in all the penitentiaries; but we should be much deceived were we to believe that uniformity exists on this point in these various prisons. Some attach to religious instruction much more importance than others. Some neglect the moral reformation of the prisoners, whilst others make it a particular object. At Sing-Sing, for instance, where the nature of things requires so severe a discipline, the directors of the establishment seemed to have in view the support of external order only, and the passive obedience of the convicts. The assistance of moral influence is disregarded; primary and religious instruction, it is true, is somewhat attended to; but it is manifest that it is considered but a secondary object. In the prisons of Auburn, Wethersfield, Philadelphia, and Boston, the reformation of the criminals occupies a much more prominent place.

In Philadelphia, the moral situation in which the convicts are placed, is eminently calculated to facilitate their regeneration. We have more than once remarked the serious turn which the ideas of the prisoner in this penitentiary take. We have seen convicts there, whose levity had led them to crime, and whose mind had, in that solitude, contracted habits of meditation and of reasoning altogether extraordinary. The system of this prison appeared to us especially powerful over individuals endowed with some elevation of mind, and who had enjoyed a polite education. Intellectual men are naturally those who are the least able to endure a separation from all society.

We can however assert, that this absolute solitude produces the liveliest impression on all prisoners. Generally, their hearts are found ready to open themselves, and the facility of being

* In Boston all are admitted who present themselves. (Report of Mr. Gray, pages 10 and 11.)

moved renders them also fitter for reformation. They are particularly accessible to religious sentiments, and the remembrance of their family has an uncommon power over their minds. One who enjoys the intercourse of society, is perhaps incapable of feeling the whole value of a religious idea thrown into the lonesome cell of a convict.

Nothing distracts, in Philadelphia, the mind of the convicts from their meditations; and as they are always isolated, the presence of a person who comes to converse with them is the greatest benefit, and one which they appreciate in its whole extent. When we visited this penitentiary, one of the prisoners said to us: "it is with joy that I perceive the figure of the keepers, who visit my cell. This summer a cricket came into my yard; it looked like a companion. When a butterfly or any other animal happens to enter my cell, I never do it any harm."* If the soul is thus disposed, it is easy to conceive what value the prisoners must attach to moral communications, and how great must be the influence of wise advice and pious exhortations on their minds.

The superintendent visits each of them at least once a day. The inspectors visit them at least twice a week, and a chaplain has the special charge of their moral reformation. Before and after these visits, they are not entirely alone. The books which are at their disposal, are in some measure companions who never leave them. The Bible, and sometimes tracts containing edifying anecdotes, form their library. If they do not work, they read, and several of them seem to find in it a great consolation. There were some, who only knew the letters of the alphabet, and have in prison learned, by themselves, to read. Others less ingenious or persevering, have succeeded in it only with the assistance of the superintendent or the inspectors.†

These are the means employed in Philadelphia to enlighten and reform the convicts.

Can there be a combination more powerful for reformation than that of a prison which hands over the prisoner to all the trials of solitude, leads him through reflection to remorse, through religion to hope; makes him industrious by the burden of idleness, and which, whilst it inflicts the torment of solitude, makes him find a charm in the converse of pious men, whom otherwise he would have seen with indifference, and heard without pleasure?

* See Inquiry into the penitentiary at Philadelphia, No. 10.

† There is no school regularly kept in the Philadelphia prison; but as soon as the inspectors or superintendent discover good dispositions in a prisoner, or, by whatever motive, feel interested in his favour, they bestow more care upon him than on others, and begin by imparting the first elements of instruction. One of the inspectors of the penitentiary, Mr. Bradford, spends much time in this good work.

The impression made by such a system on the criminal, certainly is deep; experience alone can show whether the impression is durable.

We have said that his entry into the penitentiary is a critical moment; that of his departure from it is still more so. He suddenly passes from absolute solitude to the ordinary state of society; is it not to be feared that he will greedily search for those social enjoyments of which he has been deprived so completely? He was dead to the world, and after a loss of several years he re-appears in society, to which, it is true, he brings good resolutions, but perhaps also burning passions, the more impetuous, from their being the longer repressed.

This is, perhaps, on the score of reformation, the chief inconvenience of absolute isolation * This system possesses, however, an advantage, which ought not to be passed over in silence; it is, that the prisoners subject to this discipline, do not know each other.† This fact avoids serious inconveniences, and leads to happy consequences. There exists always, a tie more or less strong between criminals, who have formed their acquaintance in a common prison; and if they meet again after having gone through their imprisonment, they stand in a reciprocal dependance. Known, mutually, the one is almost forced to assist the other, if the latter will again commit an offence; it would be necessary to have become virtuous in a very elevated degree, in order not to become again criminal. This rock, generally so fatal to delivered convicts, is, indeed, in part avoided in the Auburn system, where the prisoners, seeing without knowing each other, contract no intimate connexion Yet we are still much more certain of avoiding this danger in the Philadelphia prison, where the convicts never behold each other's faces

He who at the expiration of his punishment leaves this prison

---

* We cannot see that absolute solitude offers in this respect, any difficulty which the Auburn system does not offer in the same degree On the contrary, we believe that the convict, leaving the solitary cell of the Philadelphia prison, will, generally, be much more strengthened by continued and almost uninterrupted reflection against new temptations than a person who has undergone his imprisonment in a penitentiary on the Auburn system. That objection, which is justly made against educating young persons in convents, who, unaccustomed to the world, but too often strive to regain the time which in point of the enjoyment of pleasures seems lost to them, and thus become the prey of worldly habits, cannot be made against the Pennsylvania penitentiary system, because it is a very different thing to enter life totally inexperienced and to re-enter it from a penitentiary There is one passion, the indulgence in which we can easily conceive, may be very common with those, who leave even the Philadelphia penitentiary, because it is that deepest planted in the human frame, and more difficult to be bridled—an indulgence which may, by a necessary association with immoral persons, become the recommencement of a criminal path, but, certainly, this is a difficulty to be encountered also by the Auburn system and by every possible prison system.—Trans.

† See Second Report on the penitentiary of Philadelphia, 1831.

in order to re-enter society, cannot find in his former fellow-prisoners, whom he does not know, any assistance in doing evil ; and if he is willing to pursue an honest course, he meets nobody to prevent him from doing so. If he wish to commit new offences, he stands alone , and, as to this point, he is still as isolated in the world as he was in the prison ; if, on the contrary, he is desirous of commencing a new life, he possesses full liberty to do so.

This system of reform is undoubtedly a conception which belongs to the highest philosophy ; in general it is simple and easy to be put in practice ; yet it presents in its execution, a difficulty sufficiently serious. The first rule of the system being, that the prisoners shall be entirely prevented from holding intercourse with, or even seeing each other, it results that no religious instruction or school can take place in common, so that the teacher or chaplain can instruct or exhort but one person at a time. This occasions an immense loss of time * If the prisoners could be united to participate in the benefit of the same lesson, it would be much easier to diffuse moral and religious instruction ; but the principles of the system are opposed to it †

In the prisons of Auburn, Wethersfield, Sing-Sing, and Boston, the system of reformation does not rest upon so philosophical a theory as at Philadelphia ‡ In the latter prison, the system seems to operate by itself, by the sole force of its principles. At Auburn, on the contrary, and in the prisons of the same nature, its efficiency depends much more upon the persons charged with its execution ; we see, therefore, assistance borrowed from external means, which are not so much employed in the other prison.

The Auburn plan, which permits the prisoners to assemble

* All the prisoners of one wing of the penitentiary partake, in Philadelphia, of the same sermon but as the penitentiary will have seven distinct parts, seven consecutive religious instructions would be requisite to be given by the same minister, or else seven ministers be occupied with the same subject at once.

† As in all similar matters, the only question is, which offers the greater advantages or is the less objectionable , the advocates of the Pennsylvania system do not think it a great loss to the prisoners that they cannot participate in a form of service similar to that of free persons, because they believe this disadvantage, if it be one, vastly compensated by the powerful reflection to which solitude necessarily leads Besides it must be remembered that it is a mistake which leads to serious disadvantages, if we reason from the feelings, dispositions, and wants of free persons to those of convicts. It is a mistake but too often fallen into, and yet there is all the difference which exists between a healthy person and a reduced patient —Trans

‡ The adversaries of Auburn say, that the system of reformation has met there with so little success, that it has been entirely abandoned. It must be admitted that the efforts to regenerate the criminals are not always crowned with success, but it would not be exact to say that reformation is given up at Auburn , we can attest, on the contrary, that the gentlemen who direct the establishment, pursue this end with ardour. We refer the reader to what G. Powers says on this point to E Livingston, (Letter of G. Powers to Edward Livingston, 1829)

during the day, seems, indeed, less calculated than that of Philadelphia to produce reflection and repentance; but it is more favourable to the instruction of the prisoners; in all prisons subject to the same discipline, the instructer and the chaplain can
address all the prisoners at once. At Auburn there is a chaplain
(Mr. Smith) exclusively for the establishment. The same is the
case in Wethersfield, where Mr. Barrett, a presbyterian minister,
devotes himself entirely to the penitentiary*. After the school,
and the service of Sunday, the prisoners return to their solitary
cells, where the chaplain visits them; he visits them in a similar way on the other days of the week;† and strives to touch
their hearts by enlightening their conscience; the prisoners feel
pleasure when they see him enter their cell. He is the only
friend who is left to them; they confide in him all their sentiments; if they have any complaint against the officers of the
prison, or if they have a favour to sue for, it is he who is intrusted with their wishes. By showing the interest which he
takes in them, he gains more and more their confidence. He
soon becomes initiated into all the secrets of their previous life,
and, knowing the moral state of all, he endeavours to apply to
each the proper remedy for his evil. For the rest, the minister
interferes in no respect with the discipline of the prison. If the
convicts are in their workshops, he never draws their attention
from their work; and if a complaint is made to him, he does
not act, but merely solicits in favour of the unfortunate whose
interpreter he is. It would be difficult, indeed, to describe the
zeal which animates Messrs Barrett and Smith in the exercise
of their pious functions; yet they sometimes, perhaps, deceive
themselves respecting the results of their efforts, though they
are at all events sure to earn the veneration of all who know
them.

They are admirably seconded in their charitable office by several individuals not belonging to the establishment   The Sunday school is almost entirely managed by citizens residing near
the prison. These, guided by a sentiment of humanity with
which a profound feeling of religious duty mixes itself, pass on
every Sunday two or three hours in the prison, where they act
as primary instructers   They however do not only instruct the
prisoners in reading, but explain to them also, the most important passages of the gospel. At Auburn, this gratuitous and religious office is performed by the members of the presbyterian
seminary. School is also held at Sing-Sing, Baltimore, and Bos

---

* Mr. Barrett receives a salary of 200 dollars.
  † In the evening when they have returned to their cells, after the day's work
is over.

ton.* In the last named city, we have seen men of the highest distinction taking upon themselves this obscure office; they made several criminals, standing around them, repeat their lesson; sometimes they would intersperse their remarks and councils in so affecting a way, that the convicts shed tears of emotion. Certainly, if the reformation of a criminal be possible, it must be obtainable by such means and such persons.†

Now, to what point is this reformation actually effected by the different systems which we have examined?

Before we answer this question, it will be necessary to settle the meaning attached to the word *reformation*.

Do we mean by this expression the radical change of a wicked person into an honest man—a change which produces virtues in the place of vices?

A similar regeneration, if it ever take place, must be very rare. What would it be in fact? To give back its primitive purity to a soul which crime has polluted. But here the difficulty is immense. It would have been much easier for the guilty individual to remain honest, than it is to rise again after his fall. It is in vain that society pardons him; his conscience does not. Whatever may be his efforts, he never will regain that delicacy of honour, which alone supports a spotless life. Even when he resolves to live honestly, he cannot forget that he *has been* a criminal; and this remembrance, which deprives him of self-esteem, deprives also his virtue of its reward and its guaranty.‡

* See Report of Mr. Niles, December 22, 1829. We must say, that at Sing-Sing the school, though held with care, appeared to us to be restrained to too small a number. The number of convicts admitted to the Sunday school varies from 60 to 80, a small proportion to 1000 convicts. (See Report of 1832 on Sing-Sing.) The direction of this establishment, seems to be too little of a mental character; a circumstance caused undoubtedly by the fact that the superintendent and his inferior officers are solely occupied with maintaining the external order, which is constantly in danger. We were witnesses of a fact which proves how great the effect of the school at Sing-Sing might be, if more attention were paid to it. A poor negro, who had learned to read in prison, recited by heart to us, two pages of the Bible, which he had studied during the leisure hours in the week, and committed not the least mistake in the recitation.

† "Sabbath after Sabbath, without any considerable variation from cold, rain, or heat, twenty-five, thirty, and forty gentlemen, and this alternately, so as to make the whole number probably not less than five hundred, are found regularly at their posts at half past ten o'clock, on Sabbath morning, in the state prison Sabbath school, (in Charlestown, near Boston)." See Seventeenth Report of the Boston Prison Discip. Soc. page 12.—In New Jersey a prison instruction Society has been formed, and has published its First Annual Report, in January 1833. The second article of the constitution of this society shows its object.

Art. 2. The chief object of this society shall be, to extend to the convicts in the prisons of this state, the benefits of the Sabbath school system of instruction, and also to furnish them with preaching.—Trans.

‡ There are many criminals, indeed, who themselves must see as well as others, that a concurrence of fatal circumstances led them to crime, which, after they have really reformed, will remain a cause of self-reproach, but we do not believe need always deprive them of self-esteem. But as a virtuous life depends in all

Yet if we consider all the means employed in the prisons of the United States, in order to obtain this complete regeneration of the wicked, it is difficult to believe that it should not be sometimes the reward of so many efforts. It may be the work of pious men who devote their time, their cares, and their whole life to this important object. If society be incapable of calming the conscience, religion has the power. If society pardon, it restores liberty to the prisoner's person—this is all. When God pardons, he pardons the soul. With this moral pardon, the criminal regains his self-esteem, without which honesty is impossible This is a result which society never can attain, because human institutions, however powerful over the actions and the will of men, have none over their consciences.

We have seen some persons in the United States, who have a strong belief in this reformation from the means used to effect it. Mr. Smith said to us at Auburn, that out of the six hundred and fifty prisoners in that prison, already fifty, at least, were radically reformed, and that he considered them *good Christians.* Mr. Barrett, at Wethersfield, thought that of the hundred and eighty prisoners in that penitentiary, already fifteen or twenty were in a state of complete regeneration. *

It would be useless to investigate here, whether Messrs Smith and Barrett deceived themselves in their estimate, it seems to us that we can admit with them the existence of radical reformation. But, we must be allowed to believe that the cases are still rarer than they themselves believe. This is at least the opinion of almost all enlightened men with whom we have come into contact in the United States. Mr Elam Lynds, who has great experience in prison matters, goes much further, and considers the thorough reformation of a criminal a chimera.† Perhaps he runs into the other extreme, and so discouraging an opinion as his, ought to be founded on incontrovertible truth, in order to be adopted. There exists no human means of proving this complete reformation ; how can we prove with ciphers the purity of the soul, the delicacy of sentiments, the innocency of intentions? Society, without power to effect this radical regeneration, is no more capable of proving it if it exist. In the one and the other case, it is an affair of the interior *forum;* in the first case God alone can act; in the second, God alone can judge. However, he who on earth is the minister of God, has sometimes the privilege of reading the consciences of others; and it is thus

daily and common occurrences much more upon moral delicacy, (which is but the result of moral education or long custom) than upon reflection renewed every moment, it is perfectly true that it is a difficult task indeed, for a convict to rise again to virtue, particularly if his education has been abandoned —Trans
    * See Letter of Mr. Barrett, No. 14
    † See Conversation with Mr. Elam Lynds, No. 11

that the two ministers whom we have mentioned, affect to know the moral state of the prisoners, and what goes on in the depth of their souls. Undoubtedly they are more favourably placed than any body else, to gain the confidence of these unhappy beings, and we are persuaded that they often receive disinterested avowals, and the expressions of sincere repentance But how much risk do they run of being deceived by hypocritical protestations ! The convict, whatever may be his crime, always looks for pardon. His hope exists, particularly in the prisons of the United States, where, during a long time, the custom of pardoning has been much abused * The criminal, therefore, has an interest in showing to the chaplain, with whom alone he has moral communications, profound repentance for his crime, and a lively desire to return to virtue. If these sentiments are not sincere, he nevertheless will profess them. On the other hand, the man who sacrifices his whole existence to the pursuit of an honourable end, is himself under the influence of an ardent desire which must sometimes lead to errors. As he desires with ardour the reformation of the criminals, he easily gives credence to it. Shall we find fault with his credulity? No, because success, in which he is confident, encourages him to renewed efforts, illusions of this nature only become fatal, if on the belief of similar regenerations pardons should be multiplied, as this would encourage hypocrisy, and we should soon see the prisoners reform themselves by calculation.† We must say, that in general, this danger seems to be felt very much, and that pardons become rarer and rarer, if the wish of public opinion should be completely satisfied, the governors would make use of their privilege of pardon only in favour of convicts whose guilt has become doubtful, in consequence of circumstances having appeared after their judgment. However, we must also add, that the inconvenience of too great a number of pardons is not yet entirely avoided; at Auburn, one-third of the whole number of pardons is granted on the presumption of reformation.‡

---

* See Statistical Notes, No. 16 We shall there explain the various causes which have produced so great an abuse of the privilege of pardoning in the United States

† Mr. Smith himself said to us, that he was very cautious as to external signs of repentance in the convicts, he added, that in his eyes the best proof of the sincerity of a convict was his not desiring to leave the prison

‡ We have reason to believe that the present governor of the State of New York, follows those rules in making use of his pardoning power, which alone are conducive to the benefit both of society and the convicts, and we are glad that he will leave a sound precedent The general rule ought always to be ; make your laws as mild as you possibly can, and let them strike, if made, with their whole severity , or, in other words, " use mercy in making laws, but none in applying them." This is indeed the only merciful course, and nothing can be more cruel to the convicts themselves, than to be lax in punishing crime. We always ought to consider criminals as redeemable beings, having, in spite of

To resume, we would say positively, if the penitentiary system cannot propose to itself an end other than the radical reformation of which we have just spoken, the legislature perhaps should abandon this system; not because the aim is not an admirable one, but because it is too rarely obtained. The moral reformation of an individual, which is an important affair for a religious man, is little for a politician; or to express it better, an institution is only political if it be founded on the interest of the mass; it loses its character if it only profit a small number.

But if it be true that the radical reformation of a depraved person is only an accidental instead of being a natural consequence of the penitentiary system, it is nevertheless true that there is another kind of reformation, less thorough than the former, but yet useful for society, and which the system we treat of seems to produce in a natural way.

We have no doubt, but that the habits of order to which the prisoner is subjected for several years, influence very considerably his moral conduct after his return to society.

The necessity of labour which overcomes his disposition to idleness; the obligation of silence which makes him reflect; the isolation which places him alone in presence of his crime and his suffering; the religious instruction which enlightens and comforts him; the obedience of every moment to inflexible rules; the regularity of a uniform life; in a word, all the circumstances belonging to this severe system, are calculated to produce a deep impression upon his mind.

Perhaps, leaving the prison he is not an honest man; but he has contracted honest habits He was an idler, now he knows how to work His ignorance prevented him from pursuing a useful occupation; now he knows how to read and to write; and the trade which he has learnt in the prison, furnishes him the means of existence which formerly he had not Without loving virtue, he may detest the crime of which he has suffered the cruel consequences; and if he is not more virtuous he has become at least more judicious; his morality is not honour, but interest. His religious faith is perhaps neither lively nor deep; but even supposing that religion has not touched his heart, his mind has contracted habits of order, and he possesses rules for his conduct in life; without having a powerful religious conviction, he has acquired a taste for moral principles which religion affords; finally, if he has not become in truth better, he is at

all their vices, much in common with ourselves, but they never are redeemed by laxity, on the contrary, they are hardened by it Few, very few cases indeed, ought to be excepted, viz. those in which neither jury nor judge could help condemning according to the positive law, but in which, nevertheless, a number of circumstances render the law for this individual instance unjust, cases which no human wisdom can entirely prevent.—Trans.

least more obedient to the laws, and that is all which society has the right to demand

If we consider the reformation of convicts under this point of view, it seems to us to be obtained, in many cases, through the system which we are considering; and those Americans who have the least confidence in the radical regeneration of criminals, believe, nevertheless, in the existence of a reformation reduced to these more simple terms.

We must remark here, that the zeal of religious instructers, which is often insufficient to effect a radical reform, has yet a great influence on that of the second grade, which we have just described. It is because their aim is great, that they pursue it with ardour, and the nobleness of their undertaking elevates at once their office, and the functions of those who, in concert with them, work for the reformation of the criminals; it gives altogether to the penitentiary establishment a greater interest, and a much higher morality. Thus, though the preacher does not often arrive at his proposed end, it is yet important that he should pursue it without interruption; and, perhaps, that point which we have indicated, is obtained only because the aim is taken much higher.

The advantages of the penitentiary system of the United States may then be classed in the following manner.

First, Impossibility of the mutual corruption of the prisoners.

Secondly, Great probability of their contracting habits of obedience and industry, which render them useful citizens.

Thirdly, Possibility of a radical reformation.

Though each of the establishments which we have examined aims at these three results, there are nevertheless, in this respect, some shades of difference, which distinguish the Auburn system from that of Philadelphia

Philadelphia has, as we have already observed, the advantage over Auburn in respect to the first point Indeed, the prisoners, separated by thick walls, can communicate with each other still less than those who are separated by silence only The Auburn discipline guaranties the certainty that silence shall not be violated, but it is a mere moral certainty, subject to contradiction, whilst at Philadelphia, communications among the convicts is physically impossible.

The Philadelphia system being also that which produces the deepest impressions on the soul of the convict, must effect more reformation than that of Auburn. The latter, however, is perhaps more conformable to the habits of men in society, and on this account effects a greater number of reformations, which might be called "legal," inasmuch as they produce the external fulfilment of social obligations.

If it be so, the Philadelphia system produces more honest men, and that of New York more obedient citizens.*

SECTION II.

AFTER having shown the consequences of the penitentiary system, such as we understand them, shall we find in ciphers the proof of those facts, which we believe we can attribute to it?

It is customary, in order to know what influence the penitentiary system has upon society, to meet the question thus:

Has the number of crimes augmented or diminished since the penitentiary system has been established? (*bb*)

The solution of all questions of this kind in the United States, is extremely difficult, because it, requires statistical documents, which it is almost impossible to procure. There is neither in the Union nor in the different states, any central authority which possesses them. With difficulty the statistics of a town or county can be obtained; but never those of a whole state.†

Pennsylvania is the only state in which we have been able to learn the total number of crimes. During the year 1830, there were two thousand and eighty-four individuals condemned in this state to imprisonment; which, if compared to a population of 1,347,672 inhabitants, gives one conviction for 653 inhabitants.‡

---

* To judge from recommittals, we are authorized in saying, that as far as experience goes, the Philadelphia system produces a greater effect on convicts, whether by reformation, or by the severity of solitude, which impresses the mind of the convict with a fear of suffering it a second time, or by a combination of both.—TRANS.

† We have met, however, with extreme kindness, in the various authorities, and an extraordinary readiness to afford us all the information we wished for. Mr. Flagg, secretary of state at Albany, Mr. Riker, recorder at New York, Messrs. M'Ilvaine and Roberts Vaux in Philadelphia, Mr Gray in Boston, and all the inspectors of the new prisons, have furnished it, with a great mass of valuable documents.

Mr. Riker has procured for us the general statement of crimes committed in the whole state of New York during the year 1830. This is a very interesting document ; but we have returns for one year only.

‡ See Statistical Notes, No. 16.

In other states we have obtained very exact materials respecting the number of certain crimes, but never the totality of offences   Thus we know merely the number of burglaries committed in the states of New York, Massachusetts, Connecticut, and Maryland, which caused the criminals to be sent to the state prison.*

If we take these special convictions for the basis of our observations, we shall see that in the states of New York, Massachusetts, and Maryland, the number of criminals, compared to the population, decreases , that in the state of Connecticut it increases ; whilst it is stationary in Pennsylvania.†

Shall we conclude from this statement that the prison of Connecticut is very bad; that those of New York, Massachusetts, and Maryland, are the only good penitentiaries, and that those of Pennsylvania are better than the first, but worse than the others?

This conclusion would be strange, because it is an incontestable fact, that the penitentiary of Connecticut is better than the prisons of Maryland and Pennsylvania.‡

If we examine with attention the situation of these different states, and the political circumstances which surround them, we shall see that the number, more or less considerable, of crimes, and even their decrease or increase, may be owing to causes entirely foreign to the penitentiary system.

First, a difference must be made between the number of crimes and their increase : in the state of New York there are more crimes committed than in Pennsylvania ; yet the number of crimes is stationary in the latter state, whilst it diminishes in the former.   In Connecticut, where crimes increase, there are, in the whole, but half the crimes committed, in proportion, to those in all other states.§

We would add, that, in order to establish well founded points of comparison between the various states, it would be necessary to deduct from the population of each the foreigners, and to compare only the crimes committed by the settled population ; proceeding thus, it would be found that Maryland is that state the settled population of which commits most crimes. This fact is explained by a cause peculiar to the southern states—the coloured race. In general, it has been observed, that in those states in which there exists one negro to thirty whites, the prisons contain one negro to four white persons.‖

* See Statistical and Comparative Observations, No. 17.
† Ibid.
‡ We speak here of the old prisons of Pennsylvania and Maryland The new penitentiaries of these states are yet too recently established to occupy us here with their effects.
§ See Statistical and Comparative Observations, No. 17.
‖ Ibid.

The states which have many negroes must therefore produce more crimes. This reason alone would be sufficient to explain the large number of crimes in Maryland: it is, however, not applicable to all the states of the south; but only to those in which manumission is permitted: because we should deceive ourselves greatly were we to believe that the crimes of the negroes are avoided by giving them liberty; experience proves, on the contrary, that in the south the number of criminals increases with that of manumitted persons; thus, for the very reason that slavery seems to draw nearer to its ruin, the number of freed persons will increase for a long time in the south, and with it the number of criminals. (cc)

Whilst the southern part of the United States contains in its bosom this fertile cause of crimes, there are in the states of the North, on the other hand, such as New York and Massachusetts, several political causes which tend to diminish the number of crimes.

The coloured population decreases here every day, compared to the white population which goes on continually increasing.

Moreover, the foreigners who arrive every year from Europe without means of existence, in these states are a cause of crime which is continually becoming less

In the same measure as the population increases, the number of emigrants, though not decreasing in itself, becomes less in relation to the sum total of the inhabitants.

The population doubles in thirty years; whilst the number of emigrants remains about the same.* So that this cause of increase of crime in the North, though apparently stationary, loses every year its force in a statistical point of view; the cipher which represents it remains always the same considered by itself; but it becomes less compared with another cipher which daily increases.

Some Americans† believe also that knowledge and education, so much diffused in the states of the North, have a tendency to diminish the number of crimes.

There are in the state of New York, with a population of two millions of inhabitants, five hundred and fifty thousand children instructed in the schools, and the state alone spends for this ob-

---

* We believe that the number of emigrants has increased of late very much, but the argument of the authors remains nevertheless true in the whole. Population increases faster than the influx of emigrants.—Trans.

† Among others, Mr Edward Livingston. See his writings, especially his letter to Roberts Vaux, 1828, pp. 14, 15 Judge Powers considers ignorance and intemperance as the two principal sources of crime. (See Gershom Powers' Report of 1828, page 50.) (So far the authors) This "some Americans" is an unfortunate expression indeed, because it ought to have been " all Americans" with the exception of a few, of whom we, however, hardly know a single one. We shall say a few more words on this subject.—Trans.

ject nearly six millions of francs every year * It seems that an enlightened population, to whom no opportunity is wanting which agriculture, commerce, and manufactural industry can offer, should commit less crimes than that which possesses these latter advantages without having the same intellectual means to make use of them; nevertheless, we do not believe that to the diffusion of knowledge this decrease of crimes in the North is to be attributed, because in Connecticut, where knowledge is still more diffused than in the state of New York, crimes increase with extreme rapidity; and if we cannot reproach knowledge with this prodigious increase, we are at least constrained to acknowledge that it has not the power of preventing it,† for the

---

* This expression is not quite accurate. Society, either through government or the various communities, pays not so much According to the Annual Report of the Superintendent of Common Schools of the State of New York, January 7, 1833, the school funds paid to the trustees of the several school districts in April 1832, amounted to $805,582 78 cents. Of this sum, $100,000 were paid from the state treasury, $188,384 53 cents were raised by a tax upon the property of the inhabitants of the several towns and cities in the state, and $17,198 25 cents derived from local funds possessed by some of the towns The amount paid for teachers' wages in the several districts of the state, over and above the public money apportioned by the commissioners, is $358,320 17 cents. This sum, added to the public money, gives a total of $663,902 95 cents paid for teachers' salaries ; except about $60,000 in the City of New York, which is raised by a special tax, and applied to the erection of the school houses This whole sum then would make from three to four millions of francs But to this is yet to be added what is individually paid by the parents of children , and the whole sum amounts to what the authors state The reader, in order to have an accurate view and statement of the whole, is referred to the extracts we have given of the report above quoted, appended by us to the remarks of the authors given under the head *Statistical Details respecting the New York School System* in No 5, ON PUBLIC INSTRUCTION —Trans

† Knowledge, even if not separated from religious instruction, creates a number of new wants, which, if they are not satisfied, impel to crime It multiplies the social relations, it is the soul of commerce and industry, it thus creates a thousand opportunities for fraud and bad faith, which do not exist in the bosom of an ignorant and rude population It tends, therefore, in its nature, rather to multiply than to diminish the number of crimes This point seems, at present, pretty generally acknowledged because in Europe it has been observed that crimes progress in most countries where knowledge is most diffused. As we are on the subject, we will give our opinion on the influence of knowledge. Its advantages seem to us infinitely superior to its disadvantages. It develops the mind and supports all branches of industry It thus promotes the moral strength and the material well being of nations The passions which it excites, though fatal to society, if they are not satisfied, produce many advantages, if they obtain what they seek. Knowledge, indeed, disperses among men the seeds of corruption , but it is knowledge also which makes people richer and stronger Knowledge is, with a nation surrounded by enlightened neighbours, not only a benefit, but even a political necessity —See note on public instruction in the United States, No 5 —So far the authors [Whenever a subject begins to attract attention, and to be inquired into, it is a long time before people properly understand what others mean by certain expressions , and before they know themselves the precise meaning of their own words This is true in the whole intercourse of men, from a common conversation to national debates, religious controversies and scientific investigations , and the present inquiry, whether diffusion of knowledge increases or decreases the number of crimes.

rest, we do not pretend to explain these strange anomalies exhibited by states whose political institutions are almost the same, and in which, nevertheless, the proportion of crimes to the population is so different; these difficulties belong to that class

by no means makes an exception to the remark. It has been often asserted, in modern times, that deficiency of knowledge is the chief cause of crime, and again, in quite recent times, in equally general terms, that neither poverty nor ignorance are its most active agents, to prove which, statistical tables have been produced. (See, for instance, A Queteset's interesting Observations on the Disposition to commit Crimes in the different Ages of Human Life, reprinted, among others, in the *Courier des Etats Unis,* April 25th, 1832) But has it been settled what is meant by *knowledge,* or by *being enlightened?* are people agreed upon what they mean by increase of crime, or upon the conclusions they draw from it ? Do they mean that the criminal disposition of society has increased ? Often, the increase of crime, as derived from official statements concerning it, which are our only guide, shows a higher state of civilization, which offers of itself more chances for crime , for instance, house-breaking can only occur frequently where people in general feel secure; in the middle ages, when every dwelling of a wealthy family was a castle, no house-breaking could be committed. (See e. g. *Encyclop Americana,* vol iv , page 29, and seq) Differences also arise from a more watchful police, or a more correct record of crimes, &c , &c ; so that, in fact, it is useless to compare, in order to settle this great question, two nations, the one enlightened, the other less so or not at all , because we must take all the attending circumstances into account One means, of great assistance in settling this question, though we allow it is not the only means, is to inquire how many of all criminals in a nation have enjoyed the advantage of knowledge, and in what degree ? As to the word knowledge, and instruction, what is meant by it ? Shall it express merely that information which exercises and enriches the understanding alone, a meaning which in France it has received of late, and in her schools has been acted upon but too often? In this sense, knowledge is, in itself, in most cases, neither good nor bad , arithmetic will assist a defaulter, as much as an industrious man who works for his family, as a knife may serve the murderer as well as him who cuts a piece of bread with it for a crippled beggar , just as the sun lends his light to crime as to virtue Or have we to understand by knowledge, that light which is cast on the whole human soul , which reaches the heart as well as the head ? We allow that some nations have, since the middle of the last century, pursued their merely physical well-being with short sighted eagerness, have made, at times, productive industry almost the sole national object, and thus favoured a kind of egotism which leads to many crimes, if assisted by the *skill* (not the *light*) of knowledge. But the greatest mistake upon this point, one which is very common, and against which our authors have, in our opinion, not guarded themselves, is the confounding of knowledge with civilization in general, of which the former undoubtedly is a part, but a part only What the authors have said at the beginning of this note, on knowledge, (*instruction* is their word,) ought to have been said in relation to civilization We cannot here enter into the inquiry, often made, does man become better and happier by civilization ? Whatever may be the answer, the only alternative is between ignorant innocence, (or rather absence of crime,) and civilization, with all its opportunities for crime, in the same way as man has the alternative of ignorance or science, with all the chances of error, misconception, and mistakes , or of political stupor, or liberty, with all the chances of its abuse. The absence of crime is not what is unconditionally desirable. An American Indian can commit but few crimes—murder, treason, and perhaps some others Private property exists not with him, therefore he cannot commit crimes against it. He may repudiate his wife, that is no crime , he may steal from other tribes, that is no crime. But civilization, for which man is destined, and which is truly his " natural state," whether it make him happier or not, begins with private property ; as soon as this is established, a whole class of crimes—the most nu-

which never fails to lead to every kind of statistical labours.* But the considerations which we have just offered, serve at least to prove how many important causes, unconnected with the penitentiary system, influence the increase or decrease of crime.

Sometimes a crisis in the industry of a country, the disbanding of an army, &c , &c , &c., are sufficient to increase the number of offences during a year

Thus in the year 1816, the number of criminals increased in an extraordinary degree in all American prisons. Had the penitentiary system any thing to do with it? No, it was simply in consequence of the war between America and England, peace having been concluded, a number of regiments were disbanded, and the soldiers thus deprived for the moment of employment.

There is another difficulty; even if we agree respecting the cause of crimes, we do not know exactly that of their increase.

How shall the number of crimes be proved? By that of the convictions? Several causes, however, may produce more fre-

merous with all civilized nations—springs into existence. Civilization creates wants, as it is developed by them , all trades, all national intercourse, are founded on wants , the good strive to satisfy their desires by honest means, the bad by any means in their power   A shepherd, clothed in skin, and satisfied with his simple meal, has few wants, and few temptations   But the human mind was destined by its creator to expand, morally and intellectually, not for stagnation, but for Life , civilization is the true element of mankind, and civilization offers necessarily opportunities for crime   Without the art of writing, forgery could not exist, without the art of writing, each tribe, each generation, would be isolated , and morals would be but little developed.   Look at history   But the question now arises, what is civilization without knowledge, as we find in each civilized nation a large portion influenced by it, and yet left in ignorance, or as we find ignorant nations bordering upon civilized ones, and partially influenced by the latter?   This is in our opinion the true point to which the question must be reduced , and which not only answers the question, whether ignorance is a source of crime, but also whether poverty be such   Poverty without civilization is not any more a peculiar source of crime than ignorance, because it feels no wants , but poverty with civilization is an abounding source of crime   Whatever some writers of the European continent may maintain respecting the beneficial or injurious influence of the diffusion of knowledge, Americans and English, who know more of the practical art of government than any other nation, are agreed upon its necessity for the well being of society, and the prevention of crime among civilized nations, who, in order to avoid the dangers of imperfect knowledge, have but one resource, that of diffusing knowledge, intellectual, moral, and religious, as far and wide, and in as high a degree as possible.   We are sorry not to be able to enter fully into this subject, but we have already exceeded the limits of a note. Why crimes are committed in so disproportionate a number in New York and Connecticut, we cannot develop here, nor are we probably acquainted with all the reasons , but there is little doubt that without schools many more crimes would be committed   See, for more remarks on this subject, the note which we have added to No 17, parag. I, showing the convicts of Pennsylvania, Connecticut, New York, &c , classed according to the nature of their crimes —Trans]

* In order to know all the advantages afforded by statistics and to the art of making use of them, it is necessary to read the excellent work which Mr. Guerry has just published under the title of *Statistique Morale de la France.*—Paris, 1832.

quent convictions, though the number of crimes be the same.
(*dd*)

This may happen, if the police pursue crimes with more activity—a circumstance which generally occurs, if public attention
is more actively directed to the subject   In such case the number of crimes is not increased, but more crimes are proved. The
same is the case when courts of justice are more exact; which
happens always when the penal law is mitigated   Then the number of acquittals diminishes *   There are more convictions, though
the number of crimes has not varied.   The penitentiary system
itself, which is intended to diminish the number of crimes, has
for its first result, the increase of convictions.   In the same
degree as magistrates feel repugnant to condemn the guilty,
since they know the corrupting influence of the prison which
receives them; in the same degree, they show themselves more
ready to pronounce a condemnation as soon as they know that
the prison, far from being a school of crime, is a place of repentance and reformation. (*ee*)

However this may be, it is clear from the above, that the increase of crimes or their decrease, is produced sometimes by
general causes, and sometimes by accidental ones, which have
no direct connexion with the penitentiary system.

If we consider the object of the penitentiary system and its
natural extent, we shall see that it cannot have that general influence which is often attributed to it; and that the question is
not put as it ought to be, if we intend to judge of it by the absolute number of crimes ; a prison discipline, good or bad, cannot have any influence except on those who have been imprisoned.   Prisons may be very good in a country where there are
many crimes, and very bad in another in which few are committed.   Thus in Massachusetts, where there are less convicts,
the prisons are bad, whilst they are good in the State of New
York in which crimes are much more numerous.†   A bad prison
cannot corrupt those who have not been exposed to its influence,
any more than a good penitentiary can correct those who have
remained out of the reach of its beneficial discipline.

The institutions, the habits,‡ and political circumstances—

---

* The reader remembers a very peculiar case of this kind of very recent date.
The punishment for sheep stealing in England was, till the year 1832, death, and
numberless acquittals took place, though the crime was proved   Since, however,
the punishment has been changed into transportation for a long series of years,
no acquittals of this kind have occurred , so that actually, the milder law is
much more severe in its operation —Trans

† We say that in Massachusetts, where there are less convictions, the prisons
are bad . *they were bad,* and are not any longer so   we are obliged to speak of
the past, because the question here is to appreciate their effects.

‡ Great efforts are made in the United States to correct a vice, which is very
common—intemperance   See Note on Temperance Societies, No 9

these influence most the moral state of men in society, prisons act but on the morality of prisoners *

The penitentiary system then has not that extended circle of action which sometimes is attributed to it. If we reduce it as we ought to do, to the inmates of the prison, its influence is sufficiently important not to attribute to it another that is foreign to it; and, in fact, if this part of the social body on which the penitentiary system operates is but small, it is at all events the most diseased, and its disorder is both the most contagious and the most important to be remedied.

Hence, if we wish to appreciate the merit of a prison and the system which has been put in practice, we ought to observe not the morality of society in general, but only of those individuals who, having been imprisoned in such establishments, have returned to society; if they commit no new offence, we have a right to believe that the influence of the prison has been salutary; and if they relapse into new crimes, it is a proof that the prison has not made them better.

Whilst it is true that a large or small number of recommittals alone can prove the deficiency or excellence of a prison, we must add, that it is impossible to obtain, on this point, a perfectly exact statement.

On the one hand, it is difficult to obtain proof that liberated convicts have led an honest life; on the other, we have not always a knowledge of the new crimes which they commit

To these considerations, which appear to us necessary to reduce the question to its true limits, we shall add another, which seems to us equally important, that is, in order to appreciate the effects of the penitentiary system, we ought not to consider the epoch of its creation, but the period which follows it. This truth, which it seems idle to mention, has nevertheless been forgotten by writers of great merit, we will quote an example.

We have said already that in the year 1790, a new system of imprisonment was established in Philadelphia, and the Walnut street prison organized on a plan which we have pointed out as entirely deficient; yet by some accidental circumstance, or from some unknown reason, the number of crimes in Pennsylvania during the years 1790, 1791, 1792, and 1793, was considerably less than during the preceding years Mr Livingston and Mr. Roberts Vaux, in the United States, and in France, the Duke de Larochefoucauld-Liancourt and Mr. Charles Lucas, have drawn from this decrease of crimes, the proof of the efficiency

---

* Mr. Livingston has expressed this truth more than once, and with particular energy in his letter to Roberts Vaux, pp. 14, 15, 1828. See the Note *ff* in the Appendix.

of the system ;* but their arguments seem to be founded on a fact erroneously appreciated. To ascribe this result to the new system, it would have been necessary to prove that the individuals, once imprisoned in Walnut street, had not committed new crimes. This proof could not be made. In fact, the system commences in 1790 ; and already in the years 1791, 1792, and 1793, the effects are sought for, i. e. before most of the prisoners, on whom the new system could have any effect, were released. (*gg*)

It is easy to conceive that the effect of the penitentiary system cannot be appreciated except after a certain series of years, and only after the convicts, whose terms have expired, have had time to commit new crimes, or to give assurance of an honest life.†

On this account we shall pass over the results obtained in the new penitentiaries of Philadelphia, Sing-Sing, Boston, and Baltimore ; by giving up the arguments which we might draw from these different prisons, we shall very much narrow the circle of disagreement ; but we shall have at least the advantage of giving to our arguments none but solid foundations.

Let us then compare the effects produced by the ancient prisons of the United States, with those resulting from the new system practised in the penitentiaries of Auburn and Wethersfield, the only ones which have been established for a time sufficient to draw just conclusions as to their influence.

In the ancient prison of New York, (Newgate) recommittals took place (in proportion to the whole number of convictions) as one to nine ; in the prison of Maryland as one to seven ; in that of Walnut street as one to six ; in the ancient Connecticut prison as one to four ;‡ and in the Boston jail also, as one to six.§

The number of recommittals is considerably less in the new

* See Edward Livingston's Introductory Report to the Code of Prison Discipline, page 7   See also, Notices of the original and successive efforts to improve the discipline of the prison at Philadelphia, and to reform the criminal code of Pennsylvania, by Roberts Vaux, pp 53, 54   See *Du Systéme Pénitentiaire en Europe et aux États-Unis*   By Mr. Charles Lucas

† The authors seem to overlook one circumstance, i e that a system of imprisonment may prevent crime, and therefore have also some effect upon others than actual prisoners   And we must mention here, what, though it may sound strange, seems to us nevertheless to be a fact, from various inquiries which we have made, viz that criminals are little daunted by the prospect of hardships or cruelties awaiting them in prison, provided they are sure of finding there their old associates, but they dread a penitentiary system, in the same degree, as it offers more or less opportunity for converse with their fellow convicts, so that we hold ourselves convinced that criminals in the United States shun much more the Pennsylvania system, than the Auburn penitentiary, in spite of the whip of the latter. The reason is clear. We acknowledge that this dread may, with those who have never been imprisoned, cause as often the more cautious pursuit of crime, as a total abstinence from it —TRANS.

‡ See Statistical and Comparative Observations, No. 17.

§ See Statistical Notes, No. 16.

prisons at Auburn and Wethersfield. In the former, recommittals form the nineteenth part of the whole number; and of one hundred individuals released from the latter, since its creation, five only have been recommitted for new offences; which gives the proportion of one to twenty.*

At Auburn not only those criminals are noted down who are recommitted, but an attempt has also been made to watch the conduct of delivered prisoners who have remained in society. Of one hundred and sixty individuals, in respect to whom it was possible to obtain information, one hundred and twelve have conducted themselves well; the others have returned to bad or at least doubtful habits. (*hh*)

These ciphers, however conclusive they may appear, are the result of too short a period to justify an invincible proof of the efficiency of the system to be deduced from them; but we must nevertheless acknowledge, that they are extremely favourable to the new penitentiaries, and the presumption in their favour, caused by this result, is so much the stronger as the effect obtained perfectly accords with that promised by the theory; it must be added, that in spite of the impossibility of drawing any conclusive argument from the penitentiaries of Sing-Sing, Boston, and others of the same kind, on account of their having been so recently established, it cannot be doubted, that the success of Auburn and Wethersfield, renders that of establishments on the same model, extremely probable.

In offering these statistical documents, we have not compared the number of crimes and recommittals in the United States and in France, persuaded as we are, that the foundation for such a comparison would be imperfect.

The modes of existence in the two countries do not resemble each other, and the elements composing them are essentially different.

A young society, exempt from political embarrassments, rich both by its soil and its industry, should be supposed to furnish less criminals than a country where the ground is disputed foot by foot, and where the crises produced by political divisions tend to increase the number of offences, because they increase misery by disturbing industry.

Yet if the statistical documents which we possess of Pennsylvania, should be applied to the rest of the Union, there are in this country more crimes committed than in France, in proportion to the population.† Various causes of another nature explain

* See Statistical and Comparative Observations, No. 17.

† There are more crimes of a grave nature committed in France, but the whole number of crimes is less than in America. See Statistical and Comparative Observations, No. 17.

this result: on the one hand, the coloured population, which forms the sixth part of the inhabitants of the United States, and which composes half of the inmates of the prisons ; and on the other hand, the foreigners pouring in every year from Europe, and who form the fifth and sometimes even the fourth part of the number of convicts.

These two facts, explaining the great number of crimes in the United States, make it not a subject of comparison with the number of offences in a country where we are met with no similar facts

If we should deduct from the total number of crimes, those committed by negroes and foreigners, we should undoubtedly find that the white American population commits less crimes than ours ; but proceeding thus, we should fall into another error ; in fact, to separate the negroes from the whole population of the United States, would be equal to deducting the poorer classes of the community with us ; that is to say, those who commit the crimes. One obstacle is here avoided only to meet with another, in this respect, the only certain, incontestable fact, which we have remarked in the United States, and which may offer an opportunity for comparison, is the peculiar and extraordinary morality of the women belonging to the white race. Out of one hundred prisoners in the United States, we find but four women ; whilst with us there are twenty in a hundred.* Now this morality of the female sex must influence the whole society; because it is upon them that the morality of a family chiefly depends.

At all events, as the elements of comparison are otherwise different, we can on the whole but hazard probabilities.

Difficulties abound if we wish to make approximations of this kind between the two nations. The difference which exists between the penal laws of the United States and ours, adds greatly to them.

In the United States, things are punished as crimes which with us are beyond the reach of the laws, and again, our code punishes offences which in the United States are not considered as such. Thus, many offences against religion and morals, such as blasphemy, incest, fornication, drunkenness, &c., &c.,† are in the United States repressed by severe punishments ; with us they are unpunished. Again, our code punishes bankruptcy, against which the laws of the United States have no provisions.‡

How then can we compare the number of crimes committed

---

* See, for some points of comparison between France and America, No. 18.
† Sodomy, having intercourse with a girl under a certain age, pedrasty, &c
‡ At least none against " careless bankruptcy "—Trans.

in countries the legislation of which is so different? And yet, we must add, that this comparison, were it made exactly, would hardly afford conclusive results: thus, it may well be said, in general, that the number, more or less considerable, of convictions in a country, proves its corruption or its morality. Yet there exist exceptions to this rule, which throw a great uncertainty upon these calculations: thus, in one of the most religious and most moral states of the Union, (Connecticut,) there are more convictions for offences against morals than in any other state.* To understand this result, it is necessary to remember that crimes of this nature are punished only where they are rare: in societies in which adultery is frequent, it is not punished. No bankrupts are found in the prisons of the United States ; shall we conclude from this that the crime of bankruptcy is never committed there? This would be a strange mistake, because in no country perhaps more bankruptcies take place than there : it is necessary, therefore, in order not to admire on this point the commercial morality of the United States, to know whether a matter is in question which the law regards as a crime. Again, if we know that there are in the United States ten criminals committed for forgery out of one hundred prisoners,† we are not authorized to take this as a proof of greater corruption in that country than in ours, in which those sentenced for forgery are but two out of the hundred ‡ In the United States the whole population is in some degree commercial, and in addition, there are three hundred and fifty banks, all emitting paper money ; the ingenuity of the forger therefore has in that country a much wider field, and much stronger temptation, which is not the case with us, where commerce is but the business of a single class, and where the number of banks is so small

There is again a difficulty in comparing the crimes committed in the two countries, it is, that in those cases even, in which the legislation of both punishes the same act, it inflicts different punishments ; but as the comparison of crimes is made by that of the punishments, it follows that two analogous results, obtained from different bases, are compared together ; which is a new source of mistake.

If it is difficult to compare, for any useful purpose, the number and nature of crimes committed in the United States and in France, it is perhaps still more so to compare the number of re-committals, and to arrive by this comparison at a conclusive result, in respect to the prisons of the two countries.

---

* See Statistical and Comparative Observations, No 17
† Ibid.
‡ See comparison between France and America, No. 18

In general, those recommittals only, which bring back the prisoner to the prison where he has been detained the first time, are calculated in the United States * His return to the same prison, is in fact the only means of proving his relapse In that country, where passports do not exist, nothing is easier than to change one's name; if therefore a delivered convict commits a new crime under a fictitious name, he can very easily conceal his relapse, if he is not brought back to the prison where he underwent his first punishment There are, besides, a thousand means of avoiding the chances of being recognised. Nothing is easier than to pass from one state to another, and it is the criminal's interest to do so, whether he intends to commit new crimes, or has resolved to lead an honest life. We find therefore among a hundred criminals convicted in one state, thirty, upon an average, who belong to some neighbouring state.† This emigration is sufficient to make the proof of recommittals impossible. The tie between the various states being strictly political, there is no central power to which the police officers might refer to obtain information respecting the previous life of an indicted person : so that the courts condemn, almost always, without knowing the true name of the criminal, and still less his previous life. It is clear, therefore, that in such a state of things the number of known recommittals is never that of all the existing ones. (*u*) The same is not the case with us. There are a thousand ways in France to prove the identity of the indicted and the convicted prisoner, by means of the mutual information which all the agents of the judicial police keep up among themselves; the convictions pronounced by a *cour royal* in the south are known by a court in the north; and the judiciary possesses on this point all the means of investigation which are wanting in the United States If, therefore, in France, no more recommittals should take place than in the United States, a greater number, nevertheless, would be publicly known, and as the means of proving them in the two countries are so different, it would be useless to compare the number.

All comparisons of this kind then, between America and Europe, lead to no satisfactory result. America can be compared only with herself; yet this comparison is sufficient to shed abundant light upon the question we are considering, and we acknowledged the superiority of the new penitentiary system over the old prisons, when we found that the number of recommittals in the ancient prisons, compared to all convictions, was in the pro-

* "In using the term *first conviction* above, we mean as it respects this prison only, there are nearly twenty who have been in other prisons " (See Report on Auburn Prison, January 1, 1824, page 127.)
† See Statistical and Comparative Observations, No. 17.

portion of one to six, and in the new penitentiaries in the proportion of only one to twenty.*

* If we find in some parts of this work difficulties enumerated, which some readers as well as ourselves, consider as having been rated, perhaps, too great by our authors, we cannot pass over this passage without expressing our gratification at their minute statement of all the difficulties to be encountered in comparing the two countries; because though some details which they have explained will be considered by a few as having been stated previously, yet so much abuse has been carried on of late with statistical statements, such rash and superficial conclusions have been drawn from numbers, apparently very conclusive, and such seeming accuracy has, in many cases, been stamped on most deceptive and untenable statements, that we feel rejoiced wherever we find an application of the true principles of reasoning to such statements. That this abuse has been so frequent is not surprising The science of statistics is of recent date, and has been misunderstood by many, as consisting merely of the art of collecting certain tables. It will, after having passed through its trials, as all new sciences do, be brought to its true limits and proper sphere, and one part of it will be cultivated, which as yet is but very partially developed—the art of reasoning upon facts afforded by statistical statements.—Trans.

CHAPTER IV.

Financial Department.

SECTION I.

Distinction between the Philadelphia and Auburn systems.—The first requires a much more expensive construction —The latter very favourable to economy. —Difficulties to be avoided —Plans.—Estimate by Judge Welles —Is it advisable to have prisons built by prisoners?

AT present, after having stated the principles and effects of the penitentiary system in the United States, with regard to the reformation of the prisoners, it only remains to treat of its result in a financial view.

The latter comprises the manner of constructing prisons, and the expenses of the support of the prisoners, compared to the produce of their labour.

Construction of the Prisons.

We must in this respect distinguish between the systems of Philadelphia and Auburn

The penitentiary of Philadelphia (Cherry Hill,) will, at the time of its completion, have cost 432,000 dollars; which makes the price of each cell 1624 dollars.*

It is true that enormous unnecessary expenses have been incurred in its construction. The greater part had no other object than the ornament of the edifice. Gigantic walls, gothic towers, a wide iron gate, give to this prison the appearance of a fortified castle of the middle ages, without affording any real advantage to the establishment.†

---

* The outer wall of the Philadelphia prison alone cost 200,000 dollars, yet it is of all prisons that which requires least a high enclosing wall, because each prisoner is isolated in his cell, which he never leaves. (See Report of the Boston Pris. Discipline Soc, and Judge Powers', 1828, page 86)

† In comparing the Philadelphia penitentiary to a castle of the middle ages, we but reproduce a comparison used by the Philadelphia Prison Society, which speaks with praise of this building in the following terms · "This penitentiary is the only edifice in this country, which is calculated to convey to our citizens the external appearance of those magnificent and picturesque castles of the middle ages, which contribute so eminently to embellish the scenery of Europe." (See Description of the Eastern Penitentiary.)

Yet even if these unnecessary expenses had been wisely avoided, there would yet remain a considerable amount inherent in the Philadelphia system, which it would have been impossible to avoid. The convict being condemned, according to this system, to constant confinement, his cell must necessarily be spacious and well ventilated, provided with all proper wants, and large enough to permit him to work without much constraint. It is besides necessary that a small yard should be joined to the cell, surrounded by walls, in which he may, each day, during the hours prescribed by the rules, breathe the fresh air. Now, whatever pains may be taken to construct this cell with its appendage in the most economical manner, it must necessarily be much dearer than one that is narrower, without a particular yard, and destined only to receive the convict during night.

The prisons, constructed on the Auburn plan, are infinitely cheaper. Yet there are very considerable differences in the respective costs of their construction.

This disparity seems at first difficult to be accounted for; but upon investigating the causes, we find, that the construction of new penitentiaries is either expensive or cheap, according to the means employed in erecting them.

The penitentiary at Washington, for the District of Columbia, will have cost, when finished, 180,000 dollars. It contains only one hundred and sixty cells, each of which, therefore, will cost 1125 dollars; whilst the penitentiary at Wethersfield, established on the same plan, has cost, for two hundred and thirty-two prisoners, 35,000 dollars: so that each cell costs but 150 dollars and 86 cents.*

As all public expenses are incurred with great economy in the small state of Connecticut, we might believe that the small expense of the building of the prison is the effect of extraordinary efforts, of which a larger society, occupied with other interests, would not be capable.

But the penitentiaries of Sing-Sing and Blackwell Island, (erected for the same price as that of Wethersfield) in the State of New York, the largest of all the members of the Union, prove that Connecticut has done nothing extraordinary; and the construction of the Baltimore penitentiary has caused no greater expense.

The care which some states take to avoid in this matter every kind of useless ornament, whilst others do not pay the same attention to economy, produces this difference in the expense of construction.

The Washington penitentiary has been built on a sumptuous plan, more fit for a palace than a prison.

* For the expenses incurred in the construction of other penitentiaries, see Financial Division, No. 19.

The greatest difficulty to be avoided in similar constructions, is the ambition of the architect, who will always strive to erect an edifice of great size, and will reluctantly submit to the adoption of a simple and strictly useful plan. Several states have triumphed over this difficulty, though at Philadelphia, Pittsburg, and Washington, it has not been avoided.

Of all the establishments founded on the Auburn plan, the construction of the Washington penitentiary has been the most expensive.

The reason of this circumstance perhaps is to be found, in the nature of the authority itself, which directed this building to be constructed.

Particular states of the Union adopt generally the simplest plans for their prisons: they superintend the execution, and aim at strict economy in the most minute details. On the contrary, the administration at Washington, more elevated in its views, admits more easily of great designs; and as it is absorbed by a number of general interests, it is obliged to leave every thing which belongs to the execution of the plan, to agents whom it has neither the time nor the power to superintend.*

All practical men in the Union, believe that the Auburn system satisfies all claims of economy as far as regards construction.

In those prisons in which the whole discipline consists in the strength of the walls and the solidity of bolts, heavy walls and strong locks are requisite to master the prisoners.

In the new penitentiaries, so much material strength is not necessary, because it is not the point against which the prisoners direct their continual efforts. The moral superintendence forms the chief object with which they have continually to struggle. Isolated by the cell or by silence, they are moreover reduced to their individual strength; to curb them, therefore, does not require so much material force as if they were able to unite their efforts.

The necessity of having a cell for each prisoner, multiplies indeed the walls, and requires a greater extent of building. But this increase is compensated by a circumstance favourable to economy.

As the prisoners have no communication whatever with each other, every classification becomes useless, and it is not any longer necessary to have a separate division for young convicts, another for criminals more advanced in age, and another for recommitted convicts, &c.; in short, the principles of the penitentiary system being directly opposed to every communication of the prisoners with each other, there is no yard for recreation required in the modern penitentiaries. Much, therefore, is saved

* Why not the power ?—TRANS.

in building and enclosing walls, which exist, or at least ought to exist, in the system of our prisons.

In short, it may be said, that the construction of a modern penitentiary may be effected at a cheap rate, if proper views of economy are adopted.

Mr. Welles, one of the inspectors of the Wethersfield prison, whose correct views and experience we have always appreciated, has told us repeatedly, that in this affair every thing depended upon economy in the most minute details. He thinks that a penitentiary of five hundred cells might be constructed for about 40,000 dollars; which would make eighty dollars for each cell.*

It would be impossible to estimate exactly the cost of a prison in France, by that of one in the United States.

However, we believe that this expense would be about the same in France as in America. Because if it is true that the raw materials are much dearer with us than in the United States, it is also incontestable, that wages for daily labour are much higher in America than in France †

We have seen that in the United States the prisoners are some-times employed to build the prisons. The penitentiaries of Sing-Sing, Blackwell Island, and Baltimore, have been thus erected: yet there are many persons in America, who believe that this is not the most economical way, and that it is more profitable to have them built by free labourers. This opinion seems at first glance to be opposed to the nature of things, particularly in a country where labour is so dear as in the United States. But it is answered, that for this very reason, viz. the high price of labour, manufactured articles are sold at a high price. Thus the labour of the prisoners applied to productive industry, yields more for the state than it has to spend for the work of free la-bourers.

This question, therefore, must be decided according to place and circumstances. Its solution, says Judge Welles of Wethers-field, depends likewise upon the situation of the prisoners: it is better to leave those in their workshops whose labour is applied to branches which are very productive; but such as are not par-ticularly skilful may be used for the rougher kind of labour in the construction of a penitentiary. ‡

In France, the construction of prisons by the prisoners, might be still more advantageous than in America, if we look at the

* See Letter of Judge Welles of Wethersfield (in the Appendix,) in which the estimate of a prison for five hundred prisoners is to be found This estimate is probably incomplete ; because even the most experienced architects always omit some items. But even if his estimate were doubled, the construction of the pe-nitentiary would still be half as expensive only as our prisons. See No. 12.

† See Note *oo,* end of the Vol

‡ Letter of Judge Welles, No. 12.

question simply on account of its economy, and disregard the difficulties which, with us, the superintendence of prisoners occupied in building their own prison, would present.

The rate of manufactured articles does not present in France the same chances of profit as in the United States, and the prisoners, therefore, may be employed in the construction of the prison, without risk of loss in the productiveness of their labour.

We are sure that the walls to be erected would be profitable, since they have their destination fixed before being built: whilst nothing is more accidental and uncertain than the future profit yielded by the sale of merchandise.

If we employ free workmen, we pay their wages without diminution; whilst prisoners, occupied with any branch of industry, work with all the chances of loss and depreciation, incident to manufactured articles If, on the contrary, the prison is built by the prisoners themselves, the fruit of their labour is immediately collected; this labour does not produce a gain, properly so called; but it dispenses with an unavoidable charge.

We are well aware that in America the case is not the same; there, manufactures stand a favourable chance on account of the various fields opened to industry: the object there is to gain, whilst we only aim at avoiding losses. Finally, it is a great advantage in France to be able to employ the prisoners in a labour useful, and sometimes necessary, without injuring by way of competition the manufactories of free labour.*

SECTION II.

Expensive support of the ancient prisons —The new penitentiaries yield a revenue to the state.—Daily expense of the new prisons —Expense of food only. —Cost of *surveillance.*—Contract and *régie* —Combination of these two systems of administration.

Annual Expense of the Prisons.†

THE new system in practice in the United States, promises also great advantages on the score of *annual* expense; its effects have already, in this respect, surpassed the expectations of its promoters.

As long as the ancient prison discipline was in practice, the support of the prisoners was in all the states a source of considerable expense. We will cite but two instances: From the year 1790 to 1826, the state of Connecticut has expended for its prison, (Newgate) 204,711 dollars (see Statistical Tables, Financial

* See Note *s*, at the end of the Vol.
† See Statistics, Financial Division, Section II., No. 19, end of the Vol.

Division), and the state of New York has paid for the support of the ancient prison of Newgate, during twenty three years, (from the year 1797 to 1819,) 646,912 dollars The new system was established in 1819 in the state of New York, and in 1827 in Connecticut; in the former, the expenses immediately diminished, in the latter they changed directly into an annual revenue. (See Statistical Tables, Financial Division, No. 19.)

At Auburn, the income resulting from the labour of the prisoners, has, during the last two years, exceeded the expenses of support; and the period is already foreseen, when, after the construction of Sing-Sing shall be finished, the labour of its prisoners, applied solely to productive industry, will cover the expenses of the prison.

From the first year of its institution, the new Connecticut prison (Wethersfield,) has produced 1,017 dollars 16 cents, expenses deducted ; every year the revenue has increased ; and the gain of the year 1831, was 7,824 dollars 2 cents.

In short, the new penitentiary, which cost so much, produced during three years and a half, expenses of all kinds deducted, a net income of 17,139 dollars 53 cents.

The Baltimore penitentiary has, during three years, beginning with the day of its institution, yielded to the state of Maryland 44,344 dollars 45 cents, all expenses deducted.

These results, assuredly, are not owing altogether to the penitentiary system : and that which proves it, is the circumstance, that the Baltimore prison was productive even previously to the introduction of the penitentiary system ; we allow even, that the best penitentiary is not that which yields the most ; because the zeal and talent of the prisoners in the workshops, may be stimulated to the detriment of the discipline. Yet we are obliged to acknowledge, that this system, once established, is powerful in maintaining order and regularity in the prison ; it rests on an uninterrupted watchfulness. The labour of the prisoners, therefore, is with such a system more constant and more productive.

At all events, after having seen the above statements, it would be unreasonable to reject the penitentiary system as expensive, since the discipline which has been established in the United States with so little expense, supports itself in some states, and has become in others a source of revenue (*jj*)

Every prisoner in the new penitentiaries costs, on an average, for his support, food, clothing, and *surveillance*, fifteen cents ; in Wethersfield and Baltimore, the support of the prisoner is the cheapest ; at Auburn the dearest : the food costs in the various penitentiaries, on an average, five cents a day per head. At Wethersfield it costs but four cents, and at Sing-Sing, five cents.

The expenses for clothing and bedding, amount in general to nothing, owing to the care which is taken to have them made in the prison by the prisoners themselves. The expenses of *sur-veillance* amount on an average to six cents a day per head. At Auburn they are the least, and at Sing-Sing the most.

In all the new prisons, the expenses of *surveillance* are great-er than those incurred for food and clothing.* All economy on this point would be destructive to a system which rests entirely upon discipline, and consequently upon the good choice of offi-cers.

We see that in all the new prisons, the sum total of the ex-pense, though varying in some points, is nevertheless always, nearly the same; and it is clear, that as long as the administra-tion of these establishments is directed by men of probity, and with similar economy, the expenses of each year will not vary much: there is a minimum below which it cannot fall, without becoming detrimental to the well being of the prisoners; and a maximum beyond which it ought not to rise, without extrava-gance in the administration, or misconduct on the part of the officers.

The same is not the case with a production which by nature is variable. We may certainly presume that the prison which produces most is that in which the prisoners work most. Yet the difficulty attending the sale of the articles, produced by their labour, often defeats this presumption. Even in the United States, where labour is so dear, the demand for articles undergoes numerous variations, which raise or lower their price.†

In short, the financial administration of Auburn, Wethersfield, Sing-Sing, and Baltimore, has appeared to us to be directed with extreme skill; and the discretionary power with which the su-perintendents are invested, is perhaps one of the principal causes of economy. They govern the prison, as it seems best to them, under the superintendence of the inspectors. They are responsi-ble, but they act freely.

The administration of these prisons, which combines the sys-tem by contract with the *régie* (management of sale, &c., by its own officers,) appears to us very conducive to economy.

There are in our prisons many things for which a very high price is paid to the contractor, and which are obtained for very little expense in a prison which manages its own affairs.

---

* The expenses of surveillance cost six *centimes* more than food, for each pri-soner a day. See Statistics, Financial part, Section II , No. 19.

† These accidental causes explain why a day's labour in the prison yields on an average, in Baltimore, twenty-six cents, whilst at Auburn it produces but fourteen cents. See Report of December 21, 1829, on the Maryland State pri-son, pages 6 and 7, and the Financial Division, Section II., end of the Vol. The sale of manufactured articles also incurs sometimes difficulties in Connecticut. See Report of 1830, of the inspectors to the Legislature. With us a day's labour of 17,500 convicts, in the *maisons centrales*, produces but four cents, on an ave-rage, a day.

At Auburn* (in 1830,) one hundred and sixty prisoners out of six hundred and twenty, are occupied in the service of the prison: they make every thing which serves for the clothing, linen, and shoes, and conduces to the neatness and order of the prison; only four hundred and sixty-two work for the contractor.

At Wethersfield, the number of prisoners who work for the contractor is proportionately still smaller. It is believed in America that it is more profitable to employ a large number of contractors, because more favourable agreements can be made for each branch of industry.

Particular care is taken never to make contracts for any great length of time the contractors, therefore, cannot exact contracts disadvantageous to the prison, under the pretence of injurious contingencies to which the possible depreciation of the manufactured articles may expose them, the duration of a contract often does not exceed a year, it is sometimes of less duration for the labour, and generally of six months only for the food.

The contractor pays for a day's labour of a prisoner, about half of what he would pay to a free workman. (*kk*)

The constant renewal of the contracts makes it possible for the administration to seize upon all the chances of economy: it profits by the cheapness of provisions, and if the price of manufactured articles is high, it obtains better conditions from the contractors to whom it hires the labour of the prisoners it makes these calculations for each contract, and must on this account be acquainted with the rise and fall of the various branches of industry, one often prospers to the disadvantage of another; and in such a case the prison will regain from one contractor the loss which it has suffered with another.

It is evident that such an order of things requires in the superintendent a constant attention, an accurate knowledge of affairs, and a perfect probity, which procures him the confidence of the state, and of all those who have business with him. The superintendent is not only the director of a prison, but he is also the agent who, attentive to the movements of commerce, must watch without interruption how he can apply the labour of the prisoners in the most advantageous way, and find the most profitable sales for his products This system, which unites the contract and the *régie*, necessarily produces a responsibility of a very complicated character; and on this account will not meet with the approbation of those who, in all matters of administration, wish to see but one individual; in the accounts but one column, and in this column but one number, this simplicity is not to be found in the American prisons It requires in the superintend-

* See Report on Auburn, 1831.

11

ent constant activity, in the inspectors a minute *surveillance,* and in the comptrollers of the state a thorough examination.

We may yet remark, that this variety of duties, this power of governing the prison, or of making contracts for its labour, this vast administration at once moral and physical, serve to explain also, why the office of superintendent is sought for by persons at once intelligent and respectable.

SECOND DIVISION.

CHAPTER I.

Expensiveness of our prisons · reason of this circumstance —They do not correct the prisoners, but they corrupt them, cause of this corruption, intercourse of the prisoners among themselves —Bad use made of the prisoner's saving, (*pécule*) —The system of our prisons is fatal to the life of the convicts.

DURING the years 1827, 1828, 1829, and 1830, government paid 3,300,000 francs every year for the support of 18,000 prisoners in the *maisons centrales* (state prisons) Thus the prisons, which, in the United States, yield an income, form with us a heavy charge upon the public treasury. This difference is owing to various causes

The discipline of our prisons is less severe, and the labour of the prisoners necessarily suffers from every relaxation of discipline.

The saving (*pécule*) of the prisoners absorbs, with us, two-thirds of the produce of their labour, whilst in America it does not exist at all.

Finally, the manufactured articles are sold in France with much more difficulty, and with less profit, than in the United States.

The object of punishment is to punish the guilty and to render them better; but as it is at present, it punishes little, and instead of reforming, it corrupts still more We would develop this melancholy truth, if we believed that there is a single individual who contests it. Of 16,000 prisoners, at present in the *maisons centrales*, there are 4,000 held upon recommittals. * And it is now acknowledged by government itself, that the number of recommittals goes on continually increasing.† The same was formerly the case in America; but since the new penitentiary system has been established, the number of recommittals diminishes.

The corruption of our prisons is owing chiefly to two causes. The first and the most important, is the free communication of

* This number has been furnished to us in the office of the minister of public works, by the division, the chief officer of which is Mr Labiche. All the documents which we possess relative to the prisons of France, are from the same source.

† See Report of the keeper of the Seals on Criminal Justice, 1830, page 16.

the prisoners both night and day. How can a moral reformation of the prisoners take place in the midst of this assemblage of all crimes and all vices? The convict who arrives at the prison half depraved, leaves it in a state of complete corruption, and we may well say that in the bosom of so much infamy, it would be impossible for him not to become wicked.*

The second cause of the depravity of the prisoners is found in the bad use which they make of their saving. They spend that part of it which is allowed to them in the prison, in excess of food or other superfluities; and thus contract fatal habits. Every expense in the prison is destructive of order, and incompatible with the uniform discipline, without which there is no equality of punishments. The saving is of no real use whatever to the convict before he leaves the prison. And we must add, that, in the actual state of things, that part even of the saving which is given to the convict on his leaving the prison, is neither more useful than that which he has spent in the prison. Had he contracted, during his imprisonment, habits of order, and some principles of morality, the sum, sometimes very considerable, then placed at his disposal, might be employed in a judicious way, and for his future benefit. But, corrupted as he is by his imprisonment itself, he hardly feels himself free, than he hastens to spend the fruit of his labour in debaucheries of all kinds; and continues this kind of life until the necessity of recurring to crime brings him back to the arm of justice, and thence to the prison.

The prison, the system of which is corrupting, is at the same time fatal to the life of the prisoners. With us one prisoner dies out of fourteen in the *maisons centrales*.† In the penitentiaries of America, there dies on an average one out of forty-nine ‡

In these prisons, in which death is so rare, the discipline is austere, the law of silence is imposed upon the prisoners: all are subject to a uniform discipline, and the produce of their labour is not lost either in debaucheries or superfluous expenses; the most rigorous punishment reaches, without pity, every one who breaks orders, not one hour of rest is granted them during the day; and the whole night they are in solitude.

In our prisons, where death makes so many ravages, the prisoners talk freely together; nothing separates them during day or night, no severe punishment is inflicted upon them. Every one may, by the earning of his labour, alleviate the severity of

---

* We refer the reader again for a picture of this almost inconceivable corruption, and of the many other vices of the French prisons, as well as of the police system, to the Memoirs of Vidocq, which, we repeat, contain facts enough to make them a melancholy though interesting and important work for the student of human society.—TRANS.

† Documents furnished from the office of the minister.

‡ See Statistical Tables, end of the Vol.

his imprisonment; and finally, he can enjoy hours of recreation * * * * * *

This severe discipline of the American penitentiaries, this absolute silence imposed upon the prisoners, this perpetual isolation, and the inflexible uniformity of a system, which cannot be alleviated for one without injustice to others, do they not altogether constitute a rigour which is yet full of humanity?*

The contagion of mutual communications, which in our prisons corrupts the inmates, is not more fatal to their souls than their bodies †

We notice here the principal vices which have most attracted our attention in our central prisons It is easy to see that we do not present them as a complete picture, moreover, we add nothing on the "houses of arrest" and "of justice," the other departmental prisons and the bagnes; we only speak of the central prisons destined for great criminals, because they alone contain a population analogous to that within the penitentiaries of America.

* We think that this acknowledgment of our authors themselves, fully justifies our remark in a previous note affixed to a passage in which the severity of the penitentiary system was called barbarous —TRANS

† The defect of our *maisons centrales* is not in their government, but in the principle of their organization Perhaps it would be impossible to turn the actual system to better account. We have seen of late a "central prison" (that of Melun,) where we admired the order of the labour and the "outward discipline " The direction of the "central prisons" is confided to the minister of the interior and to very capable persons. But whatever may be done, prisoners, who have free intercourse with each other, will not be made better, and their mutual corruption will not be prevented. (So far the authors) We must add here an important fact, however offensive the subject may be to our feelings, and if we do not clothe this note in Latin, as we have done on a similar occasion in another work (Journal of my Residence in Greece,) it is because we believe this book ought to be read and fully understood by persons who are not conversant with Latin. All who have attended to the moral state of the prisons on the old plan, know in how frightful a degree two unnatural vices are practised by both sexes One of these vices is probably committed much less in English and American prisons (on the old plan,) than in the French, where not even the presence of other prisoners prevents it, because the national feeling of the English and Americans is much more decided against this vice. But the other, which may be committed in solitude, was frequent also in American prisons, and had the most fatal consequences upon the health of the prisoners We have not had an opportunity of making sufficient inquiries respecting the existence of this vice in prisons on the Auburn plan, but to judge from the general state of health in these establishments, and the effects which reasonably may be supposed to result from their discipline in general, the constant, restless labour during day, with uniform and simple food, it cannot exist to any great degree. In the Philadelphia penitentiary, we hold ourselves authorized to assert from special inquiry, that it does not exist, owing undoubtedly to the general calming tendency which uninterrupted solitude, simple food, and absence of all excitement must naturally have upon the inmates of a solitary cell.—TRANS.

CHAPTER II.

Application of the penitentiary system to France.—Examination of the objections made to this system —Theoretically it seems preferable to all others — What obstacles it would have to overcome in order to become established among us —These difficulties are in the state of things, in the customs, and in the laws —In the state of things the existence of prisons badly constructed, which it would be necessary to supplant by others —In the customs repugnance of public opinion to corporal punishment , and difficulty of procuring for the system the assistance of religious influence —In the laws punishments, inflicting infamy, variety of ways of detention and administrative centralization. —Judication of a system of local administration —The penitentiary system, even if established in France, would not produce all the effects which have resulted from it in the United States —Situation of delivered criminals —*Surveillance* of the high police —Agricultural Colonies.—Even if the system should not be introduced entirely, some of its advantages may be borrowed —A model Penitentiary.—Recapitulation.

Would it be possible to establish the American penitentiary system among us?

It seems to us that this system, considered theoretically, (if we abstract the particular difficulties which its execution would meet with in France,) is both sound and practicable.

Various objections are made against it, which we shall examine. Many persons see in the penitentiary system a philanthropic conception which has for its sole object the amelioration of the physical situation of the prisoners, and as they believe that the criminals are not too severely punished in their present prisons, they reject the system which would make them more comfortable. This opinion rests upon a fact: for a long time those who have raised their voices in France in favour of reforms in the prison discipline, have called public attention simply to clothing, food, and all those matters which contribute to make the convicts more easy.* So that in the eyes of a great number, the adoption

* The prisons have for a long time deserved most of the reproaches made against their physical management it was therefore not without reason that the abuses and vices, which infected them, were attacked , consequently, we are far from blaming the efforts of those who have succeeded in correcting the evil, except that, by the side of a wise and moderate philanthropy, there also exists a zeal which surpasses its end. There are in France prisons in which undoubtedly changes respecting their salubrity are desirable; but in general it may be said that in our prisons the prisoners are as well fed and clothed as they need to be; every amelioration on this point would become an abuse in the other extreme, not less fatal than that which it was intended to remedy. The task of those who justly called for better clothes and better bread for the prisoners, seems at an end , at present the work of those must commence, who believe that there is in the discipline of prisons a moral part, which ought not to be neglected.

of a penitentiary system, which makes innovations necessary, tends only to the physical amelioration of the prison.

Others engaged in a way entirely opposite, believe that the condition of the prisoners is so unfortunate that it would be wrong to aggravate it: and if they hear of a system which is founded on isolation and silence, they say that society has not a right to punish men with such severity.

Finally, there is a third class of persons who, without expressing themselves on the advantages or inconveniences of the penitentiary system, consider it as a eutopian scheme, destined only to enlarge the number of human errors. It must be acknowledged that the opinion of the latter has been in some cases supported by the writings of the most distinguished publicists, whose mistakes in this matter have been received together with their soundest opinions.

Thus, Bentham wishes in his *panoptic* prison the continual sound of music, in order to soften the passions of the prisoners. Mr. Livingston asks for the young prisoner, and for the convicts themselves, a system of instruction almost as complete as that established in any of the free academies ; and Mr. Charles Lucas indicates, as a mode of executing the punishment of imprisonment, a penitentiary system which it would be difficult to reconcile with the principles essential in criminal matters.*

---

* See *Du Système pénal et répressif*. Mr. Lucas finds the whole penal legislation in the penitentiary system. He says "The only question is to reform the wicked · this reformation once effected, the criminal ought to re-enter society" There is some truth in this system ; but it is incomplete. The first object of punishment is not the reformation of the convict, but, on the contrary, to give a useful and moral example to society this is obtained by inflicting upon the guilty a punishment commensurate to his crime Every punishment which is not in proportion to the offence, offends public equity, and is immoral whether from too much severity or too much indulgence.

But it is also important for society, that he, whom it punishes, in order to set an example, should correct, if possible, his morals in the prison This is the second object of punishment, less important than the first, because its consequences are less extensive. The system of Charles Lucas is defective, inasmuch as he considers the second point only, and neglects entirely the first. He invariably considers punishments as means of reformation, and not as means of example It is for this reason that he wishes to see liberty restored to the criminal, as soon as there is a *presumption* of his regeneration. Seeing in imprisonment but a time of trial (noviciate,) in which the convict shows himself more or less quick in repentance and correction, he makes the duration of his sentence depend upon the convict's behaviour in prison. However, the behaviour in prison proves absolutely nothing . on the contrary, we have seen that in many cases it is an indication rather unfavourable (See Chapter II, Section II , § 7.) Besides, who can be the judge of the reformation of convicts ? We are able to judge of a fact, but who can descend into the conscience of the prisoner, to weigh there the sincerity of his repentance ?—And further, where is the reparation due to society ?—And where is the guaranty which society requires, that the criminal has become an honest man, and that this change is equivalent to an expiation of his offence ? (So far the authors) The length of this note shows that the authors must have had good reason for combating in detail a theory, which, if it actually is meant to be such as we have it represented here, would be instantly dismiss-

Is it just to blame the severity or mildness of the penitentiary system? Must we condemn this system on the exaggeration of writers who, preoccupied with philosophical doctrines, have not guarded themselves against the danger attending any theory if carried to its full consequences?

The new system, on the contrary, seems to us to have been conceived for the very object of avoiding those excesses with which it is reproached: freed from severities which are not necessary for its success; unincumbered by indulgences which are asked for only by mistaken philanthropy.

Finally, its execution presents itself with all the advantages of extreme practical simplicity.

It is believed that two depraved individuals, kept in the same place, must corrupt each other; they are therefore separated. Their passions, or the bustle of the world, had deafened or misled them: they are isolated and thus brought to reflect   Their intercourse with the wicked had perverted them; they are condemned to silence · idleness had depraved them; they are made to work. Misery had conducted them to crime; they are taught a useful art.   They have violated the laws of their country, a punishment is inflicted upon them; their life is protected, their body is safe and healthy: but nothing equals their moral suffering.   They are unhappy, they deserve to be so; having become better, they will be happy in that society whose laws they will have been taught to respect.   This is the whole system of American penitentiaries.

But, it is objected, that this system, tried in Europe, has not succeeded; and to prove it, the instances of Geneva and Lausanne are mentioned, where penitentiary systems have been established at great expense, and without producing the results which were expected from it for the reformation of the convicts.

ed by every practical man as a futile scheme produced both by an entire want of knowledge of prisons and criminals, and by a confused conception both of political societies and others, as families, religious communities, &c —a confusion which has produced the most fatal consequences. The reader probably is aware of the fact, that a number of philosophers of late have denied the right, which has been claimed for society, of punishing in order to afford an example, and have pronounced the necessity of resting the right of punishment on other grounds (See among other works, the article Criminal Law in the Encyclop Americana)   This is not the place to give our view of the entire ground on which the whole philosophy of penal law appears to us to rest   But thus much we will say, that there is a public moral feeling as well as a public opinion, and the former cannot manifest itself, cannot stamp crime as such, cannot show that there is a moral difference between honest and wicked acts, except by punishments—a reason which remains powerful even in those cases in which the protection of society does not require any further punishment. And though the greatest punishment may be the grief which a virtuous person feels for past and now well understood offences, society has no means of punishing thus , it cannot punish but by equal, and, in their origin, physical punishments—as deprivation of liberty, &c —Trans

We believe that the example of that which has been done in Switzerland ought in no respect to influence what France might do. In fact, the same mistake in respect to the construction of prisons, has been fallen into in Switzerland, which has not been always avoided in the United States, viz. the desire of elevating architectural monuments instead of simply constructing useful establishments: the expense incurred for the Swiss penitentiaries, therefore, ought in no way to be taken as a basis for calculating the probable expenses of prisons of the same nature in France. On the other hand, if the system of these penitentiaries has not been efficient for the reformation of prisoners, we must not seek for the cause in the system of the United States: it is a mistake to believe that the discipline of the prisons in Geneva and Lausanne is the same with that of the American penitentiaries. The only point common to both is, that the prisoners pass the night in solitary cells: but that which makes a difference of primary importance in the penitentiary systems of the two countries, is, that in the United States the discipline rests essentially on isolation and silence, whilst in Switzerland the prisoners have free intercourse with each other during the day.

It cannot be denied that the liberty of communication granted to the prisoners, changes the very nature of the American system, or to speak more correctly, it produces a new system without any resemblance to the latter.

As for us, as much as we believe that the system founded on isolation and silence, is favourable to the reformation of criminals, we are equally inclined to believe that the reformation of convicts who communicate with each other is impossible.

It seems to us, therefore, that, speaking in the abstract, the penitentiary system of the United States (the superiority of which over every other prison discipline appears incontestable,) presents itself to France with all the chances of success which a theory can offer, the first experiment of which has already succeeded. In stating this opinion, we are not blind to the difficulties which this system would have to overcome in being established with us

These difficulties are in the nature of things; in our customs, and in our laws

The first of all is the existence of another order of things, founded upon a different basis, and upon principles diametrically opposed The American system has for its foundation the separation of the prisoners, and for this reason we find in each penitentiary as many cells as convicts In France, on the contrary, the system of cells established in a general way is unknown; and in all our prisons, the greater part of the convicts are huddled together during night in common dormitories. This circumstance

12

alone is sufficient to render, for the present, a system which rests entirely upon the isolation of the prisoners, impracticable with us. Should, therefore, this system be adopted, new prisons, constructed upon the model of the modern penitentiaries, must be raised, but here a grave difficulty presents itself, resulting from the first expenses of their construction.

We are far from believing that the expense of this would be as considerable as is generally presumed. Those who see in Paris a model prison, destined for four hundred prisoners, and costing 4,000,000 of francs,* conclude with apparent reason, that it would require 320,000,000 of francs, to lodge, upon the same plan, 32,000 criminals; i. e. 10,000 francs for each. But we must remember, that this enormous expense has been occasioned by the deplorable extravagance with which the construction of that prison was attended.

The elegance, the regularity of its proportions, and all the ornaments with which it is embellished, are of no use whatever for the discipline of the establishment: they exhausted the public treasure, and are of service to the achitect alone, who strove to erect a monument, to hand down his name to posterity.

We must remark again that a distinction ought to be made between the expenses of construction upon the Philadelphia and the Auburn system: we have acknowledged, that there are great advantages resulting from the plan of absolute confinement adopted in Pennsylvania, and if the question were only on a theoretical point, perhaps we should prefer it to the Auburn system; but the expense of penitentiaries built upon the Philadelphia plan is so considerable, that it would seem to us imprudent to propose the adoption of this plan for our country. Too heavy a burthen would be thrown on society, for which the most happy results of the system could hardly offer an equivalent. Yet the Auburn system, whose merit in theory is not less incontestable, is, as we have shown above, much cheaper in its execution; it is therefore this system which we should wish to see applied to our prisons, if the question were only to choose between the two.

But the Auburn system itself could not at once be established in France without great expense, which certainly would be incomparably less than that incurred for the prison which we just mentioned; we believe even that the construction, if judiciously directed, of a modern penitentiary, would in the whole cost no more here than in the United States. (*mm*) Yet, however great the economy might be, which would preside over such an undertaking, it is certain that more than 30,000,000 of francs would be necessary for the general establishment of this system: and it

* The Prison in the street de la Roquette near the cemetery Père Lachaise.

will easily be believed that France would not burthen her budget with a similar item in the midst of political circumstances, which require from her still more urgent sacrifices.

Is it not also to be feared that the grave interests which absorb the treasures of France, are injurious in another way to the reform of prisons? Do not political events preoccupy the minds of men to such an extent, that questions, even the most important, on internal reforms, excite public attention but feebly? Talent and capacity are directed towards one single object—politics. Every other interest meets with indifference, and the result of this is, that the most talented men, distinguished writers, experienced members of the administration—in one word, all those who exercise influence on public opinion, spend their energy in discussions useful to the government, but not conducive to the welfare of society. Shall we not fear the consequence of this disposition in respect to the penitentiary system? Will not this institution, which requires for its execution public attention and favour, be received with coolness?

But even if the pecuniary and political objections, just indicated, did not exist, and nothing in the actual state of things were opposed to internal reforms, the introduction of the penitentiary system into France would nevertheless meet with grave difficulties

The American discipline is, as we have seen, principally supported by corporal punishment. But is it not to be feared that a system, of which these punishments are the most powerful auxiliary, will be ill received by public opinion? If it is true, that with us an idea of infamy is attached to this punishment, how could it be inflicted on persons whose morals it is our intention to improve? This difficulty is a real one, and it appears still more serious, if we consider the nature of the discipline itself, which is to be maintained. Silence is the basis of the system: would this obligation of absolute silence, which has nothing incompatible with American gravity, be so easily reconciled with the French character? If we believe Mr. Elam Lynds, the French are, of all nations, those who submit the easiest to all the exigencies of the penitentiary system: yet the question seems to us yet undecided, and we do not know to what point Mr. Elam Lynds has had an opportunity of judging of the docility of French convicts in general, by observations made in American prisons, where he has seen but a small number of French dispersed among a multitude of Americans *

As for ourselves, without pretending to solve this problem, we believe that the law of silence would be infinitely more pain-

* See our Conversation with Mr. E. Lynds, end of the Vol.

ful to Frenchmen than to Americans, whose character is taciturn
and reflective ; and for this reason, it seems to us that it would
be still more difficult with us than in America, to maintain the
penitentiary discipline whose foundation is silence, without recurring to corporal punishment. We are the more induced to
believe so, as the discipline of American penitentiaries is favoured by another circumstance, on which we cannot calculate. There
is a spirit of obedience to the law, so generally diffused in the
United States, that we meet with this characteristic trait even
in the prisons: without being obliged to indicate here the political reasons of this fact, we only state it as such · but this spirit
of submission to the established order does not exist in the same
degree with us.* On the contrary, there is in France, in the spirit
of the mass, an unhappy tendency to violate the law : and this
inclination to insubordination seems to us also to be of a nature
to embarrass the regular operation of the discipline.†

* In the same degree as there exists liberty in a nation, is obedience to the
laws to be found. All over the continent of Europe the great mass of the people
consider the law as something imposed and foreign to them, which must be
obeyed because transgression is punished The observing traveller, who goes
from the continent to England, is struck with the moral power the word law has
in that country, but much greater still in the United States ; and why ?—Because
it is made by the people themselves, and *not* supported by a threatening executive. The most striking instances respecting what we have said, are not found
in great political actions, but in the occurrences of daily life, and can be observed
only on the spot.—Trans.

† With all deference to the opinion of the authors, whose knowledge of the
French character must be infinitely greater than ours, we cannot help thinking
that in this case they overrate the difficulty. As to silence, we acknowledge that
there must be a great difference between Americans and Frenchmen. Go to a
dinner in a French and an American public house, and you will see the truth of
the remark. But in spite of their taciturn disposition, Americans feel the urgent
necessity of communication as well as other mortals, and silence, if imposed,
must be as hard to them as others Besides, custom can do almost every thing ;
the greatest difference, we believe, between an American and a Frenchman,
would show itself in this respect, in moments of excitement. In these, an American certainly would master himself easier, but there is no excitement in the
case , and, we repeat it, as to ordinary silence, that the Frenchman would stand
on a par with an American. And is it not a fact, which goes far to prove what
we say, that the Irish, certainly not taciturn in their disposition, and at least as
easily excitable as Frenchmen, form so great a part of the population of our penitentiaries, and yet submit to the discipline ? If the law of silence is not more
severe for a Frenchman than for an American, it is much more necessary for the
former, inasmuch as roguery and crime, considered as a profession, is carried to
a much greater degree of perfection in France than here. An American criminal
is but a blunt beginner compared to a thorough rogue in France, whether we
consider their adroitness, skill, boldness, or shrewdness in conception, or their
settled views respecting moral principles. Crime is in France a much more perfected *profession,* which, as such, is of course capable of greater or less development. The French criminal, therefore, requires stronger agents to affect him,
and to make the penitentiary system become such for him , and to abandon silence in his treatment would be still more fatal to him than to our convicts, could,
indeed, any difference in the ruinous consequence of such a measure exist Respecting the whip we would say this much ; that if it is according to the authors

The penitentiary system, to which it would be difficult to give, in France, the physical support of stripes, that would seem in this country more necessary than in others, would perhaps be deprived also of a moral auxiliary, which contributes in the United States much to its success.

In America, the progress of the reform of prisons has been of a character essentially religious. Men, prompted by religious feelings, have conceived and accomplished every thing which has been undertaken, they were not left alone; but their zeal gave the impulse to all, and thus excited in all minds the ardour which animated theirs. So also is religion to this day in all the new prisons, one of the fundamental elements of discipline and reformation: it is her influence alone which produces complete regeneration, and even with regard to reformations less thorough, we have seen that it contributes much to obtain them.

It is to be feared that in France the penitentiary system would not find this religious assistance.

Would not the clergy receive with lukewarmness this new institution, on which philanthropy seems to have seized?

And on the other hand, if the French clergy should show themselves zealous for the moral reformation of the criminals, would public opinion be satisfied to see them charged with this duty?

With us there exist, in a great number of persons, prejudices against religion and her ministers, which are unknown in the United States, and our clergy in turn are subject to impressions unfelt by the religious sects of America.

In France, where, during a long period, the altar has struggled in concert with the throne to defend royal power, the people are not yet accustomed to separate religion from authority, and the feelings directed against the latter usually extend to the former.

It thus happens, that in general public opinion shows itself

themselves, not used very frequently in the penitentiaries of the United States, it would be used still less in France, because the Frenchman is more pliable, and though he may not be as much disposed to obey the law for its own sake, as the American, he, on the other hand, has been long accustomed to render obedience to power, which an American does not experience. We well know that corporal punishment has always been held in France in greater abhorrence than in other countries, their feeling of honour being more sensitive; but should we fear to lose public favour by using it in cases of infliction of discipline? How is it at present? The most merciless beating is now in use, and who has seen a chain of galley slaves conducted to the bagnes and brutally beaten in the most arbitrary manner by their guards, that does not think the public would consider a penitentiary system, even with the whip, a change for the better? and as to the degrading effect of stripes in the prisoner's own eyes, the stigma of his crime, which can never be entirely removed, must always be greater than the degradation caused by corporal punishment. We have given our opinion respecting stripes and their necessity in the Auburn system, in the article Pennsylvania Penitentiary System, at the end of the Vol. We speak now merely of the difference of their effects here and in France.—TRANS.

little favourable towards any thing protected by religious zeal ; and the clergy, on their part, show little sympathy for any thing which presents itself under the auspices of public favour.

In America, on the contrary, church and state have always been separated ; and political passions erect themselves against the government, and never against religion. For this reason, religion there always remains out of the struggle ; and there exists an absence of all hostility between the people and the ministers of every sect

We must add an observation on this point : it is, that in the United States, should the support of the clergy fail, the reform of prisons would not thereby be deprived of the assistance rendered by religion.

In fact, society in the United States is itself eminently religious—a circumstance which has a great influence upon the direction of penitentiaries , a multitude of charitable persons, who are not ministers by profession, sacrifice nevertheless a great part of their time to the moral reformation of criminals ; as their religious belief is deeply rooted in their customs, there is not one among all the officers of a prison who is destitute of religious principles. For this reason, they never utter a word which is not in harmony with the sermons of the chaplain. The prisoner in the United States, therefore, breathes in the penitentiary a religious atmosphere, and is more accessible to this influence, because his primary education has disposed him for it.

Generally speaking, our convicts have not such favourable dispositions, and without the walls of the prison, religious ardour is met with in the ministers of religion only.

If they are kept from the penitentiary, the influence of religion will disappear : philanthropy alone would remain for the reformation of criminals. It cannot be denied that there are with us generous individuals, who, endowed with profound sensibility, are zealous to alleviate any misery, and to heal the wounds of humanity : so far, their attention, exclusively occupied with the physical situation of the prisoners, has neglected a much more precious interest, that of their moral reformation. It is clear, however, that called to this field, their charity would not be tardily dispensed, and their efforts would undoubtedly be crowned with some success. But these sincere philanthropists are rare , in most cases philanthropy is with us but an affair of the imagination   The life of Howard is read, his philanthropic virtues are admired, and it is confessed that it is noble to love mankind as he did , but this passion, which originates in the head, never reaches the heart, and often evaporates in the productions of the pen.

There are, then, in our customs and morals, and in the actual disposition of the people, moral difficulties, with which the penitentiary system would have to struggle, if ever it could be established such as it exists in the United States   These obstacles certainly would not always exist. A lasting public prejudice against religion and her ministers, is not the natural state of things ; and we do not know what point a society may reach, without the assistance of religious belief. But here we must not go beyond the actual state of things ; and among the difficulties actually existing, which would injure the penitentiary system in France, that which we have just pointed out would without contradiction be one of the gravest.

Our legislation also presents difficulties.

The first results from the very nature of some of our penal laws.

At the time when the brand was prescribed by our code, the penitentiary system could not have been established; because it would have been contradictory to pursue the moral reformation of criminals who had been disgraced already with indelible infamy. This punishment has disappeared from our laws, and its abolition, which reason and humanity imperiously claimed, is one impediment the less to the efficacy of a good prison discipline.   But there are yet some provisions in our penal code, which are not less irreconcilable to a complete system of reform. We mean the infamy attached to most punishments, and their great diversity.

There are in our laws eight punishments which are expressly called infamous ; without courting public exposure, which is considered only as accessory to certain punishments, and that of the ball, which only figures in the law as a mode of enforcing labour. (Articles 6, 7, 8, 15, and 22, of the penal code.)

If you attach infamy to a perpetual punishment, we see little inconvenience in it, provided the principle of perpetuity is once admitted. But is it not an inconsistency, to declare by judgment a person infamous, who may at some future period reappear in society.   To be logical, the law should also declare, that at the expiration of the punishment the prisoner should receive back his honour and his liberty.   It does not so, because the infamy so easily imprinted on the forehead of the guilty, cannot be effaced with the same facility.   However this may be, the perpetual dishonour attached to a temporary punishment, seems to us little compatible with the object of the penitentiary system, and we do not know how it would be possible to awaken sentiments of honour and virtue in those whom the law itself has taken care to disgrace and to debase.   In order to make, in this respect, our penal legislation agree with the essential principles of the penitentiary system, few changes would be required ; it would be sufficient, not to call any longer the punishments pronounced by the code infamous, and in all cases to spare the convict the transitory shame of the pillory, and the lasting humiliation of hard labour in public.

It would be necessary, lastly, to abolish, if not the diversity of punishments, at least the difference which exists in the manner of suffering them.

The variety of punishments and of imprisonment, prescribed by each of them, have rendered necessary a great number of different prisons. As there are criminals of various degrees, and as they are thrown together in our prisons, it has been justly believed that it would be immoral to confound all, and to place under the same roof, in the same workshop, and in the same bed, the man who has been sentenced to twenty years of forced labour, and him who has to undergo but one year's imprisonment. There is, therefore, a separate prison for the galley slaves, another for *réclusionnaires*, (simply) ; and if the law were strictly executed, there would be a third class of prisons, for persons sentenced for police offences to more than a year's imprisonment, and a fourth class, for those whose confinement would be for less than a year. These classifications, the reason of which we understand, if in principle the assemblage of the prisoners is admitted, become evidently useless, if the system of separation during night and silence during day is introduced. This system once established, the least guilty of all the convicts may be placed by the side of the most consummate criminal, without fearing any contamination.

It is even well to unite the criminals of various kinds in establishments of the same nature ; all are subject to a uniform system ; punishment varies only in its duration. We thus lose the exceptionable system of the bagnes, and see the government of the French prisons freed from this strange anomaly, which places the third of all convicts under the direction of the minister of the marine.

It would then be necessary, in order to put our legislation in harmony with the penitentiary system, to abolish those provisions in the penal code which prescribe distinct prisons, subject to a special system,* for each species of convicts.

The second obstacle in our laws, is the too great extent to which the principle of centralization has been carried, forming the basis of our political society.

---

* Though but one and the same system ought to be established for all convicts, we can very well conceive that there might be differences in the discipline according to the weight of punishments, whether distinguished by their name or duration : thus prisoners for police offences might be allowed to save a *pécule*, greater than that granted to convicts sentenced for grave crimes, &c., &c. If we ask for a uniform system, we only wish for the application of the fundamental principles of the penitentiary system to all prisoners—isolation during night and silence during day ; and we assert, that these two principles once admitted, the variety of prisons becomes useless.

There are, no doubt, general interests, for the conservation of which the central power ought to retain all its strength and unity of action.

Every time that a question arises concerning the defence of the country, its dignity abroad, and its tranquillity within, government ought to give a uniform impulse to all parts of the social body; this is a right which could not be dispensed with, without compromising public safety and national independence.

But however necessary this central direction respecting all subjects of general interest may be to the strength of a country like ours, it is as contrary, it seems to us, to the development of internal prosperity, if this same centralization is applied to objects of local interest.*

---

* We wish that all France should come to a thorough conviction of this all-important truth. The tendency of the French government has been, for many centuries, towards the centralization of all power, and the annihilation of the individual life of communities, if we may so express ourselves. At the era of the French revolution, liberty was proclaimed, but life could not so easily be restored to those primary bodies, without which no liberty can be imagined; nor was this important point sufficiently understood, on the contrary, the tendency of centralization having operated for centuries, the revolution merely completed it, inasmuch as it produced greater uniformity and equality, and we find it attaining its height in the imperial government. A French republic, indeed, had been decreed, but a republic never existed, there was always a central power at Paris, under whatever name it went, which absorbed the political life of the whole country, concentrated all power, and ruled without a check, because it is, in our opinion, of little use that those who rule are elected, or of little importance how they are elected, if they are checked merely by the letter of a written constitution, and not by the vigorous, healthy, free action of every part and limb of the great body politic. It is the free action of all the minor or greater circles, the villages, towns, wards, cities, societies, companies, courts, &c &c &c. by which true liberty, which is more than a written decree, is nourished. This is the great secret why England remained free, whilst every nation on the continent of Europe hurried to the whirlpool of centralization. Her parliament has been at times servile enough, great speeches alone would not have saved her; but her people retained that manly, independent political activity, that bracing consciousness of individual right, which we have signalized as the very nerve of living liberty. Were it but the constitution of the highest national authorities which constitutes liberty, many a country would be freer than Britain. Who will deny, that, in the abstract, the constitution of Brazil promises much more liberty than that of England? But the life of the community is wanting. Liberty cannot be *made*, cannot be guarantied by a parchment, cannot be secured by an oath; (look at the history of France for the last fifty years;) liberty must be a national life, a *reality* which extends its ramifications to every part of society; or it is but little more than an empty sound. We trust no reader will charge us with agreeing with those absolutists, who, using nearly the same arguments, conclude that every attempt to establish constitutions is a folly. All we mean to say is, that a nation's attention ought always to be directed chiefly to the point indicated by us, and often, we most willingly acknowledge, is the proclamation of a constitution the first step, which possibly can be taken toward liberty. Such was the case, in our opinion, with France—France, whose governments, from Louis XIV., down to the revolution, had instilled the poison of disorganization into every vein of society; but she forgot the true end; and unless she searches for the true foundation of liberty, there, where we conceive its sole firm basis to

It has appeared to us, that the success of the new prisons in the United States, is principally owing to the system of local administration under the influence of which they have originated.

In general, the first expenses of construction are made with economy; because those who execute the plan, pay also the expenses. Little mismanagement is to be feared from the inferior agents, because those who make them work are near to them; and even after the system which they have thus introduced is put into practice, they do not cease to watch its operation. They are occupied with it as with their own work, and one, in the success of which, their honour is interested

As soon as a state has founded a useful establishment, all others, animated by a happy spirit of emulation, show themselves zealous to imitate it.

Would our laws, and our customs, which leave every thing to the central power, offer to the penitentiary system the same facilities for its foundation and support among us? We do not believe it.

If the question were, of enacting a law, this centralization would be far from throwing difficulties in the way; in fact, it would be much easier for our government to obtain from the chambers, the adoption of the penitentiary system for all France, than it has been in America, for the governors of the various

be, she may yet change her dynasties and her charters, may alter the national council in Paris, but she will not find what she is in search of, Paris will rule, but the people will not have a national liberty   Her task appears to us to be one of the most difficult recorded in history.   She has to break up centralization, and to conduct through the country the irrigating streams of liberty, without which the most active and the boldest national councils are but vast rivers, whose immense volumes receive no produce from sectional branches. We were rejoiced, therefore, as our reader will be, to find in the above passage, and still more in others, how well our authors have understood what is truly needed.

For the reasons given above, it is our opinion, harsh as it may sound, that as yet but two nations understand justly what liberty is—the British and American. With them liberty is a reality, something positive, that they can grasp—which is developed in their history—a blessing to the people, a distinct system of politics, a practical mode of government   It is exemplified in their charters and laws—in their revolutions, and parties, and elections—in their penitentiaries—in war and in peace. It is not a mere floating gossamer or a brilliant phantom.

It is a peculiar fact, that a restless disposition existed during the last century in almost all the governments of the European continent, to concentrate the whole power, nay, the whole activity of a nation in one point, a minister was appointed for every branch, even for public worship ("*cultus*"), every community was stripped of any trace of self-action—*bureaucracy* extended over knowledge, commerce, industry, law, worship, roads, canals—every thing But so troublesome has this kind of ruling become, that governments themselves, even those the least disposed to yield in any way to the wish of national liberty, have made advances towards surrendering certain branches of administration to the various communities interested in them.—TRANS.

states, to get this same principle sanctioned by the various legislatures, without whom it could not be acted upon.

But after this principle has been adopted by law, it yet remains to be executed; it is here, where with us the difficulties begin.

It is to be feared that the building which the government would cause to be erected for this purpose, would not be on a very economical plan; and that the expenses of construction, superintended by secondary agents, would much exceed the original estimates. If the first experiments prove too expensive, they will discourage public opinion, and the most zealous partisans of the penitentiary system. Supposing these first difficulties conquered, is not the indifference of the different communities towards the success of an establishment which is not their own work, to be feared? and yet this system cannot prosper without the especial zeal of the officers of the prison. Finally, how could the central power, the action of which is uniform, give all those modifications to the penitentiary system, which are necessary on account of local customs and wants?

It seems to us difficult to expect the penitentiary system to succeed in France, if its foundation and erection are to be the work of government, and if it should be thought sufficient to substitute for the central prisons (*maisons centrales de détention*) others built merely on a better plan.

Would not the chances of success be far greater, if the care of constructing, at their own expense, and of directing (according to certain general principles expressed in a law common to all) the prisons of all kinds, (those destined for great criminals not excepted) were conferred upon the departments themselves?

The laws of 1791 laid down the principle, that the superintendence of the prisons belongs essentially to the municipal authority, and their direction to the administrative authority of the department.* These same laws prescribe, as to the administration of the prisons, a great number of important innovations, and contain even the germ of the penitentiary system since adopted in the United States.†

But the principles thus proclaimed, were but imperfectly executed as soon as Bonaparte had been invested with consular dignity, he decreed the establishment of "central houses of detention," without taking the pains to cause the abolishment by

---

* See laws of July 22, September 29, and October 6, 1791.

† Article 16 of the law of October 6, 1791, decrees "Every person sentenced to confinement, shall be locked up *alone* in a place, into which daylight shines, without iron or fetters; he shall not have any communication with other convicts or with persons without, as long as his imprisonment lasts." This is exactly the theory of solitary confinement it is the system of Cherry-Hill, (Philadelphia.)

the constitutional powers, of the laws contrary to this decree. This institution was destructive to all local direction and super-intendence. In fact, most of the central prisons now existing, are nothing but ancient convents dispersed through France, some near towns, others in the midst of fields.

Bonaparte, however, declared in 1810, that each department should have, besides the "houses of justice and arrest," a prison destined to contain prisoners convicted for police offences.

If, then, the system of one general prison for each depart-ment should be adopted, we would return to the principle of the laws of 1791; and we should extend to all criminals the local imprisonment, which Bonaparte himself intended to establish for those convicted of police offences.

This extension would be without inconvenience in regard to prison discipline, since we always reason on the supposition of a change in the penitentiary system, founded on silence and isola-tion of the prisoners.

Government depriving itself of the privilege of directing the central prisons, would abandon a prerogative which is but oner-ous to itself, without being beneficial to the departments. It would retain a right of impulse, control, and superintendence; but instead of acting itself, it would make others act.

We here only throw out hints of a system, which, to be adopt-ed, ought to be matured; we have the certainty of that which exists being bad; but the remedy seems to us not so certain as the existence of the evil.

Our prisons created and entirely governed by a central power, are expensive and inefficient for the reformation of the prisoners: we have seen in America, cheap prisons, in which all contami-nation is avoided, springing up in small states under the influ-ence of local authorities: it is under the impression of this con-trast that we write.

We are well aware that the situation of the various American states and that of our departments, is not the same. Our depart-ments possess no political individuality; their circumscription has been to this day of a purely administrative character. Accus-tomed to the yoke of centralization, they have no local life; and we must agree, that it is not the duty of governing a prison which would give them the taste and habits of individual administration; but it is to be hoped that "political life" will enter more into the habits of the departments, and that the cares of government will have, more and more, a tendency to become local.*

If our hopes in this respect should be realized, the system which we indicate would become practicable, and the peniten-

* The original is: *et que les intérêts d'administration tendront de plus en plus à se localiser.*—TRANS.

tiary system in France would find itself surrounded by a great many favourable circumstances, which, in the United States, have effected its success

Each department having its central prison, would only contribute to the support of its own convicts ; whilst at present the rich and well populated department, whose inhabitants commit few crimes, pays more for the support of central prisons, than the poor department, whose population, less numerous, furnishes more criminals.

If each department should construct its own prison, it would vote with less repugnance the funds which it would itself dispose of. The construction, which would be its own work, would, undoubtedly, be less elegant and less regular than if it had been directed by the central power, assisted by its architects * * * * But the beauty of the fabric adds little to the merit of the establishment. The great advantage of a local construction would be to excite the lively interest of its founders. The French government, acknowledging how necessary local direction and superintendence are for the prosperity of the prisons, has tried at various times to interest the departments in the administration of their prisons,* but its attempts have always been without success. Whatever government may do, the various bodies will never take an interest in that which they have not made themselves.

Would not this constant watchfulness, this continual and mute care, this constant solicitude and zeal, indispensably necessary to the success of a penitentiary prison, be extended to an establishment created by the department, the witness of its birth, its development, and its progress?

Among the difficulties which would be opposed to the execution of this system, there are some which are perhaps not so serious as some think, and which we believe it our duty to indicate. It is feared, with reason, that by increasing the number of central prisons, the expense of their construction would proportionally increase. In fact, eighty prisons destined to contain 32,000 prisoners, would cost more than the erection of twenty prisons fitted to contain the same number of individuals But if the advantage of economy is inherent in vast constructions, on the other hand, that of a better discipline is inherent in establishments less considerable.

It is certain that a prison, in order to be well governed, ought not to contain too great a number of criminals , the personal safety of the officers and the order of the establishment are in continual danger in prisons, where two or three thousand male-

* See Circular of the Minister of the Interior, of March 22, 1816 , Ordinance of April 9, 1819.

factors are assembled : (as is the case in the bagnes.) It is the small number of the prisoners in Wethersfield which forms one of the greatest advantages of that penitentiary ; there the super-intendent and the chaplain are thoroughly acquainted with the moral state of each individual, and after having studied his evil, they endeavour to cure it. At Sing-Sing, where there are one thousand prisoners, a similar care is out of the question, and it is not even attempted. Supposing that the 32,000 prisoners of France were distributed in eighty-six departmental prisons, there would be on an average 400 in each of them. There are some departments, indeed, whose large and corrupted population furnishes many criminals, whilst' others, whose inhabitants are less numerous and more honest, send few criminals to the prisons ; but what would result from this fact ? that those departments in which most crimes would be committed would be forced to build larger prisons, whilst the others would erect smaller penitentia-ries. Our departments would be in this respect precisely in the same position with the different states of the American Union.

The state of New York, which contains 2,000,000 of inhabi-tants, has two central prisons ; of which one alone contains 1,000 prisoners. Connecticut, with but 260,000 inhabitants, possesses a single prison containing but 200 criminals. Few departments would have a prison so numerously filled as that of Sing-Sing, the principal defect of which consists in the great number of its inmates, and many departments, whose population is similar to that of Connecticut, would not have more criminals in their pri-sons than we find at Wethersfield ; and we have a right to believe that this limitation of number would be an advantage, since Wethersfield, the smallest penitentiary in America, is also the best. And would not the example of this penitentiary, which, though less extensive, cost less in its construction than all the others, prove that we are enabled to compensate, by a spirit of economy and by local superintendence, for the greater expense occasioned by the construction on a small scale?

It is perceived with what reserve we have communicated these ideas. In order to proceed safely and steadily on a similar path, it would be necessary to possess information which we have not, and to be supported by documents which are not at our disposal.

Deprived as we are of this guidance, we do not present a sys-tem ; we have only started a question, the solution of which is of vital interest to society, and to which we call the attention of all enlightened men.

Supposing the penitentiary system established and prospering in France, we cannot perhaps expect from it all the happy effects which it has produced in the United States.

Thus we doubt whether the labour of the prisoners would be as productive as it is in America, even allowing that the saving

l

(*pécule*) of the convicts should be entirely suppressed. Indeed it is incontestable, that manufactured articles do not find with us the same market which is offered in the United States: and in order to estimate the revenue of a prison, it would be necessary to take into account articles which would remain unsold.

The penitentiary, which on this account would be less productive with us, would for a similar reason also be less efficient in respect to the reformation of the convicts. In America, where wages are extremely high, the convicts easily find labour when they leave the prison; and this circumstance favours their good conduct, when they have re-entered society :* in France, the situation of delivered convicts is infinitely less favourable : and even if they are resolved to lead an honest life, they are not unfrequently brought back to crime by a fatal necessity. In the United States, the delivered convict generally leaves the state where his conviction is known; he changes his name and takes up his residence in another state, where he may begin a new life: with us, the convict, whose punishment has expired, meets everywhere with obstacles and embarrassments. The *surveillance* of the police, to which he is subject, obliges him to a fixed residence, which he cannot change, without committing a new offence against the laws: he is condemned to live in the place where his first crime is officially known, and every thing conspires to deprive him of the means necessary to his existence. The defect of a similar state of things is felt by all the world: and we doubt whether it will be long continued.†

The surveillance of the " high police," such as it is practised at present, is less useful to society than fatal to the delivered criminal. It would be of some advantage, if, by its influence, society, informed of the real situation of each released criminal, had some means of procuring labour for those who have none, and assistance for those who stand in need of it. Might not go-

---

* "It must not be concealed, that one great reason why crimes are so unfrequent is the full employment the whole country offers to those who are willing to labour, while at the same time, the ordinary rate of wages for a healthy man is sufficient to support him and a family. This is a point which you will not lose sight of in comparing the institutions of America with those of Europe " (Letter of the Attorney General of the state of Maryland, January 30, 1832)

† There is hardly a writer, who has touched upon this subject, who does not complain in strong terms of the unfortunate effect, which the surveillance of the French police over delivered convicts causes, by almost depriving them of the possibility of living honestly This surveillance, originally established for the benefit of society, has become one of its greatest evils for the reason stated Indeed, if we consider the whole system of imprisonment in France, with its almost infallible evil of contamination, how it regularly leads from short imprisonments to longer ones, until it brings the criminal at last to the bagne , it offers an instance of one of those unfortunate institutions, not a few in number, which, though intended for the benefit of society, have become its greatest evils Prisons were invented to repress crime , they teach it surveillance was established to protect society , it drives the criminal like a wolf back to his old haunts.—TRANS.

vernment find this means in the foundation of agricultural colonies, similar to those which at present are so flourishing.in Belgium and Holland ?* If such colonies were established in France on the yet uncultivated districts of our soil, no idler could complain of not finding labour; the beggars, vagrants, paupers, and all the delivered convicts, whose number, continually increasing, threatens incessantly the safety of individuals and even the tranquillity of the state, would find a place in the colony, where they would contribute by their labour to increase the wealth of the country.

Perhaps persons convicted for a short time, might also be sent there. There would be an incontestable advantage in introducing the greatest possible number of prisoners. One of the principal advantages of agricultural colonies, indeed, consists in not injuring the industry of citizens: they thus obviate one of the greatest dangers presented by the establishment of manufactories in prisons.† The system of agricultural colonies deserves, therefore, a serious attention on the part of politicians; it seems that after having admitted its principle, it ought to be extended as much as possible, and that it would be easy to reconcile its application with the principles of the penitentiary system. Lastly, the establishment of agricultural colonies would have, among other advantages, that of deriving happy effects from that administrative superintendence, of which almost all the consequences are otherwise fatal; and it would thus cause one of the difficulties, obstructing the introduction of the penitentiary system, to disappear. ‡

We have pointed out the difficulties which the penitentiary system would meet with in France, and have not disguised their importance. We do not deny that we see very great obstacles to the introduction of this system, such as it is in the United States, and surrounded by all the circumstances which accompany it in that country. We are, nevertheless, far from believing that nothing can be done towards the amelioration of our prisons.

We never have entertained the idea that France could attempt a sudden and general revolution in its prison system; to raze the old establishments, to erect new ones, and to sacrifice, for this single object, in one moment, enormous sums, which are urgently claimed by interests of another nature. But we can reasonably demand progressive reforms in the system of our prisons; and, if it is true, that it would be impossible to found in France a discipline supported by the assistance of the whip;

* See Note on Agricultural Colonies, No. 4.
† See Alphabetical Note *s*
‡ We refer those readers, who are unacquainted with the history and character of these agricultural colonies, as our authors call them, to the article *Pauper Colonies,* following that of *Colony* in the *Encyclopædia Americana.*—TRANS.

if it is true, that with us the assistance of local influence is wanting to the success of the establishment, and the support of religion to the progress of moral reformation, it is also certain, that, though not adopting the American prison discipline without modification, we might borrow from it a number of its principles and its advantages. Thus every new prison which would be built according to the system of cells, would have an incontestable superiority over the present prisons. The separation of the prisoners during night, would put a stop to the most dangerous communications, and destroy one of the most active agents of corruption. We cannot imagine what objection, possibly, could be made against the system of cells, if, as we believe it to be the case, the prisons built according to this system, would not cost more than the others.* We have said that it seems to us difficult to maintain absolute silence among the convicts without the assistance of corporal punishment. However, this is only an opinion, and the example of Wethersfield, where the prisoners have been governed without beating for several years, tends to prove that this severe means of discipline is not absolutely necessary. It seems to us, that the chance of success would make the trial on the part of government well worth the attempt—a trial which seems to us the more reasonable, as we would be sure at least of approaching our end, in case we should not succeed entirely. Thus even if public opinion should show itself decidedly hostile to corporal punishments, we would be obliged, in order to establish the law of silence, to resort to disciplinary chastisements of another nature, such as absolute solitude without labour, and a reduction of food; there is good ground to believe, that with the assistance of these latter punishments, less rigorous than the first, but nevertheless efficient, silence would be sufficiently maintained to avoid the evil of moral intercourse between the prisoners; the most important point would be, first to declare the principle of isolation and silence as a rule of discipline of the new prisons; the application of the principle would meet, perhaps with us, with more obstacles, because it would not be aided by such energetic auxiliaries, but we have no doubt, that regarding the great general end, much good would already thus be effected. Radical reformations, perhaps, would not be obtained by this imperfect system, but great corruptions would be prevented, and we would thus derive from the American system, those advantages which are the most incontestable.

We believe that government would do something useful in establishing a model penitentiary, constructed upon the American plan, and governed as much as possible according to the disciplinary rules which are in force in the penitentiaries of the

* See Alphabetical note, *mm.*

14

United States. It would be necessary that this construction, planned according to all the simplicity of the models we have brought with us, should be executed without any architectural elegance. Care should be taken to place in the penitentiary new convicts only ; because if the nucleus of an old prison should suddenly be introduced into the new penitentiary, it would be difficult to submit to the severities of the new discipline, individuals accustomed to the indulgent system of our " central houses."

To recapitulate, we have signalized in the two first parts of this report, the advantages of the penitentiary system in the United States. The inflexible severity of a uniform system, the equality of punishments, the religious instruction and the labour substituted for the system of violence and idleness ; the liberty of communication supplanted by isolation or silence ; the reformation of the criminals instead of their corruption ; in the place of jailors, honourable men who direct the penitentiaries ; in the expenditure, economy, instead of disorder and bad management : these are the characteristics which we have acknowledged in the new American system.

The necessity of a reform in the prison discipline in France is urgent, and acknowledged by every one : the number of recommitted criminals regularly increasing, is a fact which strikes every thinking mind. The delivered convicts, who are but criminals still more corrupted for their having been confined in the prison, become, wherever they show themselves, just objects of fear. Incapable, as society thus is, to correct the guilty, will it resort to transportation? Let France look at England ; let her judge whether it would be wise to imitate her in this respect.*

The defect is in our prisons, infected with a frightful corruption ; but cannot this cancer, which every year increases, be healed? And do we not see prisons efficient for the reformation of the wicked, in a country whose prisons, but fifteen years ago, were worse than ours are now?

Let us not declare an evil incurable, which others have found means to eradicate ; let us not condemn the system of prisons ; let us labour to reform them.

To arrive at this end, the united efforts of many are necessary. And first, it is requisite that all writers, whose talent influences public opinion, should strive to give it a new direction, and to succeed so far, that the moral part of the discipline should be no more neglected than the amelioration of the administration of the physical part. It is necessary that the interests of reform should seize every mind, and become the conviction of all. A controversy even, would be desirable between the organs

* See Appendix on Penal Colonies, No. 2.

of public opinion, in order to find out which are the disciplinary punishments that might be admitted without wounding public feeling, and which are incompatible with our civilization and our customs.

Lastly, it would be necessary that the government should put our legislation in harmony with the principles of the penitentiary system, and above all, that it invite the deliberation of the most enlightened men on these grave matters.

The future success of the penitentiary system, depends much upon the first step we take. It is important, therefore, that all possible precaution be taken to secure success to the first establishment which may be erected in France. It is particularly necessary for the success of this establishment, that public attention should be turned towards it, should receive it favourably, and instead of throwing obstacles in its way, surround it with that moral assistance, without which no institution can prosper in a free country.

PART III.

On Houses of Refuge.

CHAPTER I.

Origin of Houses of Refuge in the United States.—Their organization.—Elements composing them —The establishment has all the rights of a guardian over juvenile offenders.—The house of refuge is a medium between a prison and a school.—System of these establishments.—Houses of refuge at New York, Philadelphia, and Boston —How the time of the children is divided between labour in the workshop, and the school —Contract —Disciplinary means —Remarkable theory of a discipline established in the house of refuge in Boston —Those of New York and Philadelphia less elevated, but preferable.—On what grounds liberty is restored to the children.—Effects of houses of refuge in respect to reformation.

Governor Clinton, whose name is for ever celebrated in the state of New York, said : "The houses of refuge are the best penitentiary establishments which have been conceived of by the genius of man, and instituted by his benevolence." With an examination of them we will finish our work, as we announced in the beginning.

The first house of refuge was established in the city of New York, in the year 1825 ;* Boston followed in 1826, and Phila-

* The authors are mistaken on this point, if they mean by the above any thing more than that the first American house of refuge was established in New York. The first house of refuge, in modern times at least, (for we do not know whether a similar charitable establishment has not perhaps existed at some former period; as Sunday schools, likewise, are but reinvented in modern times, though we confess that it seems improbable that houses of refuge have existed at any former period,) was established in Germany Johannes Falk, a native of Dantzig, lost, in the year 1813, in Weimar, four promising and dearly beloved children, within a few days, and the bereaved parent resolved to become the father of those unfortunate children, who had been deprived of a sound education, and were in the path of crime and destruction He founded the "Society of Friends in Need" for children of criminals, and criminal children, and adopted, as a fit symbol for his establishment, the representation of some children converting on the anvil their chains into useful tools It shows the spirit of his establishment Count Adalbert von der Recke-Vollmarstein established, in 1819, his "Saving Institution" at Overdyck, near Bocham, in order to "save" neglected and abandoned children. In 1822 he extended this establishment, and removed it to Duesselthal, near Duesseldorf, where the children learn farming, &c. in addition to the com-

delphia in 1828 ; and there is good reason to believe that Balti-

mon trades, taught also in our houses of refuge Mr. Wadzeck founded a similar establishment in 1819, in Berlin, for "beggar-boys" Mr. Wadzeck died in 1823, but his establishment was extended, and the character somewhat changed, (a real house of refuge existing now besides). It consists, 1 of a school for 150 poor boys , 2 of another for 190 poor girls , 3 an institution for the formation of good nurses, to take the charge of children , 4 an institution for infants, remaining there day and night, but not a foundling house , 5 an institution for infants, brought there by poor parents in the morning, if they go to work, and taken home in the evening. The Institution No 3, a most salutary one, is connected with Nos. 4 and 5 In 1820, an institution precisely like that of Mr Falk in Weimar, was established in Erfurt, and in the same year another in Aschersleben. In 1824 a number of gentlemen in Berlin formed the "Society for the education of children morally neglected " By their efforts the house of refuge in that city has been founded It is in all main points similar to ours, except that no power is granted to the directors to seize any vagrant child—a power which, in a country where public opinion has so few chances of making itself heard, would be most dangerous This house of refuge is under the superintendence of Mr. Kopf, whom it gives us the greatest pleasure to place by the side of such names as that of Mr. Wells in Boston, and Mr Hart of New York We know not that we could express our respect for the excellent qualities of either of them in a better way. The Prussian government had been alarmed by various reports respecting the increase of crimes committed by youths, and on November 30th, 1825, government issued a decree, requiring every quarter a list of crimes committed by "young individuals" to be sent in , and, October 2, 1826, a decree was issued respecting the "treatment and correction of neglected and demoralized children." To be brief, there exist at present several houses of refuge in the Prussian monarchy, viz. in Memel, Breslau, Dantzig, Berlin, &c , and there is the best reason to believe that they will rapidly increase in that kingdom, as well as in other parts of Germany, where the government of France, therefore, might obtain the best information, should they contemplate the establishment of houses of refuge. For more information, the reader is referred to Annals of the Prussian Popular School System, vol. 5, Division On Institutions for the Correction and Treatment of Neglected Children This volume was published in Berlin, 1826 Still, though houses of refuge were first established in Germany, they were conceived, planned, and executed in the United States, entirely independently of those in Germany. The "Society for the Prevention of Pauperism in the City of New York," were soon led, by their inquiries into the causes of pauperism, to the melancholy consequences resulting from juvenile vagrancy, and the imprisonment of children with adults As early as January 21st, 1821, we find "juvenile delinquency" pointed out as one of the subjects recommended to the careful consideration of the Society, and particular attention is directed to the misery resulting from juvenile offenders being imprisoned together with old convicts. In the "Report on the Penitentiary System in the United States, prepared under a Resolution of the Society for the Prevention of Pauperism in the City of New York," published in 1822, we find, on page 59, and seq the idea of a house of refuge already entirely matured, both in respect to the main points of discipline, and the character of such an establishment—a medium between a prison and an institution for education , and in the Report of the same Society for 1823, the subject is still more urgently brought before the public. It is said, on page 18, that the committee cannot but indulge the belief, that the facts previously stated will convince every citizen of New York "that it is highly expedient that A HOUSE OF REFUGE FOR JUVENILE DELINQUENTS, should, as soon as practicable, be established in the immediate vicinity of New York " On March 29th, 1824, "an act to incorporate the Society for the Reformation of Juvenile Delinquents in the City of New York," was passed by the state legislature Several other acts followed, for all of which, as for any more particular information respecting the house of refuge of New York, we refer the reader to Documents relative to the House of Refuge in the City of New York, by N. C. Hart,

more will soon have a similar one.* This offers an opportunity of judging of the power of association in the United States.

Touched by the shocking fate of young delinquents, who were indiscriminately confounded in the prisons with inveterate criminals, some individuals of New York sought a remedy for the evil; they united their efforts; laboured, first to enlighten public opinion, and then, setting themselves the example of generosity, soon found sufficient funds, by voluntary subscriptions, for the establishment of a house of refuge.

The houses of refuge, thus called into existence by the combination of individual charity, are, as is seen in their origin, private institutions; yet they have received the sanction of public authority. All the individuals whom they contain are legally in custody. But in approving of the houses of refuge, government does not interfere in their management and superintendence; of which it leaves all the care to the private individuals who founded them.

Every year the state grants some pecuniary assistance to these establishments, and yet it never takes the least part in their administration.

The supreme authority over the houses of refuge, resides in the entire body of the subscribers, who have contributed to their erection, or who continue their contributions for their support.

The subscribers elect the directors (managers,) on whom they confer the power of ruling the establishment in the manner which they judge the most advantageous. These managers appoint the officers, and make all the necessary regulations for the administration of the house. Some of them compose a permanent acting committee, charged with superintending the execution of the several resolutions: this composes the executive power of the institution. The officers of the house of refuge are the immediate agents of the acting committee, to whom they submit all their acts. They give no accounts to government, which does not demand any. Among the officers, the choice of the superintendent requires the chief care of the directors, because he is the soul of the whole administration.

Thus left to themselves, and subject to the control of public

Superintendent, New York, 1832. The eighth annual report of this institution was published in 1833. The fact that two nations have come to the same conclusion in so important a matter, and have resorted to the same remedy for so great an evil, proves how urgent is the necessity of providing effectually for the rescue of abandoned children; and at the same time it encourages us to hope much from the efficiency of this measure, since it must be founded on true principles. —TRANS.

* A house of refuge has not yet, (up to the time we write, April, 1833,) been erected, owing partly to the failure of a certain revenue, destined for the erection of the establishment by the legislature of Maryland; but no reasonable doubt can be entertained that Baltimore will soon have its house of refuge, which, like every other large city, it needs so much.—TRANS.

opinion alone, the houses of refuge prosper; the efforts, through the assistance of which they maintain themselves, are the more powerful as they are spontaneous and free   The expenses which they cause are incurred without trouble or regret, because they are voluntary, and because the lowest subscriber has his share in the administration, and consequently, his interest in the success of the establishment   Though the expenses of construction and support are not paid by the state, they are not the less a charge upon society; but they weigh upon those who can best sustain them on account of their fortunes, and who find a moral indemnity in the sacrifice which they have had the merit of imposing upon themselves

The houses of refuge are composed of two distinct elements: there are received into them young people of both sexes under the age of twenty, condemned for crime , and also those who are sent there by way of precaution, not having incurred any condemnation or judgment.

Nobody contests the necessity of houses of refuge for young convicts. In all ages and in all countries, the disadvantage has been acknowledged which results from placing in the same room, and submitting to the same discipline, the young delinquents and the guilty offenders whom age has hardened in crime : the prisoner, yet of tender age, has often committed but a slight offence : how can we justly make him the associate in prison of another, who is doomed to expiate heavy crimes? This defect is so serious, that magistrates hesitate to pursue young delinquents, and the jury to condemn them. But there another danger presents itself. Encouraged by impunity, they give themselves up to new disorders, which a punishment proportionate to their offence would perhaps have prevented them from committing.

The house of refuge, the discipline of which is neither too severe for youth, nor too mild for the guilty, has therefore for its object both the withdrawal of the young delinquent from a too rigorous punishment and from the dangers of impunity.

The individuals, who are sent to the houses of refuge without having been convicted of some offence, are boys and girls who are in a position dangerous to society and to themselves : orphans, who have been led by misery to vagrancy ; children, abandoned by their parents and who lead a disordered life ; all those, in one word, who, by their own fault or that of their parents, have fallen into a state so bordering on crime, that they would become infallibly guilty were they to retain their liberty.*

* We found, when visiting the house of refuge of New York, that more than half of the children, who had been received there up to that time, were in this establishment in consequence of some misfortune. Thus of 513 children, 135 had lost their fathers, 40 their mothers, 67 were orphans, 51 had been pushed on to crime by the notorious misconduct or want of care of their parents there were 47 whose mothers had married again.

It has, therefore, been thought that the houses of refuge should contain at once juvenile criminals and those on the point of becoming such, the latter are spared the disgrace of judgment, and all protected against the pollution of the prison. And that no disgrace should be attached to confinement in the house of refuge, a name has been given to this establishment, which reminds us of misfortune only * The house of refuge, though containing a certain number of convicted youths, is nevertheless no prison. He who is detained in it undergoes no punishment: and in general the decision by which the children are sent to the refuge, has neither the solemnity nor the forms of a judgment. And it is here that we will mention a fact which seems to us characteristic of this institution. The magistrates who send the children to the refuge, never determine what length of time the delinquent must remain there; they merely send them to the house, which from that moment acquires all the rights of a guardian. This right of guardianship expires when the lad arrives at his twentieth year,† but even before he has attained this age, the managers of this establishment have the right to restore him to liberty if his interest require it.

The house of refuge is a medium between a school and a prison; the young delinquents are received much less for punishment than to receive that education which their parents or their ill fate refused them; the magistrates, therefore, cannot fix the duration of their residence in the house of refuge, because they cannot foresee how much time will be necessary to correct the children, and to reform their vicious dispositions ‡

* In Boston the name of house of refuge is given to an asylum for females of bad reputation who have resolved to reform, and what is called house of refuge in New York, is called in Boston house of reformation —TRANS.

† This is correct, speaking *generally* We believe that the guardianship of the managers of the refuge usually terminates at the age of eighteen for females, and twenty one for males We may add here, that though the state exercises no direct management of these institutions, yet their charters of incorporation require that their laws and regulations should not be inconsistent with the constitutions of the country The judiciary have a complete supervision of their rules and conduct, inasmuch as by the medium of the writ of *habeas corpus*, the legality of the commitment or detention of any child may be inquired into and tested by the courts

It may also be stated, that the solemnity of a judgment often occurs before sending a subject to the refuge, and, in some cases, is necessary.—TRANS.

‡ The various authorities which may send children to the house of refuge, are
1. The courts of justice.
2. Police officers
3. Commissioners or managers of the alms-house.
The revised statutes of the state of New York, § 17 of title 7 (chap. 1,) 4th part, declare
" Whenever any person, under the age of sixteen years, shall be convicted of any felony, the court, instead of sentencing such person to imprisonment in a state prison, may order that he be removed to and confined in the house of refuge, established by the society for the reformation of juvenile delinquents in the city of New York, unless notice shall have been received from such society, that there is not room in such house for the reception of further delinquents."

The office of judging whether a child is fit to leave the refuge, is left to the managers of the establishment, who see every day the children confided to their superintendence, judge of their progress, and designate those to whom liberty may be restored without danger: but then even when a child leaves the house of refuge in consequence of good conduct, he does not cease to be under the supervision of the managers during minority; and if he does not realize the hopes which had been entertained, the latter have the right to call him back to the house of refuge, and may employ the most rigorous means in order to effect it. *

Some objections have been made in Pennsylvania against the right granted to the houses of refuge to receive individuals who had neither committed a crime nor incurred a conviction.† Such a power, it was said, is contrary to the Constitution of the United States: it was added, that the power of the managers to shorten or prolong, at their pleasure, the duration of detention, is arbitrary, and cannot be tolerated in a free society. It would have been difficult to refute theoretically these objections, but the public saw that the houses of refuge alleviated the fate of juvenile criminals, instead of aggravating it, and that the children brought into it without being convicted, were not the victims of persecution, but merely deprived of a fatal liberty.

Nobody raises at present his voice against the houses of refuge. Yet we see with how much reserve the functions of those must be exercised, who have the power of sending children thither; if we consider that they have the right to withdraw a child from its parents in order to place it in the establishment, and that they must exercise this authority every time that the parents have to reproach themselves with the disorderly conduct of their child. The law has foreseen the possibility of abuse, and has endeavoured to provide a remedy: the child has, according to the law, the right of protection by the ordinary judge against the decision of the functionary who sends it to the refuge. The parents have the same right: and it is not unfrequently exercised.

For the rest, it is not persecution or tyranny which are to be dreaded in these establishments. However necessary it may be that a house of refuge should not present the severity and the discipline of a prison, it would be equally dangerous if it had the too indulgent and too intellectual discipline of a school. But if

* This can scarcely be the case, unless the child has been *indentured* by the managers —TRANS.

† This seems a mistake Children cannot be sent there who have not committed a crime . for poor children, who have none to take care of them, and become a charge on the public, and consequently vagrants, are considered, technically, criminal: *vagrancy* is a crime, though the result often of misfortune. The constitutional doubt was, as to the legality of confining children, merely charged with a crime, and not *convicted* of it —TRANS.

15

these establishments in America should deviate from their true end, it would be less from inclining too much to severity than leaning improperly to mildness.

The fundamental principles upon which the houses of refuge rest, are simple ; in New York and Philadelphia, the children are separated during night in solitary cells ; during the day they may communicate with each other.* The separation during night seems to be indispensably necessary from a regard to good morals; it may be dispensed with during day ; absolute isolation would be intolerable to children, and silence could not be maintained among them without punishments, the violence of which alone must make us repugnant to them. There would be, besides, the greatest disadvantages in depriving them of social relations, without which their intellectual progress would be checked.

In Boston they are separated neither night nor day. We have not remarked that in this house of refuge any disadvantage results from their sleeping together ; but their danger is, in our opinion, not the less, and it is avoided in Boston only by a zeal and vigilance altogether extraordinary, which it would be a mistake to expect, in general, even from persons the most devoted to their duties

The time of the children is divided between the instruction which they receive, and the various labours which they have to learn and to perform : they are taught that elementary knowledge which will be useful to them in the course of their lives, and a mechanical art, which, at some future period, may furnish them the means of subsistence. Their intellectual occupations give to the establishment the aspect of a primary school, and their manual labour in the workshop is the same with that in the prison. These two different traits are the characteristics of a house of refuge.

Their patrons do not limit themselves to a development of the minds of the children, and the skill of their hands ; an effort is made above all to cultivate their hearts, and to inculcate the principles of religion and morals. Mr. Hart, superintendent of the house of refuge in New York, often told us, that he should consider any success attendant on his efforts altogether impossible without the aid of religion.

When a young delinquent arrives at the house of refuge, the superintendent acquaints him with the regulations of the establishment, and gives him, for the guidance of his conduct, two rules, remarkable for their simplicity: 1. never lie ; 2. do the best you can. The superintendent inscribes his name in the great register of conduct. This register is destined to contain all the information relative to the children. It states, as accurately as

* Not, however, whilst they are engaged in labour. —TRANS.

possible, their previous life, their conduct during their stay in the house, and after they have left the establishment. The child is then placed in the class proper for its age, and its known morality.* Mr. Hart, of New York, defines the first class as that composed of the children who never swear, never lie, never make use of obscene or indecorous expressions, and who are equally zealous in the school and in the workshop. According to Mr. Wells, of Boston, this same class is composed of those who make positive, regular, and constant efforts towards being good.

In Boston, the admission of a child into the house of refuge is accompanied by circumstances which have appeared to us worthy of being reported   the establishment forms a small society, upon the model of society at large. In order to be received in it, it is not only necessary to know its laws, and to submit to them freely, but also to be received as a member of the society by all those who compose it already. The reception takes place after the individual in question has gone through the fixed period of trial, if the candidate is not rejected by a majority of the votes of the little members composing this interesting society.†

In every house of refuge the inmates are divided into good and bad classes Their conduct makes the children pass from one into the other. The good classes enjoy privileges which the bad ones are denied ; and the latter are subject to privations which the former have not to undergo ‡

Eight hours, at the least, are assigned every day to labour in the workshops, where the children are occupied with useful arts, such as shoe-making, joiner's work, cloth-making, carpenter's work, &c. Four hours daily are spent in the school. After rising, and before going to bed, prayers are offered. Three meals take half an hour each ; in short, there are about fifteen hours of the day occupied with study, labour, &c , and nine hours with rest. Such is, with little difference, the order established in New York and Philadelphia. This order is the same every day, and only varies according to the change of the seasons, which has an influence upon the hour of rising and retiring. The house of refuge in Boston differs from the above mentioned , the intellectual part of education occupies here a more prominent place. Only five hours and a half are daily occupied by labour in the work-

---

* Mr. Hart puts a child, on his arrival at the refuge, always in a good moral class, or which is the same, gives him the badge of those who conduct themselves well, whatever may have been the child's previous conduct , thus obliterating, as it were, his former misconduct, and giving him at once a chance to be and to be acknowledged a good child —Trans

† See Rules for the House of Reformation in Boston, in the Appendix.

‡ See the various regulations for the houses of refuge in Boston, New York, and Philadelphia.

shops; four hours are passed in the school, more than one hour is spent in religious instruction, and all the children have two hours and a quarter every day for recreation. These hours of recreation are not the least profitable ones to the children. Mr. Wells, the superintendent of the Boston house of refuge, takes part in their games, and whilst their bodies are developed by gymnastic exercises, their moral character forms itself under the influence of a superior man, who, we may say, becomes a child with them, and whose authority is never greater than at the moment when he does not make them feel it.

The children learn in the school, reading, writing, and arithmetic; they also receive some instruction in history and geography. The Lancasterian method of mutual instruction has been adopted in all of them. The children in general show great facility in learning It has been often remarked in America, that the houses of refuge are composed of a class of children more intelligent than others; the nature of these establishments itself explains this fact: in general, children abandoned by their families, or who have escaped from their homes, and for this reason have been early reduced to their own resources, and constrained to find within themselves the means of subsistence, are received here. It is therefore not surprising that they should make rapid progress in their learning. Most of them have, moreover, a restless, adventurous mind, anxious for knowledge. This disposition, which first led them to ruin, becomes now, in the school, a powerful cause of success. No useful books which they desire for their information are withheld from them. In Philadelphia, there are in the library of the establishment more than fifteen hundred volumes, which are all for the use of the children.

The hours of labour are fixed invariably for all, and none are absolved from them. Nevertheless, a task is given, after the performance of which, the young inmate of the house of refuge, who is more active than the others, may amuse himself.

The superintendence of the children in the school and workshops, does not cease in the hours of leisure. They play freely with each other; but gambling of whatever kind is strictly prohibited.

All things in their discipline are favourable to health. Every day they are obliged to wash their feet and hands. They are always dressed cleanly; and their food, though coarse, is abundant and healthy. None are allowed to eat any thing but what is prescribed by the ordinary discipline; water is the only beverage. There is no shop in which the children may obtain food or drink, and great pains are taken that they do not procure it by communications with persons out of the establishment.

Food, clothing, and bedding, are furnished by the administration. The labour of the children alone is let out by contract;

and the restrictions which abound in the contract are such, that the contractor can have no kind of influence in the establishment.

In New York and Philadelphia, eight hours a day are given to the contractor; in Boston, five hours and a half only. The contractor, or his agents, come into the establishment to teach the various arts. For the rest, they are not allowed to have any conversation with the children, nor can they retain them a minute longer than the fixed time. It will be easily understood, that, with such conditions, it is not possible to stipulate advantageously in a pecuniary respect with the contractors: but the children are not made to work in order to yield profit; the only object in view is to give them habits of industry, and to teach them a useful trade.*

It is therefore not surprising that the support of the houses of refuge costs more than other penitentiary establishments. On the one hand, the young inmates are better fed and clothed than convicts, and a greater expense is incurred for their instruction; and, on the other, their labour does not yield as much as that of criminals who are sent for a long time into the prisons. So also, as we shall soon see, the young pupil of the house of refuge leaves the establishment as soon as he can be placed anywhere else with advantage. Liberty is restored to him when he knows a trade; that is to say, at the moment when his labour would become productive to the establishment.

The administration of the American houses of refuge is almost entirely *en régie;* that is, it manages its own supplies without contract; it is justly believed that the system of contract, applied to all the branches of administration, would be irreconcilable with the moral management which the nature of the establishment requires.

Though, on the whole, the subsistence of the young prisoners is expensive, every thing seems to be calculated to avoid unnecessary expense. The houses of refuge contain both boys and girls, who, though under the same roof, are perfectly separated from each other. But this circumstance permits some labour to be done by the girls, which, if it were performed by others,

---

* The reader sees, that, in the United States, nothing similar exists to what is practised with us. In the *Maison des Madelonettes,* destined in Paris for young prisoners, discipline is entirely invaded by the contractor. He considers every child as his property; and, if it is intended to give instruction to the juvenile prisoners, the contractor does not permit it. "*I am robbed,*" he says, "*of the time which belongs to me.*" He regards merely his own interest, that of the children does not concern him. Thus he only thinks how he can turn their labour to the greatest profit. As it requires time to learn a mechanical profession, he rarely takes the trouble to teach it to them, he prefers occupying them with certain manual labours, which require neither skill nor experience, such as making pasteboard, *agraferie,* &c, &c. These labours, productive for him, are of no use to the children, who know no mechanical art when they leave the house.

would be a charge to the house. Thus they do the washing, mend the clothes, and make the greater part of their own dresses, and those worn by the boys, they also do all business in the kitchen for the whole house,* thus they are employed in a way useful for themselves, and for the house, whilst it would be difficult to give them any other productive work.

This order of things is established and maintained by disciplinary means, which we ought to examine. Two principal means are employed. punishments and rewards; but we must make a distinction upon this point, between the houses of refuge of New York and Philadelphia, and that of Boston.

In the two first establishments, the punishments inflicted for disobeying the discipline, are:

1. Privation of recreation;
2. Solitary confinement in a cell;
3. Reduction of food to bread and water;
4. In important cases, corporal punishment—that is to say, stripes.†

In New York, the house is expressly authorized to apply stripes. In Philadelphia, the regulations do not permit them expressly, but merely do not prohibit them. The distribution of punishments belongs to the superintendent, who has a discretionary power in the establishment.

Whilst the refractory children are subjected to these various punishments, according to the character of their offence, distinctions of honour are accorded to the children whose conduct is good. Besides the honour of belonging to the first class, those who distinguish themselves in this, wear badges of honour; lastly, the superintendent designates among the best, a certain number of monitors, to whom he confides part of the *surveillance* with which he is charged himself and this testimony of confidence is for those whom he has chosen—a distinction to which they attach great value.

In Boston, corporal chastisements are excluded from the house of refuge; the discipline of this establishment is entirely of a moral character, and rests on principles which belong to the highest philosophy.

Every thing there tends to elevate the soul of the young prisoners, and to render them jealous of their own esteem and that of their comrades: to arrive at this end, they are treated as if they were men and members of a free society.

We treat of this theory with reference to discipline, because

---

* This latter is at least not the case in the house of refuge of New York, where a few boys do the kitchen work, by a very judicious application of a steam engine. We do not know how it is in the others.—TRANS.

† We ought to add here, that the whole discipline is kept up with great paternal kindness —TRANS.

it has appeared to us, that the high opinion instilled into the child, of his own morality and social condition, is not only fit to effect his reformation, but also, the best means to obtain from him entire submission.

First, it is a principle well established in the house, that nobody can be punished for a fault, not provided for, either by the divine law, or those of the country or the establishment. Thus the first principle in criminal matters, is also established in the house of refuge. The regulations contain the following principle: "As man is not capable of punishing disrespect or irreverence to God; therefore, if a boy be irregular in his behaviour at religious services, he shall not be allowed to attend them—leaving the punishment with a higher power, and for a future day."

In the house of refuge in Boston, the child, withdrawn from religious service, incurs, in the opinion of his comrades and of himself, the severest of all punishments.

In another place it is expressed, that the children shall not be required to denounce the offences of their comrades,* and in the article which follows, it is added, that nobody should be punished for a fault sincerely avowed. We know in France, public establishments, in which this denunciation is encouraged, and where it is practised by the better subjects of the house †

A book of conduct exists, likewise, in Boston, where every one has his account of good and bad marks, but that which distinguishes this register from those of other houses of refuge is, that in Boston, each child gives his own mark. Every evening the young inmates are successively asked; every one is called upon to judge his own conduct during the day; and it is upon his declaration that the mark, indicating his conduct, is inscribed. Experience has shown that the children always judge themselves more severely than they would have been judged by others, and not unfrequently it is found necessary, to correct the severity and even the injustice of their own sentence

If any difficulty arises in the classification of morality, or whenever an offence against the discipline has been committed, a judgment takes place. Twelve little jurymen, taken from among the children of the establishment, pronounce the condemnation or the acquittal of the accused.

Each time that it becomes necessary to elect among them an officer or monitor, the little community meets, proceeds to the election, and the candidate having most votes is proclaimed presi-

* This excellent rule is as follows "No boy shall be required to give information of the faults of another, nor shall he be allowed so to do, unless he be apparently conscientious in it "—TRANS

† See in Vidocq, to what frightful consequences this evil practice leads.

dent. Nothing is more grave than the manner in which these electors and jurymen of tender years discharge their functions.

The reader will pardon us for having dwelt so long on this system; and for having pointed out its minutest details. We need not say that we do not consider this an infant republic in good earnest. But we believed ourselves obliged to analyze a system so remarkable for its originality. There is, however, more depth in these political plays, which agree so well with the institutions of the country, than we would suppose at first glance. The impressions of childhood and the early use of liberty, contribute, perhaps, at a later period, to make the young delinquents more obedient to the laws. And without considering this possible political result, it is certain, that such a system is powerful as a means of moral education.

In fact, it is easy to conceive the elasticity of which the youthful mind is capable, when all the sentiments proper to elevate it above itself are called into action.

The discipline is, however, fitted still more for those cases where the moral means which we have just indicated, prove insufficient.

Children, whose conduct is correct, enjoy great privileges.

They alone participate in the elections, and are alone eligible; the vote of those who belong to the first class, counts for two— a kind of double vote, of which the others cannot be jealous, because it depends upon themselves alone to obtain the same privilege. With the good are deposited the most important keys of the house; they go out freely, and have the right to leave their place, when the children are assembled, without needing a peculiar permission; they are believed on their word, on all occasions; and their birth day is celebrated All the good do not enjoy these privileges, but whoever belongs to a good class, has a right to some of these prerogatives. The punishments, to which the bad children are subject, are the following:

Privation of the electoral right, and the right of being elected; they are not allowed to come into the room of the superintendent, nor to speak to him without permission, nor are they allowed to converse with their comrades; lastly, if it should be required, a physical punishment is applied Sometimes "bracelets" are put on, sometimes, the offender is blindfolded; or he is shut up in a solitary cell. Such is the system of the house of refuge in Boston.*

---

* See the rules for this house of reformation at the end of the volume (So far the authors) The system of education and correction which Mr. Wells has established in the house of reformation in Boston, is one of those subjects which cannot but be misunderstood, if it be exhibited in a rapid sketch, because it is founded on so original a basis. Yet it has appeared to us to be planned with great wisdom, and to be executed with a profound knowledge of the human

That of the establishments of New York and Philadelphia, though infinitely less remarkable, is perhaps better : not that the Boston house of refuge does not appear to be admirably conducted, and superior to both the others ; but its success seems to us less the effect of the system itself, than that of the distinguished man who puts it into practice

We have already said that the great defect of this house of refuge is, that the children sleep together :* the system, moreover, which is established there, rests upon an elevated theory, which could not be always perfectly understood ; and its being put into practice would cause great difficulties, if the superintendent should not find immense resources in his own mind to triumph over them.

In New York and Philadelphia, on the contrary, the theory is simple The isolation during night, the classification during day, the labour, the instruction—every thing, in such an order of things, is easily understood It neither requires a profound genius to invent such a system, nor a continual effort to maintain it. To sum up the whole, the Boston discipline belongs to a species of ideas much more elevated than that established in New York and Philadelphia, but it is difficult in practice.

The system of these last establishments, founded upon a theory much more simple, has the merit of being within reach of all the world. It is possible to find superintendents who are fit for the Philadelphia system : but we cannot hope to meet often with such men as Mr. Wells.

In spite of the well-marked difference between the two systems, of which one can be practised only by superior men, whilst the other is on the level of ordinary minds, we must acknowledge that, both in the one and the other case, the success of the houses of refuge essentially depends upon the superintendent. It is he who puts the principles upon which the system acts into action ; and he must, in order to arrive at a happy result, unite in his person a great number of qualities, the union of which is as necessary as rare.

If a model of a superintendent of a house of refuge were required, a better one, perhaps, it would be impossible to find,

---

soul. To convey however to the reader a correct idea of this peculiar institution, a minute description, far exceeding that, for the length of which our authors even begged the reader's pardon, would be required   We can only say, that it appeared to us one of the most peculiar, most interesting, and most heart-cheering subjects, which, in all our travels, has ever come to our knowledge, and which must be seen and personally inquired into, in order to be perfectly understood   We know of no instructer who has seen deeper into the human heart, and knows more thoroughly to what principles in the human soul he safely may apply, than Mr. Wells —TRANS.

* We believe that it is no defect, as a part of Mr. Wells's whole system.— TRANS.

than that which is presented by Mr. Wells, and Mr. Hart. A
constant zeal, an indefatigable vigilance, are their lesser qualities;
to minds of great capacity, they join an equanimity of character,
the firmness of which does not exclude mildness. They believe
in the religious principles which they teach; and have confidence in their own efforts. Endowed with deep sensibility, they
obtain still more from the children, by touching their hearts,
than by addressing their understandings. Finally, they consider
each young delinquent as their child; it is not a profession which
they perform: it is a duty they are happy to fulfil.

We have seen how the youth enters the house of refuge, and
what discipline he is subjected to.

Let us at present examine by what means he may obtain the
restoration of liberty, and let us follow him into the society
which he re-enters.

The principle above laid down, that the inmate of a house of
refuge does not undergo a punishment, finds here, again, its application As he has been sent to the house for his own interest
only, he is allowed to leave it as soon as his interest requires it.

Therefore, as soon as he has learnt a trade, if, during one or
several years, he has acquired moral and industrious habits, he
is believed to be capable of becoming a useful member of society.
Yet absolute and complete liberty is not restored to him; because, what would become of him in the world, alone, without
support, unknown by any body?—He would find himself precisely in the same situation in which he was, before he entered
the house. This great danger is avoided: the superintendent
waits for a good opportunity to bind him out as apprentice with
some mechanic, or to place him as a servant in some respectable
family; he avoids sending him into a city, where he would relapse into his bad habits, and find again the companions of his
disorderly life; and every time an opportunity offers, employment for him, with farmers, is preferred.* At the moment he
leaves the establishment, a writing is given to him, which, in
kind words, contains advice for his future conduct; the present
of a Bible is added.

In general, it has been found inconvenient to restore liberty to
these juvenile offenders, before they have been in the house at
least one year, in order to acquire habits of order.†

Leaving the house of refuge, he does not cease to belong to
the establishment, which, binding him out as an apprentice, re-
serves all the rights of a guardian over him; if he leave the
master with whom he has been placed, he is, according to the
law, brought back to the house of refuge, where he must again

* Provided there is no special reason to let him enter another profession, e. g.
his peculiar wish, &c.—Trans.

† If we remember right, one year is considered to be sufficient with most.—
Trans.

remain until he has given a new proof that shows him worthy of liberty. In fine, he may be successively brought back to the establishment, and restored to liberty, as often as the managers think it necessary; and their power, in this respect, does not cease, until the individual in question has arrived at the age of eighteen, if a female; and of twenty, if a boy.

During his apprenticeship, the child is the object of continued attention, by the house of refuge. The superintendent corresponds with him, and endeavours to keep him in the path of virtue by his advice; and the youth writes on his part to the superintendent, and more than once the latter has received letters from young delinquents, full of touching expressions of gratitude.

Now, what results have been obtained? Is the system of these establishments conducive to reform? and are we able to support the theory by statistical numbers?

If we consider merely the system itself, it seems difficult not to allow its efficiency. If it be possible to obtain moral reformation for any human being, it seems that we ought to expect it for these youths, whose misfortune was caused less by crime, than by inexperience, and in whom all the generous passions of youth may be excited. With a criminal, whose corruption is inveterate, and deeply rooted, the feeling of honesty is not awakened, because the sentiment is extinct; with a youth, this feeling exists, though it has not yet been called into action. It seems to us, therefore, that a system which corrects evil dispositions, and inculcates correct principles, which gives a protector and a profession to him who has none, habits of order and labour to the vagrant and beggar whom idleness had corrupted; elementary instruction and religious principles to the child whose education had been neglected; it seems to us, we say, that a similar system must be fertile of beneficial effects

There are, however, cases in which it is almost impossible to obtain the reformation of juvenile offenders; thus experience has taught the superintendents, that the reformation of girls, who have contracted bad morals, is a chimera which it is useless to pursue As to boys, the most difficult to be corrected are those who have contracted habits of theft and intemperance; their regeneration, however, is not so desperate a task as that of girls who have been seduced, or have become prostitutes. *

It is also generally thought in the United States, that it is necessary to avoid receiving, in the house of refuge, boys above six-

---

* The experience of Mr. Kopf, superintendent of the house of refuge in Berlin, has taught him the same; and, if we recollect aright, he told us that he has found the correction of girls altogether more difficult than that of boys, though he is assisted in his laudable work by his excellent wife. The reason why it is so much more difficult to redeem a girl who has been a prostitute, than any other young delinquent, seems to us very easy to be explained, from the nature of

teen, and girls over fourteen years; after this age, their reformation is rarely obtained by the discipline of these establishments, which is less fit for them than the austere discipline of
the prisons

In Philadelphia, it is believed, that more than half of the children who have left the refuge, have conducted themselves well.*

Being desirous of ascertaining ourselves the effects produced
by the house of refuge in New York, we made a complete
analysis of the great register of conduct, and examining separately the page of each child, who had left the refuge, investigated what was its conduct since its return into society.†

Of four hundred and twenty-seven male juvenile offenders, sent
back into society, eighty-five have conducted themselves well,
and the conduct of forty-one has been excellent. Of thirty-four,
the information received is bad; and, of twenty-four, very bad.
Of thirty-seven among them, the information is doubtful; of
twenty-four, rather good than otherwise, and of fourteen, rather
bad than good.

Of eighty-six girls who have returned into society from the
house of refuge, thirty-seven have conducted themselves well,
eleven in an excellent manner, twenty-two bad, and sixteen very
bad. The information concerning ten is doubtful; three seem to
have conducted themselves rather well, and three rather bad than
otherwise.

Thus of five hundred and thirteen children who have returned
from the house of refuge of New York into society, more than
two hundred have been saved from infallible ruin, and have
changed a life of disorder and crime for one of honesty and
order.

female character, according to which, chastity has acquired a greater moral importance for women than for men Girls, destined much more for tranquil and
passive virtues than men, act still more against their nature, and, therefore, sink
deeper, by giving themselves up to vagrancy, and the crimes following from it,
(for which they are sent to the house of refuge,) than boys, whom the Creator
has destined to push, at some future period, their way in the agitated scenes of
life; and, in proportion as girls deviate from their moral nature, the difficulty increases of bringing them back, the more they degenerate, the more difficult it
is to restore their moral health —TRANS.

  * See Conversation with the superintendent of the house of refuge in Philadelphia Appendix, No 15

  † All materials which could be of any use to us in this inquiry, have been put
at our disposal with the greatest kindness; and, as we found ourselves in possession of original materials, we were enabled to form an exact opinion upon the
conduct of all children after they had left the refuge. Our inquiry extended to
all children admitted in the refuge, from the 1st of January, 1825, to the 1st of
January, 1829 Since the latter year, many individuals have been admitted, and
have left the house of refuge of New York. but the latter have been too short
a time in society to afford an opportunity of judging of their thorough or apparent
reformation; to be decisive, the proof must be of a longer continuance (So far
the authors.) We would refer the reader to the annual reports of the New York
house of refuge, for some interesting letters of persons who have been in the
refuge.—TRANS.

CHAPTER II.

Application of the system of houses of refuge to our "houses of correction."—
State of our penal legislation in relation to children under sixteen years, and
detained for crimes and offences, or by way of precaution —They corrupt each
other in the prisons —Modifications to be made in the penal legislation and in
the discipline of the houses of correction.

If France should borrow from the American houses of refuge
some principles on which these establishments are erected, she
would remedy one of the chief vices of her prisons.

According to our laws, the criminals, under the age of sixteen,
are not to be confounded with convicts of maturer years; and the
law gives the name of house of correction to the place where
they are detained. Yet, with very rare exceptions, the young
delinquents and the old criminals are placed together in our prisons Nay more: it is well known that the child not yet sixteen
years old, who has been acquitted on account of want of judgment, is nevertheless, according to circumstances, rendered to
its parents, or conducted into a house of correction, in order to
be *educated and detained (elevé et détenu)* during such a number of years as the judgment of the court shall determine, and
which never exceeds the period of his arrival at his twentieth
year.

Thus, if a child, accused of a crime, is acquitted, the courts
have the right to send it back to its parents, or into a "house of
correction." This alternative makes it easy to comprehend the
intention of the law. The parents receive it, if they show a
guaranty of morality, and the child is restored to them, that
they may correct its evil dispositions and reform its bad habits.
On the contrary, if the judges have good reason to believe, that
the faults of the child are owing to the fatal example of its own
family, they will take care not to restore the child to it, where
it would only accomplish its corruption; and they, therefore,
send it into a house of correction, which will be less a prison
than a school; it will be *educated and detained,* says the law.
Now, we ask, is the intention of the legislature fulfilled? and
do the young prisoners receive the education which it was the
intention of the law to procure for the unfortunate child?

It can be said that, in general, the prisons, in which with us
the juvenile offenders are detained, are but schools of crime; so

that all the judges who know the corrupting discipline of these prisons, are averse to condemn an arrested youth, whatever may be the evidence of his offence; they rather acquit him and restore him to liberty than contribute on their part further to corrupt him, by sending him into one of the prisons; but this indulgence, the motive of which is so easily understood, is not the less fatal to the guilty, who find in this impunity an encouragement to crime.

There is also a right sanctioned by our civil laws, and the operation of which is in some sort suspended by the defect of our prisons: we mean the power which belongs to the parents of causing those of their children, who are minors and whose conduct is reprehensible, to be detained in a prison.

What parents would use their authority, if they knew into what a den of corruption their children would be thrown?

There is then in this respect a void in the system of our prisons which it is important to fill. This would be obtained by establishing houses of refuge or correction founded upon the principles of those of which we have given a picture

It would certainly be difficult to adopt entirely the American system: thus, the power given in the United States to all officers of the police to send children, whose conduct is suspicious, into the house of refuge, though no specific offence be imputed to them; and the extraordinary right which they have even of taking a child from his parents if they do not take sufficient care of its education, would not all this be contrary to our customs and laws?*

But the discipline of the American houses of refuge would have great advantages in France if only applied to young convicts, or to those who, without being declared guilty, are to be detained during a fixed time in consequence of a positive judgment.

If our houses of correction, the viciousness of which frightens the courts, should undergo a reform, the magistrates would send

* In order to understand our authors, the reader must remember what an immense difference exists between a French police officer, the member of a powerful and independent body, extending with its million arms over the whole country, and an American police officer, a harmless and comparatively powerless single individual, under the constant *surveillance* of public opinion, which in a country where public life is so public, is a police unequalled in watchfulness by that of any body of paid officers Every thing depends in such matters upon circumstances. An officer in the United States never ceases to be and to *feel* as a citizen; he is in this respect essentially different from a government officer on the continent of Europe. We may add further the remark we before made, as to the supervisory power of the judiciary—and also, that in Pennsylvania, at least, (we are not so well informed in regard to the other states,) the power by no means exists to the extent stated by the authors The authority to commit to the refuge is confined to courts, magistrates, and guardians of the poor, and is not granted to police officers—and is limited too to the cases of crimes or offences committed by children. See what we have said on this point in a previous note —TRANS.

there without repugnance a number of young delinquents, vagrants, beggars, &c., who abound in all our cities, and whom an idle life leads infallibly to crime. This reform might be effected by building, in the houses of correction, solitary cells, which would prevent communication during night, and by the adoption of a system of instruction and labour, analogous to that which is practised in New York and Philadelphia.

It would be necessary, however, to make an important change in our legislation, in order to insure success to the houses of correction in France

The greater part of the happy results crowning the endeavours of the American houses of refuge, are principally owing to the discretionary power with which the managers of these establishments are invested, to retain or return to society according to their pleasure, the children of whom they have received the guardianship; they use this right for the interest of the young delinquent, for whom they endeavour to find an advantageous place, as an apprentice; and each time that a favourable opportunity offers itself, they can avail themselves of it, because they have unlimited authority over the children sent to the refuge.

According to our laws, the director of a house of correction could do nothing like it; he would be obliged, in order to restore liberty to a young delinquent, to wait for the expiration of the period fixed by the judgment. What would be the consequence ? that, on leaving the house of correction, the child would find itself as embarrassed respecting its fate as previously to its being sent to the refuge : it would be full of good resolutions and principles, but incapable of putting them into practice.

It seems to us that a single modification of article sixty-sixth of the penal code, would greatly remedy this inconvenience.

The young delinquents, under the age of sixteen years, are of two kinds: those who, having acted with discretion, are declared guilty and convicted, and those who, having acted without discretion, have been acquitted but are detained for the sake of their education. Respecting the first, their fate is positively settled by the judgment and ought to be so; they have committed a crime, they must suffer the punishment One is but a corollary to the other. This punishment and its duration can be pronounced only by the courts; if it is fixed, it must be suffered to its whole extent, according to the terms of the judgment: in this case, the special interest of the child is of little importance; it is not only for the purpose of correction, that it is imprisoned : it is particularly for the interest of society and the sake of example that the punishment is inflicted.

But the child acquitted in consideration of its want of discretion, stands in a different position : it is detained in a house of correction, not in order to secure its person, but because it is thought that it will be in a better place than in its own family; a good education is afforded, which it would not find elsewhere; it is looked upon as unfortunate only, and society takes upon itself to give that which fortune has denied. It is not for public vengeance, but for its personal interest, that it is placed in the house of correction : as it has committed no crime, no punishment is to be inflicted upon it.

In respect to the young prisoners who are in this position, it seems to us that the duration of their stay in the house of correction ought not to be fixed by the courts. We appreciate the position, that the judicial authority alone ought to retain the power of sending them there, according to the circumstances, of which it has the opportunity of judging; but why should they be burthened at the same time with determining the number of years during which the education of a child may be completed? As if it were possible to foresee, in each case, the time which may be requisite for the correction of the vices, and the reformation of the evil inclinations of a child!

Would it not be more judicious to invest the inspectors and directors of the house with the guardianship over children whose education is confided to them, and with all the rights which appertain to the guardianship?

If it were so, the directors of the establishment would study the dispositions of the children placed under their authority; they would be able to seize with much more advantage upon the favourable moment to restore them to liberty; the time during which a child would have to remain in the house of correction, would thus be determined in a much more judicious way. And if a good opportunity should offer itself for one among them to be indentured as an apprentice, or in any other way, the directors would make use of it.

Even if all the advantages should not result from this change which it promises, something would already be gained, by effacing from our laws the provision in question. This provision is in fact the source of the worst abuses : it will surprise us little if we consider that the law confers a power upon the courts, without furnishing, at the same time, a rule for its exercise. Thus it empowers the court to send to the house of correction, for a certain number of years, (at its discretion,) children acquitted in consideration of want of judgment; but upon what principle do they adjudge the number of years which the child has to stay in the house of correction? The law is silent on this point : the courts themselves are ignorant respecting it. If a court pronounce a punishment, it is measured by the offence; but by what standard shall the stay in the house of refuge be measured by anticipation, if the education of a child is in question, whose intellectual state is unknown to the judges, and of whose future progress they can know nothing?

This impossibility of finding a basis for the sentence, produces a completely arbitrary execution of the law. The judges will condemn a child to be detained until his fifteenth or twentieth year, without having the least standard to go by: this badly defined authority causes often the most revolting decisions.

A child of a less age than sixteen appears before a court The first question is as to its capacity: if it is adjudged to have acted with discretion, it is sentenced to be detained in the house of correction; as this is a punishment pronounced by the court, it is proportionate to the offence, which appears not very grave, considering the youth of the convicted prisoner. It will, therefore, receive a sentence of some months imprisonment only.

Let us suppose another youth of the same age indicted; his offence is light, and the court finds he has acted without sufficient discretion. This youth will be sent for several years to the house of correction, to be *educated and detained* indeed, but, in fact, to be locked up in the same prison with the first, with this difference only, that he remains there a long time, whilst the former, who has been declared guilty, passes but a short time in the same place.

Thus it may be justly said, that for offenders under sixteen years, it is better to be found guilty than to be acquitted. Whoever has any experience in the administration of criminal justice, will acknowledge the defect which we point out; it is a defect not to be imputed to the magistrate, but belongs altogether to the law and its operation. This evil would be remedied in a great degree, in all cases in which children are detained without being convicted, if the courts would merely decree their detention in the house of correction, without fixing irrevocably the period of detention; by the sentence, the directors of the house would be authorized to retain the child for a fixed period, but it would be lawful for them to restore him to liberty before the expiration of the term, if circumstances permitted. They would not retain the child longer than the fixed period, but they would be at liberty to retain him for a shorter period.

It seems, therefore, to us, that a great advantage would result from a change of the provision of the law in question. The houses of correction would then become, in the true meaning of the word, houses of refuge, and they would be able to exercise upon the mind of the young delinquent a salutary influence, which, in the actual state of our legislation, is unattainable. We only indicate here the principal changes which would be requisite to arrive at this end: many questions connected with this subject, ought to be discussed and investigated, if a reform is to be produced fertile of happy results. Thus it would first be

17

necessary to examine which would be the best means of interesting public opinion in the success of this reform; to determine
the elements which shall compose the houses of refuge ; to fix
the principles of their organization, and to discuss the question,
"where and in what number ought they to be established?" &c.
All these questions, and many others which we pass over in
silence, must be submitted to the investigation of men enlightened and versed in the knowledge of our laws, our customs, and
the actual state of our prisons.

If this discipline should be introduced among us, pains ought
to be taken to remove every thing which is of a nature to im-
pede its success in this country.

We have already spoken of the danger, which is the most difficult to be avoided in this matter, viz , the difficulty of keeping
a house of refuge in the proper medium between a school and a
prison. In the United States, the houses of refuge approach, perhaps, too much to the former, and this defect may become fatal
to them, when children, instigated by their parents themselves,
may wish to find advantages denied them in their family. It
ought, therefore, to be kept in mind, that these establishments, to
fulfil their true object, must preserve, though differing from a
prison, part of its severity, and that the comfort as well as the
moral instruction which the children are sure to find in the house
of refuge, ought not to be such as to make their fate enviable by
children whose life is irreproachable.

We may, on this occasion, remind our readers of a truth which
cannot be neglected without danger, viz , that the abuse of philanthropic institutions is as fatal to society as the evil itself
which they are intended to cure.

APPENDIX.

ON PENAL COLONIES.

Introduction.

We believe it necessary to make a few introductory observations, before we treat of the question of penal colonies, because we have observed that in France, the general opinion is in favour of the system of transportation. Many have declared themselves in favour of this punishment, and writers of talent have extolled its effect If public opinion should advance in this direction, and should induce government to follow it, France would find herself engaged in an enterprise, the expenses of which would be immense and the success very uncertain.

Such, at least, is our conviction ; and fully persuaded of these dangers, we hope to be pardoned if we treat them somewhat in detail

The system of transportation presents some advantages which we do not hesitate to acknowledge.

Of all punishments, that of transportation is the only one which, without being cruel, frees society from the presence of the guilty.

The imprisoned criminal may break his chains; restored to liberty on the expiration of his sentence, he becomes an object of well founded fear to all who surround him ; the transported criminal re-appears but rarely in his native country ; with him, a fertile germ of disorder and new crimes is removed.

This advantage is undoubtedly great; and it cannot but strike the thinking part of a nation, with whom the number of prisoners is increasing, and in the midst of whom, already arises a whole people of malefactors.

The system of exportation, therefore, rests upon a true idea, peculiarly fit by its simplicity to strike the mind of the mass, which has not the time to investigate the subject. We do not know what to do with the criminals at home ; we therefore transport them to another clime.

Our subject is to show here, that this measure, apparently so simple, is surrounded in its execution by difficulties always very great, sometimes insurmountable; and that it does not effect even the chief object which those who adopt it have in view.

———•◦●◦•———

CHAPTER I.

DIFFICULTIES PRESENTED BY THE SYSTEM OF TRANSPORTATION
TREATED AS A QUESTION OF LAW.

The first difficulties are met with in the legislation itself.

To what criminals is transportation to be applied?

Shall it be only to those sentenced for life? In that case, the utility of the measure is extremely limited. The convicts for life form always but a very small number; they are already rendered harmless.

As to them, the political question becomes one of philanthropy, and nothing more.

The criminals, whom society has really an object in exiling far from itself, are those convicted for a limited time; who, on the expiration of their sentence, recover their liberty. But to those, the system of deportation cannot be applied without reserve.

Let us suppose that any individual, who has been transported, whatever may be the gravity of his crime, is prohibited from ever re-appearing in the mother country; in this way, we would have obtained, undoubtedly, the principal object which the legislator proposes to himself; but the punishment of transportation, thus understood, would meet with numerous obstacles in its application.

Its greatest defect would exist in its being entirely disproportionate to the nature of certain crimes, and that it would affect, in a similar way, individuals, the degree of whose guilt was essentially different. Assuredly the man doomed to perpetual imprisonment, and he for whom the law decrees but five years' privation of liberty, cannot be placed on the same level. Both, however, would end their days at a distance from their family and country. For the one, transportation would be an alleviation of punishment; for the other a severe aggravation. And by this new penal graduation, the least guilty would be the most severely punished

After having kept the criminals in the place of transportation until the time of the expiration of their punishment, should they, on the contrary, be furnished with the means of returning to their country ? But then we would miss the most important object of penal colonies, which is, gradually to exhaust the source of crime in the mother country, by making its authors disappear. It certainly cannot be believed, that the delivered convict returns to his country an honest man, by the mere circumstance of his having been to the antipodes, or of having made a voyage round the world. Colonies of criminals do not correct as penitentiaries do, by reforming the individual sent there. They change him by giving him other interests than that of crime; by creating a prospect of futurity for him: he does not reform, if he retain the idea of returning

The English give to the delivered convict, the often illusory power of returning to his native soil; but they do not furnish him with the means of doing it.

This system has other inconveniences; first, it does not prevent a great number of criminals, the most adroit and dangerous of all, from reappearing in the society which has banished them,* and, moreover, it creates in the colony, a class of men, who, having had the intention during the whole time of their punishment of returning to Europe, have not reformed; after the expiration of their sentence, these individuals are connected by no tie whatever with their new country, they ardently desire to return; they have no certain plan for futurity; and in consequence, no industry; their presence threatens the peace of the colony a hundred times more than that of the prisoners themselves, in all whose passions they participate, without being restrained by the same ties †

The system of transportation, therefore, presents, as a theory of law, a problem of difficult solution.

But its application presents still greater difficulties.

* From the report of Mr Bigge it is seen that each year a certain number of convicts arrive in New South Wales, who have been there previously

† See *L'Histoire des colonies pénales,* by Mr. Ernest de Blosseville. In all that we have to say on penal colonies, we shall often have occasion to refer to Mr Blosseville's work. This work, whose author seems favourable to the system of transportation, abounds in interesting facts and curious researches. It forms the most complete statement in French literature, on the British settlements in Australia.

CHAPTER II.

DIFFICULTIES OPPOSED TO THE ESTABLISHMENT OF A PENAL COLONY.

Choice of a fit place for its foundation.—Expenses of the first establishment.—
Difficulties and dangers which surround the infancy of the colony —Results
obtained by the penal colony ; It does not produce economy , It augments
the number of criminals —Budget of the Australian colonies —Increase of
crimes in England —Transport ation considered as a means of colonization —
It creates colonies hostile to the mother country.—Colonies founded in this
way always resent their origin —Example of Australia

It is certainly not a trifling enterprise to establish a colony,
even if it is intended to compose it of sound elements, and if
the mother country has in its power all desirable means of execution.

The history of the Europeans in the two Indies, shows but
too well the magnitude of the difficulties and dangers which
always surround the growth of similar settlements.

All these difficulties present themselves likewise in the foundation of a penal colony ; and many others in addition, peculiar to
this species of colonies

First, it is extremely difficult to find a convenient place for its
foundation : the considerations which must direct such a choice
are of a nature entirely peculiar : the country must be healthy ;
and, in general, an uninhabited country is not so during the first
twenty-five years of its clearing ; and if its climate differ essentially from that of Europe, the life of Europeans will always be
in great danger.

The desired country, therefore, should be situated precisely
between certain degrees of latitude.

We say that it is important that the soil of a colony should be
healthy from the beginning ; this necessity is much greater for
prisoners than for free colonists.

The convict is already enervated by his vices. He has been
subject, before his arrival at the place of his destination, to privations and fatigue, which have almost always more or less affected his health ; at the place of his exile he seldom has that energy,
and that physical and intellectual activity, which, even in an
unhealthy climate, often support the health of the free colonist,
and permit him to brave with impunity surrounding dangers.

There are many statesmen, and perhaps even some philanthropists, who would not be disturbed in their opinion by this
difficulty, and who would answer us, with perfect sincerity :
what matters it, after all, that these guilty persons go to die at
a distance ? Society, which rejects them, would not call for an
account of their fate. This answer does not satisfy us. We are
not systematically opposed to the punishment of death ; but we
believe that it must be legally inflicted , and we do not think
that men's lives can be taken away in a circuitous or fraudulent
way.

It is certainly an advantage for an ordinary colony to be situated near the mother country ; there is no explanation necessary
to make this understood

The first requisite of a penal colony is to be separated from
the mother country by an immense distance. It is necessary
that the prisoner should feel himself thrown into another world ;
obliged to create a new futurity for himself in the place which
he inhabits, and that the hope of return should appear like a
chimera; and how much will not this very chimera trouble the
imagination of the exile ? The transported criminal of Botany
Bay, separated from England by the whole diameter of the globe,
struggles yet to find a way to his country, through insurmountable perils.* In vain does his new country offer him peace and
comfort, he meditates only on returning, and plunging again
into the miseries of the old world In order to obtain a return
to the shores of Europe, a great number submit to the hardest
conditions ; several commit new crimes to procure thus the means
of transport which they want.

Penal colonies differ so essentially from ordinary colonies,
that the natural fertility of the soil may become one of the greatest obstacles to their establishment.

Transported convicts, it is easy to perceive, cannot be subjected to the same discipline as the inmates of our prisons They
cannot be locked up within four walls; because then it would
be better to have them retained in the mother country. It is
thought sufficient to regulate their actions, but' their liberty is
not entirely revoked.

If the soil, on which the penal establishment is founded, presents natural resources to the isolated individual; if it offers such
means of existence as in general the soil of the tropics presents;
if the climate is constantly mild, wild fruits abundant, and hunt-
ing easy, it will be readily imagined, that a great number of cri-

* During the first years of the colony, a pretty general belief existed among the
colonists that New Holland was connected with the continent of Asia Several
convicts attempted to escape by reaching Asia , most of them died in misery in
the woods, or were obliged to retrace their steps. It was very difficult to convince these unfortunate persons of their mistake.

minals will profit by the half liberty left to them, to fly into the
desert, and will exchange with pleasure the tranquillity of slavery
for the perils of a contested independence. They will form so
many enemies to the growing colony; and from the first day it
would be necessary to have arms in hand in a desert country.

If the continent, where the penal colony has been planted,
were peopled by semi-civilized tribes, the danger would be still
greater.

The European race has received from Providence, or has acquired by its own efforts, so incontestable a superiority over all
the other races which compose the great human family, that the
individual, placed with us, by his vices and his ignorance, on
the lowest step of society, is yet the first among savages.

The convicts will emigrate in numbers toward the aborigines;
they will become their assistants against the whites, and, generally, their chiefs

We do not reason here on a vague hypothesis: the danger
which we signalize, has made itself already strongly felt in Van
Diemen's land. From the first period of the establishment of the
English, a great number of convicts have fled into the woods:
there they have formed associations of stragglers; they have
united with the savages, have married their daughters, and adopted, partly, their customs. From this crossing of blood, a race
of mestizos has sprung up, more barbarous than the Europeans,
more civilized than the savages, whose hostility has, at all times,
disturbed the colony and sometimes brought it to the brink of
ruin.

We have indicated the difficulties which present themselves,
from the moment of a place being selected for the establishment
of a penal colony. These difficulties are not, by their nature,
insurmountable; since, after all, the place which we describe,
has been found by England. If they were the only difficulties,
perhaps it would be wrong to lose time in describing them: but
there are several others, which have an equal claim upon public
attention.

Let us then 'suppose the place to be selected; the country
where the penal colony is to be founded, to be on the other side
of the globe, uncultivated and desert. It would be necessary to
carry every thing thither, and to provide for every thing What
immense expenses are requisite for an establishment of this nature! No calculation can be based upon the zeal and industry
of the colonists, in order to supply the want of useful things, the
absence of which will always make itself felt, however great our
exertions may be to the contrary. Here, the colonist takes so
little interest in the undertaking, that he must be forced to sow
the grain which is to feed him. He would almost resign himself to a death of hunger, could he but disappoint the hopes of

the society which punishes him. Great calamities must therefore accompany the beginning of a similar colony.

It is sufficient to read the history of the English settlements in Australia, to be convinced of the truth of this remark. Three times the young colony of Botany Bay was near being destroyed by hunger and disease, and it was only by giving limited rations to the inhabitants, as to a crew of a wrecked vessel, that it was possible to wait for support from home

Perhaps there was negligence and inactivity on the part of the British government: but can we expect to avoid all faults and mistakes in a similar undertaking?

In the midst of a country, where every thing is yet to be created, where the free population is isolated, without support, surrounded by a crowd of malefactors, it is clear that it must be difficult to maintain order, and prevent revolts   This difficulty is particularly great in the first moment, when the criminals, as well as those who watch over them, are entirely occupied with the care of providing for their own necessities. The historians of Australia speak, in fact, of incessant plots, foiled only by the wisdom and firmness of the three first governors of the colony— Philip, Hunter, and King

The character and the talents of these three men must be rated very high, in estimating the success of the colony; and, if the British government is accused of inability in the direction of the affairs of this colony, it must not be forgotten, that it ably fulfils at least the task, perhaps the most difficult and most important of all, that of selecting competent agents.

We have supposed the place of transportation to be found ; we will even admit the first difficulties conquered. The penal colony exists; let us now examine its effects.

The first question which presents itself here, is:

Is it economical for the state to adopt the system of penal colonies?

If we turn aside from facts, in order to consult theory alone, we must be permitted to doubt the affirmative of this , because, admitting that the support of a penal colony costs the state less than prisons, certain it is, that its foundation exacts much greater expenses ; and, if it is economical to feed, maintain, and watch the convict in the place of his exile, it is extremely expensive to transport him there * Besides, all kinds of convicts cannot be sent to the colonies: the system of transportation, therefore, does not allow us to dispense with the erection of prisons

The writers, who, until the present time, have shown them-

* During the years 1828 and 1829, each convict in Australia cost the government, for transportation alone, twenty-six pounds sterling. See Legislative Documents sent by the British Parliament, vol. xxiii. page 25.

18

selves the most favourable to the colonization of criminals, have not denied that the foundation of such an establishment would be extremely onerous to the state. The reasons of this fact are easily conceived, and we may dispense with their exposition.

It has not yet been possible to determine with exactness how much it has cost to establish the Australian colonies; we only know that, from the year 1786 to 1819, a space of thirty-two years, Great Britain has spent for her penal colony 5,301,623 pounds sterling. It is certain, however, that, at present, the expenses of support are much less than in the first years of the establishment; but do we know at what price this result has been obtained?

When the prisoners arrive in Australia,* the government chooses among them, not those who have committed most crimes, but those who have learned a mechanical art, or know some branch of industry useful in the colony. It subjects these to the public labour of the establishment. The criminals, thus reserved for the service of the state, form but the eighth part of all the convicts;† and their number is continually decreasing, as the public wants themselves diminish. To these prisoners, a discipline nearly the same as that in the English prisons is applied, and their support is a heavy charge upon the public treasure.

The other criminals are distributed, soon after their debarkation in the colony, among the free farmers. These pay for their services at a fixed price, and besides, furnish them with the necessaries of life.

The criminal, therefore, prisoner though he be, becomes, transported to Australia, in fact, a servant at wages. This system seems, at the first glance, economical for the state, we shall see its bad effects hereafter.

Several calculations, of which we give the bases in a note,‡ induce us to believe, that, in 1829, (the last year of which we have returns,) the support of each of the fifteen thousand convicts, who were then in Australia, has cost the state at least twelve pounds sterling §

* Inquiries made by order of Parliament, in 1812 and 1819. These inquiries are among the documents sent by Parliament to our government. Vol xc. and xci.

Report made by Mr Bigge, in 1822, in the same collection

Report of the committee charged with the examination of the budget of the colonies in 1830, same collection.

† In 1828, 1,918 convicts, of 15,668, were thus employed by government. Vol. xxiii. of the above-mentioned collection of Legislative Documents, sent by the British Parliament.

‡ See the note placed at the end of the alphabetical notes.

§ Each prisoner in the *hulks*, (a kind of floating bagnes in several ports of Great Britain,) costs annually but six pounds sterling, the price of his labour being deducted. It must be said, however, that, on the other hand, the support of each prisoner at Milbank, costs annually about thirty-five pounds. See Inquiry made by order of Parliament in 1832.

If we add to this sum the annual interest of those sums which have been spent for the foundation of the colony, and take into account the progressive increase of the number of criminals who are transported to Australia, we shall be authorized to believe that the economy which it is reasonable to expect from the system of transportation, reduces itself to very little, if it exist at all.

We willingly acknowledge, that the question of economy is but a secondary one The principal point is, to know whether the system of transportation diminishes the number of criminals. If this were the case, we might imagine that a great nation would willingly impose on itself a sacrifice of money, if the result insured its peace and well-being

But the example of England tends to prove, that, if transportation causes great crimes to disappear, it greatly increases the number of ordinary offences; and that thus the decrease of recommittals is more than outweighed by the increase of first offences

The punishment of transportation intimidates nobody, and hardens many in the way of crime

In order to obviate the immense expenses which the *surveillance* of the prisoners in Australia causes, Great Britain, as we have seen, grants, in a degree, liberty to most of them, as soon as they have been landed at the penal colony.

In order to create some prospect of futurity for them, and to fix them by moral and durable ties, the colony facilitates, in every possible way, the emigration of their family.

After their punishment has expired, the colony gives them lands, so that idleness and vagrancy shall not lead them back to crime.

This combination of efforts produces sometimes the result, that individuals, rejected by the mother country, become useful and respected citizens in the colony; but more often we see that the man, whom the fear of punishment would have constrained to lead a regular life in England, breaks the laws, which he otherwise would have respected, because the punishment with which he is threatened, has in fact no fear for *him*, and often rather pleases, than affrights his imagination

A great number of convicts, says Mr Bigge in his report to Lord Bathurst, are retained much more by the facility of subsistence in Australia, by the chances of gain, and the free manners common to the colony, than by the vigilance of the police. A singular punishment must that be which the convict fears to have withdrawn !

To say the truth, transportation is, for many Englishmen, nothing but an emigration to Australia, undertaken at the expense of government. This consideration could not but excite the attention of a nation so justly renowned for its intelligence and skill in the art of ruling society. We find, therefore, as early as in the year 1819, in an official letter by Lord Bathurst, (January 6th,) this expression: "the terror formerly inspired by transportation gradually diminishes, and the crimes increase in the same proportion.* (*They have increased beyond all calculation*)†

The number of persons sentenced to transportation, which in the year 1812 was 662, had gradually risen until 1819, when the letter of Lord Bathurst was written, to the number of 3130; during the years 1828 and 1829, it had risen to 4500.‡

* We have retranslated this passage from the French, as we had no access to this letter —TRANS

† Lord Bathurst's own words —TRANS.

‡ (We have been obliged to retranslate the passages, in the following report, quoted from English reports —TRANS)

In 1832, the British Parliament appointed a "Select Committee to inquire into the best mode of giving efficacy to secondary punishments, and to report their observations to the House of Commons " The report was made, June 22d, 1832. From this valuable document we take the following extracts · we ought to mention, however, that the committee were not unanimous, and that the report only expresses the opinion of the majority. At least we have been so informed by a very distinguished member of parliament, who belonged to the committee.

"After the evidence received by the committee, they believe that there exists frequently a belief among the people of the lowest class, that it is very desirable for them to be transported to Botany Bay, and that crimes have been committed with the sole view of effecting a transportation to Australia It seems, therefore, necessary that a real punishment should be inflicted upon the convicts, either before they leave England, or immediately after they arrive in Australia, and before they are placed as servants with the farmers " p 12.

"The committee are of opinion, that the punishment of transportation to Australia, alone, is not sufficient to check crime , and as no means has been indicated so far, to make the individuals once transported undergo that punishment which society calls for, without considerably increasing the charges upon the public treasury, it results that this punishment ought to be inflicted before their departure to New South Wales " p 14

" The punishment of transportation, such as it is put in practice in England, appears to the committee an ineffectual punishment. But it may become useful in combination with other punishments " p 16

" It appears from the declarations of witnesses, that the impression made upon the minds of the people by transportation, depends essentially upon the situation of the convicts Working men have the greatest fear of being sent to the penal colony, whilst, for unmarried people, mechanics for instance, who are sure to earn very high wages in Australia, and, in general, for all those who feel the necessity of changing their situation, and have the vague desire of improving it, transportation has nothing formidable All the reports which are sent from New South Wales and Van Diemen's Land, the committee are satisfied, are very favourable. They represent the situation of the convicts in Australia as very happy, and the chances of success before them as certain, if they conduct themselves with prudence. It is natural, therefore, that transportation should be considered by many rather as a benefit than a punishment " p 17

" It is not surprising, that in a country with an abundant population, where a number of persons suffer great privations, and where, consequently, much inducement to crime exists, those whose education has been abandoned, and who are exposed to suffering, yield without trouble to the temptation of doing evil. They rely on the incertitude of legislation, and the probability of acquittals which it presents; and if this chance fails, they know that the worst which can

The partisans of the system of transportation cannot deny these facts : but they maintain, that this system has at least for its result the rapid foundation of a colony, which soon refunds, in riches and power, to the mother country, the expenses it has caused.

Considered in this light, transportation is not any longer a penal system, but a method of colonization Under this point of view, it not only deserves the attention of the friends of mankind, but also of politicians, and all those who exercise an influence on the destinies of nations.

As for ourselves, we do not hesitate to declare, that the system of transportation appears to us as unfit for the foundation of a colony, as for the suppression of crime in the mother country. It carries, undoubtedly, to the country which is to be colonized, a population which would perhaps not have gone thither of itself; but the state gains little by gathering these premature fruits, and it would have been more desirable for it to have allowed things to take their natural course.

And first, if the colony actually grow rapidly, it soon becomes difficult to maintain the penal establishment there at little expense ; in the year 1819, the population of New South Wales amounted to about 29,000 inhabitants, and even then the surveillance became difficult, even then the idea was suggested to government, of erecting prisons for the detention of the convicts: thus we would have the European system, with its vices, transported to a distance of 5000 leagues from Europe *

The more the colony increases in population, the less is it dis-

happen is a change of their situation, which renders them scarcely worse than they were before." p 20.

" The rapid increase of the number of criminals in this country, (England and Wales,) has for some time created alarm, and baffled all the efforts of philanthropists and politicians In v un has it been tried to arrest this increase, either by amending our penal laws, or by establishing a more efficient police. All these means have not been sufficient to retard the progress of the evil, nor to diminish the frightful catalogue which the records of jurisprudence annually offer. Without recurring to distant periods, it can be shown by documents furnished to the committee, that the number of individuals committed for trial, and acquitted or condemned, for crimes and offences, in England and Wales, regularly increases.

Number of Persons Committed for Trial

From 1810	to	1817	-	56,308
1817	to	1824	-	92,848
1824	to	1831	-	121,518

Number of Convicted Individuals

From 1810	to	1817	-	35,259
1817	to	1824	-	62,412
1824	to	1831	-	85,257

* On the 27th of February, 1826, the governor of New South Wales caused a new prison, independently of that already then existing in Sidney, to be erected. Several prisons had already been built, on various points of the territory of the colony, for the most untameable convicts See the Documents printed by order of the House of Commons, and, among others, the Ordonance of Governor Darling, in 1826, and the " Regulations on Penal Settlements," printed in 1832.

posed to become the receptacle of the outcasts of the mother country. It will be remembered what indignation was excited in America, by the presence of criminals sent out from the mother country.

Even in Australia, with this young colony, composed, in a great degree, of malefactors, the same murmurs are already heard, and we believe that as soon as the colony has the power, it will refuse with energy the fatal presents of the mother country.

Thus great Britain will lose the expenses caused by her penal establishment.

The Australian colonies will strive to free themselves from the onerous obligations imposed by England so much the sooner, as there exists in the hearts of their inhabitants but little good feeling towards her.

And this is one of the most fatal effects of the system of transportation applied to colonies

There is, in general, nothing more tender than the feeling which binds the colonist to the soil of his childhood. Recollections, habits, interests, prejudices, every thing binds him still to his beloved home, in spite of the ocean which rolls between him and his country. Several nations of Europe have found and still find a great source of power and glory in these ties of a distant fraternity. But one year before the Revolution of America, the colonists, whose forefathers had, a century and a half before, left the coasts of Great Britain, yet called England their "*home.*"*

But the name of the mother country brings back to the memory of transported convicts the recollection of misery, and sometimes of unmerited misery. It is there that he has been unhappy, prosecuted, guilty, dishonoured.

What ties shall unite him to a country, where, in most cases, he has left nobody who cares for his fate? How should he wish to establish the intercourse of commerce and amity with the mother country? Of all places on the globe, that where he was born, appears to him the most odious   It is the only place where his history is known and his shame has been divulged.

It cannot be doubted but that these hostile sentiments of the colonist perpetuate themselves with his race ; in the United States, the rival nation of England, the Irish can yet be recognised by the hatred which they vow against their ancient masters.†

---

* England was called *home,* as we find the word often used to this day in Calcutta and other East India newspapers, &c   The original has it, "*chez nous,*" which undoubtedly was meant for "home," the French being unable to render this sweet and powerful word in their language —Trans

† All emigrated Irish would not be willing to subscribe to this passage.—Trans.

The system of transportation then is fatal to the mother countries, inasmuch as it weakens the natural ties which should unite them with their colonies; nay more, it prepares for these growing states themselves, a futurity replete with turmoil and misery.

The partisans of penal colonies have not omitted to cite the example of the Romans, who began with robbery and ended with the conquest of the world.*

But these facts are of a distant era: there are others, more conclusive, which have passed almost under our eyes, and we cannot believe that we ought to recur to instances exhibited three thousand years ago, if the present speaks so loud.

A handful of sectarians land, at the beginning of the seventeenth century, on the coasts of North America; and form there, almost in secret, a society on the basis of liberty and religion. This tribe of pious adventurers has become since a great people, and the nation which has grown from that nucleus, has remained the freest and the most religious in the world † On an island dependent upon the same continent, a band of pirates, the scum of Europe, seek, almost at the same period, an asylum. These depraved, but intelligent men, established likewise a society, which soon abandoned the piratical habits of its founders It became rich and enlightened, but remained the most corrupted on the face of the earth, and its vices prepared the bloody catastrophe which has terminated its existence.

But without the examples of New England and St. Domingo, it would be sufficient for us, in order to show still more strikingly what we mean, to exhibit that which is passing in Australia itself.

Society‡ in Australia is divided into various classes, as separated from and hostile to each other as the different castes of the middle ages. The convict is exposed to the contempt of him whose time of punishment has expired; the latter again is ex-

---

* A comparison of no value, since Mr Niebuhr has written his History of Rome. Nothing is, in our opinion, less useful, and in some cases more dangerous, than to refer in discussions of interests and measures, essentially modern, to the ancients How seldom do we know all the details of their situation, and if we do know them, how seldom are they applicable to our own ! Immense time and study, and much wit, have been wasted in forced comparisons with the ancients , this, for some time at least, was natural, since the light of knowledge had been rekindled by the writings of the ancients , and they became authorities for every thing Pedantry, and, not unfrequently, sophistry, seized upon this abuse It is but a few short months since we found the example of the Romans adduced in an elaborate article in defence of slavery ! Whately, now archbishop of Dublin, has in his Introductory Lectures on Political Economy, an excellent passage on the reference to the Bible, in scientific or political disquisitions —Trans.

† *La plus libre et la plus croyante* is the original —Trans.

‡ Inquiry of the years 1812 and 1829 Report of Mr Bigge. Report of the Committee on the budget in 1830. See Legislative documents sent by parliament to our government.

posed to the scoffs of his own children, who are born in freedom; and all, to the haughtiness of the colonist whose origin is without stain. They are like four hostile nations, meeting on the same ground.

We can imagine the feelings which animate these different members of the same nation, by the following passage of the report of Mr. Bigge * As long as this feeling of jealousy and hostility exists, it would be wrong, he says, to introduce the trial by jury into the colony   In the actual state of things, a jury composed of former convicts will not fail to unite against an indicted person belonging to the class of free colonists, so jurymen, taken from among the free colonists, would always be inclined to prove the purity of their class, by finding guilty the former convict a second time indicted.

In 1820, one-eighth of the children in Australia received some instruction.   The governor of the colony, however, established public schools at his own expense: he knew, as Mr. Bigge says in his reports, that education alone could overcome the fatal influence which the vices of the parents exercise.

That which is essentially wanting in Australian society, is good morals.   And how can it be otherwise?   The force of example and the influence of public opinion are hardly able, in a society composed of pure elements, to restrain human passions; of 36,000 inhabitants, which Australia had in 1828, 23,000, or nearly two-thirds, belonged to the class of convicts.   Australia, therefore, was in the rare situation where vice receives the support of the majority.   The women had lost that shame and virtue, which characterize their sex in the mother country, and of the greater part of its free colonies; though government encouraged marriage with all possible means, often even at the expense of discipline, bastards yet formed the fourth part of all the children.

There is another cause (somewhat of a physical character) of bad morals in penal colonies, which not only prevents the introduction of good morals, but facilitates disorders and prostitution.

In all countries of the world, the women commit infinitely less crimes than men.†   In France, the women form but the fifth part of the convicts, in America, the tenth.   A colony, founded by means of transportation, will therefore necessarily present a great disproportion in the number of the two sexes.   In 1828, only 8,000 women existed in Australia with 36,000 inhabitants, or less than a fourth part of the whole population; and it may

* We retranslate this passage from the French —Trans

† We refer the reader for interesting statements respecting this and other points connected with the statistics of crimes, to an article *Crimes, Statistics of*, in the *Encyclopædia Americana*, and to Mr. Ouctelet's Observations, printed in the *Courrier des Etats Unis* of April 25, 1832 —Trans.

easily be conceived, what experience besides proves, that it is necessary for a nation, in order to preserve its morals pure, that both the sexes should be nearly the same in number.

But not only are the infractions of the laws of morality frequent in Australia; but crimes against the positive laws of society are committed there more frequently than in any part of the world.

The annual number of executions in Great Britain is about sixty, whilst in the Australian colonies, ruled by the same laws, peopled with the same stock, and with a population of but 40,000 inhabitants, from fifteen to twenty executions, it is said, take place.*

Lastly, of all the British colonies, Australia is the only one which is deprived of that precious civil liberty which has been the glory of England, and the strength of her children in all parts of the world. How could the function of a juryman be trusted to an individual, who himself comes from the prisoner's box? And can the direction of public affairs be left, without danger, to a population tormented by its vices, and divided by deep-rooted animosities?

It will be acknowledged, that transportation may contribute to people rapidly an uninhabited country, it may form free colonists, but not strong and peaceful societies. The vices which we thus ship from Europe are not destroyed; they are but transplanted to another soil, and England only frees herself of a part of her misery, to assign it to the children of Australia.

—◦◦◦◦◦—

CHAPTER III.

DIFFICULTIES PECULIAR TO OUR TIME AND TO FRANCE.

Where can France hope to find a place fit for the foundation of a penal colony ? —The national character is not favourable to undertakings beyond the seas. —Facilities for Great Britain in the founding of Botany Bay, which would be wanting to France —Expenses which would be caused by a similar colony.— Chances of a maritime war.

We have shown in the preceding chapter, the reasons why we believe that the system of transportation is neither useful as a repressive measure, nor as a method of colonization. The difficulties which we have pointed out, seem to us to exist in all ages and with all nations; but in certain periods and with certain nations they become insurmountable

* This fact has been stated to us by a person who is worthy of credit, and who lived more than two years in New South Wales.

First, where should France at present go in search of a spot to found her penal colony upon? Let us begin to investigate whether that place exists, this is certainly following the natural order of ideas; and here we cannot abstain from making a remark.

If you speak with a partisan of the system of penal colonies, you will hear an enumeration of the advantages of transportation; an exposition of general, and not unfrequently ingenious remarks upon the advantages which France might derive from it; and some details on the colonization of Australia. You will hear little of the means of execution; and as to the selection of a French colony, the conversation will finish without a word on the point. If you touch upon it, the other will hasten to another subject; or perhaps will remark that the world is large, and that in some part of it, it must be possible to find the necessary corner.

As if the universe were yet divided by the imaginary line, formerly drawn by the popes, and beyond it unknown continents extended, where imagination might wander at pleasure.

Yet it is within this limited circle, that we should like to see the partisans of transportation, it is on this question of mere fact, that we the most wish for light.

As for ourselves, we confess without hesitation, that we can see nowhere the spot on which France could seize for the purpose in question. The world seems to us no longer vacant; every spot is occupied

What we have said above, respecting the selection of a place proper for the foundation of a penal colony, must be kept in mind; it is, we believe, incontestable.

Let us then here propose the question in precise terms: in what part of the world is a similar place to be found?

Fortune pointed out such a place to England fifty years ago. An immense continent, and consequently no fear of future extension; spacious ports, safe anchorages, fertile and uninhabited land, the climate of Europe—every thing was found united there, and this privileged place, too, in the region of the antipodes.

Why, it will be objected, shall we abandon to the English the free possession of a country ten times larger than England? Cannot two nations make use of this immense territory? And would a population of fifty thousand English be at all incommoded, if at a distance of nine hundred leagues from them, on the western side, a French colony were founded? Those who thus speak, are undoubtedly not aware that Great Britain, warned by what has happened in America, of the danger resulting from having neighbours, has repeatedly declared, that she would not suffer any other power to found a colony in Australia. Cer-

tainly we feel as much as any other person, the pride and inso-
lence of this declaration; but do the partisans of transportation
want us to enter into a maritime war with Great Britain for the
purpose of a penal colony?

An author who has written with talent on the penitentiary
system, Mr. Charles Lucas, indicates, indeed, to the consideration of government, two small islands of the Antilles, and the
colony of Cayenne, which might be used, he says, as places of
detention for certain convicts. He would detain there, re-committed murderers, and those who have been guilty of attempts
against the liberty of the press and religion * But transportation, confined to these two species of criminals, is of no general
use, and moreover, it is very doubtful, whether the places pointed out would be well chosen. The author of whom we speak,
who contests the right of society to punish even a parricide with
death, certainly would be averse to leave the insalubrity of the
climate, to do what, according to him, justice herself has no right
to inflict.

Nobody, so far, has, to our knowledge, seriously occupied
himself with the resolution of the question which we have pro-
pounded above And yet, would it not be necessary to agree,
first of all, upon this point?

We must, however, hasten to say, that we do not believe it
impossible to find a place fit for the foundation of a penal colony, merely because our researches have been fruitless respecting
the point.

But suppose the place to be found; there remain yet the difficulties of execution: they have been great in England; they
appear insurmountable in France

The first of all, it must be acknowledged, is found in the character of our nation, which, so far, has shown itself little favourable to undertakings beyond the seas

France has always been placed in the first rank of continental
powers, by her geographical situation, as well as her extent and
fertility. It is the *land* which forms the natural theatre of her
power and glory, maritime commerce is but secondary with
her. The sea has never with us excited, and undoubtedly never will excite, those deep feelings of filial respect which trad-

---

* Such a law, certainly would prove only to what danger the liberty of the
press and of conscience were still exposed And if there were yet so small a
majority of the French people, in favour of these liberties, a time might easily
arrive, when these laws would be disregarded or overthrown, if, in fact, society
ever could be induced to enforce them Disproportionate punishments never
prevent political offences, they merely indicate the divided state of a nation.
Teach the people to love the liberty of the press, and it will be founded on firm
ground. The British have none by the law, and who will dare to deprive them
of it ? And if the people do not love it, no threat, however severe, will protect it.
—TRANS

ing nations entertain for it.   Hence it has often been seen, that
the most powerful genius at once failed, if the question were to
combine and to direct naval expeditions.   The people, on the
other hand, have little belief in the success of distant undertakings   The money of individuals is reluctantly embarked in such
schemes; the persons who, with us, present themselves in readiness to found a colony, are generally those to whom the me-
diocrity of their talents, the impaired state of their fortune, or
the recollections of their previous life, deny the hope of future
success at home.   And yet, if any undertaking in the world depends upon the heads who direct it, it is, without contradiction,
the foundation of a penal colony.

When England, in the year 1785, conceived the project of
transporting her convicts to New South Wales, she had nearly
already acquired that immense commercial development, which
we now observe in that country.   Her preponderance on the
sea was even then an acknowledged fact.

She turned these two advantages to great account; the extent
of her commerce made it easy for her to find mariners for the
voyage to Australia.   The industry of private persons conjoined
to assist the state; vessels of large tonnage* presented themselves in numbers to transport the convicts at a cheap rate. Owing to the great number of vessels, and the immense resources
of the royal navy, the government was enabled to provide for
all contingencies.

Ever since that period, the power of Great Britain has continued: the Island of St. Helena, the Cape of Good Hope, the
Isle of France, have fallen into her hands, and offer to her vessels so many ports where they may safely stop under the protection of the British flag.

The rule of the waves is slowly acquired; but it is less subject
to the abrupt changes of fortune.   Every thing indicates, that
Great Britain will yet for a long time, remain in undisturbed
enjoyment of these advantages, and that war even would throw
no obstacle in her way.

England was, therefore, of all nations in the world, the one
which could found a penal colony with the least difficulty and
the least expense.

Nevertheless, the infancy of the colony of Botany Bay has
been exposed to great dangers, and we have seen what immense
sums England has spent in its foundation.

These results explain themselves sufficiently easy.   A nation,
whatever its advantages may be, cannot at little expense found
a penal colony at a distance of three or four thousand leagues
from the centre of its power; and particularly, if every thing

---

* No vessels under 500 tons burden are employed.

must be carried there, and nothing can be expected from the efforts and industry of the colonists.

In imitating our neighbours, we cannot hope for any of their facilities.

The French navy cannot, without a considerable increase of the budget, send annually vessels to countries so distant; and the French commerce, on the other hand, offers few resources for expeditions of this kind.

Once departed from our ports, it would be necessary for French vessels to sail over half the circumference of the globe without finding a single intermediate place where they could rely on efficient assistance.

These difficulties are expressed in a few words, but they are very great; and the more we examine the subject, the more we are convinced of them.

It could only be by means of great pecuniary sacrifices, that we ever could succeed in surmounting similar obstacles.

We cannot believe that in the present state of our finances, it can be the intention to increase, on this account, the charges of the treasury. Even if the undertaking should meet with success, nay, if at some future period it should save its expenses, France does not seem to be in a state of ability to bear the first investment. The result by no means seems to warrant such sacrifices.

And are we sure of escaping for a long time, the fruits of so expensive an undertaking?

Those who advocate penal colonies, avoid considering the chances to which a maritime war would necessarily expose the new colonies; or if they touch upon the subject, it is only to reject the idea, that France could ever fear a conflict and not have the power of making, at any time, the justice of her rights respected.

We shall not follow this example: true national as well as individual greatness has always appeared to us to consist in undertaking not any thing which is merely desirable, but every thing which *can* be effected. Wisdom as well as true courage consists in knowing ourselves and in judging of ourselves without weakness—preserving always a just confidence in our own resources.

The geographical situation, the colonial establishments, the maritime glory, and the commercial spirit of England, have given her an incontestable preponderance on the seas. In the actual state of things, France may support against her a glorious struggle; she may triumph in particular engagements—she can even efficaciously defend possessions at no great distance from the centre of the kingdom; but history teaches us, that her distant colonies almost always end by falling into the hands of her rival.

England has fixed settlements and intermediate points on all coasts; France cannot find a single support for her fleets, except on her own territory, or in the Antilles. England can disperse her forces in all parts of the globe without rendering the chances of success unequal; France cannot struggle except by collecting all her forces on the seas which surround her.

After having made great efforts and sacrifices to found her colony, France would see herself exposed to the almost certain danger of having it torn from her.

A similar colony would but little tempt the cupidity of England. Nothing authorizes us to believe it. She would always have an interest in destroying a French settlement of whatever character it might be. England, moreover, having made herself mistress of the penal colony, would certainly hasten to give it another destination, and endeavour to people it with other subjects.

But let us suppose, that the colony having had time to arrive at a considerable magnitude, England would not or could not capture it; she need not do that, in order to injure France; it would be sufficient for her to cut off the communication with the mother country.

A colony, and particularly a penal colony, (at least, if it has not arrived at a very high degree of development) cannot endure without injury a perfect separation from the civilized world. Deprived of its intercourse with the mother country, we should soon see her decay. On the other hand, if France cannot any longer transport her convicts beyond the seas, what becomes of the result of transportation, so dearly bought? Her colony, instead of being useful to her, will cause her difficulties, and expenses which did not previously exist. What becomes of the convicts who had been destined for the penal colony? They must be kept at home; no preparation made for their reception; during every maritime war, therefore, it would be necessary to establish again provisional bagnes to contain the criminals.

Such are, in the actual state of things, the almost certain results of a war with Great Britain. Now, if we open the page of history, we shall see, that the peace at present existing between England and ourselves, is one of the longest that has occurred during the space of four hundred years.

ALPHABETICAL NOTES.

(*a*). In 1804 the erection of the first penitentiary in Baltimore was decreed; and in 1809 a general reform of the criminal laws, in accordance with a new system of imprisonment, took place. See Act of Assembly Baltimore, 1819, page 24. The 28th Article of the Law decrees solitary confinement. Article 30 of the same Law prescribes labour, and Article 40 authorizes the use of the whip as a disciplinary means The law of Maryland differs in this point from that of New York.

The system of absolute isolation in certain cases, was not adopted in the Charlestown (Massachusetts) prison until June 21st, 1811. (See Rules and Regulations for the government of the Massachusetts State Prison Boston, 1823)

In New Jersey it has been put into practice since 1797.

See Fifth Report of the Boston Pris Disc. Society, page 422.

In 1820 a law was passed in New Jersey, which decreed solitary confinement, not exceeding a fourth part of the imprisonment, with labour, to which the convict would have been formerly sentenced, for arson, murder, rape, blasphemy, perjury, burglary, forgery, &c (See Letter of Mr Southard of New Jersey, of December 27th, 1831)

(*b*) On April 2d, 1821, the legislature of New York charged the director of Auburn to select a class of criminals, the most hardened, and to lock them up in solitary cells, night and day, without interruption and without labour On December 25th, 1821, a sufficient number of cells was completed, and eighty criminals were placed in them. (See Report of Gershom Powers, superintendent of Auburn in 1828, page 80, and MS note of Elam Lynds, with which he furnished us)

Judge Spencer of Canandaigua, one of the most distinguished criminal lawyers of the state of New York, was a member of a committee, which reported on this decree of the legislature. In its report, it is recommended that the convicts ought to be classed according to their morality; that *the hardened villains should be subject to solitary and uninterrupted confinement*, and those who follow next in the scale of crime, should be, part of the time, subject to the same punishment, and during the rest of their imprisonment, should have permission to work; the less depraved would have the right to work the whole day. (See Report to the Legislature, for 1821.)

(*c*) This was in the year 1822, which followed directly after experiments had been made respecting solitary confinement without labour. Judge Powers, "agent and keeper of the state prison at Auburn," relates what happened in the following terms :—

" During the year preceding January 1823, there was an average of about 220 convicts in prison From the physician's report of that year to the inspectors, it appears that the average number of sick in the hospital was between seven and eight. That there were ten deaths, seven by consumption, five of which were from among the solitary convicts The physician speaks of convicts coming into the hospital from the cells, with difficulty of respiration, pain in the breast, &c , and concludes his report as follows . ' It is a generally received and acknowledged opinion, that sedentary life, no matter in what form, disposes to debility, and consequently to local disease. It may be produced in the study or the prison , in the nursery and the college, or in any other place where muscular exertion is restrained If we review the mental causes of disease, we shall probably find, that sedentary life *in the prison,* as it calls into aid the debilitating passions of melancholy, grief, &c , rapidly hastens the progress of pulmonary disease.' From the order and cleanliness of the prison, we have no reason to conclude that any atmospheric cause reigns within its walls, calculated to produce serious disease , but confinement operates upon the existing germ of diseases, and hastens the progress of all those that must have otherwise terminated in death.'' See Report of Judge Powers, of 1828, page 81.

We shall see, further on, that labour, added to the system, changed entirely the conclusions of the physician.

(*d*). This prison is at present in a degree abandoned ; the cells destined for solitary confinement, are open to all convicts, who are at liberty to communicate with each other ; we found sixty-four in the prison , the only thing which was defective in the system—absence of labour—has been retained. The convicts, with the exception of a very few, are entirely idle, because there is no workshop for united labour. In spite of the material defects of the establishment, something better might be done, in our opinion, but the directors of the prison are disgusted with the bad disposition of the place, and as for the system, it not having had the expected success, public attention is not any longer directed towards it. In a government where power is nowhere exerted, only those things are undertaken which interest public opinion, and which, consequently, give fame or profit to those who take part in them The penitentiary of Philadelphia is conducted by individuals of great merit , that of Pittsburg, already forgotten, finds agents of but ordinary capacity for its direction.

(*e*). The Boston Prison Discipline Society was established in 1826. [Its first report bears date June 2d, 1826 —Trans] From that time to the present, i. e. during six years, it has spent 17,498 dollars 19 cents, of which 15,681 dollars were given by charitable persons [According to the last, the seventh report, bearing date May 24th, 1832, there were received during the last year 3035 dollars, of which 477 dollars 49 cents were the balance of the account of the previous year —Trans.] Mr. L Dwight is of the greatest importance to the society, for, with indefatigable zeal, he collects all possible documents for the purpose of enlightening public opinion , shunning no fatigue , visiting good and bad prisons ; pointing out the defects of the one, and the advantages of the other ; the ameliorations which have been effected or such as ought to be introduced. He labours without interruption for the reform of prisons.

The reports published by this society are like an authentic book, in which all abuses and mistakes of the penitentiary system are registered, whilst at the same time all happy results are stated.

This society, which is convinced that religious instruction is the basis of the whole system of reform of prisons, has supported, during six years, from its own funds, ministers in the prisons of Auburn, Sing-Sing, Wethersfield, Lamberton, (New Jersey,) and Charlestown.

The sum spent already for this object is 4727 dollars 29 cents. See the six reports.

(*f*). The law which orders labour in the solitary cells, is of the date of April 23d, 1829 See Section 3d of the Law entitled, An Act to reform the penal laws of this commonwealth.

It happens by no means unfrequently in the United States, that the true character of the Philadelphia penitentiary is not understood Some take it to be the same with the former Walnut street prison, so much extolled in spite of its defects, and praise or blame it accordingly , others believe still that no labour is introduced, and attack it violently on that account. [To this remark of the authors, the translator must add, that he actually found several intelligent individuals, who take a lively interest in the cause of penitentiaries, and an active part in their success, who nevertheless were utterly unacquainted with the true character of the Philadelphia penitentiary, though they live in a state not far from Pennsylvania.]

(*g*) It is truly remarkable, that the penal law, and that which regulates the mode of its execution, i e the system of imprisonment, form but one whole This way of proceeding is logical and wise. In fact, the sanction of a punishment is in its execution The judgment which condemns a convict is but a principle, an idea, if its execution does not make it something material The law, therefore, which regulates this execution, is as important as that which ordains the principle, this is the reason why all laws decreeing imprisonment, ought to state carefully how this punishment is to be inflicted This the legislature of Pennsylvania has done.

(*h*). The penitentiary of Massachusetts was organized in 1829 that of Maryland in January, 1830, those of Tennessee and Kentucky were erected at the same period. The prison of Vermont has not yet been entirely completed . [this has been done since the authors were in this country We copy the following from the Seventh Report of the Boston Prison Discipline Society, page 10 — "The new prison at Windsor, containing one hundred and thirty six solitary cells, on the general plan of those at Charlestown and Wethersfield, was finished and occupied during the last year. The effect of this change is stated, in a letter dated October 14, to be quite satisfactory to all
" The legislature of Vermont, at the last session, provided by law an additional compensation for a chaplain, so that the state now pays three hundred dollars per annum for this service, and a chaplain has been appointed to discharge the duties of the office "—TRANS] As to Maine, we consider its prison as established on the Auburn system, though, in principle, it was intended for solitary confinement without labour [We have already stated that a penitentiary on the Auburn plan at Concord, for New Hampshire, and another on the Pennsylvania principle for New Jersey, have been provided for.—TRANS.]

(*i*) The plan of a house of refuge has already been adopted, and a committee is active in establishing it [The legislature of Maryland, as we stated already, have provided for it but the source from which the funds were to be drawn, did not prove as feeble as had been supposed The legislature is immediately to be applied to again. Mr E L Finley, one of the most active citizens of Baltimore for the erection of a house of refuge, visited, with Mr. Small, an architect, in the summer of 1831, the houses of refuge in Philadelphia, New York, and Boston, to investigate both their system and plan of building, and a model has been formed, whose authors strive to combine all the advantages of the other establishments, and to obviate the admitted defects They might also consult with advantage the reports on the various houses of refuge in Germany, contained in the Annals quoted in a note to the body of the work.—TRANS]
We may quote, amongst the indifferent prisons, that of Lamberton [Instead of translating further, we refer the reader to page 46 of the Seventh Report of the Boston Prison Discipline Society, where the substance is to be found of the report of a committee of the legislature, and of the warden of the prison, and a memorial of the inspectors of the prison to the legislature, which show this institution to be in a most melancholy condition The result has been, as the reader has been informed, that provisions for a new penitentiary have been made.]

(*j*). Prisons were observed, which included persons convicted of the worst crimes, and a remedy has been applied where the greatest evil appeared, other prisons, where the same evil exists, but where it makes less fearful ravages, have been forgotten, yet to neglect the less vicious, in order to labour only for the

20

reform of great and hardened criminals, is the same as if only the most infirm were attended to in a hospital, and, in order to take care of patients, perhaps incurable, those who might be easily restored to health, were left without any attention The defect, which we mention here, is felt in America by some of her most distinguished men

Mr Edward Livingston attacks this defect with great force ·—

"After condemnation, there can be no association but of the guilty with the guilty, but, in the preliminary imprisonment, guilt is associated with innocence"

See his Introductory Report to the Code of Prison Discipline, page 31, for this and the following passages, which represent the truth in clear and powerful language

In order to show, still more clearly, the bad effects of so defective a system of imprisonment, for individuals indicted, Mr Livingston presents a table of persons arrested, tried, acquitted, or convicted at New York, from 1822 to 1826, inclusive It results from this table, that four-fifths of the persons arrested in New York, for supposed crimes or offences, and thrown, as such, into a prison, expecting the session of the court, have been acknowledged as innocent, partly by the police magistrates, partly by the grand jury, or after trial See this table at the end of this volume We have met with none, in the United States, who were more afflicted by the bad state of the houses of arrest, than Mr. Riker, recorder of the city of New York—a magistrate of rare merit and great virtue, who connects with much knowledge, great experience in criminal affairs.

(*k*) In the United States, the "heads of society" are always far advanced on the path of reform the rest of the social body, composing the mass of the population, follows generally the movement, though at a distance ; and, if it be intended to lead it too far, stops quite short It is thus that the Quakers have not been able to procure the abolition of capital punishment in Pennsylvania, its abolition, in cases of wilful murder, being repugnant to the opinions of the mass . the same would take place in other states, the most enlightened in the Union, if the attempt should be made to abolish it in cases for which public opinion considered it necessary. The legislatures of the various states do nothing but what seems right to the majority, and if, in advance of public opinion, they should attempt innovations, the want of which was not yet felt, they not only would expose themselves to the loss of public favour, but also to seeing their work destroyed the next year by their successors [It is one of the most interesting processes for the observation of a foreigner coming to this country, to see how public opinion is gradually enlightened upon certain subjects, and how the cause, on which it is to be enlightened, increases in power, until at last nothing can resist it. As to the operation of public opinion, if formed, the authors ought to have said, instead of " United States," "all countries where a free public opinion exists." Suppose a great innovation should be attempted in the management of music in Italy; there is, in many parts of Italy, a public opinion upon the subject of music, and all which is true of public opinion in England respecting civil affairs, would be so respecting music in Italy In France, a decisive public opinion exists on but few points , on most others, but a Parisian opinion , and, even then, it is generally a *coterie* opinion, (often powerful enough,) but very different from British or American public opinion—that powerful element of all their civil relations. It was natural, therefore, that the operation of public opinion should strike French gentlemen, whilst an English observer would not have been surprised at it.—TRANS]

(*l*). The substance of this note is, that some have reproached solitary confinement with injustice, because it affects an individual whose mind has been cultivated, much more than him, who, without any education, has remained in a kind of brutal condition ; but this inequality is the effect of every punishment. All infamous punishments are more cruel to one of higher social standing, than to him who has lived obscurely. One with a lively imagination suffers more than another of dull fancy. Indians cannot long endure privation of liberty ; would this be any reason for abolishing imprisonment in a society where some Indians happened to reside ?

(See Report of the Commissioners appointed to revise the Penal Code of Pennsylvania)

[In fact, the very principle of justice, without which no justice is imaginable —that of equality—is already in itself a great source of injustice , because absolute justice could only take place where a different punishment could be applied to each single case, considering the whole combination of causes, effects and circumstances in an individual—a justice which can be looked for with none but with H m whose omniscience penetrates all, and whose omnipotence can effect all   Such justice expected from man, would abolish all laws, which are general rules. It was therefore an unfounded reproach to solitary confinement.—Trans.]

(*m*) Without speaking of the monstrous intercourse of convicts during night, it suffices to say, that the conversation of criminals in a prison, is solely upon crimes they have committed or intend to commit, after the expiration of their punishment In such conversations, each boasts of his misdeeds, and all dispute for the privilege of infamy   The less advanced in crime listens eagerly to the greater villains , and the blackest individual among them becomes a type of depravity for the others.

All who have visited the prisons of France will acknowledge the truth of this picture   Mr Louis Dwight gives a multitude of facts, in the Rep of the Bost. Pris Disc. Soc , which proves that we are yet below truth in this exposition

For the rest, the contagion of prisons and the uselessness of classifications, are two points well established in the United States   Mr Livingston expresses himself on this point in the following terms "and it became evident that no reform could be expected, while it was suffered to exist   Classification had been tried in England, and partially here, but it was found to be an incomplete remedy— that system could only be perfected by individual seclusion because, even when the class was reduced to two, one of them would generally be found qualified to corrupt the other ; and if the rare case should occur, of two persons who had arrived at the same precise point of depravity, and the rarer circumstance of the keeper's discernment being successfully employed in associating them, their approximation would increase the common stock of guilt."—Letter of Edward Livingston to Roberts Vaux, 1828, page 6

(*n*) The Baltimore system is that of Geneva   In the latter place, silence has been considered a too cruel pain, which man has not a right to impose upon his fellow creature (') In order to be humane toward prisoners, they are allowed to corrupt each other.

The right of society is contested   why? Society has a right to fetter the arm which has committed murder, and should it not have a right to stifle the voice which makes itself heard merely in order to corrupt ? We also hear of the rights of men ! But is it time to speak of the rights of liberty after the individual has been thrown into prison ?

[Objections of this kind can be raised by men only who have never studied prisons, or who wish to make a show of sensitiveness   Do we not amputate both arms, if it be necessary for the preservation of the rest of the body , and should we not stop the mouth of a criminal?—Trans]

(*o*). We have met with the greatest kindness in visiting this penitentiary. Mr. Samuel Wood, warden of the prison, and a gentleman of rare merit, had given orders that we should always be admitted, whether he were present or not. All the under-officers had been instructed to open any cell for us, and to allow us to have free intercourse with its inmate   Mr. Wood often said . "We have no other interest than that of truth. If there is any thing defective in our prison, it is important that we should know it "

We have carefully noted down the conversations which we had with the prisoners   They form, under the title "Inquiry into the Penitentiary of Philadelphia," an interesting document, which shows the successive impressions which the prisoners receive in their solitude.

See No. 10.

(*p*) Mr. Elam Lynds expresses himself, in a note which he has given us, thus, on this subject

"Obedience to the law of society is all that is asked from a good citizen   It is this which the criminal ought to learn   and you teach him much better by practice than by theory   If you lock up in a cell, a person convicted of a crime, you have no control over him   you act only upon his body   Instead of this, set him to work, and oblige him to do every thing he is ordered to do; you thus teach him to obey, and give him the habits of industry, now I ask, is there any thing more powerful than the force of habit ?   If you have succeeded in giving to a person the habits of obedience and labour, there is little chance of his ever becoming a thief

Convicts in solitary cells, who ask for labour, do not so because they love labour, but because isolation is so tedious to them."

[We re-translated, of course, this note from the French.—Trans.]

(*q*). It is impossible to see the prison of Sing-Sing, and the system of working established there, without being struck with surprise and fear   Though the order is perfectly kept, it is apparent that it rests upon a fragile basis   it is owing to a power always active, but which must be reproduced every day, if the whole discipline is not to be endangered   The safety of the keepers is incessantly menaced.   In presence of such dangers, avoided so skilfully, but with so much difficulty, it seems to us impossible not to apprehend some future catastrophe   For the rest, the dangers, to which the officers of the prison are exposed, form, for the present, one of the surest guaranties of order, every one of them sees that the preservation of his life depends upon it

(*r.*) See Report of Judge Powers of 1828, page 25.

This note, in the original, relates to the necessity of having good officers, and the mistaken economy of giving them small salaries   The authors refer to page 25 of the Report of Judge Powers, of 1828, to Mr Barrett's letter, given under No. 14, to the various reports of the Bost. Pris. Disc. Soc., to the Report to Governor Martin of Maryland, of December 21, 1829, to the fact that the penitentiary of Maryland had been a burthen to the state until 1817, and that from that period it had become productive merely by having better officers, without changing the system of imprisonment, for which see Mr. Niles's pamphlet of December 22, 1828, and to the Report of the Inspectors of Auburn prison, of January 28, 1826, page 3, in which an increase of salary is asked for.

(*s*). The system of the American prisons, which is to make the labour of the prisoners as productive as possible, is perfectly correct in that country where the price of labour is so high

No fear is entertained, that the establishment of manufactories in the prisons will injure the free working classes   In truth it is generally the interest of a nation, that the mass of production should constantly increase, because prices fall in proportion as quantity increases, and the consumer, paying less, grows rich by it.   Nevertheless, in countries where the abundance of production has reduced the price of manufactured articles to its lowest term, production cannot be increased without exposing the working class to injury.   It may be said that production has its lowest price, when the gain of the workman allows him to provide for the merest necessaries of life.   If wages have sunk to this point, manufactories in prisons are much more dangerous than the erection of manufactories in society   Indeed it is not a mere competition with which the establishments of free workmen have, in such case, to contend.   The prison works, not in order to gain, but to diminish its expenses, it lowers the prices at pleasure, without endangering its existence   If the price of articles depreciate, the contractor pays less for the labour of the prisoners, and the government must pay more for their support. On the other hand, the ordinary workman can live only when he makes money , and if the price of the article becomes so depreciated that it yields no profit, either for the workman or for the owner of the manufactory, the establishment must cease

If, therefore, manufactories are established in prisons, a competition against the industry of free men takes place, which becomes fatal, if the latter are reduced to the alternative of stopping their work or working at a loss. To resume, the work of free people must cease if it yield no profit , while manufactories in prison, supported by government, stand against all chances, whether they yield much or little , because their object is not to gain as much as possible, but to lose as little as possible , the capital of a free manufactory is limited, and cannot stand against all chances, the capital of a prison—the public treasury—is infinite.

They were, undoubtedly, these considerations, which have repeatedly induced the British government to stop the labour of prisoners, and to invent "treadmills"—machines which work without producing

Looked upon merely as regards the interest of the prisoner, these machines fulfil but half the object for which the prisoner is made to work. They occupy and preserve him, indeed, against the dangers of idleness , but, if he leaves the prison, of what use is it to him to know the art of turning the tread-mill ? The tread-mill, therefore, is absolutely bad for the prisoner, but the interest of society is also to be taken into consideration The difficulty for a government to decide on this point is very great It is extremely arduous to determine the moment when manufactories, or any productive labour, may be established without detriment to free, industrious citizens , as it is also a delicate question of equity to decide to what point the interest of the state, and the moral situation of the criminal, may be taken into consideration, without oppressing the honest and free member of society Absolute theories on these questions are useless , their solution depends entirely upon a perfect knowledge of the state of things in each separate country. In one case, however, the tread-mill appears to us absolutely bad , that is, if it is used as a productive machine. It increases production, without teaching the convict any useful art.

However this may be, the special question on the tread-mill is, that of labour in general, so grave for several countries of Europe, and presenting no difficulty to the United States , in that country the tread-mill would be conducive to no good whatever.

On the contrary, as production is yet in the United States below the wants of consumption, it is the interest of society to increase production, and to teach the prisoners a useful art, by which they may support themselves at some future period.

(*t*) It is probable, that if the prison of Sing-Sing is finished, a great variety of professions will be taught in it The beautiful marble quarries on the spot, and in the neighbourhood of the Hudson, which offer so convenient an opportunity of transportation, will furnish, for a long time to come, sufficient occupation to the prisoners , but will the danger of allowing a thousand criminals to work in the open field, never be cause of fear ?

At Auburn and Baltimore, the work consists chiefly in weaving, shoemaking, joinery, cooperage, locksmith's work. (For details see the annual reports on these prisons.)

(*u*). See *cahier* of the charges for the general contract for the service of the *maisons centrales de detention*

Besides the food, clothing, and bedding of the prisoners, the cleanliness and salubrity of the prison, washing, &c , &c , are included in the contract The contractor has the convicts shaved, and their hair cut, he provides fuel and light for the prisoners and the keepers , he furnishes the officers with paper, ink, &c , &c He supplies the necessary articles for divine service, provides for interment , in short, life, religion, and death, are included in the contract

For fear that any thing is forgotten, it is said, at the end of the *cahier*, that the contractor shall provide every thing wanted, of whatever kind, specified or not.

The victual shop belongs to the contractor, who is interested in selling as much wine as possible , and, consequently, that the discipline be as much as possible disturbed—a provision so much the more dangerous, as the convict may spend half of his *pécule* or earning, which amounts to two thirds of his labour

The consequence of all this is, that the contractor is the most important person attached to the prison. The overseers of the work-shops, the *contre maitres*, cooks, bakers, victual sellers, laundresses, apothecaries, attendants of the sick, servants, *hommes de peine*, and all others, whose functions are subject to no surveillance whatever, are chosen by the contractor, who causes them merely to be approved of by the government of the prison.

The result is, that the prison and its discipline are at the mercy of the contractor and his agents. For the rest, the business of the contractor is immense ; every thing depends upon him, the most important and the most trifling operations.

There is undoubtedly a great simplicity in this system ; accounts are kept with only a single individual. But it is evident that the cupidity of this person is extremely excited , he does every thing, and must gain by every thing Added to this, his position, so complicated, is in some respects very unfavourable ; in case of dispute, the question between him and the administration is adjudged by the " council of the prefecture,"* i e by the administration itself—his adversary. It is clear that he does not accept the contract except with almost certain chances of great profit.

No essential change in the moral discipline could be effected in our prisons, without changing the functions of the contractor. At present he is in possession of the most important parts of the discipline

If we censure the inconvenience of the contract, we in no ways praise the discipline of the prisons where it does not exist. Thus we are far from advocating the system of the Walnut Street prison, the administration of which is managed by itself , we believe even that the principle of contract, prudently applied, is on the whole more useful than fatal.

(*v*). In 1828, a revolt broke out in Newgate, (New York,) and could be subdued only by firing upon the rebel-convicts; but, after their reduction, a hundred of them refused to work , they were put in solitary confinement without labour ; these means, however, remained without effect for seventy days ; thus two months' labour was lost

See Report of January 20, 1819

The superintendent of Newgate, (New York,) where solitary confinement with reduction of labour was the only disciplinary measure, said on this subject

" The actual way of punishing, whatever may be its duration, weakens the convict, without curbing him at all "—[Re-translated]

See Report of December 31, 1818

(*x*). The law of the state of New York, allowed formerly the keepers to lay on thirty-nine stripes, and no more The Revised Statutes say, " The officers of the prison shall use all suitable means to defend themselves, to enforce the observance of discipline," &c &c

See Revised Statutes of New York, tit. 2, ch 3, 4th part, art. 2, § 59.

The law of Connecticut allows stripes in positive terms " Moderate whipping, not exceeding ten stripes for any one offence " See Law of May 31, 1827, page 163, sec 3.

Twenty stripes might therefore be inflicted, for two offences, on the same individual.

The law of Maryland also permits stripes explicitly, the maximum of which must be not more than thirteen

See article 40 of the penal code of 1809.

* This " council of the prefecture" does not only decide matters between officers, but also between citizens and government, such as those relating to taxes, duties, &c., and is one of the greatest defects of the French administration of justice.—*Trans*

In a trial of an assistant keeper at Auburn, accused of having whipped a convict, Judge Walworth said, in charging the jury at Cayuga, at the Court of Oyer and Terminer, September, 1826

"That confinement with labour merely, had no terrors for the guilty. That the labour which the human body was capable of performing, without endangering its health, was but little more than many of the virtuous labouring class of the community daily and voluntarily performed for the support and maintenance of their families That to produce reformation in the guilty, or to restrain the vicious from the perpetration of crime by the terrors of punishment, it was absolutely necessary that the convict should feel his degraded situation, should feel that he was actually doing penance for his wilful violation of the laws of his country. That he must, in his own person, be made to feel the difference which should exist between the situation of the upright and honest freeman, who labours for his daily bread, and the vile and degraded convict, who, by fraud or robbery, has deprived that honest freeman, or his family, of the hard-earned rewards of his industry That mistaken or misapplied sympathy for such offenders, was injustice to the virtuous part of the community. That the system of discipline adopted by the inspectors of the prison, under the sanction of the laws, was well calculated to have the desired effect of reforming the less vicious offenders, and of deterring others from the commission of crime, by the severity of punishment inflicted, and that, too, in the best possible way A mode of punishment, where comparatively little bodily suffering is felt, and the greatest severity of the punishment is inflicted upon the culprit, through the medium of the mind. That it was, however, through terror of bodily suffering alone, that the proper effect upon the mind of the convict was produced , and thence the necessity of a rigid enforcement of the prison discipline upon every convict, by the actual infliction of bodily suffering, if he would not otherwise submit to the rules "

See Report of Judge Powers, of 1828, page 121.

(y) Messrs. Allen, Hopkins, and Tibbets, inspectors of the Auburn prison, express themselves, on the necessity of investing the superintendent with discretionary powers, thus

"The men upon whom the responsibility of the safe keeping of the convicts rests, ought to possess the authority to punish them, if they neglect or refuse to obey the laws of the establishment

"For the proper exercise of this power, they are, and ought to be, amenable to the laws. But we understand it to be a principle of the common law of this state, as it certainly is of reason and common sense, that every keeper of a prison must have such power of personal correction

"The condition of a prisoner, is that of personal restraint As the prisoners are always the most numerous, and have, therefore, the advantage of physical force, they must take the mastery whenever they think expedient, if there is no power of punishment , or when that power is fettered or imperfect, then submission will be proportionably incomplete

" Upon this method of governing, our opinions are entirely decided and unanimous , and we hesitate not to state to the legislature our settled conviction, that the government of felons in a prison must be absolute, and the control over them must be perfect. The principal keeper must be a man of firmness, discretion, and vigilance , and he ought to be the responsible person in all matters relative to the conduct and safe keeping of the prisoners Without this, there can be no discipline nor economy. Every consideration requires this , the safety of the lives of the officers, and of the prisoners themselves, requires it It is indispensable to economy, and to profitable labour , and if there can be any hope of reformation, it must not be where the prisoner stands upon his rights, and exacts conditions; but where he is brought to a sense of his degradation, and feels the sadness incident to dependence and servitude, and becomes willing to receive any indulgence as a boon, and instruction, advice, and admonition, as a favour.

" It is proper to remark, that we have been informed of complaints which had been made against the officers of the Auburn prison, of too great severity of discipline   Some of us took pains to investigate the grounds of those complaints, and sought interviews with some respectable persons who had supported them, and with some members of a grand jury of Cayuga county, before whom the subject had been brought.   In one instance, a convict had called out to the prisoners in the mess room to rise.   He was instantly struck down by the keeper attending, and, we believe, struck after he was down   In no case have the grand jury thought proper to interfere, though the subject has been more than once before them ; and we believe that the corporal punishment now inflicted at the Auburn prison, is not more than is requisite to preserve proper obedience "

(Report of Stephen Allen, Samuel M. Hopkins, and George Tibbets, of 1825. The passage above quoted, may also be found on page 108, and seq. in G. Powers's Report of 1828)

It has been often discussed in the United States, whether under-keepers ought to refer to the superintendent, before they inflict corporal punishment, or whether they shall have the power to punish "on the spot "   The inspectors of the Auburn prison have discussed this question in one of their reports, and it is their opinion, that the inferior officers ought to be invested with the power in question   "The danger of abuse, is an evil much less than the relaxation of discipline produced by want of authority "   This opinion has prevailed

See Report of the Committee, of which Judge Spencer was the organ 1820.

(z)   Among the number of estimable philanthropists, who, in our opinion, somewhat deceive themselves on this point, we will mention Mr Tukerman, of Boston, who hopes that a day will appear, when, all the wicked having been regenerated, prisons will be no longer wanted   It is certain, that, if there were many individuals as ardently devoted to the cause of humanity, his hope would be no chimera   The name of Mr Tukerman cannot be pronounced without veneration , he is the living personification of benevolence and virtue.   A disciple of Howard, he spends his life in doing good, and strives to alleviate all human miseries , though of a feeble body, pale and almost lifeless, yet, if a good act is to be done, he becomes animated, and full of energy.   Mr Tukerman, as we said, perhaps deceives himself on some questions ; yet he renders immense services to society.   His charity towards the poor of Boston, has given him the authority of their guardian , and, if his kindness for them is extreme, it must not be believed that his severity, whenever just or necessary, is less manifested · the poor love him, because he is their benefactor, and they respect and fear him, because they know the austerity of his virtue   They know that his interest in them depends upon their good conduct * * * *   Mr. Tukerman does more for the good order and police of Boston, than all the aldermen and justices of the peace.

[One of the chief endeavours of the Rev Mr Tukerman, is to procure an opportunity of offering the gospel to the poor—he visits them, he enters into all their wants, gives them advice in all matters, teaches them to lead a happier and more comfortable life with the means they possess, counsels them on the education of their children, and takes an active part in the amelioration of prisons But he is known to every Bostonian , and should we, therefore, give an exact account of this exemplary man to others—we, in the same country, and personally acquainted with him—would be in a very disadvantageous position, compared with the French authors, who, at such a distance, are at liberty to express their full opinion, which, we frankly avow, we gave with some conciseness, for fear of displeasing the venerable subject of this note   It cheers and consoles the heart to meet with such a lowly charity in the convulsive agitations of society, with all its unfeeling and unmeaning formality, and selfish weakness.—TRANS.]

(aa)   The inspectors of the Philadelphia prison, signalize in the following terms one of the advantages of solitary confinement

" Personal vanity, which so often leads a prisoner to value himself upon being regarded by his fellows as a "staunch man," there deserts him ; for there is no one to applaud, admire, or see him " Second Report of the Inspectors of the Eastern Penitentiary, for the year 1831

(*bb*) It is an opinion pretty general in the United States, that the number of crimes increases more rapidly than the population, even in the states of the North. This is a mistake, which rests on a fact misunderstood—the constantly increasing crowd of prisoners. It is true, that, on January 30th, 1832, there were 646 convicts, i e ninety-six more than cells, and at Sing Sing, at the same period, the cells, a thousand in number, were not sufficient, in each of these prisons, it was necessary to double a certain number of cells which is destructive to the whole penitentiary system, however quickly new prisons are erected, the number of convicts increases still faster   This increase of criminals is owing to three principal causes   1 The population of the state of New York increases with unparalleled rapidity, 2 The Revised Statutes have increased the number of cases in which the prisoner is sent to the state-prison, (penitentiary) And finally, infinitely less pardons are granted of late, than formerly   This last cause alone would be sufficient to explain the progressive accumulation of convicts in the prisons of Sing-Sing and Auburn   See Statistical Observations, No. 17.

(*cc*). The freed person commits more crimes than the slave, for a very simple reason, because, becoming emancipated, he has to provide for himself, which, during his bondage, he was not obliged to do   Brought up in ignorance and brutality, he has been accustomed to work like a machine, all the motions of which are caused by an external power   His mind has remained utterly undeveloped. His life has been passive, thoughtless, and unthinking   In this state of moral annihilation, he commits few crimes   why should he steal, since he cannot be a proprietor ? The day when liberty is granted to him, he receives an instrument, which he does not know how to use, and with which he wounds, if not kills himself   His actions, involuntary when he was a slave, become now disorderly. judgment cannot guide him, for he has not exercised it   he is improvident, because he never has learned to think of futurity. His passions, not progressively developed, assail him with violence   He is the prey of wants, which he does not know how to provide for, and thus obliged to steal, or to die   Hence so many free negroes in the prisons, and hence their greater mortality than that of slaves (See Statistical Note, No 15) Must we conclude that it is wrong to emancipate slaves ? Certainly not, as little as we must preserve an evil forever, because it exists Only it seems to us necessary to acknowledge, that the transition from slavery to liberty, produces a state more fatal than favourable to the freed generation, and of which posterity alone can reap the fruits.

(*dd*) With us, besides the number of convictions, the number of accusations and prosecutions, not followed by conviction, is ascertained, also the proportion of crimes committed, to the convictions, is pretty nearly known. In the United States, it would be very difficult to obtain a document of this nature, first, no officer is charged by government to draw it up, and, secondly, it may be said, that, to a certain point, the basis itself of such a document, do s not exist.

Constituted as our judicial police is, it is customary to state the crime as soon as it is committed, and then to search for the author, who is condemned, though he may be absent   In the United States, another proceeding takes place, nobody is condemned, if not present at the trial, and, as long as the criminal is not apprehended, little attention is paid to the crime, with us, it would appear, that the crime is prosecuted, in the United States, the criminal   This explains why we know better the number of crimes committed, independently of convictions pronounced upon their authors

[The conviction *en defaut*, or *in contumaciam*, so repulsive to English law in criminal matters, is legal in most, or all of the countries of the European continent. If judgment is passed in a civil action against an absent person, it stands, but, in criminal matters, it is generally set aside, if the accused person appears, and submits to trial   though not always   They are frequent in political prosecutions.—Trans]

21

(*ee*)   This is one of the causes, to which the extraordinary increase of crimes in Connecticut is attributed.   It appears to us, indeed, incontestable, that the merited reputation of the excellent penitentiary of Wethersfield, must have contributed to increase the number of convictions.   But, it is evident, that this cause is not the only one, since the increase in question is progressive, and anterior by twenty years to the foundation of the penitentiary.

(*ff*).   "I have now done, but it is 'very stuff of the conscience' with me, never to write or speak on this subject without saying, that, whatever partial good you may do by penitentiary punishments, nothing radically important can be effected, unless you 'begin (as the fairy tale has it) at the beginning' Force education upon the people, instead of forcing them to labour as a punishment for crimes which the degradation of ignorance has induced them to commit; teach religion and science, and a simple system of penal law, in your primary schools; adopt a system of penal procedure that shall be expeditious, gratuitous, easily understood, and that shall banish all hope of escape from the defects of form, as well as every vexation to the parties or the witnesses   Provide subsistence for the poor who cannot labour, and employment for those who can.   But, above all, do not force those whom you are obliged to imprison before trial, be they innocent or guilty, into that contaminating society from which, after they are found to be guilty, you are so anxious to keep them.   Remember, that in Philadelphia, as well as in New York, more than two thousand five hundred are annually committed, of whom not one-fourth are found to be guilty; and that thus you have introduced every year more than 1,800 persons, presumed to be innocent, into a school where every vice and every crime is taught by the ablest masters; and we shut our eyes to this enormous evil, and inconsistently go on preaching the necessity of seclusion and labour, and industry after conviction, as if penitentiaries were the only places in which the contamination of evil society were to be dreaded.   Why will not Pennsylvania take the lead in perfecting the work she began, and, instead of patchwork legislation, that can never be effectual, establish a complete system, in which all the different, but mutually dependent subjects of education, pauperism, penal law, and prison discipline should be embraced'"—Edward Livingston's Letter to Roberts Vaux, 1828, pages 13 and 14

(*gg*).   Those who maintain that the Walnut street prison has really produced the effects generally ascribed to it, answer our objection thus . that the rigours of solitary confinement, and all that accompanies the system of isolation, has a salutary effect not only on the prisoners, but also on all those who fear being sent there.   This influence may undoubtedly exist   but it is not the influence of a penitentiary system which reforms the guilty, it is the effect of a punishment, which acts by way of terror, in this point of view, the punishment of death would be the best punishment, now, in the opinion of the enthusiastic partisans of the penitentiary system, the merit of this system is not in its cruelty and terror.   It is necessary, therefore, in order to judge of the *penitentiary system*, properly so called, to consider merely the effect it has directly on the reformation of the prisoners.   It is remarkable that the system of Walnut street is at present acknowledged as defective, by those even who attribute to it so happy an efficacy.

[We have spoken already once of the dread which solitary confinement inspires; it is essentially different from the terror excited by bodily suffering; the former is a moral dread, and the effects of solitary confinement may therefore be very active, without giving the least foundation to say, that the punishment of death would be, on this principle, the most efficacious.   A virtuous man dreads the moral suffering of repentance, and sometimes this prevents him more powerfully from doing certain acts, than other considerations. Is, therefore, this moral dread equal to any fear inspired by physical suffering?—TRANS.]

(*hh*).   See Gershom Powers, page 64, 1828, and report of the inspectors of Auburn, of 1829.   In 1826, it was for the first time attempted to obtain, by means of circulars directed to post-masters, sheriffs, attorney generals, &c. information respecting the morality and conduct of convicts, after the expiration of their imprisonment in Auburn This correspondence lasted until 1829, when it was dropped it was considered too expensive, and its results too uncertain

Postage in the United States is very dear, (i. e. for short distances —Trans.) and this expense became too onerous for the government of the prison. For the continuance of this correspondence, the federal government ought to have granted a franking privilege It was Judge Powers who started the idea of collecting this information the state government took no part in it ⸱ when he who had conceived the idea, abandoned it, it was dropped altogether. Besides, we do not know whether the statements thus received, deserve much confidence. The person consulted, is often influenced by other motives than the interests of truth, sometimes he gives a good character from misconceived benevolence or charity; sometimes from fear. As he gives this information unofficially, he does not feel himself bound to give the strictest truth, particularly if he believes that there is danger to himself, if he gives a bad character [It is only necessary to look at a thing which happens every day, to understand how far we can trust such unofficial information. How seldom is the written character, which, in many countries, masters are obliged to give to a servant who leaves them, strictly conformable to truth ? People think it cruel to give a doubtful character. It would be very different, if such information were obtained upon the oath of some officer, always, however, carefully avoiding the great evil of a surveillance, as it exists in France, and of which we have spoken in another note —Trans.]

(*ii*). The superintendent of the prison at Columbus, (Ohio,) says in his report ⸱ " Of sixty five convicts, who are in the penitentiary of Ohio, fifteen are recommitted convicts I know that fifteen or twenty individuals, formerly imprisoned in this prison, are at this moment in the prisons of Kentucky, Virginia, or Pennsylvania "—Re-translated.

Thus more than half of the recommitted convicts have not come back to the same prison where they underwent their first imprisonment , and yet recommittals cannot be proved generally in the United States, except by the convict's returning to the same prison. It must be, however, remarked, that the Columbus prison, here in question, is one of the worst in the United States See Report of the Superintendent of the Prison of Columbus Sixth Report of the Bost. Pris Disc Soc., page 508 [And respecting the last remark of the authors, we refer the reader to the Report of B Leonard, Keeper of the Ohio State Prison, of December, 1831, and a passage of Governor M'Arthur's Message to the Legislature of Ohio, extracts of both of which are to be found in the seventh Report of the Bost. Pris. Disc. Soc., page 59 and seq —Trans]

(*jj*). We shall show that the penitentiary system in question is less expensive than the old system of prisons. Yet even if the new system should be more expensive for its establishment and support, it would be, perhaps, finally, less onerous to society, if it is true that it has the power of reforming the wicked A prison system, however economical it may be in appearance, becomes very expensive if it does not correct the majority of the prisoners Because, as Mr. Livingston has well said " Discharging an unreformed thief, is tantamount to authorizing a tax of an unlimited amount to be raised on individuals " (Livingston's Letter to Roberts Vaux, 1828, page 13.)

(*kk*). The reasons of this difference are, 1 that the contractor is obliged, by his contract, to pay the ignorant and unskilful prisoner as well as him who works with skill and talent , 2 the contractor is not sure that he can sell the article which he causes to be made, and yet he never can interrupt the labour , 3. the day's labour in the prison is shorter than that of a free mechanic the latter works in winter from six in the morning to eight in the evening, whilst the prisoner works only from eight in the morning to four in the afternoon , 4. it seems that, at this moment, the contractors, and particularly the one at Auburn, have obtained too favourable conditions. This is one of the reasons why Auburn yields less than Wethersfield and Baltimore. With us, the contractor pays for the prisoner who works for him, a little more than half the wages of a free workman. But this contractor has a general contract, and for a long term.

(*ll*). The *pécule*, or over stint, is the part which is allowed to the prisoner, of the produce of his labour. It will be conceded, that it is for the interest of the prison government itself, to give proper wages to the prisoner, in order to stimulate his zeal, and if these wages were moderate, the state itself would gain by paying them. It is thus with the bagnes, where formerly the labour of the convicts was without remuneration, at present a slight *pécule* is allowed, which, by making the convicts more industrious, has also made their labour more productive. The state gives to the convict only so much as is thought proper. According to the law it owes him nothing.

But in the *maisons centrales de détention et de correction*, two-thirds of the produce of their labour belongs to the prisoners, one-third is given to them in the prison, for the alleviation of their situation, the other third is reserved, and handed over to them only when they leave the prison, one third is retained for the government. We may say, therefore, with reason, that the convicts work on their own account. It seems to us that it would be more just to establish the contrary principle, which is not contested in the United States, viz. that the prisoners work in the prison for the interest of society, to which they owe the indemnification of the expenses of their imprisonment. We have censured the severity of the American laws, which allow no *pécule* to the convict; that which is allowed in France seems to us too much, and we believe that it ought to be reduced. For the rest, we will not criticise here the existing laws, because the order of things which we censure is not prescribed by law, and, in some respects, is contrary to its provisions. The penal code, agreeing in this respect with the previous laws, recognises no right in the convict to any *pécule*; yet the convicts, sentenced to hard labour, who are in the "houses of detention," have, like the others, the two-thirds of the produce of their labour. As to the *réclusionnaires*, Article 21 of the Penal Code says, that they shall be employed in labour, the profit of which shall be partly applied for their benefit, in such way as government may regulate; but nowhere does the law impose upon government the obligation of giving them two-thirds of the produce. It leaves this point discretionary. Thus the administration of the prison does no illegal act by allowing so considerable a *pécule* to the *réclusionnaires*, but neither would it be illegal to act otherwise.

The "correctional convicts" [prisoners confined for police offences —Trans.] are the only ones in whom the law (Art. 41 Penal Code) acknowledges this right of a *pécule* of two-thirds, which government gives to all convicts indiscriminately. But is not this privilege, explicitly conferred by the law upon prisoners whose position is more favourable than that of the convicts to hard labour, (*forçats*,) sufficient to prove, that the legislature had not the intention, that those convicted of criminal offences should be treated alike with those sentenced for police offences? We doubt very much, that the latter, sentenced for more than a year, deserve the favour which Article 41 of the Penal Code bestows upon them; and if we insist upon this point, it is only in order to prove, that in granting this favour, the law necessarily refuses it to all those who are still less worthy of it.

If the *pécule* of the prisoners had a tendency to improve them, we would be far from censuring it, however considerable it might be, persuaded as we are, that the expenses by means of which the wicked are reformed, are investments, of which society reaps the fruits at a later period. But we see, on the contrary, that the *pécule*, which causes so much expense, is itself one of the most fertile sources of the corruption of prisons. [We only add here, for the better understanding of the above, that "correctional punishments," or, as it must be translated, "punishments of the police," are sometimes imprisonment for several years, as the "correctional police" takes cognizance of offences for which the code awards heavy penalties, such as stealing wood out of the royal forests, &c. —Trans.]

(*mm*). In France, the mean term of wages for a day's labour of all sorts of workmen, may be stated at two francs fifty centimes, in the United States it is double. This price, which, in Paris, varies from three to four francs, is less by two-thirds in the other cities, except some of the largest, as Lyons, Marseilles, &c.

Labour is, therefore, infinitely lower in France than in America. The price of raw materials is, in fact, a little higher.

In the United States, the cubic foot of hard stone costs twenty-five cents, in France it costs from one franc fifty centimes to two francs, (in Paris it is double.)

In America, a thousand feet of wood for building, cost from sixty to eighty francs, whilst at Paris they cost about two hundred francs (sawing, transport, excise, &c, included.) The cost is less in the departments.

The pound of iron costs about the same in the United States as in France. It is from fourteen to seventeen centimes (cast iron) in France, and twenty-one centimes in the United States (four cents.)

See for the prices in America the note of Mr. Cartwright, a distinguished engineer at Sing Sing, and the estimate of Mr Welles of Wethersfield, No 12.

We owe our information respecting prices, to the kindness of Mr Gourlier, architect in Paris, who has furnished us with a number of useful statements.

[A *franc* is equal to eighteen cents four mills. The franc has one hundred centimes. Respecting the wages for agricultural labour in the United States, we refer the reader to an interesting statement appended by Mr Holmes, senator of Maine, to the report of his speech delivered January 22, 1832, which may be found in the Washington papers of that period.—Trans.]

(*nn*) The penal establishment of the British in Australia, is at the same time a colonial establishment, which has its own administration, magistrates, police, &c. [See the articles New South Wales and Van Diemen's Land, under Diemen's (Van) Land, in the Encyclopædia Americana —Trans.] It is almost impossible to estimate the expenses which have reference to the penal establishment only.

Thus, for instance, the transportation of prisoners in Australia requires a corps of troops. But even if there were no criminals, Great Britain would nevertheless be obliged to keep a garrison there, though smaller than at present. These difficulties present themselves at each step of inquiry into the budget of the Australian settlements.

It is, therefore, impossible to establish, by dollars and cents, the expenditure caused by the penal establishment alone, but it is clear that the English may, by way of comparison with the expenses of other colonies, arrive at an approximate result, and present a pretty accurate statement of the expenses of transportation and the establishment connected with it.

In 1829, the expenditure of the penal establishment amounted to 401,283 pounds sterling.

The reporters on the budget, who give this statement to parliament, remark, that it has been impossible for them to find out with exactness, how much of this sum had reference to the penal establishment alone. But they add that "much the greater portion" is owing to the presence of convicts in Australia.

Let us suppose that only half of this sum, or 200,641 pounds sterling, has been spent for the support and surveillance of the 15,688 convicts who were in that year in Australia, each convict then has cost about twelve pounds sterling *

It may be answered, undoubtedly, that part of the expenses has been refunded by the duties of the colony, which amounted for the same year to 226,191 pounds sterling. But this revenue belongs to Great Britain, and if they were not destined for the support of the convicts in Australia, they would be added to the public treasure. Perhaps, it is true, they would be less, if transportation did

---

* We find in the deposition of a witness, heard on March 18th, 1832, by the committee appointed by the house of commons to inquire into the efficacy of punishments, the following statement.

The expense occasioned by the transportation of a convict to New South Wales, is thirteen pounds sterling, without counting the expenses which transportation in Australia causes. See Inquiry of 1832. (*Retranslated.*)

not exist, because the colony would then be less populous We have for this consideration taken but half of the whole sum of expenditure, though, in reality, probably more than two-thirds of the 400,000 pounds sterling have been applied for transport, support, and surveillance of the convicts.

For the rest, it seems to be the opinion in England, that transportation to Australia does not cost more than imprisonment in the metropolis

In fact, we find the following statement in a legislative document of 1816 —

Estimate of what it would cost to keep, support, and employ the convicts in England during the year 1817, 75,000 pounds sterling

Estimate of the probable expense of honouring the bills drawn by the Governor of New South Wales upon the public treasury, during the same year, 80,000 pounds sterling

See Report of the Committee to examine the expenses of the colonies, November 1, 1830

This report is among the legislative documents sent by the British parliament, volume entitled . Reports of Commissioners, 1830, 1831, page 69.

For the above estimates, see the same collection, vol. 37, page 297.

No. 4.

AGRICULTURAL COLONIES.

In all countries of Europe, without exception of those where agriculture has been perfected to the highest degree, vast territories are found, the arid and unpromising soil of which has not attracted the industry of man, and which remain the property of all, because no individual would take the trouble to cultivate them.

By the side of these useless fields, a population of *proletarii* is often placed, who are in want of soil and of the means of existence. In France, nearly 2,000,000 of poor are numbered, and the uncultivated lands form the seventh part of the area of the kingdom.

Experience, however, has shown, that the greatest part of the land, thus abandoned by man, may become productive, if sufficient capital and persevering efforts are applied for its cultivation.

This suggested the idea of agricultural colonies: it was thought that it was possible to settle the poor on neglected fields by the assistance of the rich, and that the former might be caused even to fertilize the soil which was given to them by advancing the necessary capital, and by subjecting them to useful regulations.

[General van den Bosch, while in the Island of Java, had learned from a mandarin, who had under him a colony of emigrant Chinese, how to make use of land, which most farmers would despise, chiefly by the careful preparation of manure, the most remarkable feature in Chinese husbandry. When the General returned to Europe, he laid before the King of the Netherlands a plan of pauper colonies on uncultivated land. Thus the first agricultural colonies sprang into existence. We refer for the details of their origin and their organization to an article on *Colonies, Pauper,* in the *Encyclopædia Americana.*—Trans.]

If experience should answer expectation, a result would be obtained favourable to the poor, (who would exchange misery for the comfort of a farmer,) and to society, the resources of which would be increased without new sacrifices.

It was in Holland where the first attempt was made to reduce these theories to practice; and, so far it may be said, that the success has surpassed expectation.

The society which made this noble trial, was formed in 1818, at the Hague, with the approbation, but not under the direction of the government; its example was followed in 1822, in Belgium. [Pauper colonies have been formed since in other countries. See the article *Armencolonieen* in the new appendix to the German *Conversations-Lexicon.*—Trans]

According to the statistics of the society, every individual who pays three guilders, becomes a member; and as such has a part in the management of affairs.

The society soon bought a vast extent of uncultivated land, which it divided into lots of seven acres each. [We refer again to the above quoted article of the *Americana*, which gives the details of expenses for a family, their outfit and whole establishment, with greater minuteness than the original of the present work.

Those persons who pay 1,600 guilders to the society, acquire thereby a perpetual right to designate the poor family which is to have one of the lots The same privilege is enjoyed by him who, for sixteen years, pays for each pauper placed by him in the colony, the sum of 23 guilders, which is the annual sum necessary for the colonist during the first sixteen years, in order to render his land productive.

Many communities, parishes, &c, soon bought perpetual privileges to send paupers to the colonies; and the government itself conceived the idea of making an agreement with the government of the colony, in order to send there a number of vagrants and children, for whom the former had to provide.

This agreement between the government and the colony gave rise to the "forced agricultural colonies."

As it was thought that the labour of people sent there by law, and therefore forced to work, would be less productive than that of free labour, and particularly of children, it asked 45 guilders annually for each child, and 35 guilders for a pauper who had begged, or a vagrant.

The government of these latter colonists, was of course arranged so as to suit the subjects for whom it was intended, and the consequence was that these "forced settlements" prospered not less than the others. In fact it was easier to oblige a prisoner to work, than to persuade a free person, accustomed to idleness, to become industrious.—Trans.]

In 1829, the agricultural settlements of Holland and Belgium, contained already 9000 prisoners, foundlings, &c., and free colonists.

Within ten years, a vast territory had for the first time been cultivated. Society had found, in this revolution, new guaranties of tranquillity ; the public treasure, a new source of revenue, and a still greater of economy; because, in fact, the child and the beggar cost less in the pauper colony than in the asylum ; and government acquired the right of getting rid for ever of the trouble of paying for them, by furnishing for sixteen years, this sum, already less than that which it had paid formerly.

Those who wish to find further information on this interest-ing subject, are referred to the work of Mr. Huerne de Pom-meuse just published: [and the account given by Mr. Jacob, the English reporter on the corn trade —TRANS.]

No. 5.

ON PUBLIC INSTRUCTION.

[INSTEAD of translating several of the general remarks of the authors on public instruction in the United States, we refer the reader to the Division *Education*, of the Article *United States*, in the *Encyclopædia Americana*. The reason why we have referred repeatedly to that work is, because we have given there the best information we were capable of affording on the subjects in question ; and as it is quite a recent publication, we can give, of course, no better information now, than that to be found in the Encyclopædia, which, as we have reason to suppose, will be in the reach of every reader of the present work As, however, no particular account is given in that article, of the peculiar sys-tem of education in the state of New York, we translate the fol-lowing from our authors, adding some remarks of the last Report on the Common Schools, to the Legislature of New York.—TRANS.]

Public authority, therefore, does not give up the power of directing public instruction, but it does not monopolize it. We will present a picture of the system of public instruction in the state of New York, whose extent, population, and riches, have placed her at the head of the Union.

In the state of New York, the legislature has created two spe-cial funds, called the Literature Fund, and the Common School Fund; the first is destined to support the higher studies, the second for elementary instruction. We shall see below of what sums these funds are composed.

At the head of the direction of the higher studies, an adminis-trative board is placed, called the University of the State of New York. (Revised Statutes, vol. i. pages 456–466) This body consists of twenty-one members, called regents. The governor and vice-governor of the state are members *ex officio ;* the other nineteen members are chosen by the legislature.

If a particular establishment wishes to obtain a charter, by virtue of which it may officially exist as such, it must address the regents of the university; and the legislature acts in these

affairs only after having heard their opinion. As soon as an official existence has been acknowledged by a charter, numerous
relations exist between the college and the state. Each year, the
regents of the university distribute, to all colleges thus recognised, the assistance furnished by the Literature Fund; on the
other hand, they are subject to the inspection of the regents,
who report annually to the legislature. The regents also have
the right to give diplomas in matters of science and belles-
lettres.

The fund for primary instruction is infinitely larger than that
destined for the higher studies, and society takes also a more
direct part in the government of these schools.

At the head of the administration of primary instruction in
the state of New York, is placed a functionary, called *superintendent of schools* It is he who has to watch over the execution
of laws respecting public instruction, and to distribute the annual
support given by the state to the counties.

Each township is obliged to keep a school, and to support it
by a sum at least equal to that which the state gives

At the head of the schools of each township, stand the school
commissioners, who distribute to each community of the township, that portion of the sum furnished by the liberality of the
state, to which it has a right. They examine the teachers, choose,
inspect, and discharge them, but from their decisions an appeal
lies to the superintendent of schools.

The latter receives every year a detailed account of the state
of instruction in all the townships of the commonwealth, and
lays the result of these reports before the legislature, accompanying it with his remarks. (Revised Statutes, vol. i. pages 466–
488)

Besides the colleges and academies above mentioned, and the
primary schools, there exist in the state of New York a very
large number of other establishments for public instruction,
which receive no support from government, and are of course
subject to no inspection; the body politic does not recognise
them any more than other private establishments or persons.

Statistical Details respecting the New York School System.

[The authors gave these details for the year 1829 We have
substituted for them those contained in the Annual Report of
the Superintendent of Common Schools of the State of New
York, made to the Legislature January 7th, 1833.—Trans]

There are two simple systems respecting public schools: either
the government gives nothing, and leaves the whole to the various communities, or the state provides for the whole expense.

Both these systems have their advocates in the United States.

The system of the state of New York is of a mixed character:

the legislature gives annually a certain sum to each township, to assist in defraying the expenses of public instruction, and the township is obliged to furnish a sum at least equal. The results of this system are much praised. If the township had to defray the whole expense, perhaps it would not do it satisfactorily; and if the public treasury paid the whole, the community would be less watchful over the application of the funds.

There are certain states of the Union, e. g. Pennsylvania, in which the common schools, supported by the public money, are destined for the children of the poor only, who are instructed there gratuitously.

In the state of New York, as well as in New England, but one kind of common school, assisted or supported by the public, exists. The children of the rich and of the indigent meet there, and contribute according to the means of their parents. The inhabitants of the state of New York say, that the poor seize with much more zeal on the means of instruction offered to them, which cost little, but which they nevertheless think they pay, than those which they receive as a charity; they add, and justly so, that this mingling of children in the same schools is more in unison with the republican institutions of their country.

The following is the way in which the necessary sum for the support of common schools, is obtained in each township.

1. The commonwealth grants an annual supply.

2. The township levies a sum at least equal.

So far it is society, as such, which acts, pursuing a political end. The citizens, as a body, establish common schools, and contribute part of their expenses, though, of course, a number among them have no special or private interest in public instruction.

3. But the money thus obtained is far from being sufficient; it is but a premium of encouragement given by the townships to the various communities, and by the state to the various townships. Each pupil is yet obliged to pay a certain sum individually, to defray the rest of the expenses.

This will be understood better from the following:

In 1829 the state gave to the different townships the sum of 100,000 dollars, the produce of the Common School Fund, the capital of which then was 1,684,628 dollars.

The townships, in the same year, paid, for the same purpose, 124,556 dollars.

In the same year, a fund especially applied to common schools, produced 14,095 dollars. [For this fund see further below.— Trans.]

Thus society, in 1829, paid, for common schools in that state, 238,651 dollars. This was paid by all, whether they had a special interest or not; those especially interested, i. e. those who sent children to school, paid, besides, the sum of 821,986 dollars, as school money.

The sum total, therefore, paid by the inhabitants of the state of New York, in the year 1829, for primary instruction, has been about 1,060,637 dollars, of which, it must be mentioned, the greatest portion has been furnished voluntarily.

[The following are extracts of the report of A C. Flagg, superintendent of common schools, to the legislature, as above mentioned. Want of space obliged us to leave out a number of interesting facts in that able paper, to which we must refer the reader also for valuable information respecting the school system of some other states.—Trans.]

I. *As to the Condition of the Common Schools.*

There are fifty-five organized counties, and eight hundred and eleven towns and wards in the state.

There are 9,600 organized school districts in the state, of which 8,941 have made their annual reports.

In the districts from which reports have been received, there were, on the last day of December, 1831, five hundred and eight thousand eight hundred and seventy-eight children over 5 and under 16 years of age, and four hundred and ninety-four thousand nine hundred and fifty-nine scholars were taught in the same districts during the year, and eight thousand nine hundred and forty-one district schools have been kept open for the reception of pupils an average period of eight out of the twelve months.

Two hundred and sixty-seven new districts have been formed during the year for which the reports are made; and the number of districts which have made reports to the commissioners, has increased one hundred and six during the same time.

The average number of districts organized, including all the towns of the state, (773) is nearly 12½ for each town. The average number of scholars instructed in the districts from which returns have been received (8,941) is a fraction more than 55 scholars for each school. All the estimates in this report relating to the number of children taught, have reference to the whole number of scholars on the rolls of the district schools for the year; and it is not to be understood that each individual of the 494,959 scholars reported as having been taught, has had 8 months of instruction during the year, but that this is the aggregate number of scholars on the rolls of the schools receiving more or less instruction, and that eight thousand nine hundred and forty-one schools have been kept open for the reception of pupils an average period of eight out of the twelve months.

In 1816, the number of organized districts was 2,755, and the children returned as taught in the common schools, was 140,106.

The increase in 16 years, of the districts which have adopted the school system, has been 6,845, and the increase in the number of children taught in the same time, 354,853.

II. *Estimates and Expenditures of the School Moneys.*

The reports from the commissioners of the several towns show that the school moneys received by them, and paid to the trustees of the several districts in April, 1832, on the district reports of the previous January, amount to $305,582 78 cents. Of this sum, 100,000 dollars were paid from the state treasury, $188,384 53 cents, were raised by a tax upon the property of the inhabitants of the several towns and cities in the state, and $17,198 25 cents, were derived from local funds possessed by some of the towns.

The amount paid for teachers' wages in the several districts of the state, over and above the public money apportioned by the commissioners, is $358,320 17 cents This sum, added to the public money, gives a total of $663,902 95 cents paid for teachers' wages ; except about 60,000 in the city of New York, which is raised by a special tax, and applied to the erection of school-houses

The productive capital of the school fund now amounts to $1,735,175 28 cents. The revenue actually received on account of this fund, for the year ending September 30, is $93,755 31 cents.

The perpetuity of the school fund is guarantied, and its gradual increase provided for, in the following provision of the new Constitution, viz. "The proceeds of all lands belonging to this state, except such parts thereof as may be reserved or appropriated to public use, or ceded to the United States, which shall hereafter be sold or disposed of, together with the fund denominated the Common School Fund, shall be, and remain a perpetual fund ; the interest of which shall be inviolably appropriated, and applied to the support of common schools throughout this state."

This provision of the Constitution in relation to the transfer of the state lands to the school fund, took effect on the 1st of January, 1823, at which time the capital of the Common School Fund amounted to $1,155,827 40 cents. It is now, in 1833, $1,735,175.

In addition to the state fund for the support of schools, many of the towns have a local fund from which their schools derive essential aid. In most cases, these local funds were created by reservations of lots of land for school purposes, in the original grants of the townships. These lots have subsequently been sold or rented, and the fund is managed by trustees chosen by the inhabitants of the towns, who are allowed to apply to the support of the common schools, only the revenue of the fund, preserving the capital entire. Many of these school lots were very valuable, and some of the towns derive an annual revenue of more than five hundred dollars from the fund established by the sale of the school lands. In dividing any of the original townships, the school lot was also divided, which accounts for the small sums received by many of the towns, as at present organized.

In the original grants under the act of 1789, there was also a reservation of one lot for the support of the gospel in each township. By an act passed in 1798, the freeholders and inhabitants of the town in which the reserved lots lie, were authorized, in legal town-meeting, to apply the avails of the gospel and school lots, either for schools or gospel, or both. The town-meetings, it is believed, generally voted to apply the avails of the " gospel and school lots" exclusively for the support of schools. And, in 1813, it was provided by statute " that all moneys now due, or hereafter to become due, and which shall come into the hands of the commissioners of public lots, and have not been applied and paid over to religious societies, shall be apportioned among the several school districts in the several towns in the aforementioned counties,* any thing in the acts heretofore passed to the contrary notwithstanding." The annual revenue arising from the avails of the gospel and school lots in the whole state, is $14,571 24 cents, and the aggregate capital of these local school funds may be estimated at nearly 250,000 dollars.

In several of the towns, there is a local school fund derived from a different source. Before the establishment of the present poor-house system, many of the towns had a fund for the support of the poor. In those counties in which all the poor are declared to be a county charge, the town fund is no longer needed for its original object; and an act passed April 27, 1829, authorizes the inhabitants of any town thus situated, to appropriate the poor fund to any other purpose; and, if for common schools, the money thus applied is to be placed in charge of the school commissioners, as a permanent school fund for the town, and the annual interest to be apportioned to the common schools; unless the inhabitants at an annual town meeting make a different application of the capital. The revenue received from local funds, other than those derived from gospel and school lands, is 2,627 dollars; which is the interest at six per cent., of a capital of nearly 44,000 dollars.

It is evident from the data thus furnished, that the aggregate capital of the various town school funds, amounts to 294,000 dollars. Add this to the capital of the state school fund, and it

* Onondaga, Cayuga, and Seneca, were named in the act.

makes a productive capital of two millions and twenty-eight thousand dollars, set apart for the support of common schools.

III. *The Management of the Common School Fund.*

The Common School Fund is included in the general system for managing the finances of the state, and the Commissioners of the Land Office have the management and sale of the school fund lands, as well as of the lands belonging to the other funds of the state

IV. *The Organization of the Common Schools.*

The organization of the common schools, so far as relates to the distribution and application of the money, and a formal compliance with the requirements of the statute, is highly satisfactory, and the superintendent is not aware of any defects in the organization of the system, which, in his judgment, could be reached by legislative enactments. The school money is apportioned by the superintendent to 780 cities and towns—this money is paid to the treasurers of 55 counties, and by these officers to the commissioners of 780 towns and cities, and by these commissioners to the trustees of 8,941 districts. The trustees apply the money, and account for its application annually to the school commissioners, and the commissioners make an annual report through the county clerk's office to the superintendent, which contains an abstract of the trustees' reports, as well as an account of the moneys received and apportioned to the districts, by the commissioners themselves. The returns received in October and November last, from the clerks of the several counties, contained copies of the commissioners' reports from every town and city in the state. When it is considered that the district and town officers who have an agency in making these returns, form a body of thirty-eight thousand persons, it must be conceded that such results could only be produced by the most perfect organization, and an attention to their duties on the part of the officers of common schools, which is highly creditable to their zeal and intelligence. In 1822, twenty-seven towns made no returns; in 1823, twenty-one towns; in 1824, twenty-nine towns; in 1825, seventeen towns; in 1827, two towns; since which time, returns have been obtained from all the towns

Those who founded the common school system of this state, never contemplated that the public fund would at any time yield a revenue adequate to the support of such an extensive establishment. The first condition on which the public money was offered to the towns, was, that the inhabitants of each town should, by a vote at their town-meeting, authorize a tax to be raised equal at least in amount to the sum apportioned to their town from the state treasury; which sum was to be added to the apportionment from the school fund, and the amount thus made up, be applied to the payment of teachers' wages. Another requirement of the system is, that before the inhabitants of a neighbourhood can participate in the public fund, they must organize a district, erect a school-house, furnish it with fuel, and necessary appendages, and have a school taught therein at least three months by a legally qualified teacher; and, it is on a report of all these facts by the trustees, that the commissioners are authorized·to apportion the school money to a district.

The voluntary contributions of the inhabitants of the school districts, form so important a portion of the means which are necessary to give effect to the school system, that, when new forms were furnished with the Revised Statutes, a column was added, requiring the trustees in each district to report the sums paid for teachers' wages, by the patrons of the district school, over and above the sums received from the state treasury, the town tax, and the local school fund.

Seven hundred and sixty-one towns, (omitting all the wards,) have made returns the past year, exhibiting a total amount paid by individuals in the several school districts, for school bills, besides the public money apportioned to the districts, of $358,320 17 cents; which, added to the public money, ($305,582 78,) makes the aggregate amount of $663,902 95 cents paid for teachers' wages alone, in the common schools of the state. *

These returns show, that where the state, or the school fund, pays one dollar for teachers' wages, the inhabitant of the town, by a tax upon his property, pays $1 28 cents, ($60,000 deducted for New York,) and by voluntary contribution in the school district where he resides, $3 58 cents for the same object; and the proportion of 17 cents is derived from the local school fund.

The amount paid for teachers' wages, is only about one-half of the expense annually incurred for the support of the common schools, as the following estimates will show.   Taking the average between the whole number of districts organized, (9,600,) and the number from which reports have been received the last year, (8,941,) and it will give 9,270 as the probable number of schools in operation.   Deducting 30 for the city of New York, and there will remain 9,240 school-houses, which, at an average price of 200 dollars each, would make a capital of 1,840,000 dollars, add to this the cost of the school-houses in the city of New York, (say 200,000 dollars,) and it exhibits a capital of

* A part of the money received by the commissioners in the city of New York, is applied to the erection of school-houses, the purchase of fuel, books, &c. and that amount, perhaps 60,000 dollars, should be deducted from the sum applied for teachers' wages.

2,040,000 dollars vested in school-houses, which, at an interest
of 6 per cent. per annum, is -   -   -   - $122,400 00
Annual expense of books for 494,959 scholars,
  at 50 cents each,   -   -   -   -   247,479 50
Fuel for 9,270 school-houses, at $10 each,   -   92,700 00
                                          462,579 50
Add public money appearing from the returns,
  and before referred to,   -   -   -   305,582 78
Add also the amount paid in the districts besides
  public money, -   -   -   -   -   -   358,320 17
                                     $1,126,482 45

And it makes a grand total of one million one hundred and
twenty-six thousand four hundred and eighty-two dollars and
forty-five cents, expended annually for the support of the common schools of the state.

The preceding estimates show that the revenue of the school
fund, (that is, the $100,000 paid from the state treasury,) pays
a fraction less than one-eleventh of the annual expenditures upon
common schools, two-elevenths are raised by a tax upon the
several towns and cities, and the three-elevenths thus made up,
(being the item of $305,582 in the foregoing estimate,) consti-
tutes what is called the "school money," and is the sum received by the commissioners of the cities and towns, and paid
to the trustees of the several public schools. A fraction more
than two-elevenths, (being $215,110 for school-houses and fuel,)
is raised by a tax upon the property of the several districts, in
pursuance of a vote of the inhabitants thereof; and the residue,
nearly six-elevenths, (being $605,799,) is paid voluntarily by
the parents and guardians of the scholars for the balance of their
school bills, (after applying the public money,) and for school
books

There is some difference of opinion among the friends of universal instruction, as to the mode of providing funds for maintaining the schools, which is best adapted to the accomplishment
of the object. Of the three modes of providing for popular instruction—that in which the scholars pay every thing, and the
public nothing—that in which the public pays every thing, and
the scholars nothing—and that in which the burden is shared by
both—Dr Chalmers, in his "Considerations on the parochial
schools of Scotland," gives a decided preference to the latter
mode, which is the system adopted by the state of New York.

This system offers to each neighbourhood a small sum yearly,
as an inducement to the inhabitants to tax themselves, and to
establish and maintain a school. The sum distributed is not so

23

large as to induce a belief that the inhabitants have no exertions
to make themselves, on the contrary, it is coupled with such
terms as to require a school-house to be erected, and a considerable sum to be expended, before the district can participate in
the public fund : And this fund, as the returns show, pays so
small a share, (only one-eleventh of the school expenditures,)
that there is a continued necessity for individuals to tax themselves, in order to keep up the school. That feature in our system which authorizes district taxation, and which requires individuals to pay beyond the amount received from the public, has
a beneficial influence upon the school, and all the district operations The power given districts to levy taxes upon all the property of the inhabitants for school-houses, repairs, appendages,
and fuel, induces a punctual attendance of all the taxable inhabitants at the school meetings ; those citizens who have most at
stake in the district are induced to act as trustees, in order to
secure themselves against improvident taxation, and all the ills
of a careless administration of the district affairs And even the
persons who patronize the school, are induced by the assessment
to send their children with more punctuality, in order to get an
equivalent for their money ; when if the whole sum was paid by
the state, these same persons might neglect the school as a matter
with which they had very little concern.

The amount distributed from the school fund of this state, has
been eminently serviceable in arousing the public attention, and
in affording an inducement for the establishment of schools,
where otherwise they might have been neglected. This is all
that can beneficially be done by a public fund : if twenty-five
dollars induces the inhabitants of a neighbourhood to establish a
school, it answers all the useful purposes of one hundred dollars
applied for the same object ; and it is quite probable, that a district receiving twenty-five dollars annually, will support as good
a school, and be as prosperous, as if the entire expenses of the
school were paid by a public fund. The distribution of one hundred thousand dollars from the state treasury, under our system,
ensures the application of more than a million annually to the
purposes of common schools ; and in a way, too, which does as
much, if not more substantial good, than if the whole sum was
disbursed from the state treasury. What more, then, can be desired or expected from the mere appropriation of money to that
object by the state ? It is admitted that the standard of education
in the schools is below what it ought to be, but would this be
changed by paying a million of dollars annually from the state
treasury, instead of raising it in the towns and districts ? Would
the source from which the money came have any influence in
elevating the character of the teachers ? And from what source
is the capital to be derived, which is to produce annually a re-

venue of a million of dollars? If by a resort to taxation, it can
in no way be done so economically as by the people themselves,
in the present mode. With this view of the subject, instead of
repining because the revenue of the school fund apportions only
the small sum of twenty cents annually to each child between
five and sixteen years of age, we should rather rejoice that such
great results have been accomplished with such comparatively
trifling means

The incorporated academies may be relied upon as seminaries
for the education of teachers There are now fifty-five academies
in the state; in the erection and endowment of which about
four hundred thousand dollars have been expended by the state
and by individuals; and to these academies a revenue of ten
thousand dollars is distributed annually by the state In 1827,
one hundred and fifty thousand dollars were transferred from the
general funds of the state to the Literature Fund, for the avowed
object of promoting the education of teachers of common schools,
by increasing the apportionment to the academies. And it is believed that if the school districts would hold out as strong inducements as are presented by the other pursuits of life to young
men of talents, that there would be no want of a sufficient number of well qualified instructers; and that the academies would
in fact become seminaries for preparing teachers for the common
schools.

The subject of primary education in the city of New York, is
of vast importance to the well being of the city Impressed with
a belief that the arrangements for public instruction were altogether too limited for the wants of that great and growing city,
the superintendent has on several occasions called the attention
of the legislature to this subject; and in November, 1831, addressed a letter to the Commissioners of Common Schools for
the City of New York, asking their advice in relation to the
best mode of extending the means of instruction. The sum
apportioned to the public schools in New York, during the
past year, was $90,748 86, being nearly twenty dollars to each
scholar instructed in the schools which are allowed by the corporation to share in the fund. The culpable indifference of parents in availing themselves of the benefits of the public schools,
is still felt as a serious evil in the city of New York. The Public
School Society has endeavoured to counteract this deplorable
apathy, by employing a person at a salary of eight hundred dollars a year, to visit parents in all sections of the city, and to invite and persuade them to send their children to school· and it
appears by the report of the commissioners, that the corporation
of New York have passed an ordinance, "excluding from the
participation of public charity, when it may be required, all out
door poor, whether emigrants or not, who, having children be-

tween the age of five and twelve, neglect or refuse to send them
to some one of the public schools.''

Arrangements are making by the trustees of the Public School
Society, to establish ten additional schools for small scholars, in
different parts of the city The public schools in New York are
of an excellent character, and the efforts which are making to
increase their number and extend their usefulness, it is hoped,
will secure the co-operation of all the friends of popular education.

A strong conviction that something ought to be done to provide the means of instruction for the inmates of the manufacturing establishments, which are building up in various sections of
the state, induces the superintendent again to call the attention
of the legislature to this subject In many of these establishments
children are employed at a very early age, and there is great reason to apprehend, that the necessities or the cupidity of parents
and guardians, will, in too many cases, overcome their obligations
to their children and to society, and induce them entirely to neglect their education, in order to secure the comparatively miserable stipend which they can earn in these manufactories Our
laws now require the children in the poor-houses to be instructed ; and if they are bound out, the law requires a condition in
each indenture, that the master will cause such child to be instructed to read and write, and if a male, will cause him to be
instructed in the general rules of arithmetic. The returns from
the superintendent of the poor, for the year ending December
1, 1832, include more than one thousand scholars instructed in
the poor-houses. The policy of all our laws is to secure a good
common school education to every child in the state ; and the
condition of the children who are employed in the manufactories, as to their means of instruction, ought to be carefully inquired into and provided for. The diffusion of education among
all classes of our population, is deemed of such vital importance
to the preservation of our free institutions, that if the obligations
which rest upon every good citizen in this particular, are disregarded, the persons having the custody of such children, ought
to be visited with such disabilities, as will induce them, from
interest, if not from principle, to cause the children to be instructed, at least in reading, writing, and arithmetic.

Those who have considered the numerous difficulties which
present themselves at every point, in carrying into effect a system of universal instruction ; and who have witnessed the indifference of parents in sending their children to schools which
have been brought almost to their doors, cannot but regard the
Sunday schools as an important auxiliary to the cause of general
education. Thousands are induced to attend these schools, and
are taught to read, who, but for the benevolent exertions of the

Sunday school teachers, would be entirely neglected, and left a prey to ignorance and vice

The efforts made by the friends of the Sunday schools, in visiting parents and seeking out children who need instruction, in providing clothing for such as are destitute, and in removing all impediments to their attendance, give this system of instruction peculiar claims to the favour and good wishes of the friends of popular education. To ensure a good common school education to the entire mass of our population, is a work of such magnitude in itself, and of such vast importance to the well being and permanency of our republican institutions, that the friendly co-operation of all denominations of persons is desirable, if not indispensable, in carrying into effect the great purposes which the common school system of this state was designed to accomplish.

It is not only in our days, that society, in America, has taken so much interest in diffusing knowledge among its members. [Here the authors quote the law of New Haven plantation of 1660, which directs parents and masters of apprentices to take care of the instruction of the children or young persons under their protection The historian dwells with satisfaction on the facts, that ten years after the settlement of Massachusetts' Bay, Harvard College was founded, and, in 1647, the legislature of that province passed a law, requiring every town, with fifty families, to provide a school —Trans]

No. 6.

PAUPERISM IN AMERICA.

The authors give under this head a hasty sketch of the English and American views respecting paupers, according to which, charity has become, in a degree, a political institution, and close the article by giving some statistics of pauperism in the state of New York. The English and our own laws, and statistics respecting pauperism, are better known to our readers, than they could become by this sketch, intended for the French public. we therefore pass it over, and shall substitute extracts taken from the Report of the Secretary of State, giving an Abstract of the Returns of the Superintendents of the Poor in the several Counties, made January 17, 1832

"It will be seen, that 15,564 paupers have been relieved in 54 counties, during the past year. Of this number, 13,573 were county paupers, and 1,990 town paupers. The aggregate expense for the relief and support of the 15,564 paupers, has been $245,433 21 cents.

"It is shown that there has been paid for the transportation of paupers, $4,042 13 cents; to superintendents, $7,573 80 cents. to overseers, $5,396 65 cents; justices, $1,694 78 cents, to keepers and officers, $17,734 50 cents, that the value of the labour of the paupers was $12,663 26 cents; the amount saved in consequence of labour of paupers, $17,546 74 cents, and that the average expense of supporting a pauper at a poor-house, is $33 28 cents per year, or $64\frac{8}{10}$ cents per week.

"There are 5,221 acres of land attached to the poor-houses, and the total value of all the poor-house establishments in the state is $830,350 46 cents, 10,896 paupers have been received into the poor-houses during the year; there were born in the poor-houses, in the same time, 170, died during the year, 1,147, bound out, 318; discharged, 5,962; absconded, 545; total females in poor-houses, December 1, 1831, 2,532—males, 2,862—total of both sexes, 5,554, of those relieved during the year, there were 2,795 foreigners, 410 lunatics, 224 idiots, and 31 mutes.

"It is stated in some of the reports, that the poor-house system will save more than half the amount expended under the old mode of supporting the poor; and the superintendents of Dutchess, where the poor-house has been erected in the course of the last year, estimate that the saving of expense to the county, by the change in the mode of supporting the poor, will be nearly one-half.

"From the data already furnished, it is confidently believed that the poor-house system, when carried into full effect, will produce a saving in the expenditures for the support of the poor in the whole state, of at least *two hundred and fifty thousand dollars*, which is nearly equal to all the ordinary expenses of the state government "

No. 7.

IMPRISONMENT FOR DEBT IN THE UNITED STATES.

[The article on this subject, which, for about ten years, has so deservedly attracted public attention in a high degree in the United States, is treated in a very short article in the original. The reader who wishes satisfactory and detailed information on this important and melancholy subject, is referred to the Reports of the Boston Prison Discipline Society, especially to those of the years 1830, 1831, and 1832, in which Mr L. Dwight has collected a great many materials, (statements of facts and opinions of distinguished persons or bodies and laws) relating to it. The authors say, that it is thought that, in Pennsylvania, seven thousand individuals are annually arrested for debt. If we add this number to that of the convicts, which we have estimated for 1830, at 2,074, we shall find, that about one out of forty-four inhabitants, goes annually into the prison.

We have received the Report on the Debtors' Apartment of the Arch Street Prison, in Philadelphia, by Mr. Gibbon, Chairman, read to the house of representatives, March 15, 1833, which represents a state truly appalling, and, it seems inconceivable, that a society, which has, in making laws, but to follow its own dictates and interest, and especially one, which has distinguished itself, in other respects, for its humanity, from the time of its foundation, should allow such a state of things to continue any longer It is certainly an unhappy anomaly. Mr. Gibbon's report begins thus:

"From an abstract of cases of imprisonment on execution for debts *under one dollar*, taken from the prison records of the debtors' apartment, in the city and county of Philadelphia, between the 1st of May, and the 24th of September, 1830, it appears that the total amount of debts, in forty such cases, was $23 40½, upon which the costs were $70 20—making a total of debts and costs, $93 60½. Among them were debts of 2, 19, 25, and 37 cents! Such persons are generally brought to prison in a state of great destitution and misery—in rags and wretchedness—upon what are styled 'spite actions.'

"The colonial law, (which has continued obligatory since our revolution,) allows magistrates cognizance, *without appeal*, of sums below 40 shillings, or $5 33⅓ From the 1st of December, 1829, until the 1st of December, 1830, the imprisonments for debts, under $5 33⅓, in the jail of the city and county of Philadelphia, being *without stay of execution*, were as follows: Number of cases, 432, total number of days in confinement, 3,322; total amount of debts, $1,488 13; costs imposed on the above cases, $834 52. Of these, 364 cases were discharged by various processes, *without satisfying the creditors!* It appears, then, that the payment of the sums due, is defeated by the rigorous enforcement of the ultimate process for recovery. Of the 432 cases, but 68 ever paid the creditors a cent, and the total amount altogether paid, was the small sum of $160 68—after the prisoners *who paid* had suffered 214 days confinement *in idleness.*

"It is calculated that the labour lost during the imprisonment of these individuals, would have settled the whole amount of the debts which were paid, and that there is an absolute loss to the community, even when the money is eventually produced. Thirteen of the cases paid, appear to have been for *militia fines*, the whole amount for which was $26, enforced by the power delegated to the collectors."

In several late numbers of a German law periodical, called "Archives of Civil Law," Professor Mittermaier, one of the most distinguished lawyers of Germany, proves that personal arrest for simple debt cannot be justified on any principles of law.—TRANS.]

No. 8.

IMPRISONMENT OF WITNESSES.

IN the United States, if a witness cannot give bail or guarantee for his appearance, he is imprisoned, and remains in company with convicts and persons charged with crime, until the sitting of the court.

We have been told in Philadelphia, that two young Irishmen, who had been for too short a time in the country to find people who would answer for their appearance, and were too poor to give bail, had thus been imprisoned for a whole year, waiting for the time when they might give their testimony.

A foreign merchant was robbed in a public house in Baltimore; he informed the authorities of it, but as the thief had not left him enough to give bail, he was detained in prison   Thus, in order to discover who had robbed him of a part of his property, he was obliged to await justice in prison, and to abandon business which urgently called him to the west.

We mention these instances out of thousands

In Europe, people often complain of the burthensome obligations which the laws sometimes impose upon the indigent, and of the difficulties which surround them if they seek justice.

In America, the situation of the poor is harder still: if one is by chance witness of a crime, he must take care not to be seen; and if he is himself the subject, he has only to fly for fear justice will protect him.

However monstrous to us such a law may appear, habit has familiarized Americans to it in such a degree that our remarks on the subject made an impression but upon a few. The mass of lawyers see in this nothing contrary to their ideas of justice and injustice, nor even to their democratic constitution.

The Americans, descendants of the English, have provided in every respect for the rich, and hardly at all for the poor. In the same country where the complainant is put in prison, the thief remains at liberty if he can find bail. Murder is the only crime whose authors are not protected.

[He whom the authors call a thief, and who may remain at liberty, is not a thief in the eye of society, until he has been found so upon trial. Imprisonment of witnesses, however shocking at first to every person brought up in a country where nothing of this kind exists, is intimately connected with the whole English system of administration of justice, which admits, in but a limited degree, written evidence in criminal trials. Where this is permitted, or where, as in Germany, the whole process is carried on in writing, and where in fact nothing is permitted as evidence but what is taken down in writing and properly attested, no imprisonment of witnesses is necessary. Yet even there, persons are prevented from leaving the state, or any certain place, if their testimony is believed to be important; and if it is impossible at the moment to put all the necessary questions to them If then, according to the English administration of justice, the personal appearance of witnesses is necessary in most cases in criminal trials, the state must have some security, of whatever kind this may be, for their appearance at the time of trial. Where would be the justice, if this security did not exist? A persecuted man could not be sure of the means of defending himself; hatred might unjustly accuse a person of a crime, and expose him to all possible inconveniences previously to the trial, &c. But, though the appearance of witnesses is necessary, the state is satisfied in taking any sufficient guarantee, the least troublesome possible; and it is only he who cannot avail himself of this offer, who must give the guarantee in his own person. The law is not cruel or inconsistent. In a rude state of things, all witnesses would be imprisoned; but the law wishes to be as mild as safety permits; hence it allows bail for their appearance. If the poor can find a wealthy friend, or several friends, who will give bail for him, he may do so. The law is not against the poor; the state must have the certainty of the witnesses' appearance; that is all. That there is in this case a difference between the rich and the poor, is but a repetition of what we find throughout life. Mr. Edward Livingston expresses himself on this subject thus: "the temporary privation of their (witnesses') liberty is a necessary sacrifice for the safety of society; it is taken on the same principle that justifies the appropriation of private property for public purposes, and it carries with it the same right of indemnity " (Introductory Report to the Code of Prison Discipline, Philadelphia, 1827, page 35.) The same remarks apply to the imprisonment of accused persons, who may go at large if they find a guarantee, considered by the state equally safe, but more convenient to them. The cases put by the authors are

24

either very exaggerated, or very unfrequent. And their sentiments throughout, on this point, evince an ignorance of the principles of our institutions. As to the general remark, that the
law in America protects the rich but not the poor, we can only
say, that we have heard a thousand times the contrary, but never
this remark made. Have they not seen, when visiting us, the
hogs belonging to the poor, in the streets of New York and Philadelphia, contrary to constant complaint, and even positive regulation?—Trans]

No. 9.

TEMPERANCE SOCIETIES.

[The authors give, under this head, a short exposition of these
interesting and novel societies. As the Article *Temperance Societies* in the *Encyclopædia Americana* was but recently written, by one of the most competent persons in the United States,
we refer the reader to it. We would mention, besides, an Article
entitled "*A Succinct History of the Origin, Principles, Objects, and Progress of Temperance Societies in the United
States of America,*" in the first number of The American
Quarterly Temperance Magazine, Albany, February, 1833. This
article was drawn up by the corresponding secretary of the New
York State Temperance Society, in compliance with a request
of the Prussian Consul in New York, who had been directed by
the Prussian government to collect all important information
on Temperance Societies. We trust that the Prussian government has not the idea of taking any direct part in the establishment of these societies in that kingdom, as nothing could possibly be more fatal to these very societies, or, in fact, more directly
against every true idea of public right, than a similar interference
on the part of government in so private an affair as that of regu-
lating one's beverage. But we fear that government, there, though
accustomed for a long series of years to manage every thing, and
to exercise the right of interference with the most private affairs
of its subjects, will meet with no better success—though temperance societies are, in the north of Germany, urgently called for
—than the Saxon government has in the same cause, as we learn
from a letter quoted in the same number of the Temperance
Quarterly. May the slightest attempt never be made with us, to
change the character of temperance societies, as they now exist;
and to impart to them in any, the slightest degree, an official
character. The uncommon success of American temperance so-

·cieties, must be chiefly attributed to the absence even of the appearance of an imposed obligation in the pledges given by their members. Strong opposition, and ruinous hypocrisy, would be the immediate and necessary consequence of such a state of things. If temperance societies were to be established in Prussia, not directly by government, but even by its influence merely, what would follow? Part of the people would take no interest in them ; part would oppose them, (which would be the case the sooner in a country where the lower classes look upon government always as something opposed to them) , and the immense number of officers would contain among themselves many who would strictly observe the appearance, but the appearance only, of members of the Temperance Society.

We seize upon this opportunity, of mentioning a fact of melancholy interest, which is probably known to but few in the United States. Mr Ouételet, in his interesting statistical inquiries, which were reprinted in the *Courrier des Etats Unis*, of April 25, 1832, says: "It is remarkable, that, of 1,129 murders committed in France, during the space of four years, 446 were the consequences of quarrels in tippling shops; which sufficiently shows the fatal influence of the use of spirits."]

No. 10.

INQUIRY INTO THE PENITENTIARY OF PHILADELPHIA.*

(*October*, 1831.)

No. 28.—This prisoner knows how to read and write; has been convicted of murder; says his health, without being bad, is not so good as when he was free; denies strongly having committed the crime, for which he was convicted; confesses to have been a drunkard, turbulent, and irreligious. But now, he adds, his mind is changed: he finds a kind of pleasure in solitude, and is only tormented by the desire of seeing once more his family,

* Nobody is allowed to see the convicts, except the inspectors, the wardens, and the chaplain [There are some few others, who are official visitors.— TRANS.] The Philadelphia magistrates were kind enough to make an exception of the rule in favour of us. We were introduced into all the cells, and left alone with the prisoners It is the result of a fortnight's observation, which we offer above to the reader The number at the head of each article, indicates the place which the prisoner holds in the list, as to the time of his imprisonment in the penitentiary. We have often omitted to note it down, as the reader will find.

and of giving a moral and Christian education to his children—
a thing which he never had thought of, when free.

Ques Do you believe you could live here without labour?

Ans. Labour seems to me absolutely necessary for existence;
I believe I should die without it.

Ques. Do you often see the wardens?

Ans. About six times a day.

Ques. Is it a consolation to see them?

Ans. Yes, sir; it is with joy I see their figures. This summer,
a cricket entered my yard; it looked to me like a companion.
If a butterfly, or any other animal enters my cell, I never do it
any harm.

No. 36.—The prisoner had suffered previously a punishment
in the Walnut street prison; says he prefers imprisonment in
the penitentiary, to the old prison. His health is excellent, and
solitude does not seem to him insupportable. Asked whether he
is obliged to work; he says, no; but adds, labour must be regarded as a great benefit. Sunday seems interminably long, because, then, he is not allowed to work.

Ques. What is, in your opinion, the principal advantage of
the new system, to which you are subject?

Ans. Here, the prisoner does not know any of his companions, and is not known by them. It was a prison acquaintance,
who, after I had left Walnut street, again involved me in a theft.

Ques. Have you sufficient to eat?

Ans. Yes, sir.

Ques. Do you believe the yard belonging to your cell, is
necessary for it?

Ans. I am convinced, it would be impossible to do without it.

No. 41 —A young man; confesses to being a criminal; sheds
tears during our whole conversation, particularly when he is reminded of his family. "Happily," says he, "nobody can see
me here," he hopes then to return into society, without being
stamped with shame, and not to be rejected by it.

Ques. Do you find it difficult to endure solitude?

Ans. Ah! sir, it is the most horrid punishment that can be
imagined!

Ques. Does your health suffer by it?

Ans. No: it is very good; but my soul is very sick.

Ques. Of what do you think most?

Ans. Of religion; religious ideas are my greatest consolation.

Ques. Do you see now and then a minister?

Ans. Yes, every Sunday.

Ques. Do you like to converse with him?

Ans It is a great happiness to be allowed to talk to him.
Last Sunday, he was a whole hour with me; he promised to

bring me to-morrow, news from my father and mother. I hope they are alive; for a whole year, I have not heard of them.

Ques. Do you think labour an alleviation of your situation?

Ans. It would be impossible to live here without labour. Sunday is a very long day, I assure you.

Ques. Do you believe your little yard might be dispensed with, without injury to your health?

Ans. Yes, by establishing in a cell a continued current of air.

Ques. What idea have you formed of the utility of the system to which you are subject?

Ans. If there is any system which can make men reflect and reform, it is this.

No. 56.—Has been convicted three times, has a feeble constitution, has not been well during the first months of his stay in the penitentiary, which he attributes to want of exercise, and sufficient current of air. He has been brought to the penitentiary at his own request; he loves, he says, solitude; he wishes to lose sight of his former companions, and form no new ones: shows his Bible, and assures us that he draws his greatest consolations from this book.

Ques. You work here without reluctance. you have said to me that this was not the case in the other prisons, in which you have been imprisoned, what is the cause of this difference?

Ans. Labour is here a pleasure; it would be a great aggravation of our evils, should we ever be deprived of it. I believe, however, that, forced to do it, I might dispense with it.

No. 46.—Is fifty-two years old, was sentenced for burglary; enjoys good health; solitude seems to him a punishment extremely hard; the presence of the keepers even, is a great satisfaction for him, and he would consider it a happy event, if a minister would sometimes visit him; considers labour his greatest consolation. He denies having committed the crime which caused his conviction.

No. 61.—Was convicted for horse-stealing, says he is innocent. Nobody, he says, can imagine the horrid punishment of continued solitude. Asked how he passes his time; he says there are but two means—labour, and the Bible. The Bible is his greatest consolation. He seems to be strongly actuated by religious ideas; his conversation is animated; he cannot speak long without being agitated, and shedding tears. (We have made the same remark of all, whom we have seen so far.) He is a German by birth; lost his father early, and has been badly educated. Has been above a year in the prison. Health good. According to him, the adjacent yard is absolutely necessary for the health of the prisoner.

No. 65.—Is thirty years old; without family, convicted of

forgery; seven months in prison; health very good. He is little communicative, complains of solitude, which becomes tolerable by labour only. Religious ideas seem to occupy him but little

No 32.—A negro of twenty years of age; has received no education, and has no family; was sentenced for burglary; has been fourteen months in the penitentiary; health excellent; labour, and visits of the chaplain, are his only pleasures. This young man, who seems to have a heavy mind, hardly knew the letters of the alphabet, previously to his entering the penitentiary, he has, however, by his own exertions, attained to reading fluently his Bible

No 20 —Has been convicted of the murder of his wife; has been eighteen months in the penitentiary; health excellent; has a very intelligent look, at first, he says, solitude was insufferable, but custom overcomes gradually the horror, labour becomes entertaining, and the Bible a pleasure; isolation is tempered by the daily visits of the wardens. He has learned in prison the art of weaving. The turn of ideas of this prisoner, is peculiarly grave and religious, it is a remark which we have had occasion to make upon almost all whom we have visited.

No. 72.—A negro of twenty-four years, convicted of theft a second time; he seems full of intelligence.

Ques. You have been a prisoner of Walnut street. What difference is there between that prison, and this penitentiary?

Ans. The prisoners were a great deal less unhappy in Walnut street than here, because there they could freely communicate with each other.

Ques. You seem to work with pleasure · was it the same with you in Walnut street?

Ans. No; there labour was a burden, which we tried to escape in all possible ways; here it is a great consolation.

Ques. Do you read the Bible sometimes?

Ans. Yes, very often.

Ques Did you do the same in Walnut street?

Ans No; I never found pleasure in reading the Bible, or hearing religious discourses, but here.

This prisoner has been here since six months; health excellent

No 83 —Thirty years of age; is in a state of relapse. In Baltimore, where he was detained, the discipline was very hard, and the daily task of labour very considerable.

Ques. Do you prefer being imprisoned here?

Ans. No; I should prefer to return to Baltimore, because there is no solitude there.

He has been but two months here; has had the fever; but his health is entirely restored

No. 64 —A negro of twenty-six years; convicted of burglary; his intelligence seems to be but little; has learned to weave, in prison.

No 00 —Convicted of an attempt to commit murder; fifty-two years of age; has seven children; has received a good education, was a prisoner in Walnut street, makes a frightful picture of the vices in that prison, but believes most of the convicts would prefer to return to Walnut street, than to enter the penitentiary; they shun solitude so much.

Asked his opinion respecting the system of imprisonment; he says that it cannot fail to make a deep impression on the souls of the prisoners

No. 15 —Twenty-eight years old, convicted of manslaughter, has been above two years in the penitentiary; his health excellent; has learned to weave, in his cell. Solitude appeared, at first, insufferable; but one accustoms himself to it

No. 54.—Thirty-five years old, convicted of the murder of his wife; has been a year in the penitentiary; health excellent.

The remarks which this person makes on the sufferings caused by solitude, prove how much he has undergone; but he begins to accustom himself to this kind of life, and does not find it any longer as hard.

No 22.—A negro of thirty-four years, has been convicted for theft once before, eighteen months here; health pretty good.

Ques. Do you find the discipline to which you are subject, as severe as it is represented?

Ans. No; but that depends upon the disposition of the prisoner. If he takes solitary confinement bad, he falls into irritation and despair; if, on the contrary, he immediately sees the advantages which he can derive from it, it does not appear insupportable.

Ques. You have been imprisoned already in Walnut street?

Ans. Yes, sir; and I cannot imagine a greater den of vice and crime. It requires but a few days, for a person not very guilty, to become a consummate criminal.

Ques. Do you think that the penitentiary is superior to the old prison?

Ans. That is, as if you were to ask me, whether the sun was finer than the moon?*

No. 68.—Age twenty-three; convicted of theft; has been here six months, health excellent; he is cold, and little communicative; he only becomes animated by speaking of the sufferings of solitude, he works with ardour; the presence of a visitor never interrupts his labour.

No. 85.—Has been here two months; convicted of theft.

---

* We believed it necessary to give literally the answers of the prisoners

Health good, but his mind seems to be very agitated. If you speak of his wife and child, he weeps bitterly. In short, the impression produced by the prison, seems very deep.

No. 67.—Age thirty-eight; convicted of theft; has been here eight months. Health good. Became a shoemaker in the prison, and makes six pairs of shoes a week.

This individual seems to have naturally a grave and meditative mind. Solitude in prison, has singularly increased this disposition. His reflections are the results of a very elevated order of ideas He seems to be occupied only with philosophical and Christian thoughts

No. 52 —Age thirty-nine; is in a state of relapse; has been formerly in Walnut street; says that that prison is a shocking place; one cannot leave it honest. If I had been, he says, at first in this penitentiary, I should not have committed a second crime.

Ques. Have you accustomed yourself easily to solitude?

Ans. At first, solitude seemed to me horrid · gradually I accustomed myself to it; but I do not believe that I could live here without labour Without labour, there is no sleep.

This person has been nearly a year in this prison; enjoys good health.

No. 1.—This prisoner, the first who was sent to the penitentiary, is a negro. Has been here more than two years. His health is excellent.

This man works with ardour; he makes ten pair of shoes a week. His mind seems very tranquil; his disposition excellent. He considers his being brought to the penitentiary, as a signal benefit of Providence. His thoughts are in general religious. He read to us in the gospel the parable of the good shepherd, the meaning of which touched him deeply—one who was born of a degraded and depressed race, and had never experienced any thing but indifference and harshness

No. 17.—Is a mulatto, convicted of theft; confined twenty months; was never ill. Charitable persons have taught him to read; he learned here shoemaking The necessity of labour was so great, that at the end of the first week, he was able to make coarse shoes.

No. 50.—Thirty-seven years old; in relapse; paints energetically the vices which prevail in Walnut street, where he has been imprisoned

If they had put me here for my first crime, he said, I never should have committed a second; but one always leaves Walnut street worse than he enters it. Nowhere but here, is it possible to reflect.

Ques. But the discipline of this penitentiary is very severe?

Ans. Yes, Sir; particularly in the beginning. During the

two first months, I was near falling into despair. But reading and labour have gradually comforted me.

This prisoner has been twenty months here. Health excellent.

No. 62.—A well educated man, thirty-two years old. He was a physician.

Solitary confinement seems to have made a profound impression upon this young man. He speaks of the first time of his imprisonment with horror; the remembrance makes him weep. During two months, he says, he was in despair; but time has alleviated his situation. At present, he is resigned to his fate, however austere it may be. He was allowed to do nothing; but idleness is so horrid, that he nevertheless always works. As he knew no mechanic art, he occupies himself with cutting leather for the shoemakers in the prison. His greatest grief is not to be allowed to communicate with his family. He ended the conversation by saying: Solitary confinement is very painful, but I nevertheless consider it as an institution eminently useful for society.

Health good. He does not complain of the physical part of the discipline to which he is subject.

No 4.—Age twenty years; has been imprisoned already once in Walnut street. He ascribes his relapse to the pernicious influence of that prison "We are here much happier," he says; "not that the discipline of the penitentiary is mild; far from it; the first days, particularly, are horrid; I believed despair would kill me. Yet I have never been ill, though I have been here now for two years."

No. 35.—This prisoner is above eighty. When we entered he was reading his Bible.

No. 73.—A negro woman, twenty years of age, in relapse. She says the penitentiary is very superior to Walnut street prison.

Ques. Why so?

Ans. Because it makes one think. She has been seven months here; health very good.

No. 63.—Twenty-three years old; sentenced to thirteen months imprisonment for fornication.* Has been here nine months; health excellent His dispositions seem good. He congratulates himself on having been imprisoned in this penitentiary.

No. 6 —Has been two years in this prison, arrived here unwell; and his health has been re-established in the cell.

No. 69.—Thirty years old; convicted of theft; has been five months in prison; health apparently very good, but his mind dejected. "I do not believe," he says, "that I ever shall leave

* So in the original. This must be a mistake. Qu.' *adultery*'—TRANS.

25

this cell alive; solitude is fatal to the human constitution; it will 'kill me."

Ques. What are your consolations?

Ans. I have but two: labour, and the perusal of my Bible.

No. 51.—Forty-four years old; in relapse. He regrets bitterly having the first time been imprisoned in Walnut street. "Nowhere but here," says he, "can one reflect."

He has been here ten months; his health was never better.

No. 47.—Has been a year in the penitentiary; health apparently excellent.

His dispositions appear good, but it is difficult to attach much importance to his words, as he expects soon to be pardoned.

No. 66.—Twenty-one years. Contrary to the ordinary course, he refused at first to work, and it required a long diet to subdue him. At present he is perfectly subdued, he has felt the necessity of labour in solitude, and works with ardour. He has learnt in a short time shoemaking, and makes now from eight to nine pair of shoes a week.

Has been here eight months; health excellent. ·

No. 00.—Aged forty. Imprisoned for robbery on the highway with arms in his hand; seems very intelligent; told us his story in the following terms:

"I was fourteen or fifteen years old when I arrived in Philadelphia I am the son of a poor farmer in the west, and I came in search of employment. I had no acquaintance, and found no work; and the first night I was obliged to lie down on the deck of a vessel, having no other place of rest Here I was discovered the next morning; the constable arrested me, and the mayor sentenced me to one month's imprisonment as a vagrant. Confounded during my short imprisonment with a number of malefactors of all ages, I lost the honest principles which my father had given me; and on leaving the prison, one of my first acts was to join several young delinquents of my own age, and to assist them in various thefts. I was arrested, tried, and acquitted. Now I thought myself safe from justice, and, confident in my skill, I committed other offences, which brought me again before the court. I was sentenced to an imprisonment of nine years in Walnut street prison."

Ques. Did not this punishment produce in you a feeling of the necessity of correcting yourself.

Ans. Yes Sir; yet the Walnut street prison has never produced in me any regret at my criminal actions. I confess that I never could repent them there, or that I ever had the idea of doing it during my stay in that place But I soon remarked that the same persons reappeared there, and that, however great the finesse, or strength of courage of the thieves was, they always ended by being taken; this made me think seriously of my life,

and I firmly resolved to quit for ever so dangerous a way of living, as soon as I should leave the prison. This resolution taken,
I conducted myself better, and after seven years' imprisonment,
I was pardoned. I had learnt tayloring in prison, and I soon
found a favourable employment. I married, and began to gain
easily my sustenance; but Philadelphia was full of people who
had known me in prison; I always feared being betrayed by
them. One day, indeed, two of my former fellow prisoners came
into my master's shop and asked to speak to me; I at first feigned
not to know them, but they soon obliged me to confess who I
was. They then asked me to lend them a considerable sum; and
on my refusal, they threatened to discover the history of my life
to my employer. I now promised to satisfy them, and told them
to return the next day. As soon as they had gone, I left the shop
also, and embarked immediately with my wife for Baltimore.
In this city, I found easy employment, and lived for a long
time comfortably enough; when one day my master received a
letter from one of the constables in Philadelphia, which informed
him that one of his journeymen was a former prisoner of Walnut
street. I do not know what could have induced this man to such
a step. I owe to him my being now here. As soon as my employer had read the letter, he sent me indignantly away. I went
to all the other taylors in Baltimore, but they were informed of
what had happened, and refused me. Misery obliged me to seek
labour on the rail road, then making between Baltimore and Ohio.
Grief and fatigue threw me after some time into a violent fever.
My sickness lasted a long time, and my money was at an end.
Hardly recovered, I went to Philadelphia, where the fever again
attacked me When I was convalescent, and found myself without resources, without bread for my family; when I thought of
all the obstacles which I found in my attempts to gain honestly
my livelihood, and of all the unjust persecutions which I suffered, I fell into a state of inexpressible exasperation. I said to
myself: Well then! since I am forced to do it, I will become
a thief again; and if there is a single dollar left in the United
States, and if it were in the pocket of the president, I will have
it. I called my wife, ordered her to sell all the clothes which
were not indispensably necessary, and to buy with the money
a pistol. Provided with this, and when I was yet too feeble to
walk without crutches, I went to the environs of the city; I
stopped the first passenger, and forced him to give me his pock-
et-book. But I was arrested the same evening. I had been followed by the person whom I had robbed, and, my feebleness
having obliged me to stop in the neighbourhood, there were no
great pains necessary to seize me. I confessed my crime without
difficulty, and I was sent here

Ques. What are your present resolutions for the future?

Ans. I do not feel disposed, I tell you freely, to reproach myself with what I have done, nor to become what is called a good Christian; but I am determined never to steal again, and I see the possibility of succeeding. If I leave in nine years this prison, no one will know me again in this world; no one will have known me in the prison; I shall have made no dangerous acquaintance. I shall be then at liberty to gain my livelihood in peace. This is the great advantage which I find in this penitentiary, and the reason why I prefer a hundred times being here to being sent again to the Walnut street prison, in spite of the severity of the discipline which is kept up in this penitentiary.

Has been in prison a year; health very good.

No. 00.—Age forty years; has been in the penitentiary but eight days. We found him reading the Bible. He seemed calm and almost contented. He said, that during the first days, solitude seemed insufferable to him. He was neither allowed to read nor to work.

But the day before we saw him, books had been given to him; and since then, he found his condition entirely changed. He showed us that he had read already almost the whole volume which contains the four Gospels. This perusal furnished him with several moral and religious reflections. He could not conceive that he had not made them sooner.

No. 00.—Has been two years in the penitentiary. His punishment was to expire within a few days. Health excellent. Hope and joy gave an expression to his face which it was a pleasure to contemplate. He assured us of his having firmly resolved to commit no new faults. Every thing indicates that the intentions of this young man are good, and that he will act up to them. He has been convicted for an act of violence. His conduct in prison has always been exemplary.

Nos. 00 and 00.—These two individuals are insane. The warden of the prison has assured us that they arrived in this state at the prison. Their insanity is very tranquil. Nothing appears in their incoherent speeches which would justify a suspicion that their unhappy disorder is attributable to the penitentiary.

No. 00.—Age sixty-two; has arrived at the last stage of a pulmonary phthisis. He is occupied with ideas of a future life alone.

No. 00.—Was a physician; has the charge of the pharmacy of the penitentiary. He converses intelligently, and speaks of the various systems of imprisonment, with a freedom of thought which his situation makes very extraordinary. The discipline of this penitentiary appeared to him, taken in its entire operation, mild, and calculated to produce reformation. "For a well educated man," he says, "it is better to live in absolute solitude than to be thrown together with wretches of all kinds. For all, isolation favours reflection, and is conducive to reformation."

Ques. But have you not observed that solitary confinement is injurious to health? In your quality of prisoner and physician, you are more able to answer this question than any body else.

Ans. I have not observed, that, on the whole, there are here more diseases than in society. I do not believe that people here feel worse as to health.

No. 00.—Age fifty-five; enjoyed a comfortable fortune previously to his imprisonment, was a justice of the peace in his county. He was confined for having killed his wife's lover.

This prisoner, who speaks French, seems to be occupied but by one idea—that of obtaining his pardon We never could make him speak of any thing but of his trial, and the causes which produced it. He is drawing up a memorial to the governor; we were obliged to hear a part of it, and to examine with him his papers.* He is sentenced to a long confinement; he feels himself old, and only lives upon the hope of soon being delivered. This man seemed to us to believe in the efficiency of the kind of imprisonment which he suffers. He finds it peculiarly fit to correct the guilty, with whom, however, he takes good care not to number himself.

Health very good.

No. 00 —Age twenty years; is an Englishman by birth, and arrived in America but a short time ago; has been sentenced for forgery. He seems intelligent, mild, and resigned. Health excellent. His dispositions for the future seem good.

No. 00.—Age twenty years; Englishman by birth He seems to be irritated, and not subdued by the punishment It seems he dislikes visits; he does not interrupt his work when he speaks to you, and hardly answers the questions you put to him He shows no repentance, and is not the least given to religious contemplations.

Health good.

No. 00.—Age thirty-eight years; has been but three weeks in the penitentiary, and seems to be plunged in despair. "Solitude will kill me," he says; "I never shall be able to endure my sentence until its expiration. I shall be dead before that time arrives."

Ques. Do you not find some consolation in your labour?

Ans. Yes, Sir, solitude without labour is still a thousand

---

* Every reader of these lines, who is acquainted with the individual here mentioned, his crime and trial, will allow that he has good reason to make them the constant theme of his conversations He excited the interest of all who knew him the governor has, perhaps, already made an exception in his favour, in the general and just rule adopted since the foundation of the eastern penitentiary, not to grant a pardon easily.—Trans.

times more horrible; but labour does not prevent me from thinking, and being very unhappy. Here, I assure you, my soul is sick.

This unfortunate man sobbed when speaking of his wife and children, whom he never hoped to see again. When we entered his cell, we found him weeping and labouring at the same time.

No 00 —Age twenty-five; he belongs to the most comfortably situated classes of society. He expresses himself with warmth and facility. He has been convicted of fraudulent bankruptcy.

This young man shows a great pleasure in seeing us. It is easily seen that solitude is for him a terrible torment. The necessity of intellectual intercourse with others seems to torment him much more than those of his fellow prisoners who have received a less careful education. He hastens to give us his history; he speaks of his crime, of his standing in society, of his friends, and particularly of his parents; his feelings towards his family were extraordinarily developed. He cannot think of his relations without melting into tears; he takes from under his bed some letters which his family has succeeded in sending to him. These letters are almost in pieces, in consequence of being read so often; he reads them still, comments upon them, and is touched by the least expression of interest which they contain.

Ques. I see that the punishment inflicted upon you seems extremely hard. Do you believe it conducive to reformation?

Ans. Yes, Sir, I believe that this whole system of imprisonment is better than any other. It would be more painful to me to be confounded with wretches of all kinds, than to live alone here. Moreover, it is impossible that such a punishment should not make the convict reflect deeply.

Ques. But do you not believe that its influence may injure the reason?

Ans. I believe that the danger of which you speak must exist sometimes. I remember, for my part, that during the first months of my solitude, I was often visited by strange visions. During several nights in succession, I saw, among other things, an eagle perching at the foot of my bed. But at present I work, and am accustomed to this kind of life; I am not any longer troubled with ideas of this kind.

One year in prison. Health good.

No. 11.

CONVERSATION WITH MR. ELAM LYNDS.*

*   *   *   *   I have passed ten years of my life in the administration of prisons, he said to us, I have been for a long time a witness of the abuses which predominated in the old system ; they were very great. Prisons then caused great expenses, and the prisoners lost all the morality which they yet had left. I believe that this system would have led us back to the barbarous laws of the ancient codes. The majority at least began to be disgusted with all philanthropic ideas, the impracticability of which seemed to be proved by experience. It was under these circumstances that I undertook the reform of Auburn. At first I met with great difficulties with the legislature, and even with public opinion : much noise was made about tyranny ; nothing short of success was requisite for my justification.

Ques. Do you believe that the discipline established by you might succeed in any other country than in the United States ?

Ans. I am convinced that it would succeed wherever the method is adopted which I have followed. As far as I can judge, I even believe that in France there would be more chances of success than with us. I understand the prisons in France stand under the immediate direction of government, which is able to lend a solid and durable support to its agents : here we are the slaves of a public opinion which constantly changes. But, according to my experience, it is necessary that the director of a prison, particularly if he establish a new discipline, should be invested with an absolute and certain power ; it is impossible to calculate on this in a democratic republic like ours. With us, he is obliged to labour at once to captivate public opinion, and to carry through his undertaking—two things which are often irreconcilable. My principle has always been, that in order to reform a prison, it is well to concentrate within the same individual, all power and all responsibility. When the inspectors wished to oblige me to act according to their views, I told them : you are at liberty to send me away ; I am dependent upon you ; but as long as you retain me, I shall follow my plan ; it is for you to choose.†

---

* If the following lines should be read by the gentleman whose words they pretend to give, the translator trusts that he will take them for nothing more than a faithful re-translation from the French. The facts only in this work seemed to be of importance.—Trans.

† Mr Lynds, we have not the slightest doubt, is, in the main, perfectly right, but, unacquainted as he probably is, with the operation of concentrated and powerful governments, he mistakes, in our opinion, the facility with which an

Ques. We have heard it said to Americans, and we are inclined to believe it, that the success of the penitentiary system
must be partly attributed to the habit, so general in this country, of obeying scrupulously the laws.

Ans. I do not believe it. In Sing-Sing, the fourth part of
the prisoners is composed of foreigners by birth. I have subdued them all, as well as the Americans. Those whom it was
most difficult to curb, were the Spaniards of South America—a
race which has more of the ferocious animal, and of the savage,
than of the civilized man. The most easy to be governed were
Frenchmen, they submitted the most readily, and with the best
grace to their fate, as soon as they considered it inevitable. If I
had the choice, I should prefer superintending a prison in France,
to directing one in the United States. *

agent of such a government can carry on his plans. First, as to the general success of the penitentiary system, with absolute or even merely concentrated governments, we refer the reader to the just remarks of the authors on page 97,
and seq , and to our note to that passage   There is an essential and total difference between an officer who feels himself the servant of a *government,* and him
who feels himself the servant of the *public.* Wherever you require unremitted
energy in a cause, which, by its character, does not stimulate ambition, or the
love of gain, you need the public eye, public approbation, and a servant of the
people   The servant of the *government,* who feels himself to be such for life,
may do his *prescribed* duty, but there are many affairs in which this is of very little avail, and such is the direction or reform of a prison   But there is a second
consideration equally powerful   If the officer of a popular government is dependent upon the tide of public opinion, the servant of a concentrated government is dependent upon a minister, or his secretary—upon a hundred persons,
who may take it into their heads to propose something new, to direct him to do
this, to omit that, and all this from the *bureau* in a distant place, and unacquainted with the matter in question   How many thousand wise plans have been
crippled, or blasted, by this bureaucratic intermeddling.   A minister often, nay
generally, believes he can and must do every thing, his secretary has the same
opinion; and so on   If public opinion changes quickly, that of an individual
changes a hundred times quicker, and, if he has the power of executing his
opinion, what restrains him ?   Hence we see, in some absolute governments, interminable changes, and, on the other hand, we will find everywhere in history, that the freest nations, or bodies politic, retain more of their historical elements, if we may so call them, than absolute governments—actually stagnant
governments only excepted   It is a very great mistake to consider popular governments only as fickle   But to return to our subject. Mr Lynds would find
it difficult to get himself invested with such a power as he justly claims for the
reformer of a prison, under a concentrated government.   No head of a department would part with the right of constant interference, and, in most cases,
ought to part with it, because, if the watchful control of public opinion does
not exist, who shall watch over him ?   This is the reason why we can delegate
powers in many cases, which it would be of the greatest danger to delegate in
an absolute government.   Suppose a person in Russia had the power to take
children from their parents, and to put them into a house of correction, as the
managers of the New York house of refuge actually have.   And yet, who feels
unsafe on that account in New York ?—TRANS.

* Which assertion would somewhat militate with the opinion of the authors,
that it would be probably necessary to modify the prison discipline of the United
States, if it should be applied to the French prisons, on account of its austerity.
—TRANS.

Ques. What is then the secret of this discipline so powerful, which you have established in Sing-Sing, and of which we have admired the effects?

Ans. It would be pretty difficult to explain it entirely; it is the result of a series of efforts and daily cares, of which it would be necessary to be an eye-witness General rules cannot be indicated. The point is, to maintain uninterrupted silence and uninterrupted labour; to obtain this, it is equally necessary to watch incessantly the keepers, as well as the prisoners; to be at once inflexible and just.

Ques. Do you believe that bodily chastisement might be dispensed with?

Ans. I am convinced of the contrary. I consider the chastisement by the whip, the most efficient, and, at the same time, the most humane which exists; it never injures health, and obliges the prisoners to lead a life essentially healthy. Solitary confinement, on the contrary, is often insufficient, and always dangerous. I have seen many prisoners in my life, whom it was impossible to subdue in this manner, and who only left the solitary cell to go to the hospital. I consider it impossible to govern a large prison without a whip. Those who know human nature from books only, may say the contrary.

Ques. Don't you believe it imprudent at Sing-Sing, for the prisoners to work in an open field?

Ans. For my part, I should always prefer to direct a prison in which such a state of things existed, than the contrary It is impossible to obtain the same vigilance, and continual care from the guardians, in a prison surrounded by walls Moreover, if you have once completely curbed the prisoner under the yoke of discipline, you may, without danger, employ him in the labour which you think best. It is in this manner, that the state may make use of the criminals in a thousand ways, if it has once improved the discipline of its prisons.

Ques. Do you believe it absolutely impossible to establish sound discipline in a prison, in which the system of cells does not exist?

Ans. I believe that it would be possible to maintain considerable order in such a prison, and to make labour productive: but it would be quite impossible to prevent a number of abuses, the consequences of which would be very serious.

Ques. Do you believe that it would be possible to establish cells in an old prison?

Ans. This depends entirely upon the state of those prisons. I have no doubt, that, in many old prisons, the system of cells might be introduced without great difficulties. It is always easy, and not expensive, to erect wooden cells; but they have the in-

26

convenience of retaining a bad smell, and consequently of be-coming sometimes unhealthy.

Ques. Do you really believe in the reform of a great number of prisoners?

Ans. We must understand each other, I do not believe in a *complete* reform, except with young delinquents. Nothing, in my opinion, is rarer than to see a convict of mature age become a religious and virtuous man. I do not put great faith in the sanctity of those who leave the prison; I do not believe that the counsels of the chaplain, or the meditations of the prisoner, make a good Christian of him. But my opinion is, that a great number of old convicts do not commit new crimes, and that they even become useful citizens, having learned in prison a useful art, and contracted habits of constant labour. This is the only reform which I ever have expected to produce, and I believe it is the only one which society has a right to expect.

Ques What do you believe proves the conduct of the prisoner in the prison, as to his future reformation?

Ans. Nothing. If it were necessary to mention a prognostic, I would even say that the prisoner who conducts himself well, will probably return to his former habits, when set free. I have always observed, that the worst subjects made excellent prisoners. They have generally more skill and intelligence than the others, they perceive much more quickly, and much more thoroughly, that the only way to render their situation less oppressive, is to avoid painful and repeated punishments, which would be the infallible consequence of insubordination; they therefore behave well, without being the better for it. The result of this observation is, that a pardon never ought to be granted, merely on account of the good conduct of a prisoner. In that way, hypocrites only are made.

Ques. The system, however, which you attack, is that of all theorists?

Ans. In this, as in many other points, they deceive themselves, because they have little knowledge of those of whom they speak. If Mr. Livingston, for instance, should be ordered to apply his theories of penitentiaries to people born like himself, in a class of society in which much intelligence and moral sensibility existed, I believe that he would arrive at excellent results, but prisons, on the contrary, are filled with coarse beings, who have had no education, and who perceive with difficulty ideas, and often even sensations. It is this point which he always forgets.

Ques. What is your opinion of the system of contract?

Ans. I believe it is very useful to let the labour of prisoners by contract, provided that the chief officer of the prison remains perfect master of their persons and time. When I was at the

head of the Auburn prison, I had made, with different contractors, contracts which even prohibited them from entering the
penitentiary. Their presence in the workshop cannot be but
very injurious to discipline.

Ques. Wages for the labour of a prisoner, are very low in
France.

Ans. It would rise in the same degree as discipline would
improve. Experience has taught us this. Formerly, the prisons
were a heavy charge to the state of New York; now they are
a source of revenue. The well-disciplined prisoner works more;
he works better, and never spoils the materials, as it sometimes
happened in the ancient prisons

Ques. Which is, in your opinion, the quality most desirable
in a person destined to be a director of prisons?

Ans. The practical art of conducting men. Above all, he
must be thoroughly convinced, as I have always been, that a
dishonest man is ever a coward. This conviction, which the
prisoners will soon perceive, gives him an irresistible ascendency, and will make a number of things very easy, which, at
first glance, may appear hazardous. *

During all this conversation, which lasted several hours, Mr.
Elam Lynds constantly returned to this point—that it was necessary to begin with curbing the spirit of the prisoner, and convincing him of his weakness This point attained, every thing
becomes easy, whatever may be the construction of the prison,
or the place of labour.

No. 12.

EXTRACTS

*Of a Letter addressed to us by Judge Wells of Wethersfield,
former Commissioner and Director of the State Prison of
Connecticut, October, 1831.†*

"Since building the prison at Wethersfield, I have been of
the opinion, that had we to build it a second time, we should be

---

* In saying this, Mr. Lynds probably alluded to a fact, of which we had been
informed a few days before at Sing Sing.

An individual, imprisoned in that penitentiary, had said that he would kill Mr.
Lynds, the superintendent of Sing-Sing, upon the first opportunity. The latter, informed of the prisoner's resolution, sends for him, makes him come into
his bed room, and, without appearing to perceive his agitation, makes him shave
him He then dismisses him with these words I knew you intended to kill
me, but I despise you too much to believe that you would ever be bold enough
to execute your design Single and unarmed, I am always stronger than you are.

† We have reason to believe these extracts to be correct. We know that the
original, given by Judge Wells to the authors, was, though but hastily drawn
up, much more complete, and, besides, had been written with constant reference to conversations which had passed between those three gentlemen.—TRANS

able to do it at much less expense. In the present structure many useless expenses were incurred ; for example, we have a roof covered with slate, gutters of copper, and cornices. In a climate like ours, it is better that the eaves should drop directly upon the ground, otherwise the water is liable to freeze in the gutters.

"It appears to me, that in constructing a prison, two great errors may easily be committed

"The first consists in the want of a proper proportion of strength in the different parts of the building. Thus it happens, that we often see walls of five or six feet in thickness, composed of enormous blocks of stone, bound together by cramp-irons ; to these are joined doors and windows which in strength are not equal to a wall of one foot in thickness ; and a massive and expensive door is sometimes mounted upon hinges, and secured by fastenings, proper only for much lighter ones.

"The second error arises from the idea that the edifice must be so constructed as to endure through all coming ages. Public spirited and benevolent individuals are devoting much of their time and talents to devising improvements in the construction of prisons. One improvement suggests another, and it is not in the power of any man to foresee the result of these different efforts. By them public opinion is changed ; and society at length looks with an unfavourable eye, upon an establishment which is not capable of admitting all the improvements suggested by experience. Within twenty years, an entire revolution of opinion often takes place ; the old prisons do not any longer meet the wants of the community, and they are abandoned. Such is the history of the greater part of the prisons of the United States. It is, therefore, very important that these establishments should be built upon the least expensive plan, since otherwise they become obstacles to improvement ; obstacles, the more difficult to be overcome, the greater the expense bestowed upon their construction.

"The distinguishing feature in the modern system, consists in the substitution of vigilance in the place of strength of material. In the modern prisons, the eye and ear of the watchman are incessantly on the alert, and should never be withdrawn. Absolute silence should be maintained by day and by night.

"This constant vigilance contributes to render the construction of our penitentiaries less expensive. Experience has shown that no greater strength of walls is necessary in a prison, than that requisite to withstand the elements, to secure stability to the structure, and to resist the sudden attempts of the prisoners to escape. It is unnecessary to give to them greater strength than to ordinary public buildings.

"The prison at Wethersfield is built of sandstone in irregular blocks. The walls are three feet in thickness at the base, and two at the top. Two and a half at the base, and one and a half at the top, is sufficient, with external buttresses to strengthen the walls

" The top of the walls should be on a level with the ceiling of the upper tier of cells.

" The walls cost 10 cents per cubic foot ; say 4 for the stone, 4 for the work, 1 for the mortar, and 1 for scaffolding and other incidental expenses

"The cells are of brick, and cost 20 cents per cubic foot. Many of them are floored with a single stone. Each of these stones cost us four dollars. The floor of the others consists of plank 3 inches in thickness, covered with a layer of brick. The whole is covered with cement, and cost $2 for each cell. The doors of the cells are composed of oak plank, 3 inches thick, strengthened by four bolts, running through them transversely. Each door, deducting the iron work, cost $2 50. I have estimated the cost of each cell at $28, comprising the mason-work, hinges, locks, and grates.

" I have subjoined the plan of a prison having five hundred cells. (Vide subjoined plan.)

" It may be a question, whether, in building a prison, it is more advantageous to employ convicts or free labourers. I should say, that this would depend upon the manner in which they are already employed. If they are engaged in profitable labour in their workshops, it is better to leave them there. If, on the contrary, they are not so engaged, they may be put to a business which requires no great degree of intelligence, or with which they are already acquainted. They may do the iron work, prepare and carry the materials, make the mortar, &c But the expense for additional guard, which is necessary if the convicts are thus employed, will be so great as nearly to counterbalance any advantage.

" It has been asked, whether the avails of the labour of the convicts will probably be sufficient to cover the annual expenses of maintaining the prison? Upon this point I will make but a single remark, in addition to what I have already stated to you in conversation If in France it has been thought questionable, whether the labour of the convicts would be sufficient for their support, I can say, that previously to the establishment of the new prison, we had in Connecticut as strong reasons for supposing that the labour of the convicts would be inadequate to this object, as the French themselves. Our former prison was a continual source of expense During the last ten years of its existence, it received from the public treasury, over and above all that was earned, $8,400 per annum. Few individuals dared to hope that the new prison would support itself, and nothing but the highest evidence would have led us to believe, that adding the former annual loss to the present annual gain, the difference to the state treasury would be more than $16,000 per annum—but such is the fact

"It is said, that free labourers in France do not find employment as readily as in America; and, as a consequence, it is more difficult to render profitable the labour of convicts But if the free labourer is able to support himself and family, although with great effort, the convict ought to do equally well, since his maintenance costs less; and if the edifices are favourable to inspection, they may be superintended by a small number of individuals, and consequently at small expense.

"If the price of labour be less, then the expenses of support will also be less; these two things are correlative, and between them, there exists of necessity an exact proportion.

"I remain, therefore, strong in the belief, that in a prison advantageously constructed, the labour of the convicts, if well directed, ought completely to indemnify the state.

Estimate of the expense necessary to build a prison capable of containing five hundred convicts.

Length of the building, - - - -	250 feet.
Breadth of the building, - - -	50 "
Thickness of wall at the base, - - -	2½ "
Thickness of wall at top, - - -	1½ "
Average thickness of the whole height, - -	2 "
Breadth of wall at foundation, - - -	3 "
Depth of foundation, - - - -	3 "

The whole makes 49,800 cubic feet of stone laid in mortar, at 10 cents per foot

The entire expense of which will be - -	$4,980
Shingle roof,* - - - - -	1,250
Five hundred cells, arranged in 5 stories, at $28 each,	14,000
Plastering, - - - - -	600
Floor of bricks, 4½ bricks to the foot, - -	200

Offices.

Two ranges of buildings—one upon each side of the yard, at 15 feet from the external wall, to contain the shops, store-rooms, kitchens, and schools, &c.

Length, - - - -	270 feet †
Breadth, - - - -	30 "

---

* The French had here *ardoise,* but the authors were mistaken. It is precisely the slate which Judge Wells considers unnecessary at the beginning of these extracts The original, from which the authors translated, had *shingle* —TRANS
† The floor of each story in these buildings, has 8,100 superficial feet which gives in all, 32,400 feet, this is more than 40 feet shop room per man. A

Two stories high, covered with shingle roof,				
at $3,000 each, - - -	-			$6,000
External walls of the yard, in height, -		18 feet.		
Below the surface of the ground,	-	3 "		
Thickness at base, - - -		2 "		
" " top, - - -		1½ "		

Containing of cubic feet of stone, 31,500, laid
  in mortar, at 10 cents per foot.

Whole expense of this wall, - - -		$3,150
Buttresses to support the walls on the outside,	-	200
A walk upon the top of the yard wall,	- -	200
Bars for the windows, - -	-	500
House of the warden, attached to the prison,	-	2,500
Incidental expenses, - - -	-	6,420
Total, - - -	-	$40,000

Expense for each prisoner, $80.

" This estimate is made according to the actual cost of the raw material; which is as follows, viz.

Stone, (sand or free-stone,) per foot, -	-	4 cents.
Timber, (1 inch in thickness,) per 1,000 feet,	$10 00
Day's work for ordinary labourers, -	-	1 00
Iron, per pound, - - -	-	4 "

" In building the prison, it is not necessary that hewn stone should be used, except for the caps and sills of the windows and doors

" It should be observed, that nothing has been said in the above plan respecting windows and doors. In making the estimate for the walls, I have left out of account the apertures, and have considered the wall as forming a solid mass. The walls would therefore cost less than I have stated, and the excess would cover the expense of the doors and windows, together with a part of the grating

" At Wethersfield, the locks were made by the convicts, and cost about $2 25 each

Estimate of the Expense of guarding and supporting five hundred prisoners, in a prison similar to that of which the above is a plan and estimate.

EXPENSES.

Food, clothing, and bedding of each prisoner per annum, $22.

---

shoemaker requires but 20 feet, 500 men would therefore occupy 20,000 feet, leaving 12,400 feet for store-rooms, offices, &c. This would abundantly answer every purpose.

Total expense of prisoners per annum,	-	-	$11,000
Expense of Guard. 1 warden,	-	-	800
1 deputy warden,	-	-	400
8 overseers of shops,	-	-	2,800
8 guards,	-	-	2,000
Medicine and hospital expenses, -	-	-	700
Chaplain, - - - -	-	-	400
Lights, fuel, and other incidental expenses,		-	1,000

$19,100

" From the 500 prisoners, I have deducted fifty for those who are aged, sick, and engaged in unproductive labour. The remaining 450, ought to earn, one day with another, 25 cents each.

In computing the year at 300 days, the total gain should amount

to 450 men, at 25 cents each, -	-	-	$33,750
Deducting the amount of expenses, viz. -		-	19,100

There remains a net gain of   -   -   - $14,650

" This result will not appear exaggerated, if it is recollected, that, during the last year, the one hundred and sixty men confined in the prison at Wethersfield, earned for the state more than half the above named sum, ($14,650,) viz. $7,824.

"I have no doubt, that, at Wethersfield, the entire annual expense of a prison containing five hundred convicts, would be covered by $19,100.

"And I am of opinion, that I have estimated the income to be derived from such a prison, sufficiently low.

" In estimating the expense, I have taken as a basis, the actual cost of supporting and guarding the prisoners at Wethersfield; and, when I have spoken of the profits, I have taken care, on the other hand, to estimate the labour of the convicts at less than its actual value, in the same prison.

"The value of a day's work, on an average, in the above calculation, is put at 25 cents per man, although, at Wethersfield, no convict is now hired at less than 30 cents per day, and some of them have produced to the state $1.''

[To this estimate of a penitentiary on the Auburn plan, we will add the estimate of a penitentiary on the Pennsylvania plan, with 300 cells. It is taken from the report on the penitentiary, to be erected in New Jersey, to the legislature of that state, and has been drawn up by John Haviland, of Philadelphia, after whose design, and under whose direction, the Eastern penitentiary has been constructed. He has, of course, great experience in this kind of construction, and has made the plan and estimate according to the latest improvement, and on the most economical scale. The report above mentioned, says:

" The plan submitted is substantially upon the principle (with several improvements) of the Eastern penitentiary, varying, however, in its application, correspondent with a scale of reduction. It is plain, simple, and economical; and susceptible of extension, according to the increasing demands of the state, and this too, not only without marring its original design, but by carrying the same into complete effect."

The architect, in his estimate, says: "I have made the accompanying drawing, model, and estimate, for your contemplated new state penitentiary, designed for 'solitary confinement with labour.' Since the commencement of our Eastern state penitentiary, much valuable experience has been obtained, and considerable improvements made in the desired properties of security, ventilation, light, warming, and supervision of the cells, and location of the operative offices of the institution.

"In the estimate, I have calculated every feature of the design, to be executed in the most substantial and approved manner, and of the best materials of their several kinds, avoiding useless ornament, and employing members best calculated to perfect the desired properties of the institution. The value of labour and materials taken from the best information and experience.

" The whole plan will accommodate three hundred prisoners, and admit the erection of any one of the radiating blocks, as circumstances may require, from time to time, without interfering with each other."

External wall, - - - - -	$14,000
Front building containing the culinary, laundry, and bathing offices, store-rooms, keeper's chambers, observatory, reservoir, belfrey, and other fire-proof rooms, expressed in the plan, -	15,000
Culvert, sinks, cast-iron pipes, covered ways, apparatus for cooking, warming, and raising water into reservoirs, - - - -	13,000
Five radiating blocks of cells	
Block A, containing 50 cells, - - -	18,000
" B, " 75 " - - -	27,000
" C, " 50 " - - -	18,000
" D, " 75 " - - -	27,000
" E, " 50 " - - -	18,000
300 cells	$150,000

Philadelphia, January, 1833.

TRANS.]

27

No. 13.

RULES AND REGULATIONS FOR THE CONNECTI-CUT STATE PRISON.

SECTION I.

Duties of the Warden.

1. He shall reside at the prison, and shall visit every cell and apartment, and see every prisoner under his care, at least once every day.

2. He shall not absent himself from the prison for more than a night, without giving notice to one or more of the directors.

3. It shall be his duty to cause the books and accounts to be so kept as clearly to exhibit the state of the convicts, the number employed in each branch of business, and their earnings, the number in the hospital, the expenses of the prison, and all re-ceipts and payments. purchases and sales; and to exhibit the same to the directors at their quarterly meetings, or at any time when required. The quarterly accounts of the warden shall be sworn to by him, and shall specify minutely the persons from whom or to whom moneys are received or paid, and for what purpose.

4. It shall be the duty of the warden to make all contracts, purchases, and sales, for and on account of the prison—to over-see and command all the inferior officers in all their various duties, and see that they conform to the law, and the rules and regulations prescribed by the directors. He shall see that the prisoners are treated with kindness and humanity, and that no unnecessary severity is practised by the inferior officers—but if the security of the prison shall be in danger, or personal violence should be offered to him or any of the officers or guards, then he or they shall use all lawful means to defend themselves, and secure the authors of such outrage. In executing the duties of his office, the warden should never lose sight of the reformation of the prisoners, and should carefully guard himself against per-sonal and passionate resentment. All orders should be given with mildness and dignity, and enforced with promptitude and firmness.

5. It shall be his duty to treat persons visiting the prison with uniform civility and politeness, and to see that they are so treated by the inferior officers.

6. As it is by law the duty of the directors to see personally

to the condition and treatment of the prisoners, no regulation or order shall be made to prevent prisoners having ready access to the director who shall be present, nor shall any punishment be inflicted upon them for speaking to a director.   In discharging this part of their duty, the directors will deem it proper not to suffer a convict to hold any conversation with them in the hearing or presence of other prisoners.

7. The warden may, with the advice and consent of the directors in writing, appoint one person to be a deputy warden, and may, with such consent and advice in writing, remove him.

SECTION II.

Of the Deputy Warden.

1. He shall be present at the opening and closing of the prison, during the performance of religious services, and also at all other prison hours.

2. He shall daily visit the hospital, cookery, cells, and see that every part of the institution is clean and in order.

3. It shall be his duty to exercise, under the direction of the warden, a general inspection and superintendence over the whole establishment, and all its concerns, to see that every subordinate officer strictly performs his appropriate duties, to visit frequently the places of labour and yards without notice, and see that the convicts are diligent and industrious, and generally to see that the rules and regulations of the institution are enforced, and that every precaution is taken for the security of the prison, and the prisoners therein confined.

4. He shall attend to the clothing of the convicts, and see that it is whole, properly changed, and in order.

SECTION III.

Of the Overseers.

1. There shall be an overseer of each shop, to be appointed by the warden.

2. Each overseer shall, on entering upon his duties, take an accurate account of the various implements and tools belonging to his department, with the value of the same in money, and shall lodge a copy of such account under his hand with the warden, and such account shall be corrected quarterly, by adding such new implements as may have been purchased, or such as may have been broken, damaged, or lost   He shall keep an account of the stock furnished his department, and of the articles manufactured there and taken therefrom, and also of the daily

and weekly earnings of each convict. He shall see that all the property belonging to his department shall be carefully preserved, and that the work is well and faithfully done, and shall consult and promote the interest of the state, or the contractor who may employ the convicts. It is especially enjoined upon each overseer, to preserve in his department the most entire order.

No conversation between prisoners shall be allowed. Nor shall any overseer converse with a prisoner, except to direct him in his labour If any prisoner is idle, careless, or refractory, he shall be forthwith reported to the warden or deputy warden for punishment. Each overseer shall enter upon his book the name of each sick or complaining prisoner, and shall, before 9 o'clock A. M., deliver to the warden or deputy a list of such names, with the date, which list shall be placed in the hospital.

3. Each overseer shall perform his regular tour of night duty, as he may be directed by the warden.

SECTION IV.

Of the Watchmen.

1. It shall be the duty of the several watchmen to perform all such various duties and services, for the safety and security of the prison, as may be directed by the warden, both by day, and during the night; to be vigilant and active while on post, and to maintain, while off from duty, and in the guard room, both towards each other and all other persons, a gentlemanly deportment ; to refrain from all those acts which are inconsistent with the strictest decorum—treating with an uniform politeness and civility, all persons who shall visit the prison ; recollecting that the reputation, as well as the safety of the institution, depend essentially upon them, individually as well as collectively. They are to be cautious they are neat and cleanly in their own persons, and that the guard room shall at all times exhibit a specimen of neatness and order ; and that their arms are always in repair, and ready for service. No watchman shall be allowed to hold any conversation with a prisoner, except to direct him in his labour. Nor shall he receive from, or deliver to a prisoner, any article or thing, without the knowledge of the warden or his deputy.

2. It shall be the duty of the warden to designate some person who shall be employed at the prison, to see, personally, that the various rations ordered by these rules are weighed or measured for the day, according to the number of prisoners, and delivered to the head cook , and he shall keep an exact account of all such rations, so by him delivered, and shall, under oath, render the

same quarterly to the warden, under his hand, to be laid before the directors

3. Each and every person who shall by the warden be appointed to any office in or about said prison, shall be held as engaged to, and attached to the institution ; and if in office at the time a vacancy shall happen in the office of warden, as bound to continue his services at the prison, for at least one month after the death, removal, or resignation of the warden, unless sooner discharged by his successor , and in case any such officer shall refuse or neglect to perform his duty, he shall forfeit three months' wages, to be recovered by any succeeding warden, and this by-law shall be considered as one of the terms on which each officer shall contract, and as assented to by him.

SECTION V.

Of Cleanliness.

1. The hall and cells shall be swept daily, and the sweepings carried outside of the wall The floor of the hall shall be washed once a fortnight through the year. The cells shall also be frequently washed and whitewashed.

2. The beds and bedding shall be taken out of the prison and aired in the yard, once a week in the warm season, and once a fortnight during the rest of the year, when the weather will allow ; and each prisoner is to take the utmost care that his cell be kept neat, and that his furniture be not injured : and in default of observing this rule, his bed, bedding, and bedstead, to be taken from him until he will conform.

3 The utmost care is to be taken that the persons of the prisoners are kept clean. For this purpose they shall have suitable accommodations for washing.

4. The night pails shall be kept carefully clean, and their contents carried without the walls, and covered in the manner now practised.

5 No filth, nuisance, or offensive matter, shall be suffered to remain in or about the prison, shops, or yard ; but the whole establishment must be made to exhibit throughout, a specimen of neatness, good order, and cleanliness.

SECTION VI.

Of the Hospital and Physician.

1. The warden, with the approbation of the directors, shall appoint some proper person to be the physician, who shall re-

ceive such compensation as shall be fixed and agreed upon by the directors.

2 The hospital shall be furnished with the necessary beds, bedding, bedsteads, tables, and all other necessary utensils, for the comfort and accommodation of the sick, and shall at all times be kept in a state of readiness to receive such patients as are ordered there by the physician.

3. The physician shall direct such supplies, stores, and furniture, as may be necessary in his department, and his order in writing shall authorize the warden to procure the same. He shall record in a book all the orders so given, designating the articles and the time when given He shall also keep an account of the various articles belonging to his department. He shall also record in said book, his visits, the names of the patients reported as sick or complaining, the names of such as are ordered to the hospital, or as are ordered to their cells on sick diet, or are ordered to their shops He shall visit the institution every other day through the year, and oftener if it shall be necessary, or if sent for, and shall personally see every patient or prisoner, who may, by the respective overseers, be reported as sick or complaining. He shall also enter the names of such as shall be discharged from the hospital, or shall die, the nature of the complaint and the prescription, and shall subjoin such other remarks as he may deem expedient, respecting the nature of each case, and the treatment thereof, or in relation to the general health, diet, or employment of the prisoners, or cleanliness of the prison, which book shall remain at the prison, and shall be always open to the inspection of the warden and directors.

He may apply to the warden for the assistance of such convicts as may be necessary to nurse and attend upon the sick, and he, as well as the warden, shall endeavour to render the condition of the sick prisoner, in all respects, as comfortable as his situation will admit. Whenever any prisoner shall not be sufficiently ill, as to make it necessary that he be ordered to the hospital, the physician may direct such diet to be prepared for him, from the hospital or prison stores, as he may deem necessary.

4. If it shall so happen that the directions or prescriptions of the physician shall not be complied with, or duly observed, it shall be his duty to enter such failure or omission in his book, with the reason thereof, if he shall be acquainted with the same, to the end that proper measures may be taken to prevent future omissions.

SECTION VII.

General Regulations.

1 No officer or person connected with the institution, shall

be permitted to buy from, or sell to any convict any article or thing whatever, or make with him any contract or engagement whatsoever, or cause or allow any convict to work for him or his benefit, or grant any favour or indulgence to a convict, except such as the laws allow. Nor shall he receive from any convict, or from any one in behalf of such convict, any emoluments, presents, or reward whatever, or the promise of any for services or supplies, or as a gratuity. Nor shall he take or receive to his own use and benefit or that of his family, any fee, gratuity, or emolument, from any person committed to his custody, nor, from any of their friends or acquaintances, or from any person whomsoever, and every officer offending herein, shall be forthwith dismissed.

2. The compensation to each and every officer, shall be fixed and settled by the directors before he enters upon the duties of his office, and no officer shall be allowed or permitted to take or receive any other or greater compensation than the sum so fixed; nor shall he take or receive either from the public property or in the labour or services of the convicts, any perquisite whatever, without the consent of the directors in writing.

3. Spirituous liquors shall in no case be furnished to the convicts, except on the prescription of the physician. And each and every officer is hereby required wholly to abstain from their use, during the period of his employment at this institution, on penalty of being dismissed.

4. No officer except the warden, shall strike, beat, or punish corporeally any prisoner, except in self-defence.

5. In case any officer shall be absent from the prison, except upon the public business of the same, the rateable compensation of such officer shall be stopped during the time of such absence.

6. Each cell shall be furnished with a Bible, and the convicts may have such other religious books and attendance, as the warden, with the assent of the directors, may think suited to improve their morals and conduct.

7. All sums which shall be received from persons visiting the prison, shall be accounted for to the state, and deemed a part of the income of the prison, and such sums shall be included in the quarterly accounts of the warden.

SECTION VIII.

Duties of the Convicts.

1. Every convict shall be industrious, submissive, and obedient, and shall labour diligently and in silence.

2. No convict shall secrete, hide, or carry about his person, any instrument or thing with intent to make his escape.

3. No convict shall write or receive a letter to or from any person whatsoever, nor have intercourse with persons without the prison, except by leave of the warden.

4. No convict shall burn, waste, injure, or destroy any raw materials or article of public property, nor deface or injure the prison building.

5. Convicts shall always conduct themselves toward the officers with deference and respect; and cleanliness in their persons, dress, and bedding, is required. When they go to their meals or labour, they shall proceed in regular order and in silence, marching in the lock step.

6. No convict shall converse with another prisoner, or leave his work without permission of an officer. He shall not speak to, or look at visitors, nor leave the hospital when ordered there, nor shall he make any unnecessary noise in his labour, or do any thing either in the shops or cells, which is subversive of the good order of the institution.

SECTION IX.

Of the Rations, Bedding, &c.

1. The rations for each convict per day, shall be one pound of beef, one pound of bread, to be made of rye flour and corn meal unbolted Five bushels of potatoes to each hundred rations, and a porridge for supper, to be made of twenty pounds of corn meal, and six quarts of peas, to each hundred rations. Each convict to be furnished with pepper and salt.

2 Each convict shall have a straw mattress, three blankets in winter, and two in summer, and two coarse cotton sheets of sufficient size—the whole to be kept carefully clean. They shall not be permitted to sleep in their clothes, nor to lie down or rise until notice shall be given by the bell. Their meals shall be taken in their cells.

No. 13.—bis.

RULES

For the House of Reformation, South Boston. Reported by the Chaplain, E. M. P. Wells, to the Board of Directors, and by them approved.

Of Initiation.

1. WHEN a boy is received into the institution, his person shall be examined and washed, and new dressed, if there be oc-

casion therefore; and if medical or surgical aid be required, it shall be administered as soon as may be.

2 The chaplain shall also examine him, as to his habits of life, principles, and passions—state to him the cause of his coming, the object of his remaining, and the improvement and time necessary for his leaving.

3 He shall then be introduced by name to the boys, while assembled, and receiving a copy of these laws (if he can read,) he shall be placed in the second or third mal grades, as his case may require; in both or the former of which, he shall remain one week on probation. If, during this probation, he has behaved well, he shall be so reported to the boys, and their vote taken whether he shall be received into their community —If there be one of the first bon grade; two of the first two; four of the first three, or five in all, who vote against him, he shall not be admitted till another trial.

4. If a boy of peculiar circumstances, extra age, or committed by the Municipal Court, be received, he shall remain in a solitair one or more weeks before being introduced to the boys.

Division and Occupation of Time.

1. There shall be in each day three meals—the time for eating which shall not be less than one hour for the three: three seasons for play, three-quarters of an hour each: two seasons for school, and two for work—except Sundays

2. The exact time of beginning and ending each division of time, as also the hour for rising from and going to bed, shall be definitely fixed and regularly marked by the ringing of the bell as often as necessary. This division of time may be varied according to the season of the year, by consent of the committee.

3. On Sundays, the chaplain may regulate the exercises as he pleases, except that there shall be the two usual morning and evening services. There shall be prayers every morning and evening.

The Discipline

Shall be chiefly moral, rather than physical

1. No member of the community (see Initiation, *art.* 3d) shall be punished by whipping, or the cells, but solitary rooms, visors to obscure the sight, bracelets to restrain the hands, privation of conversation, of play, of work, of the regular food, or of one meal entirely, shall be substituted therefore.

2. A boy shall not be punished for a fault not expressly prohibited, either by the laws of God, of the country, or of the institution; and not unless he knew it was so prohibited, as far as can be judged from circumstances.

3. No boy shall be required to give information of the faults

28

of another, nor shall he be allowed so to do, unless he be apparently conscientious in it.

4. No boy shall be punished for a fault, however great, which he frankly and honestly confesses, unless he is influenced by his being suspected, or partially known; nor shall any boy be punished for faults which come out in the confession of another, except by consent of the one confessing.

A Dr. and Cr. account shall be kept with each boy;—Dr. marks shall be given for small faults, and at the close of each day the names shall be called over, and every boy shall pass judgment on his own conduct, and answer to his name, good, bad, or indifferent. No opinion shall be given to a boy by which to regulate his answer, but if his answer be given better or worse than it should be, it shall be corrected by the instructors, or monitors. And if it be and ought to be good, he shall receive a Cr. mark.

6. There shall be a court held in each day, before morning or evening prayers, for the examination and settlement of cases of conduct.

7. As man is not capable of punishing disrespect or irreverence to God · therefore, if a boy be irregular in his behaviour at religious services, he shall not be allowed to attend them—leaving the punishment with a higher power and for a future day.

8. The accounts shall be settled every Saturday night. If a boy have a balance of two bad marks, they may be carried to a new account, but for a greater number of marks, he shall be degraded one or more grades, according to the rules of those grades; except in the first mal a boy may lose his supper on Sunday night for his bad morals, if they do not exceed four.

If the balance of marks be Cr, they shall be passed to new account, for the purchase of passers to the city, books, paper, pencils, combs, handkerchiefs, and various other advantages.

9. In cases of extraordinary bad conduct, whether from its nature or long continuance, a boy may be expelled from the community; after which he shall have no intercourse with the boys; and if circumstances should again favour a readmission to it, shall not be except by the regular course of probation.

10. As the government of the institution is in part committed to monitors, the following regulations respecting them are adopted.

The monitors to whom the government and business of the house are at all committed, shall be appointed at the beginning of each month: A head monitor who shall preside in the absence of the officers: Two keepers of the keys, who shall take charge of the keys, ring the bells, open and shut the doors, morning, night, and other set times, and tend the door bells: A sheriff and his two deputies, who shall take charge of the second and third mal grade, one of them at all times, except sleeping hours, and the first mal grade during play hours: A steward, who shall have a boy with him, and shall attend to the marketing; the boys' meals, and provisions: A monitor of police, who shall have two or three boys under him, who shall daily sweep clean and arrange the boys' part of the house, except the chambers and dining-room: A monitor of the chambers, who shall attend to their daily and weekly clearing and arranging, who shall also keep order in the upper entry at night A monitor of the wardrobe, who shall attend to the brushing, putting up, and giving out of the clothes: Three door-keepers, who shall attend to particular doors or gates, as may be required: other monitors may be occasionally appointed. The monitors of divisions and of the first grade, shall be elected monthly by the boys of such divisions and grades, and shall march them, and see that their heads are combed, and their faces and hands washed before breakfast.

The principal enforcement of discipline shall be by promotion or degradation, according to the following system of grades of character with their privileges and privations.

The members of the community shall be divided into the following grades of character.

Bon Grades—First Grade.

Those who make *positive*, REGULAR, and CONTINUED effort to do right.

Their faults can be those only of mistake, or very rarely those of carelessness.

Privileges.

1. The same as the inferior grades, and also
2. To walk without the stockade, without a monitor; to sail and swim without a monitor.
3. To go to their rooms without permission, and into the dining room, when necessary.
4. To leave their seats in the assembling room, without permission.
5. Other things being equal, this grade have a choice before all others.
6. The use of the recreation room.
7. To be intrusted, when necessary, with the most important keys
8. To have their word taken on all common occasions.
9. To have their birth-days celebrated.
10. To wear the undress uniform.

Second Grade.

Those who make *positive* and REGULAR effort to do right.

Their faults are those only of carelessness, faults not evil in themselves, or if so, not intentional; or a balance of bad marks. Also faults which are simply legal.

Privileges.

1. The same as all inferior grades.
2. To go to the city for twenty-five good marks, without a monitor, if it is the third time
4. To be intrusted with keys of secondary importance.
5. To be capable of holding the offices of appointment.
6. To take books from the reading-room.
7. To use the papers in the assembling room, without permission.
9. Other things being equal, this grade have a choice before all inferior.

Third Grade.

Those who make *positive* effort to do right.

Their faults are those only of carelessness or of momentary erring; faults evil in themselves, perhaps, but immediately repented of, on reflection; or a balance of three bad marks.

Privileges.

1. The same as the inferior grades, and also
2. To go to the city for twenty-five good marks under a monitor.
3. To walk about the grounds under a monitor.
4. To go to the gymnasium and reading room.
5. To use the books and papers in the assembling room by permission.
6. To hold offices by election.

Mal Grades—First Grade.

Those who are *positively* inclined to do wrong.—Their faults are only legal faults, (that is, things not wrong in themselves) or moral faults rarely committed, or a balance of five bad marks.

Privations.

1. To be deprived of play and of conversation except with those of this grade, or when necessary to those they are at work with.
2. Not to go to the superintendent's rooms.
3. Not to vote at elections.
4. For faults committed while in the grade, marks or degradation.

Second Grade.

Those who are *positively* and REGULARLY inclined to do wrong. Their faults are moral or legal ones often committed, or a balance of ten bad marks.

Privations.

1. The same as the first grade.

2 Not to converse with any boys, except when necessary about their work.

3 Not to speak to the superintendent except when permitted.

4. To be deprived of their regular seats, and kept distinct under a sheriff and never be dismissed, except when in their bed rooms.

5. To be deprived of cake, or any other extra food.

6. For faults committed while in this grade, to be degraded, unless for trifling ones, which *may* be settled by bad marks.

Third Grade.

Those who are *positively*, REGULARLY and CONTINUALLY inclined to do wrong.

Their faults are moral faults often committed, or a single instance of doing wrong, without any other motive than the love of the wrong.

Privations.

1. The same as all others

2. To have their food bread and water, to wear bracelets or a visor, or to be put in a solitary room. The first of these, deprives of the use of the hands, the second, of the eyes, and the third, of the usual liberty.

3. For faults committed while in this grade, or if a boy be degraded to this grade for any extra fault, such as lying, dishonesty, profane language, or such faults, he may be deprived as above.

The time necessary to remain in the above grades before promotion is four weeks in the second Bon, two weeks in the third Bon, one week in the first mal, and in the second or third mal grade one day each, and the term for each must be correctly passed according to each grade.

12. The following things not before mentioned are also forbidden.

1. To use profane, vulgar or angry language.

2. To use tobacco.

3. To pass through any door or gate or up and down stairs without permission.

4. To cut, scratch, break, write upon or in any other way disfigure the buildings, furniture or fences.

5. To engage in any game or play which is not specially allowed of.

6. To fire stones about the house, or any thing in the house.

7. To go out of the paths in the garden or pull up or eat any thing except by permission.

8. To carry food from the dining room to throw it about or pass it to others

9. To bring any thing to the house without permission.

10. To have any buttons belonging to the clothes.

11. To converse with different grades except among the Bon Grades.

12. To have any thing of the knife or cutting kind except regular pocket knives

13. To have yarn, thread, twine or balls except by permission.

14. To run in any part of the house except the two arches.

15. To climb any where except in the Gymnasium.

Bed Rooms.

Every boy shall have a bed to himself, and he shall not change his bed or sleep in the bed clothes of another or wear his clothes without permission.

There shall be no playing, laughing, singing or other noises except that of conversation in a low voice, in the chambers.

The boys shall make their beds and do the other chamber work immediately after the ringing of the first bell and the opening of the doors, between which there shall be one quarter of an hour.

No boy shall keep any thing whatever in his room except books without permission.

⊦ No boy shall go into his own or any other boy's room (except he be of the first Bon Grade) without permission.

Cleanliness.

The bed rooms, assembling room, reading room, and wardrobe, entries and stairs, shall be washed and scoured alternately once a week when in use. The winter bed clothing shall be washed in the spring before putting away. The sheets shall be changed at least once in two weeks—The shirts shall be changed once a week at all seasons, and in the summer twice a week as circumstances require. The summer jackets and trousers shall be changed every week, extraordinaries excepted. The chamber utensils shall be rinsed every day and washed every week.

2. During the warm weather the boys shall bathe in salt water three times a week unless the weather prevent.

3. Out of the bathing season the small boys shall be washed all over and the large boys the upper and lower part of their bodies

at least once a week, and their heads shall be combed twice a week specially.

4. The hair shall be cut once a month.

Food.

The breakfasts and suppers shall consist of one pint of tea or shells, and as much bread as each boy wishes, but he shall return all that he does not want

2 The Dinners, as nearly as convenient, shall be as follows.
Baked Beef with vegetables once per week.
Boiled   "   "   "   "   "   "
Stewed "   or soup   "   "   "   "
Fish or Beef minced   "   "   "   "
Baked Beans   "   "   "
Puddings   "   "   "

3. On Christmas, Thanksgiving, 4th of July and Election day, the boys shall have extra food and recreation.

4. A boy shall not be deprived of his food more than one meal for the same fault, nor in ordinary cases shall he be kept on bread and water for more than three or four days.

Dress.

1. On Sundays and on special occasions the boys shall be dressed in a uniform to consist of a blue cap and jacket single breasted and white trowsers in summer, and in winter some other light colour.

2. The ordinary dress shall be of a plain and durable kind, except the first Bon Grade, who shall wear the first grade uniform

The foregoing rules apply to females as well as males, varying only as circumstances dictate

---

No. 14.

LETTER OF MR. BARRETT, CHAPLAIN OF THE PENITENTIARY OF WETHERSFIELD.*

Wethersfield, October 7th, 1831.

To Messrs. de Beaumont and de Toqueville:

Gentlemen,—

The population of Connecticut amounts to about 280,000 souls During thirty-six years, the old shafts near Timesbury, and

---

* Re-translated.—The Rev. Mr Barrett is no longer the chaplain. His place is occupied by the Rev. Mr. Whittelsey.—Trans.

called Newgate, served as a state prison. The new prison has been inhabited only for about four years.

During the forty years preceding the month of July, 1831, the number of individuals sent to these two prisons amounted to 976. Their crimes were of the following classes; 435 had committed burglary; 139 horse stealing, 78 passing counterfeit money; 41 assault and battery; 47 attempt to commit rape; 3 attempt at poisoning; 1 murder (the punishment had been commuted); 11 robbery on the highway, 1 robbing the mail; 1 bestiality; 60 forgery; 25 misdemeanors; 15 had been committed for attempting to deliver prisoners, 34 for arson; 9 for manslaughter; 4 for rape (the punishment had been commuted); 2 for cheating, 5 for bigamy, 23 for adultery, 16 for breaking fences, 3 for attempts at escape; 9 for theft, to the injury of the prison; 4 for incest; 3 for perjury; and 5 for crimes not known.

There are, in Connecticut, about 3 coloured people to 100 white. In the prison, the proportion of the negroes is about 33 to 100.

Of 182 convicts whom I have examined, there were 76 who did not know how to write, and 30 who had not learned to read.

Sixty had been deprived of their parents before their tenth year; and 36 others had lost them before their fifteenth year

Of 182, 116 were natives of Connecticut.

Ninety were from twenty to thirty years old, and 18 were sentenced for life

The prison contains at present 18 women. Some are employed in the kitchen, and in washing for the prisoners; others in sewing shoes.

For a pair of shoes they receive 4 cents; a woman can finish from 6 to 10 pair a day. During night they are in separate cells.

Morning and evening, prayers are said in presence of the prisoners; passages of the Bible are read and explained to them. The convicts show themselves attentive and collected on these occasions Every one finds in his cell a Bible furnished by the state, and in which he may read when he likes Generally, they are disposed to this kind of reading The other day, passing by their cells, I observed 23 prisoners out of 25, who were seriously occupied in reading.

On Sunday, a sermon is preached in their presence, which they never fail to hear with great attention. They often make, afterwards, curious questions respecting the meaning of what they have heard.

When the principles of the Holy Scriptures are impressed on the heart of a convict, it certainly may be believed that his reform is complete: we have reason to believe that this result has been sometimes obtained. I should think that fifteen or twenty of the actual number of prisoners are so affected in this case. It is, however, impossible, so far, to establish this point in a positive way. It is necessary to wait until the state of liberty, and resistance to temptations, finally prove their reformation.

None of the convicts refuse at least religious instruction ; and I have not yet found a single one who has shown the least want of respect, when I have come to visit him in his cell.

I have observed, that ignorance, neglect on the part of parents, and intemperance, formed, in general, the three great causes to which crime must be attributed

The majority of convicts show themselves anxious to be instructed. There were some who arrived without knowing a letter, and learned to read within two months. Yet they could make use of the Bible only, and received no other lessons than those which could be given through the grates of their cell.

The result to be expected from a prison depends much upon the character of the keepers They ought to have moral habits, to speak little, and to be ready to see every thing.

If the keepers are what they ought to be ; if the convicts, separated during night, labour during day in silence ; if continued surveillance is joined with frequent moral and religious instruction, a prison may become a place of reformation for the convicts, and a source of revenue to the state.

I am, respectfully, &c.

G BARRETT, *Chaplain of the Prison.*

[To the above letter, we will add some extracts of the Report of the Chaplain of Auburn Prison, the Rev. Mr. B. C. Smith, contained in the Annual Report of the Inspectors of that prison to the Legislature, January 8th, 1833.—Trans]

The fact which, of all others, is the most striking to a person conversant with the religious history of convicts, is that of their great and general *ignorance of the Bible*—and consequently, of the nature of the relations which they sustain to God and to their fellow men, and of the obligations which arise out of those relations. Without mentioning particular instances of this ignorance, which would scarcely be credited, it is sufficient to remark, that many, upon being questioned, have betrayed their inability to name any one of the books or parts of which the Bible is composed ; and expressions of surprise at finding it to be such a book as it is, are so common as to be very remarkable.

It is not, however, to be denied, that there are many, too many, among this guilty and degraded class of men, who have broken through all the restraints of a religious education, and urged their way to prison against all the powerful motives presented to their minds in the Bible , but they are *so few*, compared with those who have been brought up without instruction

29

in the great doctrines and duties of religion, that the observer cannot fail to be struck with the disparity, or to see in it a direct and conclusive proof of the salutary influence of the Holy Scriptures, and of the importance of their universal diffusion and inculcation.

It is gratifying to be able to add, in corroboration of the same point, that, of more than two thousand convicts who have been sentenced to this prison, only two or three are known to have previously received instruction in Sabbath schools.

Another fact, little less remarkable, respecting this class of men, is their general *ignorance of letters.* Since the establishment of our Prison Sabbath School, nearly seven years since, about five hundred and fifty convicts have been brought into it for instruction.—Of these, a great majority could read only in the easiest reading lessons, by spelling many of the words ; and more than one hundred commenced with the alphabet. They were selected, it is true, (from the younger portion of the convicts,) on account of their illiterateness , but yet it is clear, from this statement, that the education of these men, as a class, is far inferior to that of our citizens generally. The pupils in our school are, almost exclusively, between the ages of eighteen and thirty ; and the whole number, of all ages, from which they have been selected, is not more than $1640 - 550 = 1090$. The proportion of illiterate men above the age of thirty is at least equal—few, if any of whom, it will be observed, have been brought into this account. For the honour of our country, it is to be hoped that no spot can be found exhibiting such a proportion of men so illiterate, between the ages of eighteen and thirty, compared with the whole population above the age of eighteen. Where is the community, whose every eleventh adult, even of the whole population, has yet to learn the letters of the alphabet?

Another fact, which, though already notorious, is worthy of repetition here, is the remarkable *prevalence of intemperance* among this class of men. It will be seen in a striking light in the following statement. The number of convicts now in this prison is 683, of whom there had been,

Grossly intemperate,	230
Moderately intemperate, (regular drinking, and occasional intoxication, or either,) -	278
Temperate drinkers, -	156
Total abstinents, or nearly so, -	19
	683

The first two classes, making 508, or nearly three-fourths of the whole number, may with propriety be accounted intemperate.

Of these, 385 were under the influence of ardent spirits at the time they committed their crimes; and of the whole number, 219 have acknowledged that either one or both of their parents, or their masters, were more or less intemperate.

Multitudes of facts like these, most fully attest that intemperance is the great and overflowing source of crime in our land; and, after what I have seen in this prison, I cannot doubt, that the decrease of criminal convictions will almost keep pace with the progress of temperance, nor that its universal reign would, in the end, well nigh depopulate our prisons. To what cause but the temperance reform is it to be ascribed, that the number of state prison convictions in this state, during the year 1832, is nearly a hundred less than that of the preceding year?

Is not the *proportion of unmarried convicts* also worthy of remark? It would be an interesting subject of inquiry, and perhaps lead to some important conclusions, to ascertain and compare this proportion between married and unmarried adults in the community at large. I have not the means at hand of ascertaining the proportion of marriages among the latter, but give that of the former in this prison, to enable any one, who may be curious enough, to prosecute the inquiry.

Married convicts,	-	-	-	-	364
Unmarried convicts,	-	-	-	-	319
					683

Instances of separation between husband and wife, by desertion, previous to conviction, 62—by death, 38.

Is not this proportion of unmarried men in prison, much greater than that of the unmarried to the married among our adult male population in general? And if so, what is the inference respecting any doctrines tending to repudiate a certain "arbitrary custom" that prevails in society "under its present organization?"

The married convicts left, under age, 901 children :—

With a competence for their support,	223	} 901
Without property of any amount, -	678	
Among relatives who could assist them,	180	
Without property or assistance of friends,	498	

The resident chaplain's weekly routine of duties is too well known to need now to be particularly described. The most prominent are, the general superintendence of the Sabbath school, the public exercises of the chapel, and the private instructions at the cells, on the Sabbath, and the daily evening devotions in front of the cells, and the visiting of the hospital, during the week.

Of the manner in which these and the various other duties .

have been performed, it does not become me to speak. I trust, however, I shall be indulged in saying, that, in all my instructions and admonitions to the convicts, I have *dealt plainly with them* I have dwelt, emphatically, upon their depravity and guilt in trampling upon the laws of God and of their country; endeavoured to awaken remorse in their consciences, to convince them of the justice of their punishment, to induce them to yield strict and humble obedience to all the regulations of the prison, to press home upon them the duty of immediate repentance and amendment, and to persuade them to take refuge in the mercy of Him who says, " Let the wicked forsake his way, and the unrighteous man his thoughts, and let him return unto the Lord, and he will have mercy upon him, and to our God, for he will abundantly pardon."

Great pains have also been taken to dissuade them from the future use of ardent spirits, by portraying the ruinous effects of intemperance, as exhibited in their own wretched condition, and that of their distressed families and friends, and by giving them appropriate tracts, and frequently reading the best essays on the subject in the chapel.

The Sabbath school still proves to be a very important and efficient auxiliary to the labours of the chaplain During the past year it has consisted of about two hundred pupils, under the immediate instruction of thirty-five of the students of the theological seminary, whose benevolent, discreet and zealous efforts for the benefit of these men, deserve the highest commendation. The primary object of the school is to instruct the illiterate to read ; but in doing this, the teachers avail themselves of the opportunity of dropping useful incidental remarks, and of making such explanations and applications of the great truths of the Bible, as are calculated to enlighten the understanding and affect the heart. The happy tendency of this system of instruction is clearly apparent, not only in the remarkable progress of most of the scholars in reading and religious knowledge, but also in their more ready and cheerful compliance with the rules of the prison, and, as we trust, in some instances of that moral transformation which is the surest pledge of a virtuous life here, and the only ground of hope for the future.

And what has been said of the apparent influence of the Sabbath school instruction, may, if I mistake not, be said also of the other modes of instruction. The convicts in general appear to be affected in view of divine truth. Their fixed attention, and often their deep solemnity, during the public exercises of the Sabbath, as well as the impressive stillness of the hour for evening devotions, is a subject of general remark. In private conversation, after the first few interviews, they manifest, almost without exception, a kind, tender, subdued state of feeling, and not merely a willingness, but more or less eagerness, to receive instruction. And it is so common to hear them, with bursting tears, utter expressions of gratitude that they were arrested in their infatuated career, and lodged in the state prison, that it has almost ceased to be remarkable. We do not dream, that the hopes which such appearances are calculated to awaken, will always or even generally be realized; but that they have been, in many instances, we have the most satisfactory testimony. We have documents to show that a great number who were once convicts in this prison, are now useful and respectable citizens. It is known, also, that not a few of them, in various parts of the country, are consistent professors of religion, and that several are exemplary members of churches in our own village.

Let me here disclaim any intention of arrogating to our system of moral and religious instruction, simply, and independently, all or any of the merit of working such changes in the feelings and conduct of such men. Under a system of unrestrained association and intercourse among them, it would, I have no doubt, prove to be utterly inefficient. Its success depends upon the rigid enforcement of such a system of discipline as your Board have adopted in this institution. Confident as I am, that your system of physical coercion and discipline, merely, without its accompaniment of moral motives, would only make bad men worse, I am no less confident that without such a system of strict seclusion and non-intercourse, religious motives would have no power to make bad men better. Of this I have been more fully convinced than ever, since our number of convicts became so large as to make it necessary to confine several together at night, in each of our large cells. The mischievous effects of this association, partial as it was, have been plainly perceptible, not only upon those convicts themselves, but upon others with whom they have laboured by day. But I rejoice to find that this evil is entirely remedied now, by the completion of the new and admirable block of cells in the south wing.

It gives me the sincerest pleasure, too, that your Board will be able to represent to the legislature a great improvement in the condition of the female department. Since it has been under the superintendence of our pious and capable matron, by day, with the means of a partial separation, or rather classification, at night, the appearance and conduct of these females have certainly been very strikingly improved. We are no longer disturbed by their boisterous mirth, their infuriate shrieks, their shocking oaths, or the sound of the missile brickbat. We hear no more the clank of their chains, nor see upon their faces the marks of savage combat. With only an occasional exception, all now is silence, order, neatness, and cheerful industry. It is truly surprising, that the presence of a matron, under all the disadvantages which must be encountered in apartments so ill adapted to the purpose, should ever have wrought so great a change   *   *   *   *   *

But if all these inconveniences were obviated, there would still remain one, which, of itself, ought to be sufficient to decide the matter at once,—and for which *there is no remedy*, as stated in the last report of your Board, " without incurring an expense, in the re-organization of the male department, more than equal to that of erecting an entire new institution for females." I allude to the fact of their being necessarily confined, day and night, perpetually, within walls which almost exclude the air and light of heaven They never do, and never can, step out of their close apartments, for one moment, to breathe the fresh air, or enjoy the broad light of day. The consequence is, a great amount of disease, and a general lassitude and inertness almost as bad. A proportionate amount of sickness among the male convicts, would throng the hospital with from fifty to a hundred men constantly, instead of six or eight. In this situation, many of the females have endured long sentences, and others remain who have spent more than half of their terms, of seven, ten, twelve, and fourteen years. Who can hesitate to pronounce it inhuman—barbarous—unworthy of the age? And why is the penalty of the law allowed to fall with more severity upon this class of convicts than upon the other? To be a *male* convict in this prison, would be quite tolerable; but to be a *female* convict, for any protracted term, would be worse than death.

No. 15

CONVERSATION

With the Superintendent of the House of Refuge in Philadelphia, November, 1831

Ques. Of how old a child, do you believe, the reformation may be obtained?

Ans. Experience has shown, that after fifteen or sixteen years, there is little hope of reformation. Almost all young persons, who had passed this age when they entered the refuge, have conducted themselves badly after leaving it.

Ques. How many young persons have left the house of refuge since its foundation?

Ans. One hundred boys and twenty-five girls.

Ques. Do you believe that a great number of these persons have been reformed?

Ans. About two-thirds of them have conducted themselves, so far, well; at least, to judge by the reports of the people with whom they are as apprentices.

Ques. What vices, do you believe, are the most difficult to be corrected?

Ans. The habit of theft with boys; immorality with the girls. A girl who has lived in prostitution must be considered nearly hopeless.

Ques Do you find that the children make rapid progress?

Ans. Yes: I believe that they learn with greater ease than honest children.

Ques. Do not the regulations permit them to borrow books every week from the library?

Ans. Yes.

Ques. Do they like reading?

Ans. Of one hundred and fifty-one young delinquents, eighty seem to like reading very much.

Ques. What disciplinary punishments are in use with you?

Ans. The whip, solitary imprisonment, and reduction of food to water and bread.

Ques. Do you believe that it is dangerous to allow the young subjects to have free communication with each other during the hours of recreation?

Ans. This indulgence may, undoubtedly, present some dangers, and absolute silence might here, as in the great penitentiaries, be established; but I doubt that it would be wise to do so; children need activity and gaiety for the development of their body and the formation of their character.

Ques. What have been the first expenses of the house of refuge?

Ans. About 65,230 dollars

Ques. What are the annual expenses?

Ans. About 12,000 dollars, including every thing. The salaries of officers amount to 2,953 dollars.

Ques. How much does the labour of the young persons annually yield?

Ans. About 2,000 dollars, which leaves 10,000 dollars to be otherwise defrayed.

Ques. How many books have you in the library of the house?

Ans. 1,500 volumes. These books have been given by charitable persons. The state has made no provision on the subject.

No. 16.

STATISTICAL NOTES.

No I Divers documents relative to the sanatory state of the penitentiaries at Auburn and Philadelphia II Documents relative to individuals who have been pardoned in Auburn and Sing-Sing, from 1822 to 1831. Also some observations on the prerogative of pardon in the United States III Some penal laws of the State of Maryland relative to slaves IV Difference between the mortality of negroes and of white persons, of manumitted persons and slaves. V. Sum total of persons sentenced to imprisonment in the State of Pennsylvania in 1830 VI Number of executions in the State of Maryland from the year 1785 to 1832. VII Table of individuals who, from 1821 to 1827, have been detained in the prisons of New York, tried, acquitted, and convicted. VIII. Influence of the City of New York on the morality of the State. IX Sum total of convictions pronounced in 1830 in the whole State of New York by the ordinary tribunals

No. I.—*Documents relative to the sanatory state of the penitentiaries at Auburn and Philadelphia.*

[The authors give, under this head, short extracts from the annual reports of the physician at Auburn, and from Dr. Bache's report for the years 1829-30-31, on the Pennsylvania penitentiary system and that of Walnut street, in respect to their influence on the health of the prisoners. The subject is of the greatest importance, and we prefer, therefore, to refer the American reader to those reports themselves, or the extracts of them in the annual reports of the Bost. Pris. Disc Society, where he will find them in a more convenient form than we should be able to give them in this place. The American reader has in this respect sources of information so near at hand, that he can dispense with statements calculated for a public at such a distance. The Asiatic cholera has afforded a peculiar test of the penitentiary system in respect to health. As far as we have been able to ascertain, the result is in an extraordinary degree in favour of the penitentiaries compared to prisons on the old plan ; nay, we might almost say, compared to society in general. We have no doubt that Mr. Dwight will pay particular attention to this important point in the eighth report of the Bost. Pris. Disc. Society. It is an opportunity, which, we pray God, may not be afforded a second time. Whilst the information which we have been able to gather so far, some of which is of an official character, (e. g. See the Ann. Rep. of the Insp. of the Auburn State Prison, January 8, 1833) is very satisfactory respecting penitentiaries, it is, to judge from statements in the papers of the day and from some official papers (e. g. Report of the Committee appointed to investigate the local causes of the cholera in the Arch street Prison in Philadelphia, Mr. Gibbon chairman, read to the House of Representatives February 21, 1833) the contrary, as regards the prisons on the old plan ; and we have little doubt, but that it will be found the same all over the world, wherever cholera exists. It may be objected, that the cholera is of a peculiar character : that, whether it be contagious or epidemic, the separation of individuals necessarily must be advantageous, but that the favourable result in this special case, does not prove any thing in respect to the general state of health. But it will be allowed that if we consider, first, all the favourable reports of former years, which have we think established the fact, that the penitentiaries are highly conducive to health, whether compared to other prisons, or to the state of health of that class of persons in society to which the majority of convicts belong ; and secondly, that in most countries, those who were attacked by cholera did not previously enjoy sound health, so that victims would not have been wanting in the penitentiaries, had their inmates not been in general healthy—we think it will be allowed, that the fact of the cholera having so much spared the penitentiaries, goes far to prove their general state of health. The report of Mr. Gibbon, above quoted, is a valuable paper in several other respects.—TRANS.]

No. II —*Documents relative to individuals, who have been pardoned in Auburn and Sing-Sing, also some observations on the use of the prerogative of pardon in the United States.*

We have thought that some details respecting the manner in which the right of pardon is exercised in the United States, and especially in the state of New York, would be interesting to our readers.

From 1822 to 1831, in Auburn as well as in Sing-Sing, 130 individuals, sentenced to three years imprisonment, were pardoned.

Among these the one who remained longest in prison, had been confined two years.*

The minimum of a prisoner's stay in prison before being pardoned has been 17 days.

Eighty-six, or more than half, have been pardoned before half of their sentence had expired.

In the same period, 49 individuals, sentenced to 5 years imprisonment, had been pardoned.

Maximum of the stay in prison before pardon : 4 years.

Minimum : 3 months.

Twenty-seven, or more than half, have been pardoned before the expiration of half of their punishment.

---

* We omit the fractions of months and days.

30

Nine individuals, sentenced to six years imprisonment, were pardoned.

Maximum of the stay in prison: 5 years.

Minimum: 1 year.

Six prisoners were pardoned before half of their sentences had expired.

Eighty-three individuals, sentenced to seven years imprisonment, were pardoned.

Maximum of time spent in prison: 6 years.

Minimum: 4 months.

Fifty-three, or nearly two-thirds, had not yet been there half the time allotted to them by the court.

Thirty-eight individuals, sentenced to ten years imprisonment, were pardoned.

Maximum of their imprisonment: 9 years.

Minimum: 2 months

Twenty-eight, or nearly two-thirds, have been pardoned before half of their sentence had expired.

Thirty-six individuals, sentenced to fourteen years, were pardoned.

Maximum: 10 years.

Minimum: 1 year.

Twenty-two, or nearly two-thirds, were pardoned before half of their sentence had expired.

At length, sixty individuals, sentenced for life, were pardoned.

All obtained their pardon before having passed seven years in the prison.

Several of them before having spent two years, and one after having passed eight months in the prison.

It is thus seen, that all prisoners sentenced for life, who have obtained pardon in the course of these eight years, remained imprisoned for a less time than the persons sentenced for fourteen years and even for ten years

It is easy also to prove, that the authority which pardons more frequently chooses these convicts than the others.

Thus the prisoners convicted for life formed about the eighteenth part of all convicts sent annually to Auburn and Sing-Sing, from 1822 to 1831; it is therefore to be believed, that they form equally about the eighteenth part of the prisoners.

Now, of 477 pardoned convicts, 60 had been sentenced for life, or the seventh part of the pardoned.

There is then one convict for life to eighteen prisoners, and one to seven pardoned.*

Thus convicts for life find themselves doubly privileged, and it may be said without exaggeration, that, in the state of New

* From the following table, taken from the Annual Report of the Inspectors of the Auburn Prison, it will be seen, that, during the year ending December

York, it is the interest of the criminal, that the heaviest punishment his case permits be pronounced against him.

It is easy to indicate why the privilege of pardon is so frequently made use of in the United States, and particularly in favour of prisoners sentenced for life.

Without examining the question whether it is absolutely necessary for society that some authority should have the right to suspend punishments, it may be said, that the less this authority is elevated above the rest of society, and the less independent it is, the greater will be the abuse of pardoning.

In the United States, the governor of each state alone has, generally, the dangerous privilege of pardoning; he may do even what no sovereign, the most absolute, of Europe, does; he may dispense with the obligation of being judged. [See our remarks

31, 1832, there were pardoned eight prisoners sentenced for life of twenty-seven pardoned prisoners, which would be nearly as one to three. But before we could give any remarks on this extraordinary proportion, it would be necessary to know the particulars of these cases. Thus, we believe, that the present governor, averse to pardoning in general, grants pardons to those prisoners who have been imprisoned for a time equal to that awarded by the new laws for the crime they committed. He, of course, has nothing to do with the pardons enumerated below.—Trans.

Crimes.	Term.	Age.	Term unexpired.
Assisting felon to escape, - - -	5 years	46 years	3 years 5 months
Arson, - - - - -	10 "	32 "	5 " 3 "
Passing counterfeit money, - - -	7 "	35 "	2 " 8 "
Ditto, - - -	15 "	36 "	10 " 6 "
Robbery, - - - - -	Life	19 "	
Burglary, - - - - -	"	28 "	
Maliciously maiming, - - -	"	31 "	
Petit larceny, second offence, - - -	7 years	30 "	3 " 9 "
Burglary, - - - - -	Life	30 "	
Grand larceny and perjury, - - -	13 years	32 "	6 " 9 "
Burglary, - - - - -	Life	24 "	
Assault and battery, to rape, - - -	5 years	57 "	1 " 11 "
Petit larceny, second offence, - - -	4 "	43 "	1 " 8 "
Passing counterfeit money, and grand larceny,	14 "	2d con.	9 " 1 "
Perjury, - - - - - - -	2 "	51 years	9 "
Petit larceny, second offence, - - -	5 "	19 "	8 "
Rape, - - - - - -	Life	23 "	
Passing counterfeit money, - - -	10 years	31 "	5 " 8 "
Burglary, - - - -	5 "	30 "	2 " 6 "
Forgery, - - - - -	7 "	22 "	3 " 7 "
Manslaughter, - - - -	4 "	35 "	3 " 1 "
Grand larceny, - - - -	5 "	52 "	1 " 11 "
Burglary, - - - - -	Life	28 "	
Robbery, - - - - -	"	18 "	
Assault and battery to kill, - - -	4 years	47 "	3 " 3 "
Grand larceny, - - - -	5 "	29 "	1 " 10 "
Forgery, - - - - -	7 "	24 "	3 " 10 "

below. TRANS.] In this respect the Americans rather follow
the traditions of the ancient colonial constitutions, than a logical
order of ideas. Now, in spite of the extent of these rights in
special matters, the governor of a state occupies a social station,
by no means elevated. Every one may approach him at any
time; press upon him any where and at any moment Thus
given up, without an intermediate person, to urgent solicitations,
can he always refuse? He feels himself the slave of the public
caprice; he depends upon the chances of an election, and he is
obliged to treat his partisans with extreme care. Would he dis-
satisfy his political friends by refusing a slight favour? Moreover, being invested with little power, he loves to make as
much use of it as possible. All these causes, added to the embarrassment occasioned for a long time by want of room, explain
why the right of pardoning has been made use of so often in the
United States The excess of the evil has attracted public attention only a few years back. Pardons, which are yet granted in
too large a number, are, nevertheless, much less frequent than
formerly.

The same reasons explain, partly, why those prisoners who
are convicted for life are treated more favourably than others.

In the first place, these have the greatest interest in obtaining
a pardon, as they are the most punished. Moreover, a man submits more easily to a punishment whose duration is fixed. His
imagination and that of his friends is more easily calmed, because
they see some fixed limits; authority, too, on its side, refuses to
shorten a punishment which has a certain termination.

But he who is sentenced for life sees no end, no limits to his
hopes or fears; he and his friends use the most pressing means
to obtain a pardon, which may be granted to-morrow, or may
be delayed for years.

The governor thus finds himself much more obstinately so-
licited in favour of a convict for life than for any other, and he
grants much sooner the request, because, not wishing to refuse
always, he does not clearly see why he should not yield in one
moment as well as in another.

It thus happens that the most guilty are precisely those who
have the greatest chance.

To conclude, nothing exposes the abuse of pardoning and its
extent in the United States, in a clearer light than the following
passage of an American publication:—

"The New York committee ascertained that there are men
who make a regular trade of procuring pardons for convicts, by
which they support themselves. They exert themselves to obtain signatures to recommendations to the executive authority
to extend pardon to those by whom they are employed. And in
this iniquitous traffic they are generally successful through the

facility with which respectable citizens lend their names, without any knowledge of the merits or demerits of the parties. Few men have the moral courage necessary to refuse their signatures, when applied to by persons apparently decent and respectable, and few governors have the fortitude to refuse. I have, however, recently seen stated in the message of one of our state governors, I forget which, that he had pardoned only two or three convicts during his administration.

"It is obvious that the grant of pardon does not depend on the degree of guilt, but on the pecuniary means of the convict to hire the members of this corps A person convicted of murder in the second degree, attended with the most aggravating circumstances, who has powerful friends, or is plentifully supplied with money, has tenfold more chance of pardon, than a poor wretch found guilty of petty larceny." Mathew Carey's Thoughts on Penitentiaries and Prison Discipline. Page 59.

[We would recommend the reader to read the whole division, headed " *Power of Pardoning,*" of the above work, from page 58 to 61.—Trans.]

[It is this passage, we believe, which contains the greatest mistake in the whole book; not that we are not strongly opposed to the abuse of the pardoning privilege. No citizen of the United States can dislike it more than ourselves, whether the matter is considered as a question of law and justice, or of charity and humanity. The power of pardon, given to protect in some individual cases, when the law, by its inherent generality, strikes too hard, has been wielded like a poisoned sword against the society which conferred it. It has taken away much of the awe of crime. We know of no safer rule for a society, than this : make your laws merciful, and your prisons humane ; but having done this, look neither to the right nor the left, but let the law strike, and the prison punish. Some very rare cases, indeed, ought alone to form exceptions.

But what we cannot understand, is by what mistake the authors were led to the statement, that the governor of a state can dispense with the obligation of being judged. This assertion is erroneous in two respects. 1. All the monarchs of the European continent *have* this privilege ; they can stop a process—whether the King of the French has this right to the whole extent which the other monarchs of the continent possess, we do not know. This prerogative of the monarch is by no means unfrequently made use of, almost always if a high officer is accused of an act which was for the interest of government. When Dr. Jahn was arrested, in 1819, the minister of the police published, in the daily papers, malicious insinuations and distorted statements against him, when his trial had not yet begun. Dr. Jahn immediately instituted a suit against him, and when the trial was going

on, the process was "stopped" by royal order; which meant
that it was to be abandoned; the word "stopping" having been
chosen as a technical term, merely to make the sound at least
more agreeable to the idea of justice, as if the process were
merely adjourned to be taken up at another time. 2. No governor, and no person or body whatsoever in the United States, can
dispense with the obligation of being tried. As we said, we cannot see the cause that led our authors to so gross a misconception.
They cannot have meant, that government may, for certain considerations, not prosecute a crime. Government can do so, of
course, everywhere. Thus a person having killed another in a
duel, may perhaps not be prosecuted for it, if he return after
some years of absence. But that has nothing to do with the
governor. If nobody accuses, there can be no trial. If a grand
jury find a true bill, no power on earth can stop the trial. Or do
the authors allude to the power of the governor to grant pardons
to state witnesses? We shall not investigate here, whether this
making of state's-evidence, so shocking to every one who comes
from a country where it does not exist, (and certainly it is in
the abstract extremely immoral, that the state, or society, should
know of a crime without prosecuting it, nay, even negotiate with
it,) is an evil essentially inherent in the "process of accusation,"
during which the prisoner himself appears entirely passive, and
is never called upon to testify against himself—a process which,
in other respects, has many advantages—or whether the "process
of accusation" might exist without this offensive anomaly; but it
is certain that the King of England has the same power, and, in
a degree, the French government also. So much are the authors
mistaken in their position, that it may be said with truth, that the
governors of the several states are even limited in their pardoning
power, in cases where the heads of the European governments are
not so; e. g. they cannot generally affect the judgment consequent
upon an impeachment.—As to the causes detailed above, of the
great abuse of pardoning, that of the facility of access to the governor is undoubtedly the most correct; in the same manner as so
many pardons have been granted in Europe, where a friend of
the prisoner succeeds in penetrating to the monarch. In this, as in
other things, all depends upon public opinion. If public opinion
support a governor in refusing pardons, we will not see so many.
The next reports, we trust, will show that we are right. Respecting the other cause assigned for frequent pardons, we mean the
political one, the authors have not lived long enough among us,
to know that the people, being here the sovereign, naturally see
many things in a very different light from that in which people
view them who have no part in the government. In Italy, if a
man commit murder, the first thing that happens is, that every
person gives him all possible aid to ensure his escape from the arm

of the government. In the United States, where no hatred exists against the police, it is totally different. We do not believe that a governor ever has pardoned a criminal for the purpose of courting a political party, nor has it ever been the case in those parts of our country where there exists a large population of foreigners or descendants of foreigners, in order to get their numerous votes. At all events we do not know of such a case; it can be but very rare; not more frequent than a pardon obtained through the mistress of a monarch, or a bribe given to a minister's secretary. It is a good sign, that the Quakers, the most zealous, and so successful in the cause of humanity, are, if we mistake not, the most strongly opposed to pardoning.— TRANS.]

Proportion of Convicts, who, after having been pardoned, are recommitted.

Of six hundred and forty-one prisoners, who, from 1797 to 1811, have been pardoned in Newgate (New York), fifty-four have committed new crimes, and have returned to the same prison. This makes about one out of twelve. (Extract from the old register of Newgate.)

No. III.—*Some Penal Laws of Maryland, referring to Slaves.*

In Maryland, as well as in most states of the South, different penal laws are applied to slaves and to free coloured people.

The latter are subject to the same laws with the whites, but the slaves are, in penal matters, as in every other respect, in a position peculiar to themselves.

If a slave is found guilty of a misdemeanor, the whip is administered to him, and the master pays damages to the injured party, as in a case where domestic animals have done injury to others. Slaves who commit grave crimes are hung; and those who commit crimes which are not punished with death, though they are considered heinous, are sold out of the state.

This kind of legislation is economical, it rests on simple ideas, the execution of which is easy and quick—qualities peculiarly appreciated in democratic governments. It must be considered as one of the numerous anomalies presented by American society.

If the sale of a slave is thus ordered by the tribunals, the convict is given to one of the slave dealers, whose business it is to carry slaves from the northern slave-holding states, where their number surpasses the demand, to the southern slave-holding states, where they are more wanted. The criminal slave is confounded with the others; care is taken that his character and former life be not known, because it would lessen his price. The state which thus sells a slave, does nothing else than freeing itself of a germ of crime, in order to introduce it furtively among its neighbours. In one word, it is an act of brutal egotism, tolerated and sanctioned by a moral and enlightened society.

No. IV.—*Difference, remarked in the United States, between the mortality of Negroes and Whites, Free Coloured people and Slaves.*

In examining the bills of mortality in America, a fact has surprised us, which shows how privileged the ruling race is, even in respect to longevity.

In Philadelphia, there died, from 1820 to 1831, but one white out of forty-two individuals of the white race; whilst one negro died out of twenty-one individuals of the coloured race.

If we compare the mortality of the slaves with that of free people of colour, we arrive at a still more surprising fact: during the last three years, there died at Baltimore, one out of twenty-eight free negroes,* and one out of forty-five slaves.

Thus the free coloured people die sooner than the slaves.

This is easy of explanation: the slave has no agitation of mind, because he has no care for future plans; he has not to struggle with misery, and his actions, deprived of the character of morality or immorality, as he is not a free agent, are at least regular.

The freed slave, without capital and industry, is exposed to every misery; he does not know the art of conducting himself, he has not learned to use his reason, which nevertheless is to be substituted for the impulse, which he formerly received from his master. That happens to him on a small scale, which happens to all nations of the world, whenever they suddenly shake off arbitrary power. Liberty is something great and noble, indeed, but those who first acquire it rarely reap the fruits.— *Emerson's Medical Statistics,* page 28; *Reports of the Health Office of Baltimore.*

No. V.—*Sum total of persons sentenced to imprisonment in the State of Pennsylvania, in* 1830.

In order to discover, by approximation, the total number of persons sentenced to imprisonment during 1830 in Pennsylvania, we have proceeded in the following way:

There are in that state 51 counties, each of which has a prison for convicts sentenced for a short imprisonment. Besides

---

* Strange! Free people of colour die in less numbers in Baltimore, where the government is hard and oppressive to them, than in Philadelphia, where they are the object of philanthropy and public attention.

these, there are two central prisons, to which the counties send all criminals sentenced to one year's imprisonment or upwards.

We knew the exact number of individuals which the county of Philadelphia, the most populous of all, had sent in 1830 to the county jail. We knew also the number of criminals, who, in the same year, had been sent to the central prisons from all the counties We had, therefore, yet to ascertain the number of convicts sent to the various county jails, in order to know how many criminals had been convicted in 1830.

The following is the method which we adopted to ascertain this number.

We thought that the number of individuals sent by the county of Philadelphia to the central prisons in 1830, which is 229, is to the number of convicts, sent in the same year, by the same county of Philadelphia, to the county jail, viz 1431,* as the number of individuals sent by the other counties of Pennsylvania to the central prisons, which is 98, is to the number of prisoners sent in 1830 by the same counties to their special prisons—the number in question, in other words, we adopted the following proportion: $229 : 1431 = 98 \cdot X$ which gives $X = 612$. Six hundred and twelve individuals, then, were sent in 1830 to the various county jails, exclusive of Philadelphia, provided our calculation be strictly correct.

But we believed we could not take the number 612 as the true one. There is, in fact, a number of petty offences which only occur in cities, and there is a number of others which are prosecuted only where justice is in full activity. Proportionally, therefore, a less number of small offences, and a greater number of more heinous crimes, are committed in the country than in cities

On the other hand, Pennsylvania has many boroughs, and even considerable towns, as Pittsburg, Harrisburg, and Lancaster, where the number of small offences must be great †

We believe therefore, that, in reducing the number 612 to one half, we must approach the truth. This gives 306, but six convicts for each of the fifty counties.

We are by this calculation rather below than above the truth. But, supposing it to be exactly true, it would result that in 1830 there were 2064 individuals sentenced to imprisonment.

The population was in the same year 1,347,672, one convict out of 658 inhabitants.

---

* This number seems undoubtedly very large nevertheless, it is the mean number of the four years preceding 1830

† The first and the last of these are *cities* —TRANS.

No. VI.—*Number of executions in Maryland from* 1785 *to* 1832.

From 1785 to 1832 there have been executed 78 persons, which gives nearly two per year.

There were nineteen in the twelve last years

During this same period, the mean population of Maryland has been 380,072 ; there was thus one execution to 219,600 inhabitants.

(M S. document furnished at Baltimore)

[We refer the reader to the Report of the Boston Prison Discipline Society for similar statements relative to other states.— Trans.]

No. VII.—*Table of individuals who, from* 1821 *to* 1827, *have been imprisoned in the city of New York, tried, acquitted, and condemned.*

[The authors give here a translation of the important note to page 32 of Edward Livingston's Introductory Report to the Code of Prison Discipline, Philad., 1827, which proves conclusively the necessity of providing for a better system of imprisonment before trial.—As Mr. Livingston mentions the still greater disproportion between commitments and convictions in Great Britain, we would again refer the reader to Mr Ouételet's observations published in the *Courrier des Etats Unis,* April 22, 1832, respecting trials and acquittals in France and Belgium, and also to the article Statistics of Crimes, under *Crime,* in the *Encyclopædia Americana.*—Trans.]

No. VIII.—*Influence of the city of New York on the criminality of the state.*

The city of New York, having, in 1830, a population of 207,021 inhabitants, furnished 400 convicts out of the 982 individuals sentenced by the ordinary courts of the state.

Thus, in 1830, the inhabitants of the city were to those of the state as 1 to 9.24.

Whilst the convicts of the city to those of the state were as 1 to 2.45.

No. IX.—*Total number of condemnations pronounced in* 1830 *in the whole state of New York by the ordinary tribunals.*

The number of individuals who, during 1830, have been sentenced, either to death, imprisonment in the state or county jails, or to pay a fine, amounted to 982.

Of these 982, there were 903 men and 79 women.

The convictions divide themselves thus:

To death, - - - - - -	3
To the state prison, - - - -	461
To the house of refuge, - - -	12
To county jails, - - - - -	295
To fine alone, - - - - -	211
Total, - - - - - -	982

The statistical statement from which these details are taken, is an official document, which has been furnished to us by the authorities of New York at our request

It would be wrong, however, to believe, that the number 982 exactly represents the total number of convicted individuals in the state of New York during the year 1830.

The official statement of which we speak, contains only the number of individuals condemned by the ordinary tribunals, i. e. the Mayor's Court, Court of Oyer and Terminer, and Court of Quarter Sessions. Besides these tribunals, there is a semi-administrative and semi-judiciary authority, that of the police officers These functionaries have the right to imprison a great number of petty offenders, vagrants, disturbers of the peace, &c. who in France would be judged by the correctional tribunals, and who would figure in the statistical tables of criminal justice. The number of individuals, thus sent to prison, must be very great in the United States, if we judge by the authentic documents which we have collected in Philadelphia. The prison of that city alone has received, on an average, from 1825 to 1831, not less than 1263 prisoners every year. The greater part among them were sent thither by the police magistrates

[See, among other documents, the above quoted Report on the Cholera in Arch Street Prison, 1833; and the Report of the Committee appointed to visit the Eastern (Philadelphia) Penitentiary, Mr. Ringland, Chairman, Harrisburg, 1833.—TRANS.]

No. 17.

No. I. Comparative table of individuals sent to the various Penitentiaries, classed by their offences —II. Mean number of deaths in the Penitentiaries —III. Comparative table of recommittals —IV Comparative table of men and women in the prisons of the United States —V Proportion of coloured people in prisons and in society —VI Proportion of Americans not belonging to the state where they committed their crime —VII Proportion of foreigners among American prisoners —VIII Proportion of Irish and English among the prisoners —IX Proportion of natives —X Proportion of convicts who are natives of the state where they committed their crime, to the population of the same state.—XI Statement of pardons — XII Age of convicts —XIII. Proportion of individuals sentenced to the state prison to the population of the various states.

No. I.—*Table of individuals sent to the Penitentiaries of Pennsylvania, New York, Connecticut, and Massachusetts, classed by the nature of their offences.*

Connecticut, (1789–1830.)

Convicted for crimes committed against
property, - - - - 87 93 out of 100 crimes.
Ditto   ditto   persons, 12 06   "

Pennsylvania, (1789–1830.)

Convicted for crimes against property, 90 03 out of 100 crimes.
Ditto   ditto   persons, 9 97   "

Massachusetts, (1820–1824–1830.)*

Convicted for crimes against property, 93 64 out of 100 crimes.
Ditto   ditto   persons, 6.36   "

New York, (1800–1830.)

Convicted for crimes against property, 93.56 out of 100 crimes.
Ditto   ditto   persons, 6.26   "

Convicted for crimes against morals.

New York, (same period,) - 2 78 out of 100 convicts.
Massachusetts, (id) - 2 79 "
Pennsylvania, (id) - 2 72 "
Connecticut, (id.) - 7 93 "

* We have not been able to obtain the table of convictions in the state of Massachusetts, but we have found in the prison, by the side of the names of the prisoners in 1820, 1824, and 1830, the crime mentioned for which they were imprisoned, which is pretty much the same.

Convicted for forgery.

Pennsylvania, (same period,)		-	3 91	out of 100 convicts.
Massachusetts,	(id)	-	9.60	"
New York,	(id)	-	13 28	"
Connecticut,	(id)	-	14 26	"

If we take the mean of these four states, the inhabitants of which amounted in 1830 to the third of the population of the whole Union, (4,168,905,) we shall arrive at the following result:

Convicted for crimes against property,			91 29	out of 100 crimes.
Ditto	ditto	persons,	8 66	"
Ditto	ditto	morals,	4 05	"
Ditto	for forgery,*	- -	10 26	"

Comparison between the different periods.

In comparing the different periods which we have indicated above with each other, we arrive at the following.

Connecticut, (1789–1800)

Convicted for crimes against property,			95.40	out of 100 crimes.
Ditto	ditto	persons,	4 60	"
Ditto	ditto	morals,	3 44	"
Ditto	for forgery,	- -	10 34	"

(1819–1830.)

Convicted for crimes against property,			83 10	out of 100 crimes.
Ditto	ditto	persons,	16 90	"
Ditto	ditto	morals,	11.34	"
Ditto	for forgery,	- -	13.65	"

Pennsylvania, (1789–1800)

Convicted for crimes against property,			94.35	out of 100 crimes.
Ditto	ditto	persons,	5 65	"
Ditto	ditto	morals,	2.74	"
Ditto	for forgery, -	- -	4.97	"

(1819–1830.)

Convicted for crimes against property,			94.61	out of 100 crimes.
Ditto	ditto	persons,	5.34	"
Ditto	ditto	morals,	1 72	"
Ditto	for forgery,	- -	4.84	"

* We have used throughout this statement *forgery* for *crime de faux* Whether the authors included in this term counterfeiters, we do not know, we believe, however, not. Yet forgers of bank notes are included.—Trans.

State of New York, (1800–1810.)

Convicted for crimes against property, 96.45 out of 100 crimes.
Ditto   ditto   persons,   3 54   "
Ditto   ditto   morals,   0 87   "
Ditto   for forgery,   -   -   8.88   "

(1820–1830.)

Convicted for crimes against property, 90 12 out of 100 crimes.
Ditto   ditto   persons,   9 37   "
Ditto   ditto   morals,   5 06   "
Ditto   for forgery,   -   -   16.76   "

We have not made the same calculation for Massachusetts, because that state furnishes us with but one period.

It is pretty generally acknowledged in Europe, that the more society advances in civilization, the more the number of crimes against persons decreases.

The number which we have just exhibited, proves, that in the United States at least, this is not the case. On the contrary, we see, that in the state of Pennsylvania the number of crimes against persons does not decrease with the advance of time, and that in Connecticut and New York, it seems even to increase with the increase of civilization. This increase takes place in a uniform and steady way · it is difficult to attribute it to chance. It can neither be said that it is owing to causes foreign to America, such as emigration, the presence of Irish, &c. Never, as we shall soon see, have strangers been less numerous than at present in the prisons of the United States, speaking comparatively to the whole population; and the number of Irish has not varied in the last thirty years.

Other observations give still more weight to this remark.

Thus, not only two out of three states present a greater proportion of crimes against persons in 1830 than in 1790; but in 1830, the state where we find most of this species of crimes, is the state of Connecticut, which, in respect to instruction and information, occupies the first rank in the whole Union; and the state, which shows least of this class of crimes, is Pennsylvania, where the population is, in comparison with that of Connecticut, ignorant.

[Referring the reader to our note on the relation of instruction to the progress of crime in general, we will quote, in reference to this special case, a passage of the Report of the Directors and Warden of the Connecticut State Prison, submitted to the legislature in May, 1830, which refers to the apparent increase of crime in Connecticut. Though the authors distinctly say, in another passage, that the reasons given to them on the

spot to explain this phenomenon have not appeared to them satisfactory, we must declare, that the citizens of Connecticut agree
in the firm belief, that there are fewer crimes committed, and
that less breaches of the peace take place now than formerly.
Formerly, when every body was fully convinced, that being
sent to the state prison was the total ruin of a person and an
endless charge upon the state, many offences were put up with
and allowed to pass by unprosecuted   At present, the whole is
changed.   The state prison is considered by the public as an institution which may redeem an individual who has entered on
the path of crime, and at all events, does not corrupt him still
more , and the public, jury, and court are more willing to allow
the law to take its free course.   The consideration that the state
expenditure is not increased by convictions, has also its share in
the increased number of prosecutions   We would also refer the
reader to Governor Tomlinson's message to the legislature, May
7, 1829, partly reprinted on page 19 and sequel of the 4th Report of the Boston Prison Discipline Society.   The passage
above alluded to is the following·

"The whole number of prisoners on the first day of April
was 167, of whom 13 are females and 39 coloured persons The
number received during the last year is 72, of whom 49 are natives of Connecticut. At the date of this report, the whole number is 171, of whom 14 are females.   In our last report, we
alluded to the causes which had, as we supposed, enlarged the
number of prisoners, while there was no evidence of a corresponding increase of crimes.   We still entertain the opinion
which was then expressed, that this increase is to be attributed
principally to a diminished reluctance to prosecute and convict
offenders.—That since the system of discipline had been changed,
and the prison was a source of revenue to the state, there had
been a more thorough execution of the criminal law, and that
many persons, who, under our former system would have escaped with impunity, are now subjected to trial and imprisonment.

"A great change is also apparent in the character or quality
of the prisoners. Formerly, our prison was filled with men from
other states, who had, as a matter of calculation, selected a criminal course, and were professionally rogues—ingenious and
shrewd men, who had been tenants of half the prisons in the
country, and who designed to maintain themselves, not by
honest labour, but by a course of violence and fraud, and who
are properly styled ' *State Prison characters.*' "

The question, " Does diffusion of knowledge increase or diminish crime, or has it no influence at all upon it," is of vital
interest to society , and thorough inquiries ought to be made
upon all sides, searching unflinchingly for truth.   It would be

well if those who purpose to investigate this important subject, would make a marked difference between mere knowledge and education. A certain kind of knowledge and the skill of a nation may greatly increase, and yet education stand very low; and thus, as we observed above, partial civilization may very much advance, and yet education be comparatively neglected; which is, in our opinion, the worst of all conditions. We repeat it once more, go to the prisons, and inquire into the history of each convict, and then see, whether knowledge or its want is the chief cause of crime. We would suggest, that, in future reports of our state prisons, one or two divisions should be added, in which the education a convict has enjoyed should be indicated in a few words We want facts to appear against statements founded on apparent facts. As to the special point in question, we are not prepared to explain why crimes against persons increase in Connecticut in comparison to the increase of crimes against property. We have little doubt, but that it is owing to some peculiar and special cause unconnected with the main question; but we call the attention of the friends of humanity to contribute as much as is in the power of each to elucidate this phenomenon. Besides; what is Connecticut? A few crimes, more or less, which may be owing to some very special reasons, have a great influence on the proportional statements of so small a community. If several nations of many millions have invariably proved a fact, certainly a comparatively small number of persons cannot at once evince the contrary. We, however, most earnestly invite the attention of those who are able to solve the question to this point. Let the truth prevail. —Trans]

It will be seen, that among the crimes against property, there is one which increases regularly and very quickly in proportion as civilization increases. We mean the crime of forgery

In the state of New York, a very enlightened state, and which stands at the head of the commercial activity of America, the forgers form already about the sixth part of all convicts. In Connecticut, which has but little commerce, but where the whole population knows how to read and to write, forgers form about the seventh part of all criminals; whilst in Pennsylvania, peopled in a great degree by a German population, with whom instruction, and particularly the wish to become rich, is far from existing in an equal degree, not one forger is counted among twenty convicts.

[Respecting the proportion of crimes against property and persons, we again refer to the often quoted article on Criminal Statistics in the Encyclopædia Americana, and to Mr. Ouételet's remarks.—Trans.]

No. II.—*Sanatory State.*

The mortality in those prisons of which we have been able to collect documents, is in the following progression:

At Walnut street, (Philadelphia,)	1 died of 16.66 prisoners.	
At Newgate, (New York,) -	1 " 18.80	"
At Sing-Sing, - - -	1 " 36.58	"
At Wethersfield, - - -	1 " 44.40	"
In the Penitentiary of Maryland,	1 " 48 57	"
At Auburn, - - - -	1 " 55.96	"
At Charlestown, (Massachusetts,)	1 " 58.40	"

It must not be forgotten that for three of these prisons, Sing-Sing, Wethersfield, and the Penitentiary of Maryland, we have been able to obtain the mean term of three years only.

In the city and suburbs of Philadelphia the annual mortality has been, from 1820 to 1831, as 1 out of 38.85 inhabitants.

At Baltimore, in 1828, one individual died out of 47 inhabitants.

Thus in two prisons, Newgate and Walnut street, mortality has been much greater than in the cities of Philadelphia and Baltimore. (These are old prisons.) In one (Sing-Sing) mortality has been nearly equal, and in four (the Wethersfield, Auburn, Charlestown, and Maryland penitentiaries) the mortality has been less.

Among those who people prisons, fewer elderly people are found than in society;* it ought therefore not to surprise us, at the first glance, that mortality is less in prisons than in society; the result which we have given will, however, appear not the less remarkable, if we consider the sedentary life of the convicts; and if we reflect particularly, that all classes of society have furnished their part to the number of prisoners in the above mentioned prisons of Philadelphia and Baltimore, whilst the poorest, the most vicious, and the most disorderly classes alone have contributed to the others.

Nature of the diseases which caused death.

In the penitentiary of Wethersfield the predominating diseases have been those of the stomach and bowels. In 1819 they even assumed an epidemic character. Nine-tenths of the prisoners were affected by it. The physician of the prison, in his annual report, cannot think that it was owing to diet, as the prisoners are better fed than most farmers.

* And no very young children, which is a most important item, whilst, on the other hand, the disordered state of most convicts before they enter the prison must be taken into account.—TRANS.

In the prisons of Auburn and Philadelphia, the predominating diseases have been those of the lungs. Of sixty-four persons who died from 1825 to 1832 at Auburn, thirty-nine were carried off by pulmonary disorders. Of sixty individuals who died in the prison of Walnut street in 1829 and 1830, thirty-six died of the same cause.

During these same years, but one death caused by diseases of the lungs, out of four and a half, took place in Philadelphia.

· *Daily Number of the Sick.*

At Auburn, there was, from 1828 to 1832, every day one sick person out of one hundred and two.

No. III.—*Comparative Table of Recommittals in the different prisons of America.*

It is very difficult to compare the results obtained in the various states of America, in respect to recommittals, with each other. In fact, the documents which have a reference to this subject of our inquiries, indicate three bases which differ one from the other.

In certain prisons, the number of recommittals is ascertained by comparing the persons who *re-enter* the prison, with the totality of individuals who *enter* the same prison.

In others, the recommitted convicts who *are* in the prison, are compared with the sum total of criminals who *are* in the prison.

In others still, the number of individuals who *return* to the prison is compared with the whole number of those who have *returned to society.*

It would be of little use to compare the numbers, so differently obtained, with each other.

We cannot, for instance, compare the proportion of reconvicted and convicted persons, with the proportion of recommitted and committed persons. It is the prisoners, indeed, entering the prison, who form the population of a prison; but these prisoners do not remain there, all during the same time; and if the recommitted prisoners leave it sooner than the others, fewer of them will be found in the prison at the end of a certain period, (considering the proportion,) than there were among the convicts who successively have entered the prison. If, on the other hand, which happens every day, the recommitted convicts remain longer in the prison than the others, there will be found more (considering the proportion) at the end of a certain time, than there were among the convicts of each year.

It is still more difficult to compare the results obtained by the two operations indicated above, with the results obtained by comparison of recommitted convicts with the sum total of delivered prisoners.

In one case, you compare the recommitted individuals with the prisoners sentenced for the first time, and arriving in prison, or the prisoners of the same prison ; in the other case, you compare the same individuals with those who have been in the prison, but are no longer there. The terms of comparison are entirely different.

As we were not able to reconcile these three bases, we have thought it best to compare those states only with each other where the same bases had been used.

First method of comparison.

During 10 years (from 1810 to 1819), there entered into the Walnut Street Prison, 1 recommitted criminal out of 5.98.

In the Maryland Penitentiary, during 12 years (1820 to 1832), 1 recommitted criminal out of 6.96.

In Newgate (New York), during 16 years (1803 to 1820), 1 out of 9.45.

At Auburn, during 6 years (from 1824 to 1831), 1 out of 19.10.

Second method of comparison.

At Walnut street, in 1830, there was 1 recommitted prisoner, of 2 57 prisoners.

At Newgate, old prison of Connecticut, in 1825, 1 recommitted convict, of 4.50 prisoners

In Auburn (1824 to 1831), 1 out of 12. [We find, in the Report for 1832, that there were 50 recommitted, of 683 convicts.]

Third method of comparison.

Of 6.15 prisoners who left the Massachusetts prison during the last 25 years, 1 has returned as recommitted.

Of 19.80 prisoners who have left the Wethersfield prison since its commencement (1826) until this time, 1 has returned as recommitted.

It will be seen, whatever method is adopted, that the new penitentiaries have a decided advantage over the old prisons.

But there is one difficulty—we compare a new prison with an old one. It is clear, that those who return to the former, are less in number than those who return to the latter. The first has returned but a small number of prisoners to society, whilst the other has sent back many. The criminals of the latter have had a much longer time, and, therefore, many more chances and temptations to relapse into crime.

If we consider the history of the majority of recommittals,

and reflect on that which particularly happens in the United States, this observation is less striking than at first glance. It is certain, that, in general, recommittals take place soon after liberty is restored. If the delivered convict triumphs over the first temptations, and conquers his passions, so much the stronger for having been so long constrained, it may be believed that he will not so easily fall again.

Let us add, that in proportion as we are distant from the period of the first crime, it becomes difficult to prove the recommittal. This difficulty is so much the greater, where men change their abodes incessantly, and where no records are kept.

It must be, therefore, taken as a fact, that if a convict has escaped committing a new crime within the first four years after the expiration of his imprisonment, he has escaped altogether the danger of a second crime, or at least that of having his recommittal proved.

Newgate proves what we say. Newgate was founded in 1797. Four years after, in 1802, the proportion of recommittals was already the same as ten years later. It was at least double that which existed at Auburn four years after the foundation of the penitentiary system.

[We will add a passage of the last Message of the Governor of Pennsylvania to the Legislature of that state, December 6th, 1832, which appears to us important. He says: "One fact in reference to this institution, (the Philadelphia Penitentiary,) bears strong testimony in favour of its discipline. It appears that not a single convict discharged from this prison has ever been returned to it; which would seem to prove pretty clearly, either that a thorough reformation has been produced, or that a dread of a repetition of the unsocial manner of life which had proved so irksome before, had deterred from the commission of crimes within those limits of the state in which a conviction would ensure a sentence to the Eastern Penitentiary.—Trans.]

No. IV.—*Comparative Table of Men and Women in the Prisons of the United States.*

We are not in possession of the number for the penitentiary of Charlestown (Massachusetts). The women in Massachusetts are not in the same prisons with the male prisoners, and we have not learned their number.

At Sing-Sing, from 1828 *to* 1831.

One woman of 19.24 prisoners of both sexes.
One white woman of 33.73 white prisoners of both sexes.
One negro woman of 9.87 coloured prisoners of both sexes.

At Auburn, from 1826 *to* 1831.

One woman of 19 prisoners of both sexes. [We find in the Report for 1832, 25 women of 683 of both sexes, which would make 1 to 27.—TRANS.]

Connecticut, from 1827 *to* 1831.

One woman of 14.60 prisoners of both sexes.
One white woman of 16.14 white prisoners of both sexes.
One coloured woman of 11 coloured prisoners of both sexes.

Pennsylvania, in 1830.

One woman of 7.30 prisoners of both sexes.
One white woman of 15.64 white prisoners of both sexes.
One negro woman of 3.40 coloured prisoners of both sexes.

Maryland, in 1831.

One woman of 6.27 prisoners of both sexes.
One white woman of 86 white prisoners of both sexes.
One coloured woman of 3.56 coloured prisoners of both sexes.

The mean of these proportions shows, that in the four penitentiaries just mentioned, one woman is found in 11.85 prisoners of both sexes.
One white woman in 37.88 white prisoners of both sexes.
One coloured woman in 6.96 coloured prisoners of both sexes.
[The following is taken from the Report on the Auburn Prison for 1832 :

White males,	-	-	-	592
White females,	-	-	-	10
Black males, -	-	-	-	66
Black females,	-	-	-	15
Total,		-	-	683—TRANS.]

The proportion of women in the prisons of the Union, must become the more considerable the more you approach the south, where negroes are more numerous, because the coloured women commit more crimes than the white women.

No. V.—*Proportion of Coloured People in Prisons and in Society.*

In Massachusetts, there have been, from 1822 to 1831, annually, 1 coloured prisoner out of 6.53.
In Connecticut, from 1828 to 1832, 1 coloured prisoner in 4.42.
In the state of New York, from 1825 to 1830, 1 coloured

prisoner in 4 67. [We find, in the Report of the Auburn Prison for 1832, 81 blacks, of 683 prisoners of both colours —Trans.]

In Pennsylvania, in 1830,* 1 coloured prisoner, of 2.27.

In Maryland, in 1831, 1† coloured prisoner out of 1 82.

The number of coloured people in the prisons increases towards the south, the same as in society.

In 1830, the coloured people in society were, in these same states, in the following proportion :

In Massachusetts, 1 coloured person to 87 inhabitants.

Connecticut,	1	ditto	37	do.	
New York,	1	ditto	42	do.	
Pennsylvania,	1	ditto	36	do.	
Maryland,	1‡ free	ditto	6	do.	

Taking the mean term, we see that there is in prison, in the five states, 1 coloured person out of 4 prisoners

In 1830, there was (in the same states) 1 free coloured person out of 30 inhabitants.

No. VI.—*Comparative table of prisoners, who, natives of the United States, are strangers in the states in which they committed their crimes.*

There has been found :

In Maryland, from 1827 to 1831, one prisoner of this kind to 5.14.

In New York, from 1824 to 1832, 1 to 3.48.

In Connecticut, 1827 to 1831, 1 to 2 86

In Massachusetts, from 1826 to 1831, 1 to 2.82.

In Pennsylvania, from 1829 to 1830, 1 to 2 15.

[The following is taken from the Report on Auburn prison for 1832 :

New York,	-	-	-	-	100
Massachusetts,	-	-	-	-	13
Amount carried forward,					113

---

* It is probable, that, in Pennsylvania, the proportion of coloured people in the prisons is a little less than it appears here The above number is that of one year only, and chance may have contributed to form it We believe this the more, as in taking the number of all convicts, white and coloured, sent to the penitentiary from 1817 to 1824, (which is 1510,) there is 1 coloured prisoner, of 2.61 convicts Now the number of coloured people must have a tendency to decrease rather than increase in the Pennsylvania prisons, as it constantly decreases in society.

† We have seen before, (Statistical Notes, No. 3,) that when we speak of negroes in the prisons of Maryland, we refer to *free* negroes.

‡ As free coloured people only are sent to the prisons, we have also counted these only in society. Without this, the argument would have rested on a defective basis. All the coloured people of Massachusetts, Connecticut, New York, and Pennsylvania, are free.

	Amount brought forward,	113
Vermont,	- - - -	11
Connecticut,	- - - -	10
Pennsylvania,	- - - -	8
New Jersey,	- - - -	5
Maine,	- - - -	1
Virginia,	- - - -	2
New Hampshire,	- - -	3
District of Columbia,	- - -	2
Delaware,	- - - -	1
Ireland,	- - - - -	13
England,	- - - - -	9
Canada,	- - - - -	7
Scotland,	- - - - -	4
Germany,	- - - - -	1
Italy,	- - - - -	1
Corsica,	- - - - -	1
Total,	- - - - -	192

These are the convicts received at Auburn during the year 1832 —Trans.]

Why is the proportion of Maryland so low? Because it does not yet attract much American industry. In Maryland the stationary population commits annually more crimes than in other states;[*] if the total number of convicts is compared with the strangers, it is natural that the proportion should be small.

Pennsylvania offers great opportunities to the industry of her neighbours, and her stationary population commits few crimes.[†]

No. VII.—*Proportion of foreigners among prisoners in American prisons.*

In proportion as our inquiry approaches to the present period, the number of foreigners in the prisons becomes less, as it decreases, i. e. proportionally, in society.

This result, so natural, shows itself by the following facts:

From 1800 to 1805 there was in the state prison of New York, 1 foreigner to 2.43 prisoners.

From 1825 to 1830 there was but 1 to 4.77 prisoners.

From 1786 to 1796 there was in Pennsylvania 1 foreigner to 2.08 prisoners.

From 1829 to 1830 there was but 1 to 5 79.

The following shows the proportion of foreigners in the year 1830 and thereabouts, in the different penitentiaries:

[*] 1 Convict native of Maryland, out of 3954 inhabitants.
[†] 1 Convict native of Pennsylvania, to 11,821 inhabitants

From 1827 to 1831 there was in Connecticut 1 foreigner to 13.27 prisoners.

From 1827 to 1831 in Maryland 1 to 12.65.

In 1829 and 1830 in Massachusetts 1 to 6.

　　Do.　　　　in Pennsylvania 1 to 5.79.

From 1825 to 1830 in the state of New York 1 to 4.77.

Those states, as the reader will have remarked, which have the largest cities and present most resources to industry, show the greatest number of foreigners. This result explains itself.

No. VIII.—*Proportion of Irish and English among the foreigners in the prisons.*

The proportion of the Irish among the foreigners in the prisons of the United States is as follows:

There has been numbered

In Connecticut,	from 1827 to 1831,	1 Irishman to	3.66	foreigners.
Massachusetts,	"　1822 to 1831,	1　"	3.06	"
New York,	"　1825 to 1830,	1　"	2.11	"
Maryland,	"　1827 to 1831,	1　"	1.85	"
Pennsylvania,	"　1829 to 1830,	1　"	1.75	"

It would appear that the proportion of Irish people among prisoners to foreigners has always remained the same for thirty years. Because from 1800 to 1805 there was in the prisons of New York 1 Irishman to 2.05 foreigners, which is almost the same with the proportion in 1830.

It is easy to indicate the reasons which bring so large a number of Irish into the prisons.

Of all foreigners who emigrate to the United States, the Irish are, without any comparison, the most numerous; they arrive poor and burthened with children. In the beginning of their emigration they are exposed to misery; afterwards they find, on the contrary, an ease and comfort to which they never have been accustomed, and which their long privations as well as their violent habits frequently cause them to abuse.

Excess of misery as well as prosperity impels more among them than among other emigrants to crime.

The two states where the proportion of the Irish is the smallest, belong, as it will have been remarked, to New England. The Irish do not emigrate much to that part of the Union, and especially to Connecticut, where no populous cities exist. On the contrary, Englishmen emigrate to that part much more frequently. They find the habits, manners, and ideas much more in harmony with their own; the country offers more opportunity to their modes of industry.

This fact, which we have ascertained on the spot, is exhibited by the following numbers: in the greater part of the Union the proportion of English among foreigners in general in prison is very small. In the penitentiary of Massachusetts, on the contrary, there is 1 Englishman to 3.74 foreigners; in Connecticut 1 to 2.50.

It will have been seen, that the Irish increase in number the further you go to the south, this is chiefly owing to a cause which it is as well to know. In the north, the white population begins already to be crowded, the coloured race is reduced, slavery abolished; and a great number of white people are found willing to do any work. There, moreover, labour is honourable.

In the south, on the contrary, and particularly in the slave-holding states, there are fewer persons of white colour willing to do the harder labours of husbandry or industry This trouble is left to the negroes. Labour is not honoured in the south, it is detested as a servile thing.

Now, these humiliating duties, this rude and little productive labour, are those to which education and misery condemn the Irish emigrant; and he goes where the competition of *white labour* is the least to be feared

The Irish disperse in the cities and not in the country; they arrive in the United States poor and ignorant; they have neither money to buy land, nor industry to cultivate it. The singular inconstancy of their national character makes them moreover little fit for the cares of husbandry and the stationary life of an agriculturist. The activity and the wants of cities alone suit them.

No. IX.—*Comparative table of convicts, natives of the state in which they have committed their crimes.*

In Pennsylvania, in the years 1829 and 1830, there was 1 Pennsylvanian to 2 76 criminals.

In Massachusetts, from 1826 to 1831, there was 1 native of the state to 2.14 prisoners.

In the state of New York, from 1827 to 1832, 1 New Yorker to 2.12 prisoners.

In Connecticut, from 1827 to 1831, 1 Connecticut man to 1.77 prisoners.

In Maryland, from 1827 to 1831, 1 Maryland man to 1.43 prisoners.

We must remark, however, that there is an inaccuracy in this calculation. Our chief object, in making it, was to know in what proportion the imprisoned *inhabitants* of the states were to the prisoners in general. Now, in the statements from which we made our calculations, the place of birth, and not of domicil

33

has been taken. It is, however, chiefly the domicil which is important for us. It is certain that a great number of criminals represented by the statements as strangers, were yet domiciliated in the states where they committed the crimes.

[It depends, in our opinion, upon what is the object of inquiry. Sometimes the domicil would be the most important, sometimes the place of residence for the last ten years, often the place of education, sometimes the place of birth.—TRANS.]

No. X.—*Proportion of the convicts, natives of the state in which they committed their crime, to the population of the same state.*

In Massachusetts, from 1826 to 1832, one native of the state, has been sentenced annually out of about 14,524 inhabitants.

In Pennsylvania, from 1827 to 1831, there has been sentenced annually, one native of the state out of 11,821 inhabitants.

In the state of New York, from 1827 to 1832, one New Yorker has been annually sentenced out of 8,600 inhabitants.

In Connecticut, from 1827 to 1832, annually one native of the state out of 8,269 inhabitants.

In Maryland, from 1827 to 1831, annually one Maryland man out of 3,954 inhabitants.

No. XI.—*Comparative table of pardons.*

From 1799 to 1820 there has been pardoned, annually, in Newgate, (New York,) one prisoner of 4 07.

At Auburn, from 1823 to 1832, 1 of 10.17.

At Sing-Sing, from 1828 to 1832, 1 of 23 97.

In Walnut Street Prison, in 1829 and 1830, 1 of 9 59.

In Maryland, from 1827 to 1831, 1 of 21 25

In Massachusetts, from 1827 to 1831, 1 of 21.

In Connecticut, from 1827 to 1831, 1 of 57.

Thus there has been pardoned during the three or four last years, in these five states, 1 of 26 56 prisoners

The abuse of pardon seems to have been general in America for 25 years, but a decided tendency is observable at present in public opinion against this abuse.

In several states, however, the executive still makes use of its prerogative without measure.

Of 638 individuals, who, from 1815 to 1832, have left the state prison of Ohio, 493, more than two thirds, have been pardoned; 145 only have left the prison after the expiration of their punishment.

In 1831 there were pardoned 59 of 163 convicts in the prison.

See, respecting the use made of the privilege of pardoning,

the details and observations contained in the Statistical Notes, No. 16, § 2.

No. XII.—*Age of the prisoners at the period of their sentences.*

No table of this kind exists for Maryland.

Prisoners under twenty years of age.

In Massachusetts, 1826–1831,	1 of 12 prisoners,	⎫
New York, 1826–1832,	1 of 11 "	⎬ mean term:
Pennsylvania, 1830, -	1 of 10 "	⎪ 1 of 10.
Connecticut, 1827–1832,	1 of 8 "	⎭

From twenty to thirty years:

In New York, - -	1 of 2 prisoners,	⎫
Pennsylvania, - -	1 of 2 "	⎬ mean term:
Massachusets, - -	1 of 2 "	⎪ 1 of 2.
Connecticut, - -	1 of 2 "	⎭

From thirty to forty years:

In New York, - -	1 of 4 prisoners,	⎫
Massachusetts, - -	1 of 4 "	⎬ mean term:
Pennsylvania, - -	1 of 4 "	⎪ 1 of 5.
Connecticut, - -	1 of 7 "	⎭

From forty to fifty years:

In New York, - -	1 of 11 prisoners,	⎫
Pennsylvania, - -	1 of 9 "	⎬ mean term:
Connecticut, - -	1 of 9 "	⎪ 1 of 9.
Massachusetts, - -	1 of 9 "	⎭

From fifty to sixty years:

In Connecticut, - -	1 of 29 prisoners,	⎫
New York, - -	1 of 24 "	⎬ mean term:
Pennsylvania, - -	1 of 24 "	⎪ 1 of 25.
Massachusetts, - -	1 of 24 "	⎭

There are a few prisoners above sixty years of age, but their number is too small to be mentioned with any utility.

No. XIII.—*Proportion of convicts in state prisons to the whole population of the states of Massachusetts, Connecticut, New York, Pennsylvania, and Maryland.*

It seems, at first glance, pretty difficult to compare these five states upon this point.

First, there exist considerable differences in the penal laws.

Thus there are crimes for which, in some states, the convict is sent to the state prison, in others, to the county jail.

Secondly, the minimum of a punishment for which a convict is sent to the state prison, varies very much. Now, it is reasonable to believe, that the prison which contains convicts sentenced to a year's imprisonment, will contain more prisoners, comparatively, than that which holds convicts sentenced to three years imprisonment.

The differences arising from these varieties in the laws, are, however, not so great as upon first consideration they may appear. We have found that the crimes for which offenders are sent to the state prison, are every where nearly the same. These crimes are punished with imprisonment of longer or shorter duration, according to the legislation of each state; but all those who are guilty of such crimes are sent to the state prison; whether the minimum is fixed at one or two years. Thus the adulterous husband is punished with one year's imprisonment in Connecticut, and with two years' imprisonment in the state of New York: but both are sent to the state prison.

Yet it is necessary not to lose sight of these preliminary observations in comparing the following results:

From 1820 to 1830, there was annually,

In Connecticut,	-	1* convict to	6,662	inhabitants.
Massachusetts,	-	1 "	5,555	"
Pennsylvania,	-	1 "	3,968	"
Maryland,	-	1† "	3,102	"
State of New York,	1	"	5,532	"

The proportion of criminals to the population increases in proportion to the number of foreigners and of coloured people in each state. Thus, Connecticut, where but few foreigners and coloured people live, has less convicts than Massachusetts, which, without having more people of colour, attracts more foreigners.

Massachusetts has less criminals than the state of New York,‡ which has more coloured and foreign people. This state again has less criminals than Pennsylvania; and the state which presents most criminals, without comparison, is Maryland, where the coloured race forms the sixth part of the population.

[It is hardly necessary to mention here, that it would be rash indeed to conclude from the above facts, that in general any greater tendency to crime, or less susceptibility of the ideas of

---

* The minimum of a punishment requisite to qualify the convict for these three penitentiaries is one year

† Minimum : two years

‡ Especially if we consider the difference in the minimum of punishment.

right and wrong, were inherent in the coloured race. No experiment whatever, so far, authorizes us to make this conclusion. Coloured people are free citizens indeed in many states; no legal disability is attached to their race, and a governor of Massachusetts might be, according to the law, a coloured man. But what is legal disability compared to social ? History invariably shows that a degraded race, a race which does not fully and freely partake of the great amount of national civilization, which by prejudice or circumstances, labours under social disabilities, is also that which commits most offences, if some very peculiar and special circumstances do not prevent it, e. g such a race being kept so entirely separate from the other members of society, that they live in a kind of semi-barbarous state, which offers in itself few opportunities for crime, as the Russian bondman. In such case, the oppressed part of the population commits few crimes, for similar reasons with those which cause the slave in this country to appear less criminal than the free coloured person. Social oppression operates much more powerfully than legal.—T𝚛ᴀɴs.]

Let us examine, at present, whether, in the five states above mentioned, the number of crimes increases or diminishes with the progress of time.

Pennsylvania.

1795–1800,*	1 convict to	4,181	inhabitants.
1800–1810,	1 "	4,387	"
1810–1820,	1 "	3,028	"
1820–1830,	1 "	3,968	"

[The reader will bear in mind the period when the Pennsylvania Penal Code was revised. It may be set down as an almost invariable rule, that there appear more convicts after the revision of a Penal Code. The very desire of the public to adapt their penal laws more to the existing circumstances, explains why the laws thus revised, and therefore fit to meet the circumstances, are more strictly enforced.—T𝚛ᴀɴs.]

---

* We have not been able to begin our comparison at an earlier period than 1795, though the Walnut Street Prison was erected several years previously But before the year mentioned, convicts of the city and county of Philadelphia alone were imprisoned there. On March 22d, 1791, a law was passed, allowing the judges to send to Walnut Street all convicts sentenced to more than a year's imprisonment.

The reader has seen, that the law of March 22d, 1794, authorized the judges to send convicts to Walnut Street, but it did not oblige them to do so It is possible, therefore, that some prisoners, sentenced to more than one year's imprisonment, have been retained in the county jails Yet, we allow, it is not probable.

Connecticut.

1789 to 1800, 1 convict to 27,164 inhabitants.
1800 to 1810, 1   "   17,098   "
1810 to 1820, 1   "   13,413   "
1820 to 1830, 1   "   6,662   "

[We refer the reader to our note above, respecting the reasons of increasing criminality in Connecticut.—Trans.]

Massachusetts.

From 1820 to 1830, the only period of which we have any knowledge, the number of crimes has continually decreased in Massachusetts. In fact, it results from the reports of the prison, that during these ten years, the annual number of convicts has constantly remained the same The population has constantly increased; it was, in 1820, equal to 523,287 inhabitants, and in 1830, 610,014.

Thus, whilst the population increased one-seventh, the amount of crime remained stationary, hence the relative number of crimes diminished.

Maryland.

The same observation is applicable to Maryland; for ten years the annual number of convicts has remained stationary, whilst, during this period, the population of the state increased one-eleventh.

New York.

1800 to 1810, 1 convict to 4,465 inhabitants.
1810 to 1820, 1   "   4,858   "
1820 to 1830, 1   "   5,532   "

These tables show that the number of convicts in the state prison diminishes, comparatively speaking, to the population, in New York, Massachusetts, and Maryland.

After having increased in Pennsylvania, during the period of war,* it resumes nearly its former level, and seems to tend to a decrease rather than an increase.

---

* This war has had a great influence upon the number of crimes It will be the same in all wars undertaken by the United States The Americans, strange as it is, have preserved in their armies the old regulations of Europe [Ought to be—Continent of Europe —Trans] The soldier is a bought mercenary, who fights without chance of promotion To the privileged class of officers belong the honours and the glory If a war is at an end, the greater part of the army is disbanded The soldiers, who in general have no home, and have learned no useful profession, disperse in the country, and crime soon increases with rapidity. In 1814, more than two hundred thousand French, it is said, left the army, and yet crime did not increase in France These men belonged to the honest population of the kingdom, almost all of them knew a useful art or profession, or

In Connecticut, the progress is inexplicable: it doubles almost every ten years   The reasons which have been given to us in the country itself, are not sufficient to explain completely this phenomenon. The excessive increase of convicts in Connecticut, is owing, in all probability, to some local circumstances with which we are unacquainted.   Connecticut is, of all the states compared above, that which least deserves our attention.   Its population does not exceed that of our smallest departments.

[Here is also a reason, which tends, together with others, to explain the increase of crimes in Connecticut. A few criminals, say four or five, who happen to go there and to be caught, have a decided influence upon the annual proportion, whilst the fraction becomes almost inobservable in states with a large population.—Trans.]

In general, it may be said, that, according to the natural course of things, the number of criminals must continually tend to diminish in most parts of the Union, though this would not precisely prove an increase of morality.

The population of the United States is composed of three very distinct elements.

1. Of whites born in the country ; 2. of coloured people ; 3. of foreigners.

The morality of these three classes is very different.   The white person, surrounded by his parents and friends, and owner of the soil, must necessarily be less inclined to commit a crime than the foreigner, who arrives, unknown to anybody, exposed to a thousand passing wants, or the negro, degraded by public opinion and the law.

Now, the more time advances, the more also will the native white race preponderate over the two others. In fact, the natural progress of population will not be the same for the black and the

---

had other means of supporting themselves. [That armies on the continent of Europe have totally changed their moral character since enlisting has been abolished, and every citizen is obliged to serve for a certain period in the standing army, and since there is no barrier between the lowest soldier and the highest commander, except that which the service requires, as every one must begin from the grade of a private, is a fact well known to every body who is acquainted with the present armies and those of the last century. There are some, as for instance the Prussian, which, as a body, must be considered to possess great intelligence and morality, both as to officers and privates (numerous establishments of instruction for both exist), nor is it less doubtful that these armies are, in respect of moral elevation, incomparably superior to the English and American standing armies ; yet a citizen of the United States, or an Englishman, would consider it strange doings were he to be forced to serve in the standing army. See Story's Commentaries on the Constitution of the United States, vol iii p. 65.—We cannot consider a detached subject in judging of a body politic , we must consider the whole organization   A French or German theatre is undoubtedly less riotous, and for decent people much more agreeable than English or American theatres.   But if you desire this result, do not forget the police and gend'armes who produce the effect —Trans]

white race. In the north and centre of the Union, comfort and ease are to be found with the white, and poverty with the coloured people. Moreover, the whites continually receive additional members, the coloured, on the contrary, lose them. If we compare the native whites to the foreigners, we arrive at the same result. There are, undoubtedly, now, more Europeans annually emigrating to the United States, than thirty years ago; but the natural increase of the American population is still faster, by far, than the increase of emigrants. Besides, the emigrant counts but for himself in the class of foreigners: his children increase the number of Americans.

Each year, therefore, comparatively speaking, there must be, among the convicts, more native white Americans, and fewer coloured persons and emigrants, which, in fact, is the case. (See the Tables.) The sum total of convicts, in proportion to the whole population, must thus be annually less, because that class, which, according to circumstances, furnishes most crimes, is, at the same time, that in which criminals, in proportion to the population, are and must be less in number. Does it follow that the morality of the country increases? By no means; because the native white, the emigrant, and the negro, may each remain stationary in their respective morality, and yet the result be favourable. The decrease of crimes proves, not that the elements which compose population become more moral, but only that their relative proportion changes.

That which can be affirmed with greater certainty, is, that as long as the increase of crime in the United States, follows merely the progress of population, far from concluding from it, that the morality of the people remains the same, we must, on the contrary, conclude that it diminishes. Because, if the natives, the true population, did not commit, every year, more crimes, the total number of convicts ought to decrease continually, instead of remaining stationary.

The south of the Union alone makes an exception to this principle.

In slave-holding countries, there is a special cause, which continually tends to increase the number of persons sentenced to imprisonment;* this is manumission. The slaves, as we have seen before, are not subject to the Penal Code of the whites; they are hardly ever sent to prison. To manumit a slave, therefore, actually amounts to introducing into society a new element of crime.

It results from all that we have said, that in the actual state of the statistics of the United States, it is almost impossible to deter-

---

* It must not be forgot, that those alone who are condemned to prison, serve as a basis for the calculation of the number of crimes in America.

mine with exactness, which, in respect to morality, of the different states, compared among themselves, or to Europe, has the pre-eminence ; or to establish whether there is an increase or decrease in crime.

In order to obtain a fair and truly significant result on this point, it would be necessary to know the number of crimes committed by the native population, the only one which can be called American. If this number were known for several different periods, then, and then only, it would be possible to say with certainty whether morality increases or decreases in America. But it was impossible for us to obtain a similar document, except for the three years previously to 1831. Incomplete as it is, we will give it here : it will throw a new light upon our argument.

From 1827 to 1831, there has been sentenced :

1 native of Massachusetts, of	14,524	inhabitants.
1 "	Pennsylvania, of	11,821	"
1 "	State of New York, of	8,610	"
1 "	Connecticut, of	8,269	"
1 "	Maryland, of	3,954	"

Thus Pennsylvania, one of the states where, from 1820 to 1830, most convicts were imprisoned,* shows herself in reality one of the most moral states of the Union ; whilst Connecticut, placed at the head of the scale of legal morality, in the tables to which we allude, is in fact one of the states, which, from 1827 to 1831, sent most natives to prison.

[It would not have been uninteresting, had the authors been able to show, in a table, how many convicts escaped under the old system, and how few under the new. In fact, we know of but one single escape from the Auburn prison, when a visiter entering with two cloaks, gave one to a convict, who passed out with the visiters. None have escaped from Wethersfield. Escapes were very frequent under the old system We find, in a report to the Legislature of New Jersey, in January, 1830, the following passage :

" We have obtained information, from the records of the prison, concerning escapes which have actually been effected since the prison was built This list is now before us. It contains the names of one hundred and eight convicts who have made their escape. This is more than one-twelfth part of all who have been committed to the prison—a proof of the insecurity of the prison, so far as our knowledge in the history of prisons extends, without a parallel "

Though the number of escaped criminals was not everywhere so large, it was sufficiently so to become very alarming to society. We consider it barbarous not to keep a prisoner perfectly safe.

---

* The table at the beginning of this chapter

34

The desire of liberty, common to living beings, prompts him to seize on every opportunity of escape; the consequence of which, if he is retaken, is an increase of the physical means by which it is attempted to secure him. From whatever point of view we may look at the old prison system, we find that one evil engenders a still greater one   There is no doubt, that solitary confinement during night is a great safeguard against attempts at escape, which require more or less the combined efforts of many.

Vidocq, in his Memoirs, quoted several times in this work, says distinctly, that on days of rest, most plots are formed in the bagnes and other prisons. We would also refer to the remark on safety produced by solitary confinement, in Judge Wells's estimate, given above. "Divide and rule" is nowhere better exemplified than by the penitentiary system. It might be said: "divide and rule—even criminals."—Trans.]

No. 18.

Some Comparisons between France and America.

No. I Classification of convicts according to their offences, in France and in America.—II. Comparative Table of mortality in the "central prisons" of France, and the penitentiaries of America —III Comparative Table of recommittals in both countries —IV Proportion of men and women in the prisons of France and America —V. Tables 1 of the foreigners imprisoned in France and in America , 2 of the number of Frenchmen not born in that department where they were tried, compared to the number of Americans not born in that state in which they were tried —VI. Age of convicts in France and America.—VII. Proportion of convicts to the population in France and in America.

No. I.—*Classification of Convicts in France and in America.*

In the year 1830 there were sentenced 10,046 individuals in France, criminally and "correctionally,"* to one year's imprisonment or more Of these 10,046 individuals :†

1208 had committed crimes against persons, or 12 02 of 100 ;
8838 had committed crimes against property, or 87.98 of 100 ;
 195 had committed forgery, or 1.94 of 100 ;
 208 had committed crimes against morals, or 2 07 of 100.

In the same year, 1830, the average of condemnations pronounced in the states of Massachusetts, Connecticut, New York, and Pennsylvania, presents the following :

---

* Or by the police courts, of which we have spoken above —Trans.

† In the division of crimes against persons and property, we have not adopted precisely the order of the tables of criminal justice, in order to be able to establish a more correct comparison between France and the United States.

Convicted for crimes against persons,   8.66 of 100.
    Ditto   crimes against property, 91.29 of 100.
    Ditto   forgery,   10.26 of 100.
    Ditto   crimes against morals,   4.05 of 100.

The proportion of crimes against persons, has been, as will be seen, a little larger in America than in France. *

A great difference shows itself in the crime of forgery.

The state of knowledge in the United States, the immense number of banks, and the great commercial activity in that country, explain easily this difference.

In France, it has been observed that crimes against persons had a slight tendency to decrease Thus in 1825, they formed 22 of 100 ; in 1826, 22 ; in 1827, 22 ; in 1828, 19 ; in 1829, 18 ; and in 1830, 17 of 100 crimes.

For thirty years, however, the crimes against persons seem to have become more frequent †

Statistical Notes, No 17, First Division.

Tableaux de la justice criminelle en France, 1830, page 2, 114 ; 1829, page 2 ; 1828, page 2 ; 1827, page 2 , 1826, page 2 ; 1825, page 2.

No II.—*Comparative Table of mortality in the central houses of France, and in the penitentiaries in the United States.*

In 1828, there were imprisoned in "the central houses" in France, 17,560 individuals ; of these, 1,372 died during the year, or 1 of 12 79.

In 1829, the number of prisoners was 17,586 ; died, 1,386, or 1 of 12 68.

In 1830, the number of prisoners was 16,842 , died, 1,111, or 1 of 15.16.

Thus, during the three last years, the mortality has, on an average, been, in the "central houses" of France, about 1 out of 14 prisoners

In America, during the same years, there died, on an average, in the five penitentiaries, at Sing-Sing, Auburn, Wethersfield, Baltimore, and Charlestown, but 1 of 49 prisoners.

This result will appear still more extraordinary, if it is considered, that there are in the United States, in the five penitentiaries of which we speak, but few or no women. But if we would deduct the number of women imprisoned in France, the

---

* But it must be remembered, that in the United States it is almost always the injured party who prosecutes, and not unfrequently it is his interest not to complain. In France, in most cases, public authority takes care to revenge the offended, and government pays the expenses of the process

† Owing, undoubtedly, in a great measure, to an improved state of police.—
TRANS

mortality would show itself still greater. Thus, we have said, that in 1830, the average mortality had been 1 of 15.16 prisoners; it would have been 1 of 14.03 had the male prisoners alone been considered.

Documents, furnished by the Minister of Public Works and Commerce.

Comparative Tables respecting the State of New York, paragraph 2.

No. III.—*Comparative Table of recommittals in France and the United States.*

In France, during the years 1828, 1829, and 1830, there have been sentenced 95,876 individuals, of whom 13,622 were recommittals.

Proportion : 1 recommittal of 7 convicts.*

In Pennsylvania, from 1810 to 1819, there was 1 recommittal of 6 convictions.

In Maryland, from 1820 to 1832, 1 of 7.

In the State of New York, from 1803 to 1820, 1 of 9.

At Auburn, from 1824 to 1831, 1 of 19.

Thus France has had annually less recommittals than Pennsylvania, from 1810 to 1819, as much as Maryland, and nearly three times more than New York since the foundation of the Auburn penitentiary.

It must be kept in mind, however, that these comparisons can never furnish anything more than approximations. The number of recommittals in the United States cannot be exactly compared to the recommittals in France. In the United States no *criminal administration,* properly so called, exists. Generally speaking, it is but the return of the criminal to the same prison which proves the recommittal. In France a thousand means exist to know the previous conviction of a criminal

The result therefore is, that whilst the stated number of recommittals in the United States is the same with that in France, it may be believed, that in reality there are more recommittals in the United States than in France. It cannot be doubted, for instance, that there are less recommittals in France than in Maryland, though the numbers of both countries are precisely the same.

[But there was no better way of finding out a recommittal in

* This number only represents the recommittals legally testified in 1828, 1829, and 1830 But however great the activity of the judicial police may be, there exists even with us, a number of individuals, whose previous life remains unknown to the courts, and whose recommittal is found out only in prison There were in 1830, of the 16,000 prisoners in the " central houses," 4,000 in a state of recommittal, which gives one recommittal out of four prisoners.

the United States before the foundation of penitentiaries than after; on the contrary, a recommittal is at present in many cases more easily detected, and how does the proportion of recommittals immediately fall with the establishment of penitentiaries! It is not only Auburn which affords such favourable results; it is the same with Charlestown, Wethersfield, &c. See their reports.—TRANS.]

Comparative Tables of recommittals, No. 17, *paragraph* 3.
Compte rendu de la justice criminelle en France, 1828, p. 192 and 112, 1829, p. 193 and 114 ; 1830, *rapport au Roi,* p. xi. xvii. and xviii.; p. 165 and 94.

No. IV.—*Comparative number of women in the prisons of France and the United States.*

Of 22,304 individuals who were sentenced for crimes in France, from 1825 to 1831, there were 3,911 women.

Proportion : 17.53 women to 100 convicts of both sexes.

Of 31,655 individuals, sentenced by the " correctional courts"* to one year and more, during the same period, were 8,087 women.

Proportion : 25.54 women to 100 convicts of both sexes.

If we sum up these two numbers in order to make the comparison with the United States easier, we find, that of 53,959 individuals, sentenced from 1825 to 1831, criminally or " correctionally" to one year's or more imprisonment, there were 11,998 women.

Proportion : 22.23 women of 100 prisoners of both sexes.

Of 104,709 individuals, sentenced during the same period, correctionally, to less than one year's imprisonment, there were 20,542 women.

Proportion : 19.27 women of 100 prisoners of both sexes.

In the United States, in the state prisons of New York, Connecticut, Pennsylvania, and Maryland, the women were in proportion as 9.34 to 100 of both sexes

If we compare to this number that of individuals sentenced, criminally and " correctionally," in France, to one year's imprisonment and more—a number composed nearly of the same elements—it will be seen, that the number of imprisoned women in France is nearly double that of the imprisoned women in the United States.

Still more, it must be remarked, that the proportion of 9 to 100 applies to all American women, white and coloured ; but if we should take only the number of white women, the difference between France and the United States would be much greater

* See our previous note on this subject.—TRANS.

still; because, in the American penitentiaries, the white women are, to all white prisoners of both sexes, as 3.87 to 100.*

We cannot compare the number of women sentenced to less than one year's imprisonment, with any corresponding number in the United States We only know, that in the United States, in proportion as the punishment becomes less severe, the number of convicted women becomes greater; this at least we have observed in the states of New York and Pennsylvania. It is not so in France. The proportion of women sentenced to less than one year's imprisonment, is not so large as that of women sentenced to more than one year.

Proportion of men and women in the different penitentiaries, No. 17, paragraph 3

Tableau de la justice criminelle en France. 1826, p. 9 and 121; 1827, p. 9 and 132, 1828, p. 14 and 149; 1829, p. 14 and 151; 1830, p. 14 and 125.

No. V.—COMPARATIVE TABLE,

1. *In France, of the number of foreigners among the committed, and of the number of Frenchmen not born in the department where they have been tried.*
2. *In the United States, of the foreigners among the convicts, as also of the Americans not born in the state where they have been tried.*

In France, of 21,731 individuals accused, from 1827 to 1831,
    697 were not French;
  15,691 were born in the department where they were tried;
   5,303 were natives of other departments.

---

* It would be wrong, however, to compare the number of white women in the American penitentiaries with that of the women in the French prisons The white women in the United States, even those who belong to the lower classes of society, occupy, in comparison to coloured women, an elevated station in society. To be confounded with the latter, seems to them the highest degree of ignominy. [A white servant generally, perhaps always, refuses to wash linen for a coloured fellow servant —TRANS.] The fear of a similar shame prevents many of the white women from committing crimes Often, also, the jury themselves shun the application of a punishment to which the idea of infamy is attached. [The authors have not understood this country in this respect It is not the station of the white women compared to the coloured women alone which prevents crime among them, it is the absolutely elevated station of the white woman (and comparatively also of the free coloured woman) in the United States, incomparably higher than the station of women in any other nation, which prevents crime If we consider, that, in some states, many or most of the imprisoned women, white and coloured, have been sentenced for adultery, (in the Wethersfield prison they are nearly all imprisoned for this reason,) whilst adultery is not punished in France with imprisonment, the difference becomes still more striking A table, showing the per centage which imprisoned emigrant women bear to all imprisoned women in the penitentiaries, would have been very interesting.—TRANS.]

Thus the foreigners were to the whole of the accused as 3 to 100.

The accused born in the department were to all tried in the same department as 72 to 100

The accused not born in the department, to the whole of the individuals tried in the same department, as 23 to 100.

In America, (in the states of Massachusetts, Connecticut, New York, Pennsylvania, and Maryland,) the individuals sentenced to the state prison, are thus classified:

14 foreigners to 100 convicts;

51 individuals born in the state where they were tried to 100 convicts;

33 individuals not born in the state where they were tried to 100 convicts.

The comparison of these numbers establishes a fact with which the reader is already acquainted, viz. that the population of the United States is infinitely more transitory than that of France.

It becomes the more convincing if we consider that our departments in general are much smaller than the states of the Union, and that no political tie attaches those who have been born there. It ought to be, therefore, more common with us than in the United States to change the domicil, however, the contrary happens; [and quite of course, because communication between the different parts of the Union is so great, the vast field of industry so open to every one, and the population so homogeneous and enterprising —Trans.]

Statistical Notes, No. 17, *paragraphs* 7, 8, 9.

Tableau de la justice criminelle en France: 1828, p. 26; 1829, p. 26; 1830, p. 27.

No. VI.—*Comparative table of the age of convicts in France and in America*

Of 21,703* individuals, who, from 1825 to 1831, have been sentenced in France, for crimes:

4,251 were under 21 years of age, or about 1 of 5 convicts.
7,504 were from 21 to 30 years of age, or 1 of 3 convicts.
5,195   "   30 to 40   "   or 1 of 4   "
2,800   "   40 to 50   "   or 1 of 8   "
1,211   "   50 to 60   "   or 1 of 18   "
  483   "   60 to 70   "   or 1 of 46   "

---

* There have been in reality, during these five years, 21,740 convicts; but there were 37 whose age is unknown.

There arc a few convicts over the age of 70, but their number is too small to need determination in the present place.

If we compare these numbers with corresponding ones obtained for the United States, little difference is observable.

The convicts under 20 years of age, are, in the United States,
in the proportion of   -   -   -   -   1 to 10
Those between 20 and 30   -   -   -   -   1 to 2
Those between 30 and 40   -   -   -   -   1 to 5
Those between 40 and 50   -   -   -   -   1 to 9
Those between 50 and 60   -   -   -   -   1 to 25

The two first proportions present the greatest differences in the two countries.

But it must not be forgotten, that for France, the first proportion is composed of those under 21 years of age, in America, of those under 20 years. This one year causes the apparent but merely apparent difference. [We cannot see that this one year can double the proportion. Mr Ouételet, in his Observations, reprinted in the *Courrier des Etats Unis,* April 25, 1832, gives an interesting table on this point, also in respect to women of the different ages]

Statistical Notes, No. 17, *paragraph* 12.

Tableau de la justice criminelle en France, 1826, p. 14; 1828, p. 22; 1830, p. 22; 1827, p 14; 1829, p. 22.

No. VII.—*Proportion of convicts to the population in France and in the United States.*

In France in 1830, there were sentenced 10,261 individuals to one year's imprisonment and more.

Proportion : 1 convict to 3118 inhabitants. *

This proportion is not the result of chance, because it is nearly the same in 1829, 1828, and 1827.

In the United States, from 1820 to 1830, if we take the average of all the results obtained in the penitentiaries of Massachusetts, Connecticut, New York, Pennsylvania, and Maryland, we find 1 convict sent to the state prison to 4,964 inhabitants.

In France there are, therefore, more people sentenced for grave crimes than in the United States. But, we must remember, that for France we have adopted as the basis of our calculations, the minimum of convictions to one year's imprisonment, whilst in two of the largest states here compared, the minimum is two year's imprisonment †

---

* Taking 32,000,000 as the population of France.

† Nor must it be forgotten, that, in France, criminal justice is infinitely more active than in the United States.

We have reason to believe, that, if it were possible to compare in the two countries the total number of individuals sentenced to any kind of imprisonment, the advantage would remain on the side of France.

This opinion is founded upon the following fact:

In 1830 there were sentenced in Pennsylvania 327 persons to the state prison; there was then 1 convict of this kind to 4,121 inhabitants, a proportion which approximates the average number indicated above.

In Pennsylvania, during the same year, there were sentenced to less than a year's imprisonment, in the county of Philadelphia, 1,431 individuals.

This number is not produced by the view of one year. It forms about the average number of four years previously to 1830.

In adding 1,431 and 327, we obtain 1,758

It is clear, that this number is far from representing the whole number of individuals sentenced to prison in 1830 in the state of Pennsylvania; since one of the elements which compose it is furnished by a single county, and the results of the fifty other counties are not known to us.

We will, however, compare this number, incomplete as it is, with that of the inhabitants of Pennsylvania in 1830, and we will have one prisoner to 767 inhabitants.

Now, in France, in 1830, there was but one person sentenced to imprisonment of 1,043 inhabitants, and this proportion has been about the same in 1829, 1828, and 1827.

The individuals, therefore, sentenced to the state prison in Pennsylvania, added to the individuals sentenced to less than a year's imprisonment only in the county of Philadelphia, are already more numerous in proportion to the population of Pennsylvania, than the individuals sentenced to any imprisonment in France in proportion to the population of the kingdom

The comparison would be still more favourable to us, if we could obtain the results of criminal justice in the 50 counties in Pennsylvania of which we have no reports.

We estimate, that if this were done, we would have found at least one person sentenced to imprisonment out of 600 inhabitants,* whilst, in France, but one of 1000.

This great number of imprisonments must be attributed to two causes chiefly:

1. To the severity of principles which the first settlers imprinted on the laws There is a number of little disorders which our codes leave unpunished, and which the American codes re-

---

* See the details on this point in the Statistical Notes, No. 16, § 5.

35

press : such as gambling of all kinds, swearing, noise, intoxication, idleness in many cases.

2. These laws are severe ; their application is still more so. They contain much that is arbitrary.

[The most satisfactory results would be obtained by comparing the number of crimes of various classes committed in two different countries, e. g. in France so many burglaries, in the United States so many burglaries, in France so many thefts, in the United States so many thefts. This comparison, together with the careful consideration of attending circumstances, such, for instance, as the authors have mentioned in regard to forgeries committed in France and in the United States, would lead to more satisfactory results respecting the morality of two given countries. It cannot be too often repeated, that it is indispensably necessary to keep always distinctly in view, what you wish to ascertain by any statistical inquiry—a rule which sounds very plain, and yet is every day neglected. Nothing is more liable to mislead in statistical inquiries than names. Crime, imprisonment, schools, &c. are names which signify very different things in different countries —TRANS.]

In general the liberty of the poor is badly guarantied in the United States.* One of the principles of the British Constitution is to allow the upper classes the right of constituting the police of society. In the United States the English aristocracy does not exist, but part of its attributes has remained with the municipal administrations, which, composed of plebeian magistrates, have nevertheless adopted the same doctrines. [We cannot give any comment or refutation on this passage, because we are unable to understand the authors. The reader will have observed ere this, that they had not an opportunity, when writing this work, of investigating deeply the British institutions; a consequence of which was, that they misunderstood this country almost always where the British Constitution alone offered a key.—TRANS.]

Statistical Documents on Pennsylvania, p. 15.

Tableau de la justice criminelle en France, 1830, p. 12, p. 125.

---

* We have spoken of this opinion above.—TRANS.

No. 19.

FINANCIAL DIVISION.

SECTION FIRST. (*Old System.*)

STATISTICAL TABLE, REPRESENTING THE EXPENSE OF THE
SUPPORT OF THE OLD PRISONS, PREVIOUSLY TO THE INTRO-
DUCTION OF THE PENITENTIARY SYSTEM.

***

Daily expense, after deduction of the produce of labour.

Newgate (Connecticut).

The maintenance of the old prison of Newgate (Connecticut)
has cost, during the last ten years of its existence, as follows:

In 1817	-	-	-	-	$12,679 51
1818	-	-	-	-	12,494 27
1819	-	-	-	-	11,403 73
1820	-	-	-	-	9,704 11
1821	-	-	-	-	6,000 00
1822	-	-	-	-	5,263 65
1823	-	-	-	-	5,500 00
1824	-	-	-	-	8,002 80
1825	-	-	-	-	7,284 90
1826	-	-	-	-	6,301 08
Sum total,	-	-	-	-	$84,634 05

In 1828 there were, in the new state prison, 93 prisoners:
suppose an equal number in the old prison, during the ten years
above mentioned, each of which caused an average expense of
$8,863 40, produce of labour deducted, it results, that each pri-
soner cost the state, daily, 26 cents and 10 mil. But in taking
the number 93 for the average number of prisoners in the old
prison, from 1817 to 1826, we certainly take too high a number, since it has been shown that crime increases in Connecticut: it is therefore probable, that the support of prisoners cost
still more; but it is certain that it cannot have cost less.

From 1797 to 1829, the state of New Jersey has paid for the

support of its prison $164,963 81. (See 5th Report of the Boston Prison Discipline Society, page 423)

It must be remarked, however, that of late the Lamberton prison has singularly improved in a financial respect   In 1831 its expenses surpassed its revenue only by $1,038 65. See Report on the Prison of New Jersey, included in a Letter of Judge Coxe of Philadelphia.

Walnut Street (Pennsylvania.)

During eleven years, from 1819 to 1829, inclusive, the state of Pennsylvania has paid, for the support of Walnut Street prison, the following sums:

In 1819	-	-	-	-	-	$8,234 46
1820	-	-	-	-	-	7,110 75
1821	-	-	-	-	-	4,330 00
1822	-	-	-	-	-	3,050 40
1823	-	-	-	-	-	4,118 13
1824	-	-	-	-	-	4,065 83
1825	-	-	-	-	-	6,046 80
1826	-	-	-	-	-	4,046 80
1827	-	-	-	-	-	5,095 17
1828	-	-	-	-	-	56 80
1829	-	-	-	-	-	256 22
Total,	-	-	-	-	-	$46,411 36

In 1827 there were 576 prisoners in Walnut Street prison : suppose an equal number there during the preceding years and the two following ones, each of the eleven years has cost, on an average, $4,191 94, a deduction of the produce of labour being first made; and consequently every prisoner has cost the state, per day, at least 1 cent 99 mil

See 5th Report of the Boston Prison Discipline Society, page 354.

The causes which influence the economy or expensiveness of the administration of a prison, are very well shown in the above quoted passage of the Report of the Boston Society.

Newgate (New York).

In twenty-three years, from 1797 to 1819, inclusive, the old prison of New York has cost, for construction as well as support, $646,912. It seems that about $200,000 have been spent for construction; $446,912, therefore, remain for the support alone, a deduction of the produce of labour being made. Each of the twenty-three years then has cost, on an average, $19,432.

There were 440 prisoners in Newgate, during the above years; from which it results, that each prisoner in this prison has cost the state, per day, 12 cents 32 mil.

SECTION SECOND. (*New System.*)

§ 1. *Construction* $\begin{cases} \textit{Pennsylvania System.} \\ \textit{Auburn System.} \end{cases}$

EXPENSE OF CONSTRUCTION. (*Pennsylvania System*)

Penitentiary of Cherry Hill, near Philadelphia.—262 *Cells.*

$432,000, which makes each cell $1,648 85
(*Document obtained by us on the spot.*) See also Report of the Commissioners of Revision, also that of Judge Powers, 1828.
[See the estimate of the new penitentiary of New Jersey, on the Pennsylvania plan, which we have inserted after Judge Wells's estimate, No. 12 —TRANS.]

Penitentiary of Pittsburg —190 *Cells.*

$186,000, which makes each cell $978 95. (See *Carey.*)
We mention the penitentiary of Pittsburg under the title of Pennsylvania system, because it has been erected for solitary confinement during day and night, which forms the characteristic of this system: we ought to observe, however, that the prisoners at Pittsburg do not work, their cells having more resemblance to those at Auburn than to those at Cherry Hill.

EXPENSE OF CONSTRUCTION. (*Auburn System*)

Washington Penitentiary —160 *Cells.*

$180,000, which makes for each cell $1,125.*

Charlestown Penitentiary, near Boston.—300 *Cells.*

$86,000, which makes each cell $286 66.†

Sing-Sing Penitentiary—1,000 *Cells.*

$200,000, which makes each cell $200 ‡

---

* This statement has been furnished to us by the present superintendent. The finished part of this penitentiary has not yet cost more than $120,000, but that which is yet to be done is estimated at $60,000. It is possible that the expenses will be greater than the estimate
† See the pamphlet which contains the regulations of the new prison at Charlestown.
‡ See MS. note of Mr. Cartwright, engineer at Sing-Sing

Wethersfield Penitentiary.—232 Cells.

$35,000, which makes each cell $150 86.*

Baltimore Penitentiary.—320 Cells.

$46,823 44, which makes each cell $146 32.†

Blackwell Island Penitentiary.—240 Cells.

$32,000, which makes each cell $133 33.‡

We do not exactly know the expenses of building the penitentiary at Sing-Sing, which we have given as amounting to $200,000.

It appears from documents, which we find partly in the reports to the legislature, partly in a note of Mr Cartwright, that the construction of the penitentiary has cost the state about $150,000. But to this sum must be added the price of labour of the prisoners, employed in building instead of free labourers. It is for this reason that we add $50,000. It is evident that $50,000 exceeds much the value of the work done by the prisoners. The reader is certain, therefore, that in estimating the expense of construction of Sing-Sing at $200,000, we go beyond the real expense.

It is seen from the above table, that a cell costs, on an average, $257 47; it must be added, that this high price is caused by the Washington Penitentiary, and is disproportionate to the others; and it would be, perhaps, more just to find the average price of the others, as the Washington penitentiary has been built without regard to economy. Doing this, we would obtain the average expense of $191 for each cell. It must not be forgotten, that the question is here of the price of each cell and all accessory buildings of the prison.

* See MS. notes of Judge Wells of Wethersfield, and Reports to the Legislature on the Connecticut State Prison.

† See page 10 of the Report of the Inspectors of the Penitentiary of Maryland, of Dec 23, 1828

‡ See Carey, page 38.

§ 2.—EXPENSE OF SUPPORT. $\left\{ \begin{array}{l} \textit{Expense.} \\ \textit{Produce.} \end{array} \right.$

The Statistic Tables which follow, are but the very succinct *resumé* of an immense labour, which we have undergone on the financial situation of the prisons of America, and the extent of which itself prevents us from giving it here. We can, however, assure the reader, that not one of our numbers is given without being founded on official documents All justificatory papers have been deposited with the Minister of Commerce and Public Works.

FINANCIAL SITUATION OF AUBURN.

Year 1825—386 *Prisoners (average).*

Expenses of the prison,	-	-	-	$24,275 92
Produce of labour,	-	-	-	13,976 10
Balance against the prison,	-	-	-	10,299 82

Year 1826—433 *Prisoners (average).*

Expenses of the prison,	-	-	-	$30,736 05
Produce of labour,	-	-	-	20,522 13
Balance against the prison,	-	-	-	10,213 92

Year 1827—476 *Prisoners (average).*

Expenses of the prison,	-	-	-	$36,543 91
Produce of labour,	-	-	-	25,191 17
Balance against the prison,	-	-	-	11,352 74

Year 1828—547 *Prisoners (average).*

Expenses of the prison,	-	-	-	$33,571 84
Produce of labour,	-	-	-	33,460 56
Balance against the prison,	-	-	-	111 28

Year 1829—604 *Prisoners (average).*

Expenses of the prison,	-	-	-	$38,200 80
Produce of labour,	-	-	-	34,056 17
Balance against the prison,	-	-	-	4,144 63

Year 1830—609 *Prisoners (average).*

Produce of labour,	-	-	-	-	$36,251 79
Expenses of the prison,	-	-	-	36,226 42

Balance in favour of the prison, - - 25 37

Year 1831—643 *Prisoners (average).*

Produce of labour,	-	-	-	-	$36,209 44
Expenses of the prison,	-	-	-	34,405 60

Balance in favour of the prison, - - 1,803 84

(See Reports of the Inspectors of the Auburn prison for the years 1825, 1826, 1827, 1828, 1829, 1830, and 1831.

[To this we will add the following passage of the Annual Report of the Inspectors of the Auburn Prison, January 14, 1833. —Trans.

Including those brought from Sing-Sing, the number of convicts in this prison has increased during the last year 27; but excluding those, there has been a decrease of 23. But by a law of the last session of the legislature, the territory from which convicts are sent to this prison has been enlarged, so as now to embrace five out of the eight senate districts, which law went into practical operation about the time that the said convicts from the Sing-Sing prison were received. Since that time the number of convicts in this prison has gradually increased from 666, to the present number, 683. It appears to us, therefore, highly probable, that with the present territory, there will be a gradual increase of convicts at this prison.

The *earnings* of the convicts for the year ending on the 30th day of September last, and which have been charged to contractors, amount to $37,951 26

The *earnings* of convicts, not employed by contractors, as charged to individuals, and cash received from visiters, and for articles sold, and other incidental sources, amount to - - 3,882 21

The earnings and profits of the prison as above, for the past year, amount to - - - - $41,833 47

The expenditures during the same period, for the general support of the prison, and which includes all expenses, except those authorized by the act of the 25th April, 1832, for building 220 cells, amounts to - - - - - - - $38,305 31

Leaving a balance in favour of the prison, of $3,528 16]

Financial situation of Wethersfield.

Year 1828—(half a year)—95 Prisoners (average).

Expenses of the prison, - - - -	$2,598 31
Produce of labour, - - - - -	3,615 47
Balance in favour of the prison, - -	1,017 16

Year 1829—115 Prisoners (average).

Expenses of the prison, - - - -	$5,876 13
Produce of labour, - - - - -	9,105 54
Balance in favour of the prison, - -	3,229 41

Year 1830—150 Prisoners (average).

Expenses of the prison, - - - -	$ 7,295 00
Produce of labour, - - - -	12,363 94
Balance in favour of the prison, - -	5,068 94

Year 1831—174 Prisoners (average).

Expenses of the prison, - - - -	$ 7,342 16
Produce of labour, - - - -	15,166 18
Balance in favour of the prison, - -	7,824 02

The new penitentiary of Wethersfield has, then, within three years and a half, produced a revenue to the state, deduction of all expenses made, of $17,139 53.

The ancient prison of Connecticut (Newgate) cost the state, from 1790 to 1826, not less than $204,711, for the support of prisoners, over and above the produce of the labour of the prisoners

(See Reports of the Inspectors of the Penitentiary of Connecticut for the years 1828, 1829, 1830, and 1831.)

Financial situation of the Penitentiary at Baltimore.

Year 1828—317 Prisoners (average).

Expenses of the prison, - - - -	$15,883 79
Produce of labour, - - - -	27,464 31
Balance in favour of the prison, - -	11,580 52

Year 1829—342 *Prisoners (average).*

Expenses of the prison,	-	-	-	-	$16,265 00
Produce of labour,		-	-	-	36,216 25
Balance in favour of the prison,		-	-	19,951 25

Year 1830—*for nine months*—363 *Prisoners (average).*

Expenses of the prison,	-	-	-	-	$13,292 61
Produce of labour,		-	-	-	26,105 29
Balance in favour of the prison,		-	-	12,812 68

Thus the penitentiary at Baltimore has yielded to the state of Maryland a revenue, over and above all expenses for the state prison, within two years and nine months, $44,344 45.

(See Reports of the Inspectors of the Penitentiary of Maryland for the years 1828, 1829, and 1830.)

FINANCIAL SITUATION OF SING-SING.

Years 1828 and 1829—541 *Prisoners (average).*

Expenses of the prison,	-	-	-	-	$33,654 00
Produce of labour,		-	-	-	4,648 19
Balance against the prison,		-	-	-	29,005 81

(See Report of January 6, 1830.)

Years 1829 and 1830—669 *Prisoners (average).*

Expenses of the prison,	-	-	-	-	$36,606 00
Produce of labour,		-	-	-	13,253 01
Balance against the prison,		-	-	-	23,352 99

(See Report of the Inspectors of January 5, 1831.)

Year 1831—875 *Prisoners (average).*

Expenses of the prison,	-	-	-	-	$51,703 31
Produce of labour,		-	-	-	40,205 33
Balance against the prison,		-	-	-	11,497 98

(See Report of the Inspectors of January 12, 1832.)

In all the reports upon which we have made the above calculations, the annual expenses are given as much exceeding the number which we have stated, because the reports include the

expenses occasioned by the construction of the prison, whilst
we only state the expenses of support.

The number indicating the expenses, thus reduced, is exact :
that of the produce of labour is not. The reason is this : until
1831 the majority of prisoners were employed in constructing
the prison; it follows that their labour, which was productive,
inasmuch as it saved an expense, nevertheless produced no revenue, and was therefore not enumerated as produce of the labour or revenue of the prison. In 1831, there have been 526
prisoners out of 875 employed in productive labour; and the
number indicating the revenue strikingly increased ; we might,
in establishing a proportion, calculate how much must be produced by the labour of 875 prisoners, by taking as a basis, that
which has been produced by 526 prisoners. But, in this respect, there would be a danger of making an erroneous calculation. In fact, the produce of labour does not always double
with the prisoners at work: it often happens, that the production
of articles exceeds the consumption and the wants of commerce;
and we do not know whether 1,000 prisoners, breaking and cutting stones in the quarries of Sing-Sing, would yield proportionally as great a revenue as 526 convicts

All that may be said is, that according to all probability, the
prison will support itself, and will cost absolutely nothing to the
state, when the labour of all the prisoners shall be employed in
a productive way.

PENNSYLVANIA SYSTEM.

We do not give any statistic table of the financial situation
of the penitentiary in Philadelphia, because it has been impossible for us to obtain the necessary documents respecting the
point.

However, it results from the 2d Report to the Legislature, in
1831, that during the first year of its operation, the support of
the prisoners has been covered by the produce of their labour;
and the state had only to add the salaries of the officers. The
report of the following year seems to announce a similar result.
Yet no number is given. It must be remarked, that the number
of prisoners in the new penitentiary of Philadelphia is very
small; and Mr. Samuel Wood, the director of this penitentiary,
believes, that the labour of the prisoners will become more productive in proportion as the prisoners become more numerous.

(See 2d Report on the Penitentiary at Philadelphia.)

[To this we will add the following passage, taken from the
Message of the governor of Pennsylvania to the legislature of
that state, Dec. 6, 1832:

,‟ The annual accounts of the prison are not closed until November 30.   I have not, therefore, been able to ascertain with accuracy how far the earnings of the prisoners will be available to defray the expenses of the institution.   It is believed, that, for the present, they will pay all except the salaries of the officers; and it is not doubted, that, as soon as the prison shall have been fully organized, the entire expenses will be defrayed out of the proceeds of the establishment.”

There is no good reason why labour in solitary confinement should not be made as productive as in the Auburn system ; because, it must be remembered, that the principles of the latter do not permit any united labour in which several convicts come too closely together; the species of labour in which they can be employed, must be therefore pretty nearly the same with that in which the solitary convict can be employed. This is not only our opinion, but also that of Judge Wells of Wethersfield, and a better authority respecting the economy of penitentiaries we do not know.—Trans.]

EXPENSES AND INCOME COMPARED.

SUPPORT AND LABOUR.

Auburn.   (Average of seven years.)

Total expense of each prisoner per day,   - 17 cents 16 mil.
Labour of each prisoner produced per day, - 14 " 59 "

Sing-Sing. (Average of the three last years.)

Total expense for each prisoner per day,   - 16 cents 33 mil
Labour of each prisoner produced per day, - 10 " 26 "

Wethersfield. (Average of four years.)

Total expense of each prisoner per day,   - 13 cents 55 mil.
Labour of each prisoner produced per day, - 23 " 35 "

Baltimore. (Average of the three last years.)

Total expense of each prisoner per day,   - 13 cents 36 mil.
Labour of each prisoner produced per day, - 26 " 31 "

FOOD ALONE.

Food alone of each prisoner has cost, on an average, per day :

At Auburn, (average of 6 years,)   - 4 cents 36 mil.
At Sing-Sing, (average of 2 years,) - 6 " 00 "
At Wethersfield, (average of 4 years,) - 4 " 72 "

Expense of guarding alone.

The surveillance of each prisoner, (i. e. watching, salary of officers, &c) costs, on an average, per day :

At Auburn, (average of 6 years,)   - 6 cents 17 mil.
At Sing-Sing, (average of 3 years,) - 6 " 83 "
At Wethersfield, (average of 4 years,) - 6 " 87 "

EXPENSE OF FOOD, CLOTHING, AND BEDDING.

The food, clothing, and bedding of each convict cost, on an
average, per day :

At Auburn, (average of 3 years,)   - 5 cents 76 mil.
At Sing-Sing, (average of 3 years,) - 8 " 07 "

If we compare the above table with the statistical table of the ancient system, it will be seen, that, in Connecticut, every convict has earned for the state, during the four last years, 46 cents 65 mil. over and above the expenses which he caused; whilst, during the ten years which preceded the establishment of the new system, each prisoner cost the state per day, on an average, 26 cents 10 mil.; which makes a difference of 34 cents 90 mil. for each prisoner per day.

ANNUAL EXPENSE OF SUPPORT. (*Auburn.*)

During the seven years which elapsed, from 1825 to 1831, each prisoner has cost, on an average, per year, 63 dollars, 76 cents, 6 mil.

The most a prisoner has cost per year, is 76 dollars and 77 cents.

The least is 53 dollars, 50 cents, 8 mil.

SALARY OF OFFICERS.

	AUBURN. 1831. 643 *convicts.*	SING-SING. 1831. 875 *convicts.*	BOSTON. (Old prison.) 1829. 276 *convicts.*	WETHERSFIELD. 1831. 174 *convicts.*
Superintendent, Other officers,	$ 1,250 13,700	$ 1,750 18,370	$ 1,500 11,671 55	$1,200 2,513 33
Total, - - -	$14,950	$20,120	$13,171 55	$3,713 33

Note.—The superintendent of the Virginia state prison receives $2,000.

PENITENTIARY SYSTEM OF PENNSYLVANIA.

An Article reprinted from the Encyclopædia Americana.

[We reprint here the above named article, because, as we stated in the preface, some gentlemen, whose opinion on matters connected with prison discipline cannot but have great weight with us, requested us to do so. Besides, there is no reference in the Encyclopædia, in which the article *Prison Discipline* stands in its proper place, made to this article in the Appendix, and it may therefore easily escape the notice of many readers. We shall add at the end of it some remarks.—TRANS.]

One of the points which have occasioned the greatest division of opinion among the friends of the penitentiary system, relates to solitary confinement. One party contend that this should be made the very basis of prison discipline, and have carried their principles into effect in the Eastern Penitentiary of Pennsylvania: others strenuously oppose it. The opinions expressed in the article *Prison Discipline*, in this work, are rather unfavourable to the plan adopted in Pennsylvania. As the question is one of great interest, and as many misconceptions on this subject exist among those who are sincerely devoted to the reformation of prisons, we have thought it not improper to give, in this place, a view of some of the arguments which may be urged in support of the principle of uninterrupted solitary confinement. All that will be attempted will be to touch upon the main features of the question, and to offer some suggestions, derived from the writer's own experience, with the view of making it appear that the system of solitary confinement, as now practised in the Eastern Penitentiary in Philadelphia, is the only effectual mode of making prisons schools of reformation, instead of schools of corruption. The more light there is thrown upon this subject, the better for the cause. Strong, and, in our opinion, unfounded prejudices against the system of solitary confinement, are entertained even by men justly esteemed for their enlightened views and strenuous labours for the good of mankind. The late William Roscoe, for instance, was extremely hostile to the system, as appears from several pieces which he has written on

the subject of prison discipline.*   Mr. Roberts Vaux, of Philadelphia, addressed to him a Letter on the Penitentiary System
of Pennsylvania (Philadelphia, 1827), from which, and from another production of this gentleman, we shall present to our readers
various extracts in the course of this article.   We would also
refer the reader, for more particular information than our limits
will allow, to other publications of Mr. Vaux, who is indefatigable in promoting the education of children and the correction
of criminals.   The publications to which we allude are Notices
of the Original and Successive Efforts to improve the Prison
Discipline in Philadelphia, and to reform the Penal Law of
Pennsylvania (Philadelphia, 1826); a Discourse delivered before the Historical Society of the State of Pennsylvania on
New-Year's Day, 1827 (Philadelphia, 1827); and a Letter to
Bishop White, the President, and other Members of the Philadelphia Society for alleviating the Miseries of Public Prisons,
in No. 8, vol. i. of the Journal of Law (Philadelphia, 1830) †—
Before going into the subject of this article, we would remark
that it is believed by many foreigners, that the Pennsylvania
penitentiary system has been abandoned in the very state from
which it takes its name.   The following passage from the message of the governor of Pennsylvania to the legislature of that
state (Dec. 6, 1832), shows that this is a mistake, and throws
light upon other points in question :—" Our penitentiary system," says Governor Wolf, "as immediately connected with
the administration of criminal justice, is to be regarded as being
of the first importance, in reference as well to the security of the

* We learn, from Doctor T S Traill's memoir on that distinguished scholar,
read before the Literary and Philosophical Society of Liverpool, in October,
1832, that he said " that no literary distinction had ever afforded him half the
gratification that he received from the reflection on the part he had taken on this
great question, and he expressed his satisfaction that he now might be permitted
to think that he had not lived altogether in vain " And yet—to such mistakes
are great men liable—we believe that Mr Roscoe had but a very imperfect
knowledge of the effects of solitary confinement, and that his conclusions on the
subject were drawn from unfounded suppositions.—Since the above and this
note were written, we saw the letter of Mr Roscoe to Doctor David Hosack,
New York, dated, Liverpool, Tonleth Park, July 13, 1830, of which also the
French authors make mention It appears, that Mr. Roscoe's chief objection
was against solitary confinement without labour. He distinctly says, that, in his
opinion, the great question is labour or no labour, in general he seems, however,
to prefer the Auburn system. Whether Mr. Roscoe was, at that distance from
our penitentiaries, sufficiently informed upon the two penitentiary systems, their
principles and operation, we are unable to say
† These writings are known beyond the limits of the United States We find
them mentioned with respect in the Lectures on Prisons, &c , by Nicholas Henry
Julius (Berlin, 1828), and in the Annals of Institutions for Punishment and Correction of Paupers, their Education, &c , published monthly at Berlin, by the
same author (both in German)—works little known in this country, on account
of the language in which they are written, but which contain a great mass of information on the subjects mentioned in their titles

persons and property, as to the general morals of our citizens ; and, so far as regards the Eastern Penitentiary, the philanthropic advocates of penitentiary reform may justly congratulate themselves upon the success with which their exertions have been crowned, in bringing so near to perfection a system surrounded by so many difficulties. The government of this prison has been conducted, in regard as well to its economy as its discipline, in a manner worthy of all commendation ; and the experiment of the efficacy of solitary confinement with labour, so far as there has been opportunity to test it, has exceeded the expectations of the most sanguine among its friends.   On the 25th October, 1829, the first convict was received into the Eastern Penitentiary ; and from thence until the 1st November, 1832, the whole number admitted amounted to 132 males, and 4 females, convicted of various offences. On the day last mentioned, there remained in confinement 90 male and 4 female prisoners. The whole number discharged between the above dates, by reason of the expiration of sentence, was 28 : 9 died and 5 were pardoned. One fact, in reference to this institution, bears strong testimony in favour of its discipline. It appears that not a single convict discharged from this prison has ever been returned to it; which would seem to prove pretty clearly, either that a thorough reformation has been produced, or that a dread of a repetition of the unsocial manner of life which had proved so irksome before, has deterred from the commission of crimes within those limits of the state in which a conviction would ensure a sentence to the Eastern Penitentiary. The annual accounts of the prison are not closed until the 30th of November.   I have not, therefore, been able to ascertain, with accuracy, how far the earnings of the prisoners will be available to defray the expenses of the institution. It is believed that, for the present, they will pay all except the salaries of the officers ; and it is not doubted that, as soon as the prison shall have been fully organized, the entire expenses will be defrayed out of the proceeds of the establishment * The experiment made in the Eastern Penitentiary has demonstrated the fact, that solitary confinement with labour does not impair the health of those subjected to that species of discipline The prisoners work to more advantage : having no opportunity for conversation or amusement, they eagerly desire employment ; here all communication is cut off ; no one knows his fellow prisoner; no acquaintance is formed , no contamination takes place; the convict sees no one, holds communion with no one, except such as will give him good advice ; he is placed in a situation where he has every inducement to grow better, but little temptation to

* See our previous remark on the productiveness of labour in solitary confinement in No. 19, Financial Division, Section 2d, § 2, Part, Pennsylvania System.

grow worse; here thought and reflection will crowd upon the mind, and prepare it for solemn impressions, and for moral and religious instruction. The discipline established in this prison; the manner of the construction and arrangement of the building itself, and of the cells in which the prisoners are confined and employed, are admitted, by all who have turned their attention to the subject of penitentiary reform, to possess decided advantages over those of any other establishment designed for similar objects, in this or any other country. Foreigners, whose especial business it has been to visit the penitentiaries in this country, generally, for the purpose of acquiring information in reference to the subject of penitentiary punishment, and its efficacy in producing reformation in those subjected to its discipline, have, with one voice, awarded the meed of merit to that established in the Eastern Penitentiary of Pennsylvania. I have the satisfaction to inform you, that, of the 400 additional cells recently directed by the legislature to be constructed, 100 are finished, and will be ready as soon as the plastering shall have become sufficiently dry to receive prisoners: 118 more are in a state of forwardness, and the whole number will be completed in the course of the ensuing season."* The report to be made upon the Eastern prison during the present session of the legislature of Pennsylvania, we understand, will contain satisfactory proofs of the advantages of the system, and an account of essential improvements in the architecture of the prison. In the article on *Prison Discipline*, in the body of this work, (the *Encyclopædia Americana*,) it is said that, "unless some decided advantage is to be gained by a more expensive system (the Pennsylvania plan of separate confinement), it (the Auburn system) ought to be preferred." We believe that the Pennsylvania system affords many advantages which can be but partially attained by the Auburn system, or not at all; and that it is the best suited, of all the prison systems yet devised, to the demands of the

* The governor continues as follows "From the last report of the inspectors of the Western Penitentiary, as well as from a partial personal inspection of it, I am satisfied that its condition, and the fruits of the course of discipline there exercised, are directly the reverse of that which I have just attempted to describe. From the imperfect plan of the building itself, and the inconvenient, injudicious arrangement of the cells, the discipline of solitary confinement with labour cannot be enforced, the prisoners cannot be restrained from conversing with each other, every prisoner may acquire a knowledge of the individuals confined within its walls, contamination from conversation with his fellow prisoners may take place, the cell of the prisoner cannot, as in the case of the Eastern Penitentiary, be used as his workshop, in which he may always be usefully and profitably employed; there are no separate yards connected with the several cells, which renders it necessary, for the health of the prisoners, to allow them frequently to associate with each other in the common yards Many other defects exist, and many important alterations will be required to fit this establishment for the same course of salutary discipline so successfully practised in the Eastern Penitentiary."

age.   All persons agree that it is of the first importance to prevent prisoners from contaminating each other.   It is a melancholy fact, that, wherever a number of persons, who have openly transgressed the laws of society, or whose characters are corrupt, are brought together, and allowed to have free intercourse with each other, each individual has a tendency to sink to the level of the worst.   The intercourse of the vicious is mutually corrupting, in the same manner as the intercourse of good men is mutually improving.   To prevent this contamination, all agree that, during the night, every prisoner should be separately confined; but many have thought that, during the day time, the criminals engaged in common work may be so strictly watched that no communication can take place among them.   In order to effect this—which is the system followed at Auburn—a very severe discipline has necessarily been resorted to.   No criminal is allowed to speak to a fellow prisoner: the meals are taken in the separate cells.   Beating by the keepers must be allowed, or the discipline cannot be enforced; and it can easily be imagined how severe a discipline is required to suppress that desire of communication which is so deeply planted in human nature, and to counteract the artifices of a host of adepts in cunning, to suppress looks, signs, &c.*   Mr. Lynds, who built the prison at Sing-Sing, in the state of New York, and who must be considered as the inventor of the system of discipline pursued in the prisons of Auburn and Sing-Sing, says that his greatest difficulty has been to find keepers who were not too lenient.

We would also refer the reader to a letter written by Mr. Edward Livingston (the present secretary of state, and the framer of the code of Louisiana) to Mr. Roberts Vaux, Oct. 25, 1828 (and which appeared at the time in the public prints), concurring in the opinion that communication can be prevented only to a certain degree, and only by the use of very great severity, if the convicts work together in the day time   See also the In-

* We do not believe that absolute silence is or can be enforced. The convicts learn to speak without moving the lips, and a gentleman who was for a series of years one of the directors of a penitentiary on the Auburn plan, informed us, that, during his visits to the workshops of the convicts, he sometimes heard the sound of whispering without being able to discover which of the convicts spoke, except by continued attention   We know of two facts in two different penitentiaries, celebrated for their excellent discipline, which prove that the convicts communicate with each other   We admit that this communication cannot be such as to expose the convict to any great danger of contamination, as long as active keepers enforce the system, but two things cannot be prevented, 1. the convicts knowing each other; 2 their attention being drawn from themselves and their accustoming themselves to a (most injurious) feeling of being part of a community of villains.   The abovementioned gentleman, in whose experience we have great confidence, considers it visionary to believe, that absolute silence can ever be obtained without absolute solitude; but that farther corruption certainly can be prevented, which we do not deny to be one great point gained.

troductory Report to the Code of Prison Discipline, explanatory
of the Principles on which the Code is founded, being Part of the
Penal Law prepared for the State of Louisiana, by Edward Livingston; printed separately by Carey, Lea and Carey (Philadelphia, 1827).—But all this severity is avoided in the system of
permanent separate confinement. Communication, and consequent contamination, cannot take place; and yet the system requires neither stripes nor any punishment in order to enforce it.
It works calmly and steadily, without subjecting the convict, by
continually repeated punishment, to a continual recurrence of
disgrace for misdemeanors which the common principles of
human nature are sufficient to induce him to commit. But even
if we could obtain entirely the desired end—interruption of
communication—by the Auburn system, would this system be
desirable on other accounts? The article on *Prison Discipline*,
speaking of solitary confinement, says, " In the silence and
darkness of night the voice of religious instruction is heard; and,
if any circumstances can be imagined, calculated to impress the
warnings, the encouragements, the threats or the hopes of religion upon the mind, it must surely be those of the convict in
his cell, where he is unseen and unheard, and where nothing can
reach him but the voice which must come to him, as it were,
from another world, telling him of things which, perhaps, never
entered into his mind; telling him of God, of eternity, of future
reward and future punishment, of suffering far greater than the
mere physical endurances of the present life, and of joy infinitely
beyond the pleasures he may have experienced." This effect
certainly may take place; but it cannot occur often if the convict
is in his cell only during the night, when his time will be principally spent in sleep; and, though the nights of winter afford
much more time than is required for this purpose, men can accustom themselves to very protracted slumbers, especially if
they have never been accustomed to reflection, which must be
the case with most convicts. The great object referred to in the
above passage can be obtained, in our opinion, only by separate
confinement day and night. The greatest step, we believe,
which a convict of the common sort can make towards reformation, is from thoughtlessness to thoughtfulness. Few of those
committed to prisons are accustomed to think : it is for want of
thought that they became guilty. Surrounded as they are, in the
Auburn system, by a variety of objects during the day, they
cannot feel the same inducement to reflection as under the pres-
sure of constant solitude.   It is difficult, even for a man accustomed from his youth to reflection, and to a mode of life which
offers a great variety of objects and subjects, to entertain himself
in long-continued solitude. He must occupy his mind with himself. The writer may be permitted to refer to his own expe-

rience, having been imprisoned for a considerable period during
a time of political persecution; and, though he was not haunted
with remorse, and had more resources, from the habits of his
past life, than can fall to the lot of most of the inmates of prisons, he can testify to the power with which solitude forces a
man to make himself the subject of his contemplation—a power
which can hardly be realized by one who has not felt it. How
strongly must it operate on the common convict! Deprived of
most of the resources of educated men; constantly reminded of
the cause which brought him into this situation, undisturbed by
any distracting objects, enveloped in silence—he needs must
think. This power of solitude was acknowledged by the wisest
and best of antiquity, who retired from the walks of men to prepare themselves for great tasks by undisturbed contemplation.
The labour which the convict performs in his cell, and which is
indispensably necessary, does not disturb him, because it soon
loses the distracting power of novelty; and, though it will engage him sufficiently to prevent him from sinking into torpid
sullenness (as experience shows), it does not interrupt his contemplations.   When he has once begun to reflect, he must come
to the conclusion that virtue is preferable to vice, and can tran-
quillize his troubled mind only by resolving on reformation: he
must at last seek comfort in the mercy of that Being who created
him in his goodness, and who will receive him, notwithstanding
his guilt, if he is sincere in his repentance.   This will be the
natural course of most prisoners in uninterrupted solitary confinement, judging from the observation which we have made on
convicts thus confined. All agree that prison discipline ought to
be such as to afford a possibility for the reformation of the prisoner; and this seems to us possible only in the Pennsylvania
penitentiary system.   The cases must be very rare in which a
person, in the moment of his conviction, feels the entire justice
of it, and resolves to become better   it requires a moral energy
of which very few are capable.   The feeling usually produced
in any man, by any punishment, is that of offended pride, of
irritated self-love.   The prisoner, at the moment of conviction,
does not reflect on the justice of his punishment, but places himself in opposition to the rest of mankind, as an injured man, or, if
he be of a better nature, with the embittered feeling of an outcast.   In this state of mind he enters the prison.*   If uninter-

* It has been often observed, that the moment when a convict for the first
time enters the inner prison, when the door closes behind him, and his clothes
(those of honest men) are changed for the prison dress, is most impressive upon
him. Many show the state of mind into which shame, repentance, and horror
throw them, by abundant tears   Could but that precious moment be made use
of' In the old system the convict soon became ashamed of his shame This unfortunate effect is avoided by the Auburn system, but does not the mere sight
of a number of fellow convicts somewhat reconcile him to his unhappy situation'

rupted solitude awaits him, he will, if he is capable of reformation by any means but the devoted labours of personal friends (in which character, of course, the government cannot address him), become thoughtful. When he has reached this state, no new punishment awaits him; no new shame, no corrupting and degrading company; no new cause for considering himself an outcast, and fit associate for the worst. His solitary confinement hangs over him, indeed, as a severe dispensation, but does not daily renew the irritation of his pride. However much he may have been offended by his sentence, the prison in itself inflicts no further degradation. The keeper appears as a friend rather than a severe overseer. If he is disposed to reform, his weakness is not constantly put to the trial by offended shame, by the consideration that he is an outcast and associate of outcasts We have asked many prisoners, in permanent solitary confinement, whether they would prefer to be placed together with others; and they have almost invariably answered that they considered it as the greatest privilege to be left alone It ought not to be supposed that solitude bears so hard upon the mind of the prisoner, that he would exchange it for any other situation which would bring him into contact with other human beings. When the writer, after an imprisonment of eight months, was offered the company of another prisoner in his cell, confined also on political grounds, he refused the offer, though it was repeated at several different times. If the prisoner has made any step towards reformation, he always will wish to remain alone How different from this is the operation of the Auburn system! As soon as the convict leaves his cell, he sees and feels anew that he is degraded: he knows and is known by his fellow convicts; the keeper is (and necessarily must be) a severe, inexorable overseer. He is treated every day anew as an outcast from society; his pride is constantly offended; or, if he has no pride, no opportunity is afforded for the feeling of self-respect to spring up. We hardly see how the slow process of reformation can go on under these circumstances. Yet the most humane of all systems of prison discipline—that of Pennsylvania—has been called, and by an excellent man too (Mr. Roscoe), " the most inhuman and unnatural that the cruelty of a tyrant ever invented, no less derogatory to the character of human nature than it is in direct violation of the leading principles of Christianity." We have already shown why we believe that it is not only not " unnatural," but founded on the deepest principles of human nature; that, so far from being " inhuman," it is founded on the very principles of

Man is always more easily reconciled to any idea or situation in company than alone. But in the Pennsylvania penitentiary system, this moment, so precious, because if allowed to pass unheeded, irretrievably lost, retains its full power.

mercy, because it affords the fullest opportunity for reformation, and prevents all exposure to shame and contamination. And is it cruel? All agree, that contamination must be prevented at any price, or reformation entirely given up. The question, then, can only be a comparative one—What is the cruelty of this compared with the Auburn system? Perfect solitude, alleviated only by the permission to work, and to read the Bible, may be a hard situation; but is it more so than being placed in the company of many fellow-prisoners, with whom all intercourse is prevented by the threat of whipping? This must be torture indeed, like that of Tantalus, with the tempting viands constantly before him, and constantly receding from the approach of his famished lips.

Solitary confinement, as practised in the Eastern Prison of Pennsylvania, is rather a deprivation of most of the comforts of life, than the infliction of positive punishment. It is severe ; it ought to be so ; it ought to be feared. Is it cruel in a physical respect? Let us answer this question in the words of Mr. Vaux, page 7 of his Letter to Mr. Roscoe, who represents the cells to be "destined to contain an epitome and concentration of all human misery, of which the Bastile of France, and the Inquisition of Spain, were only prototypes and humble models." To which Mr. Vaux replies—"The rooms of the new penitentiary at Philadelphia are fire-proof, of comfortable dimensions, with convenient courts to each,* built on the surface of the ground, judiciously lighted from the roof, well ventilated and warmed, and ingeniously provided with means for affording a continual supply of excellent water, to ensure the most perfect cleanliness of every prisoner and his apartment. They are, moreover, so arranged as to be inspected and protected without a military guard, usually though unnecessarily employed in establishments of this kind in most other states. In these chambers, no individual, however humble or elevated, can be confined, so long as the public liberty shall endure, but upon conviction of a known and well-defined offence, by the verdict of a jury of the country, and under the sentence of a court, for a specified time. The terms of imprisonment, it is believed, can be apportioned to the nature of every crime with considerable accuracy, and will, no doubt, be measured in that merciful degree which has uniformly characterized the modern penal legislation of Pennsylvania. Where, then, allow me to inquire, is there, in this system, the least resemblance to that dreadful receptacle constructed in Paris during the reign of Charles V., and which, at different periods, through four centuries and a half, was an engine of oppression and torture

---

* The exact size of the chambers is 8 feet by 12 feet, the highest point of the ceiling 16 feet. The yards are 8 feet by 20 feet.

to thousands of *innocent* persons? Or by what detortion can it
be compared to the inquisitorial courts and prisons that were instituted in Italy, Portugal, and Spain, between the years 1251
and 1537 ?" Or is it believed that the influence of solitary confinement on the mind is cruel? that the human mind cannot bear
it, and must be driven to madness? We believe this by no means
to be the case. Mr. Vaux's testimony on this point is important.
Cases of insanity, he says, in the pamphlet just quoted, seem not
to be more frequent in jails than among the same number of
persons in the ordinary condition of life. The cells of the old
penitentiary are small and badly contrived, and yet many individuals have, for acts of violence committed in the prison, been
confined in them for six, nine, and twelve months in succession,
generally in irons, and always on a low diet; but no case of
mental alienation has ever occurred there. When the mind becomes hardened by a career of vice, ultimately reaching a point
of degradation which fits it for the perpetration of those crimes
that are punishable under the penal statutes, no fear of exciting
its tender sensibilities need be entertained, by its mere abstrac-
tion from equally guilty minds, so as to induce either melancholy
or madness All experience proves how difficult it is to make
any impression whatever upon the feelings of the benighted and
unhappy subjects of criminal punishment. As to the influence of
this system upon the health, we refer the reader to Dr Franklin
Bache's Letter to Mr. Vaux, contained in No. 8 of the Journal
of Law (Philadelphia, October, 1830), which concludes with the
words—" We may assert, that the entire seclusion of criminals
from all association with their fellow criminals, is altogether
compatible with their profitable employment at useful trades,
and with the preservation of their health." And in his Letter
to Bishop White and others, Mr Vaux adduces facts to confirm
this statement. Not one case of the Asiatic cholera appeared in
the Eastern Prison of Pennsylvania, whilst the disease swept
away numbers in the city of Philadelphia and its environs; and
the prison stands close by the city.* The report mentioned
above, will be, we understand, entirely satisfactory on the point
of the health of the prisoners The expense of the Pennsylvania
system has always been considered a great objection to it. It is
true that the Eastern Prison has cost much; but another prison
could be built much more cheaply; and, probably, experience
will show the possibility of further reductions, though this system may always be more expensive than the other. Yet the ad-

* The appalling Report of the Committee appointed to investigate the local
causes of cholera in the Arch Street Prison (Philadelphia), Mr. Gibbon Chairman, February, 1833, forms a striking contrast with the above statement.—See,
respecting the state of health of the prisoners in the Eastern Penitentiary, the
Inquiry into the Penitentiary of Philadelphia, No. 10.

vantages are so great; the final saving of the government, by preventing all the prisoners from leaving the prison worse than they were at the time of entering it, and by dismissing many who will return to duty and usefulness, is so decided, and the necessity of the system, if any of the desirable objects are to be obtained, so imperious, that we believe the greater expense ought not to be considered an objection wherever means exist to meet. it.* We shall quote Mr. Vaux also respecting this point It is certain that the prisoners do not leave the Pennsylvania penitentiary worse than they entered it, are not irritated and embittered against mankind, and, if they have truly resolved to become better, are not exposed to be driven by associates in the prison to the commission of new crimes, which has hitherto been so common an occurrence, as every one knows who has paid attention to the history of convicts. Men confined in common prisons, or even in those conducted on the Auburn system, find it extremely difficult, after their release, to disentangle themselves from the net of vice, though they may earnestly wish to do so. But the Pennsylvania system does not even allow the convict to know the names of his fellow prisoners. The wish to return to a life of honest industry is not so rare in released convicts as most persons suppose, provided the prisoner has not been kept in a state of constant contamination. A vicious life is not comfortable; generally, the causes which make a wicked person prefer the path of crime to an honourable life, are twofold— idleness, reluctance to regular labour, and the love of excitement. If you can overcome these two dispositions; if you can instil into the convict a love of labour, and make it a habit with him ; and if you can cure him of the craving for excitement, you will, in most cases, have laid the firmest foundation for a thorough reformation. Now, labour appears to the prisoner in solitary confinement as the sweetest comfort. He asks, he begs for it ; and no punishment could be harder than denying him the comfort of labour in his lonely cell They all will tell you so. And as regards the second point, what more effectual means can be found of curing a man of a vitiated love of excitement, (such as is found

* If the question of deciding between the Pennsylvania and Auburn systems is reduced to this point, it is, of course, a mere question of expediency. And this is, in our opinion, the only question which can exist respecting this subject. We know that it will be found, sometimes, impossible to induce a community to go to the expense necessary for erecting a prison on the Pennsylvania plan ; and if there is no hope for a change of public opinion for some time to come, it will be advisable to adopt the Auburn plan rather than no penitentiary plan at all. As to the absolute question, which of the systems is better, we have the opinion of Judge Wells of Wethersfield on our side, though, as we just admitted, he considers it impossible, in some cases, to gain public opinion for the first outlay of money for the erection of a penitentiary on the Pennsylvania plan But we have little doubt but that public opinion will gradually become more and more favourable to this plan.

in robbers, pirates, burglars, &c.) than uninterrupted confinement in solitude for years? It is a severe infliction, indeed, but it is effectual, and not more severe than is necessary. Another objection to perpetual solitude, is that the convicts cannot worship together; but in the Eastern Prison of Pennsylvania, they have preaching addressed to them. A curtain is drawn along the corridor, the sound-hole of each cell is opened, (see the description of the building in the Article *Prison Discipline,*) and the preacher stands at one end of the corridor, from which he may be heard by all the prisoners in that corridor, though no convict can see into the opposite cell, being prevented by the curtain.— In our opinion, the Pennsylvania penitentiary system is the creation of a spirit of enlightened humanity, which reflects the greatest honour on the disciples of Penn, and has solved one of the most difficult problems presented to the lover of mankind. If widely adopted, as it probably will be, it bids fair to accomplish all that can be attained in the way of prison discipline. We would direct our reader's attention to an interesting letter on the subject of solitary confinement, written by a convict, and appended to Mr. Vaux's letter, quoted above, and will conclude our remarks with a summary taken from Mr. Vaux's letter to Mr. Roscoe:—"By separate confinement, it is intended to punish those who will not control their wicked passions and propensities, and, moreover, to effect this punishment without terminating the life of the culprit in the midst of his wickedness, or making a mockery of justice, by forming such into communities of hardened and corrupting transgressors, who enjoy each other's society, and contemn the very power which thus vainly seeks their restoration, and idly calculates to afford security to the state, from their outrages in future. In separate confinement, every prisoner is placed beyond the possibility of being made more corrupt by his imprisonment. In separate confinement, the prisoners will not know who are undergoing punishment at the same time with themselves, and thus will be afforded one of the greatest protections to such as may happily be enabled to form resolutions to behave well when they are discharged. In separate confinement, it is especially intended to furnish the criminal with every opportunity which Christian duty enjoins, for promoting his restoration to the path of virtue; because seclusion is believed to be an essential ingredient in moral treatment, and, with religious instruction and advice superadded, is calculated to achieve more than has ever yet been done for the miserable tenants of our penitentiaries In separate confinement, a specific graduation of punishment can be obtained, as surely, and with as much facility, as by any other system. Some prisoners may labour, some may be kept without labour, some may have the privilege of books, others may be deprived of it; some may experience total seclusion, others may enjoy such intercourse as shall comport with an entire separation of prisoners. In separate confinement, the same variety of discipline, for offences committed after convicts are introduced into prison, which any other mode affords, can be obtained (though irregularities must necessarily be less frequent), by denying the refractory individual the benefit of his yard, by taking from him his books or labour, and lastly, in extreme cases, by diminishing his diet to the lowest rate. By the last means, the most fierce, hardened, and desperate offender, can be subdued. From separate confinement, other advantages, of an economical nature, will result · among these may be mentioned a great reduction of the terms of imprisonment, for, instead of from three to twenty *years,* and sometimes longer, as many *months,* excepting for very atrocious crimes, will answer all the ends of retributive justice, and penitential experience, which, on the actual plan, the greatest detention in prison altogether fails to accomplish. Besides this abatement of expense in maintaining prisoners, very few keepers will be required on the new system; and the females should be intrusted wholly to the custody of suitable individuals of their own sex, whose services can, of course, be secured for less compensation than those of men. Such of the prisoners as may be employed, will necessarily labour alone; and, the kinds of business in which they will be engaged, not being as rough and exposing as those now adopted, the expenditure for clothing must be much diminished. On the score of cost, therefore—if that indeed be an object in a work of this magnitude—the solitary plan recommends itself to the regard of the public economist. But the problem of expense, in my opinion, can only be truly solved by showing the cheapest method of keeping prisoners to be that which is most likely to reform them, to deter others, by the imposing character of the punishment, from preying upon the honest and unoffending members of society, afterwards involving heavy judicial costs to establish their guilt, and becoming, at last, a charge to the country as convicted felons."—So far the Article of the *Americana.*

Those prisoners who *wish* for books, (because their moral and intellectual faculties ought to be awakened and called forth as much as possible, as it is one of the best means to improve their inward condition,) ought to be provided with suitable works, which might be had for a very reasonable expense. Among these books ought to be, in our opinion, 1. Extracts of the Bible. We believe it to be advisable not to give the whole of the Scriptures at once to an individual who has never paid any attention either to the general character of the Bible, or the different nature of its component parts, and who cannot have, according to his situation, the constant and various explanations of those who have made the Bible a subject of attentive study. A vitiated mind, like that of a convict, would be liable to very great mis-understandings of some parts of it, and sometimes, even, would select those from which his uncultivated and corrupted soul would derive no profit. 2. A brief catechism of our duties as men and citizens, which would acquaint the prisoners with their obligations to society, as well as to their family and others The ignorance which the greater number of convicts show on all these points, is inconceivable for those who do not know it by experience. 3 A book on history, particularly of their own country, with an account of the organization of its society, to which they shall return, if possible, as useful citizens. 4. A col-lection of contemplations and prayers, peculiarly adapted to their situation.   There are but too many convicts who never have learned to appear before their Creator, and such a-work would assist in obtaining one great end of solitary confinement—that of producing reflection in the thoughtless criminal. These books might easily be adapted to the various moral and intellectual stages of the different prisoners. It ought always to be borne in mind, that the elements of knowledge are of the greatest im-portance to a prisoner.   They have acquired so universal an in-fluence in our society, that he who is deprived of them, stands in a very disadvantageous position to the rest of his fellow men —a position which will increase the difficulty of returning to the path of honesty. An individual who does not know how to read, is in our times very differently situated from what per-sons, equally untaught, were, a century ago.   Let us *un-bru-talize* the convict as much as it is in our power; we can return him to society with so much less fear.

In countries in which persons are sometimes imprisoned for offences, which, though declared by society or government to be such, are yet essentially different from those crimes which the code, written in every man's heart, acknowledges as grave offences, a different imprisonment ought to be applied to the for-mer from that inflicted on persons guilty of the latter description of crimes, if solitary confinement were introduced in such coun-tries, as in fact a difference is made even now in many cases. An individual confined for political offences is, in the more civilized monarchies of Europe, rarely exposed to all the rigours of imprisonment, which common criminals have to endure. Political offences are often of so delicate a nature, they become so often offences only because success favoured an opposite party, right and wrong is often in these cases so equally divided, that it would be in very many cases cruel indeed to inflict all the rigours of permanent solitary confinement, such as it is applied to the common criminal, upon political offenders Be-sides, the avowed objects of permanent solitary confinement are the prevention of contamination and the effecting of reflection in the thoughtless, and the acknowledgment of guilt before his own conscience. But many political offenders do not only not believe themselves guilty, but very often exult in what they have done. And have they not sometimes good reason to do so? It is thus, that La Fayette says, he never dreamed of revolutions more often than in the solitary prison at Olmutz This is undoubtedly true; but to conclude from this fact, that the thief, the defaulter, the robber, will also dream of theft, forgery and robbing in their solitary cells, would be a rash conclusion. These deeds are written down as crimes in every body's soul; and if you can bring the criminal to reflect on them, he will soon acknowledge their total immorality It is not so with the political offender. Whether right or wrong, he will, in many cases, reflect on them with pleasure. The great object of permanent solitary confinement, therefore, would be lost in these cases. Yet, it might be said, that even in these cases, it would be serviceable, inasmuch as it would more effectually deter men from their commission. But, if we allow this, we render that system of imprisonment, which recommends itself for its principles of humanity and its merciful disposition, a more cruel one than those already existing. Every advocate of permanent solitary confinement would be grieved to see this. We allow, that in no case whatever, can the mixture of prisoners be conducive to any good; but offenders, of the kind we have mentioned, might be allowed favours, to go out into the garden, to receive visiters, &c. which are and ought to be denied to common convicts. The best mode would always be, to confine them in entirely different places, such as forts, &c. where the commandant of the place might allow them all the favours compatible with safety, because the great object in confining political offenders is to make them harmless. We have not mentioned this case in the original article, because political offenders, strictly so called, are unknown to our laws. No proscription can exist. It will, therefore, be considered pardonable that such cases escaped our attention It is in respect to prison discipline, as in every thing else, one of the wisest rules:—guard against extremes, and do not allow the zeal with which you advocate certain means, to obscure the object sought to be obtained by them.

FINIS.

BRIDGEWATER TREATISES.

CAREY, LEA & BLANCHARD

HAVE PUBLISHED,

ASTRONOMY AND GENERAL PHYSICS, considered with reference to Natural Theology, by the Rev. WILLIAM WHEWELL, M. A , Fellow and Tutor of Trinity College, Cambridge; being the *Third Part* of the Bridgewater Treatises on the Power, Wisdom, and Goodness of God, as manifested in the Creation. In one vol. 12mo.

"It is a work of profound investigation, deep research, distinguished alike for the calm Christian spirit which breathes throughout, and the sound, irresistible argumentation which is stampt upon every page "—*Daily Intelligencer.*

" Let works like that before us be widely disseminated, and the bold, active, and ingenious enemies of religion be met by those, equally sagacious, alert and resolute, and the most timid of the many who depend upon the few, need not fear the host that comes with subtle steps to 'steal their faith away.' "—*N Y. American.*

" The present Treatise is written with great ability."—*Balt. Weekly Gazette.*

" That the devotional spirit of the work is most exemplary, that we have here and there found, or fancied, room for cavil, only peradventure because we have been unable to follow the author through the prodigious range of his philosophical survey—and in a word, that the work before us would have made the reputation of any other man, and may well maintain even that of Professor Whewell." —*Metropolitan.*

" He has succeeded admirably in laying a broad foundation, in the light of nature, for the reception of the more glorious truths of revelation, and has produced a work well calculated to dissipate the delusions of scepticism and infidelity, and to confirm the believer in his faith "—*Charleston Courier*

" The known talents, and high reputation of the author, gave an earnest of excellence, and nobly has Mr Whewell redeemed the pledge —In conclusion, we have no hesitation in saying, that the present is one of the best works of its kind, and admirably adapted to the end proposed ; as such, we cordially recommend it to our readers "—*London Lit Gazette.*

" It is a work of high character."—*Boston Recorder.*

A TREATISE ON THE ADAPTATION OF EXTERNAL NATURE TO THE PHYSICAL CONDITION OF MAN, principally with reference to the supply of his wants, and the exercise of his intellectual faculties. By JOHN KIDD, M. D. F. R. S., Regius Professor of Medicine in the University of Oxford, being Part II. of the Bridgewater Treatises on the Power, Wisdom, and Goodness of God, as manifested in the Creation. In one vol. 12mo.

" It is ably written, and replete both with interest and instruction The diffusion of such works cannot fail to be attended with the happiest effects in justifying ' the ways of God to man,' and illustrating the wisdom and goodness of the Creator by arguments which appeal irresistibly both to the reason and the feelings. Few can understand abstract reasoning, and still fewer relish it, or will listen to it. but in this work the purest morality and the kindliest feelings are inculcated through the medium of agreeable and useful information."—*Balt. Gaz.*

"Dr. Kidd has fulfilled his task, and may claim the gratitude of those who delight to contemplate the wisdom of Providence in the works of nature, and to discover the adaptation of the vegetable to the animal world, and the subserviency of the whole to the high destinies of man."—*U. S. Gazette.*

"The subject has been ably treated by a learned professor, and though it is not the most captivating topic in the world, has certainly served to display the ability of a sound thinker, who might rise, on other themes, to eloquence."— *Sat. Evening Post.*

"We congratulate Professor Kidd on the production of his work, and repeat the commendation, to which, as a popular treatise, it is indisputably entitled."— *Christian Remembrancer.*

A TREATISE ON THE POWER, WISDOM, AND GOODNESS OF GOD, as manifested in the adaptation of External Nature to the Moral and Intellectual Constitution of Man. —By the Rev. THOMAS CHALMERS, D.D., Professor of Divinity in the University of Edinburgh; being the First Part of the Bridgewater Treatises.—In 1 vol. 12mo.

The remaining parts will be published as fast as received.

The series of Treatises, of which those published form a part, are published under the following circumstances :—

The Right Honourable and Rev. FRANCIS HENRY, Earl of Bridgewater, died in the month of February, 1825; he directed certain trustees named, to invest in the public funds the sum of eight thousand pounds sterling ; this sum, with the accruing dividends thereon, to be held at the disposal of the President, for the time being, of the Royal Society of London, to be paid to the person or persons nominated by him. The Testator further directed, that the person or persons selected by the said President, should be appointed to write, print, and publish, one thousand copies of a work, on the Power, Wisdom, and Goodness of God, as manifested in the Creation ; illustrating such work by all reasonable arguments, as, for instance, the variety and formation of God's creatures in the Animal, Vegetable, and Mineral Kingdoms ; the effect of digestion, and, thereby, of conversion ; the construction of the hand of man, and an infinite variety of other arguments ; as also by discoveries, ancient and modern, in arts, sciences, and the whole extent of literature.

The late President of the Royal Society, DAVIES GILBERT, Esq., requested the assistance of his Grace, the Archbishop of Canterbury, and of the Bishop of London, in determining upon the best mode of carrying into effect the intentions of the Testator. Acting with their advice, and with the concurrence of a nobleman immediately connected with the deceased, Mr. Davies Gilbert appointed the following eight gentlemen to write separate Treatises on the different branches of the subjects here stated :—

I. The Adaptation of External Nature to the Moral and Intellectual Constitution of Man, by the Rev. THOMAS CHALMERS, D.D., Professor of Divinity in the University of Edinburgh.

II. The Adaptation of External Nature to the Physical Condition of Man, by JOHN KIDD, M.D., F.R.S., Regius Professor of Medicine in the University of Oxford.

III. Astronomy and General Physics, considered with reference to Natural Theology, by the Rev. WILLIAM WHEWELL, M.A., F.R.S., Fellow of Trinity College, Cambridge.

IV. The Hand: its Mechanism and Vital Endowments as evincing Design, by Sir CHARLES BELL, K.H., F.R.S.

V. Animal and Vegetable Physiology, by PETER MARK ROGET, M.D., Fellow of and Secretary to the Royal Society.

VI. Geology and Mineralogy, by the Rev. WILLIAM BUCKLAND, D.D., F.R.S., Canon of Christ Church, and Professor of Geology in the University of Oxford.

VII. The History, Habits, and Instincts of Animals, by the Rev. WILLIAM KIRBY, M.A., F.R.S.

VIII. Chemistry, Meteorology, and the Function of Digestion, by WILLIAM PROUT, M.D., F.R.S.

JUST PUBLISHED BY CAREY, LEA, & BLANCHARD.

CHARACTERISTICS OF WOMEN. By Mrs. JAMIESON, Author of the Diary of an Ennuyée. In 2 vols.

"Nothing can be finer than the tact with which Mrs. Jamieson enters into the infinite varieties of feminine character,—nothing more delicate than the discrimination with which she marks the boundaries of feeling; and there is a lofty purity, a generous warmth, which pervades the whole work, and gives a singular truthlike life to its delineations."—*Lit. Gazette.*

"Few books have ever come under our notice better deserving the strongest recommendation it is in our power to bestow, than the work of Mrs. Jamieson. Her talents are not only of the highest, but also of the rarest order—of such order, indeed, as it is the lot of few women to possess. Her work, taken altogether, is one of the most delightful of modern times."—*N. Monthly Mag.*

LEGENDS OF THE LIBRARY AT LILIES, By the Lord and Lady there. In 2 vols, 12mo.

"Two delightful volumes, various, graceful, with the pathos exquisitely relieved by gaiety; and the romantic legend well contrasted by the lively sketch from actual existence."—*Literary Gazette.*

NEW GIL BLAS, or Pedro of Penaflor. By R. D. Inglis, Author of Spain in 1830, &c.

"The whole work is very amusing."—*Lit. Gaz.*
"Those who want a few hours' pleasant reading are not likely to meet with a book more to their taste."—*Athenæum.*

THE BUCCANEER. By Mrs. S. C. HALL. In 2 vols.

"The perusal of these volumes warrants our preconceived impressions of the ample capacities of Mrs. Hall to sustain the bolder flight she has undertaken."—*United Service Journal.*

"The work now before us belongs to the historical school; but it has that talent which bestows its own attraction on whatever subject its peculiar taste may select. We sincerely congratulate Mrs. Hall on the interest and the talent displayed in the Buccaneer."—*Lit. Gazette.*

SWALLOW BARN, or, A SOJOURN IN THE OLD DOMINION. In 2 vols. 12mo.

"We cannot but predict a warm reception of this work among all persons who have not lost their relish for nature and probability, as well as all those who can properly estimate the beauties of simplicity in thought and expression."—*New York Mirror.*

"One of the cleverest of the last publications written on this or the other side of the Atlantic."—*New York Courier and Inquirer.*

"The style is admirable, and the sketches of character, men, and scenery, so fresh and agreeable, that we cannot help feeling that they are drawn from nature."

IVAN VEJEEGHEN, or LIFE IN RUSSIA. By Thaddeus Bulgarin. 2 vols. 12mo.

"This is a genuine Russian novel, and a tale, which, with the interest of a fictitious story, presents many details of a state of society of which nothing can be learned from books of travels. It is in every respect equal to Hope's Anastasius, and well deserves to equal that renowned romance in popularity; it has all the novelty and the ability."—*Monthly Magazine.*

THE ALHAMBRA; a series of Tales and Sketches of the Moors and Spaniards. By the Author of the Sketch-Book, &c. 2 vols. 12mo.

"Mr. Irving has fairly trusted himself 'to the golden shores of old romance,' and yielded to all their influences. He has carried us into a world of marble fountains, moonlight, arabesques, and perfumes. We do not know whether reform and retrenchment have left any imagination in the world, but this we know, that if there be any fantasies yet slumbering deep within the souls, the tales of the Alhambra must awaken them."—*London Literary Gazette.*

THE HEIDENMAUER; or, THE BENEDICTINES. By the Author of the Spy, Pilot, Red Rover, &c. 2 vols. 12mo. bds.

"We cannot but remark on the versatility of Mr. Cooper's genius, which imparts equal life to the wild Indian, the weatherbeaten sailor, the picturesque pirate, the romantic and mysterious tyranny of Venice, and the bold feudal spirit of the middle ages. In this very work, Heinrich, the burgomaster, is a complete Flemish picture."—*Literary Gazette.*

FRANKENSTEIN; or, THE MODERN PROMETHEUS. By MARY W. SHELLEY, Author of the Last Man, Perkin Warbeck, &c. 2 vols.

"Vigorous, terrible, and with its interest sustained to the last, Frankenstein is certainly one of the most original works that ever proceeded from a female pen."—*Literary Gazette.*

THE RECTORY OF VALEHEAD. By the Rev. ROBERT WILSON EVANS, M. A.

"Universally and cordially do we recommend this delightful volume. Impressed with the genuine spirit of Christianity; a diary, as it were, of the feelings, hopes, and sorrows of a family,—it comes home to all, either in sympathy or example. It is a beautiful picture of a religious household, influencing to excellence all within its sphere. We believe no person could read this work, and not be the better for its pious and touching lessons."—*Literary Gazette.*

"We fearlessly pronounce this delightful little volume to be not only one of the most faultless, but every way valuable works it has ever fallen to our lot to recommend to public perusal."—*Stamford Herald.*

"The Rectory of Valehead is a beautiful model of domestic life in the Christian home of a well-regulated family, and combines literary amusement with the most refined and intellectual improvement."—*Scotsman.*

"The domestic worship, duties, comforts, joys, and sorrows of a truly Christian pastor and his flock, are portrayed in so effective a manner as to raise, almost unconsciously, an inward aspiration after similar holiness, similar blessedness, and similar consolation under affliction..... Be the reader who he may, he will scarcely rise from the perusal of the 'Rectory of Valehead,' without having his heart touched, his devotion excited, and his moral feeling elevated."—*Christian Remembrancer.*

"The Rectory of Valehead may be briefly characterized as a truly pious work, without the slightest taint of bigotry or sectarianism: a work conceived in the gentlest spirit of benevolence, and from which the Christian reader, to whatever denomination he may belong, cannot fail to derive much advantage."—*La Belle Assemblee.*

MISS AUSTEN.

ELIZABETH BENNET; or, PRIDE AND PREJUDICE. In 2 vols. 12mo. By Miss AUSTEN.

"One of the first female novelists."—*Sir Walter Scott.*
"The most correct of female writers, Miss Austen."—*Miss Mitford, in Our Village.*

"Her fables appear to us, in their own way, nearly faultless. * * * She conducts her conversations with a regard to character hardly exceeded by Shakspeare himself. Like him, she shows as admirable a discrimination in the character of fools, as of people of sense: a merit which is far from common. * * * Those who delight in the study of human nature, may improve in the knowledge of it, and in the profitable application of that knowledge, by the perusal of such fictions as those before us."—*Quarterly Review.*

PERSUASION, a Novel. By the same Author. In 2 vols.

"It is one of the most elegant fictions of common life we ever remember to have met with."—*Quarterly Rev.*

MANSFIELD PARK. By the same Author.

"Mansfield Park contains some of Miss Austen's moral lessons, as well as her most humorous descriptions."—*Quarterly Review.*

By the same Author—
NORTHANGER ABBEY, 2 vols.
EMMA, 2 vols.
SENSE AND SENSIBILITY, 2 vols.

MISCELLANEOUS.

TOUR OF A GERMAN PRINCE, (PUCKLER MUSKAU,) through the Southern and Western parts of England, Wales, Ireland, and France. In 8vo.

" It contains the least prejudiced and most acute notices we have read of the habits and modes of thinking of Englishmen, and the merits and defects of the country and society."—*Globe.*

CONVERSATIONS WITH LORD BYRON ON THE SUBJECT OF RELIGION. By KENNEDY. 12mo.

GLEANINGS IN NATURAL HISTORY, with Local Recollections. By EDWARD JESSE, Esq. To which are added, Maxims and Hints for Anglers. From the second London edition.

" A work that will be fondly treasured by every true lover of nature."—*New Monthly Mag.*
" We hazard but little in predicting that this volume will be a favorite with a large class of readers. It is written by a true lover of nature, and one who most pleasantly records his actual observations."—*Lit. Gaz.*

A MEMOIR OF FELIX NEFF, Pastor of the High Alps, and of his Labors among the French Protestants of Dauphiné, a remnant of the Primitive Christians of Gaul. By WILLIAM STEPHEN GILLY, M. A. 18mo.

" It is a history which no Christian can read without profit—it depicts scenes of discouragement and severe trial, surmounted by an ardent devotion to the cause of religion; and presents a plain unvarnished narrative of the life of an humble but good man, whose Christian labors may be safely and profitably imitated."—*Ev. Post.*

THE ECONOMY OF MACHINERY AND MANUFACTURES. By CHARLES BABBAGE. 18mo.

" Of the many publications which have recently issued from the press, calculated to give a popular and attractive form to the results of science, we look upon this volume as by far the most valuable. Mr. Babbage's name is well known in connexion with the general subject of which he has here undertaken to treat. But it will be difficult for the reader who does not possess the volume itself, to understand the happy style, the judgment and tact, by means of which the author has contrived to lend almost the charm of romance to the apparently dry and technical theme which he has chosen."—*Monthly Rev.*

OUSELEY'S REMARKS ON THE STATISTICS AND POLITICAL INSTITUTIONS OF THE UNITED STATES.

" The author is a man of solid sense, friendly to this country, and his remarks have the value and interest of which his character and inquiries authorized the expectation."—*National Gazette.*

TWO YEARS AND A HALF IN THE NAVY, or, JOURNAL OF A CRUISE IN THE MEDITERRANEAN AND LEVANT, ON BOARD THE U. S. FRIGATE CONSTELLATION, IN THE YEARS 1829, 1830, and 1831. By E. C. WINES. In 2 vols. 12mo.

" The author is a gentleman of classical education, a shrewd observer, a lively writer, whose natural manner is always agreeable; whose various matter is generally entertaining and instructive; and whose descriptions are remarkably graphic. The greater portion of his pages have yielded us both profit and pleasure."—*Nat. Gaz.*

THE NATURAL HISTORY OF SELBORNE. By the late Rev. Gilbert White, A. M., Fellow of the Oriel College, with additions, by Sir William Jardine, Bart., F. R. S. E. F. L. S. M. W. S., Author of " Illustrations of Ornithology." 1 vol. 18mo.

" White's History of Selborne, the most fascinating piece of rural writing and sound English philosophy that

LADY'S MEDICAL GUIDE. By RICHARD REESE, M. D. 18mo.

MILITARY MEMOIRS OF THE DUKE OF WELLINGTON. By CAPT. MOYLE SHERER, Author of Recollections of the Peninsula. In 2 vols. 18mo.

" The tone of feeling and reflection which pervades the work is in the characteristic mood of the writer, considerate, ardent, and chivalrous; his principles, as might be expected, are sound and independent, and his language is frequently rich in those beauties which distinguish his previous writings. To us it appears a work which will not discredit its illustrious subject."—*United Service Journal.*

AN HISTORICAL INQUIRY INTO THE PRODUCTION AND CONSUMPTION OF THE PRECIOUS METALS, from the Earliest Ages, and into the Influence of their Increase or Diminution on the Prices of Commodities. By WILLIAM JACOB, Esq. F. R. S. In 8vo.

" Mr. Jacob's Historical Inquiry into the Production and Consumption of the Precious Metals, is one of the most curious and important works which has lately issued from the press."—*Spectator.*
" It was written at the suggestion of the late Mr. Huskisson, and displays the fruits of much industry and research, guided by a sound judgment, and embodying more learning than is usually brought to bear on statistical or economical subjects. We recommend the book to general attention."—*Times, Sept. 2, 1831.*

NARRATIVE OF A VOYAGE TO THE PACIFIC AND BEHRING'S STRAIT, to co-operate with the Polar Expeditions: performed in his Majesty's ship Blossom, under the command of Capt. F. W. Beechey, R. N., in the years 1825, 26, 27, 28. 8vo.

" The most interesting of the whole series of expeditions to the North Pole."—*Quarterly Review.*
" This expedition will be for ever memorable as one which has added immensely to our knowledge of this earth that we inhabit."—*Blackwood's Mag.*
" Captain Beechey's work is a lasting monument of his own abilities, and an honor to his country."—*Lit. Gaz.*

A GENERAL VIEW OF THE PROGRESS OF ETHICAL PHILOSOPHY, chiefly during the Seventeenth and Eighteenth Centuries. By SIR JAMES MACKINTOSH, M. P. In 8vo.

" The best offspring of the pen of an author who in philosophical spirit, knowledge and reflection, richness of moral sentiment, and elegance of style, has altogether no superior—perhaps no equal—among his contemporaries. Some time ago we made copious extracts from the beautiful work. We could not recommend the whole too earnestly."—*National Gazette.*

HISTORY OF ENGLAND, by SIR JAMES MACKINTOSH. Octavo edition. In the press.

*** The first volume of this edition will contain the same matter as the first three volumes of the 18mo. edition.

A COLLECTION OF COLLOQUIAL PHRASES, on every subject necessary to maintain Conversation, the whole so disposed as considerably to facilitate the acquisition of the Italian language. By an Italian Gentleman. 1 vol. 18mo.

NOVELLE ITALIANE.—Stories from Italian Writers, with a literal, interlinear translation on Locke's plan of Classical Instruction, illustrated with Notes. First American from the last London edition, with additional translations and notes.

CABINET CYCLOPÆDIA,

CONDUCTED BY THE

REV. DIONYSIUS LARDNER, LL. D. F. R. S. L. & E.

M. R. I. A. F. L. S. F. Z. S. Eon. F. C. P. S. M. Ast. S. &c. &c.

ASSISTED BY

EMINENT LITERARY AND SCIENTIFIC MEN.

Now publishing by Carey, Lea, & Blanchard, and for sale by all Booksellers.

This work will form a popular compendium of whatever is useful, instructive, and interesting, in the circle of human knowledge. A novel plan of publication and arrangement has been adopted, which presents peculiar advantages. Without fully detailing the method, a few of these advantages may be mentioned.

Each volume will contain one or more subjects uninterrupted and unbroken, and will be accompanied by the corresponding plates or other appropriate illustrations. Facility of reference will be obtained without fettering the work by a continued alphabetical arrangement. A subscriber may omit particular volumes or sets of volumes, without disintegrating his series. Thus each purchaser may form from the "CABINET" a Cyclopædin, more or less comprehensive, as may suit his means, taste, or profession. If a subscriber desire to discontinue the work at any stage of its publication, the volumes which he may have received will not lose their value by separation from the rest of the work, since they will always either be complete in themselves, or may be made so at a trifling expense.

The purchasers will never find their property in this work destroyed by the publication of a second edition. The arrangement is such that particular volumes may be re-edited or re-written without disturbing the others. The "CABINET CYCLOPÆDIA" will thus be in a state of continual renovation, keeping pace with the never-ceasing improvements in knowledge, drawing within its circle from year to year whatever is new, and casting off whatever is obsolete, so as to form a constantly modernized Cyclopædia. Such are a few of the advantages which the proprietors have to offer to the public, and which they pledge themselves to realize.

Treatises on subjects which are technical and professional will be adapted, not so much to those who desire to attain a practical proficiency, as to those who seek that portion of information respecting such matters which is generally expected from well-educated persons. An interest will be imparted to what is abstract by copious illustrations, and the sciences will be rendered attractive, by treating them with reference to the most familiar objects and occurrences.

The unwieldly bulk of Encyclopædias, not less than the abstruse discussions which they contain, has hitherto consigned them to the library, as works of only occasional reference. The present work, from its portable form and popular style, will claim a place in the drawing-room and the boudoir. Forming in itself a *Complete library*, affording an extensive and infinitely varied store of instruction and amusement, presenting just so much on every subject as those not professionally engaged in it require, convenient in size, attractive in form, elegant in illustrations, and most moderate in expense, the "CABINET CYCLOPÆDIA" will, it is hoped, be found an object of paramount interest in every family.

To the heads of schools and all places of public education the proprietors trust that this work will particularly recommend itself.

It seems scarcely necessary to add, that nothing will be admitted into the pages of the "CABINET CYCLOPÆDIA" which can have the most remote tendency to offend public or private morals. To enforce the cultivation of religion and the practice of virtue should be a principal object with all who undertake to inform the public mind; but with the views just explained, the conductor of this work feels these considerations more especially pressed upon his attention. Parents and guardians may, therefore, rest assured that they will never find it necessary to place a volume of the "CABINET" beyond the reach of their children or pupils.

CONSIDERABLE progress having been made in this work, the publishers wish to direct the attention of the public to the advantages by which it is distinguished from other similar monthly publications.

It is not intended that the Cabinet Cyclopædia shall form an interminable series, in which any work of

interest which may present itself from time to time can claim a place. Its subjects are classified according to the usual divisions of literature, science, and art. Each division is distinctly traced out, and will consist of a determinate number of volumes. Although the precise extent of the work cannot be fixed with certainty, yet there is a limit which will not be exceeded; and the subscribers may look forward to the possession, within a reasonable time, of a complete library of instruction, amusement, and general reference, in the regular form of a popular Cyclopædia.

The several classes of the work are—1, NATURAL PHILOSOPHY; 2, The USEFUL and FINE ARTS; 3, NATURAL HISTORY; 4, GEOGRAPHY; 5, POLITICS and MORALS; 6, GENERAL LITERATURE and CRITICISM; 7, HISTORY; 8, BIOGRAPHY.

In the above abstruse and technical departments of knowledge, an attempt has been made to convey to the reader a general acquaintance with these subjects, by the use of plain and familiar language, appropriate and well-executed engravings, and copious examples and illustrations, taken from objects and events with which every one is acquainted.

The proprietors formerly pledged themselves that no exertion should be spared to obtain the support of the most distinguished talent of the age. They trust that they have redeemed that pledge. Among the volumes already published in the literary department, no less than four have been the production of men who stand in the first rank of literary talent,—Sir James Mackintosh and Sir Walter Scott. In the scientific department, a work has been produced from the pen of Mr. Herschel, which has been pronounced by the highest living authority on subjects of general philosophy, to contain "the noblest observations on the value of knowledge which have been made since Bacon," and to be "the finest work of philosophical genius which this age has seen."

The following is a selection from the list of Contributors.

The Right Honorable Sir JAMES MACKINTOSH, M. P.
The Right Rev. The Lord Bishop of Cloyne.
Sir WALTER SCOTT, Bart.
JOHN FREDERICK WILLIAM HERSCHEL, Esq.
THOMAS MOORE, Esq.
J. B. BIOT, Member of the French Institute.
ROBERT SOUTHEY, Esq. Poet Laureate.
The Baron CHARLES DUPIN, Member of the Royal Institute and Chamber of Deputies.
THOMAS CAMPBELL, Esq.
T. B. MACAULEY, Esq. M. P.
DAVID BREWSTER, LL. D.
J. C. L. SISMONDI, of Geneva.
Capt. HENRY KATER, Vice President of the Royal Society.
The ASTRONOMER ROYAL.
DAVIES GILBERT, Esq. M. P.
S. T. COLERIDGE, Esq.
JAMES MONTGOMERY, Esq.
The Right Hon. T. P. COURTENAY, M. P.
J. J. BERZELIUS, of Stockholm, F. R. S., &c.
The Rev. G. R. GLEIG.
T. PHILLIPS, Esq. Prof. of Painting, R. A.
Rev. C. THIRLWALL, Fellow of Trinity College, Cambridge.
ANDREW URE, M. D. F. R. S. &c. &c. &c.

DR. LARDNER'S
CABINET CYCLOPÆDIA.

VOLUMES PUBLISHED.

Volumes in immediate preparation.

"BOOKS THAT YOU MAY CARRY TO THE FIRE, AND HOLD READILY IN YOUR HAND, ARE THE MOST USEFUL AFTER ALL. A MAN WILL OFTEN LOOK AT THEM, AND BE TEMPTED TO GO ON, WHEN HE WOULD HAVE BEEN FRIGHTENED AT BOOKS OF A LARGER SIZE, AND OF A MORE ERUDITE APPEARANCE."—*Dr. Johnson.*

"We advisedly call the Cabinet Cyclopædia a great undertaking, because we consider, that in its effects on the tone and habits of thought of what is known by the phrase, 'the reading public,' it will be, if carried through in the spirit of its projection and commencement, one of the most invaluable productions of modern literature. * * "But these advantages, eminent as they undoubtedly are, are not the sole nor the chief recommendations of the Cabinet Cyclopædia. Neither is it on the extreme cheapness of the publication, nor the federal independence —if we may so speak—of its several volumes, that we rest our prediction of its influence on the tone of thinking of the present, and on the literature of the next generation—but on the promise, amounting almost to a moral certainty, of the great excellence of its execution. A multitude of persons eminent in literature and science in the United Kingdom are employed in this undertaking; and, indeed, no others should be employed in it; for it is a truth that the profound and practised writer alone is capable of furnishing a 'popular compendium.'

"What parent or guardian that throws his eye over the list of its contributors but must be rejoiced by meeting the names of those who are in themselves a guarantee of intellectual and moral excellence?"—*Literary Gazette.*

"The plan of the work appears well adapted to the purpose it is proposed to fulfil—that of supplying a series of publications, embracing the whole range of literature and science, in a popular and portable form; while the excellence of the execution is guarantied by the judgment displayed in the selection of writers. The list of authors employed in this ambitious undertaking comprises some of the most eminent men of the present age."—*Atlas.*

"The Cyclopædia, when complete, will form a valuable work of reference, as well as a most entertaining and instructive library. It is an essential principle in every part of it, that it should be clear and easily understood, and that an attempt should everywhere be made to unite accurate information with an agreeable manner of conveying it. It is an experiment to try how much science may be taught with little crabbed or technical language, and how far the philosophical and poetical qualities of history may be preserved in its more condensed state. It possesses also the most indispensable of all the qualities of a work intended for general instruction—that of cheapness. Whatever the plan might be, it was evident that the grand difficulty of Dr. Lardner was to unite a body of writers in its execution, whose character or works afforded the most probable hope that they were fitted for a task of which the peculiarity, the novelty, and even the prevalent relish for such writings greatly enhance the difficulty. We do not believe, that in the list of contributors, there is one name of which the enlightened part of the public would desire the exclusion.

"In science, the list is not less promising. The names of the President, Vice-Presidents, and most distinguished Fellows of the Royal Society, are contained in it. A treatise on astronomy, by Herschel; on optics, by Brewster; and on mechanics, by Lardner; need be only recommended by the subjects and the writers. An eminent Prelate. of the first rank in science, has undertaken a noble subject which happily combines philosophy with religion. Twelve of the most distinguished naturalists of the age, Fellows of the Linnæan and Zoological Societies, are preparing a course of natural history. Others not less eminent in literature and science, whose names it is not needful yet to mention, have shown symptoms of an ambition to take a place among such fellow-laborers."—*Times.*

"The topics, as may be supposed, are both judiciously selected and treated with ability. To general readers, and as part of a family library, the volumes already published possess great recommendations. For the external beauties of good printing and paper they merit equal commendation."—*Balt. American.*

"The uniform neatness of these volumes, their very moderate price, and the quantity of information which they contain, drawn from the best and most attractive sources, have given them deserved celebrity, and no one who desires to possess such information, should hesitate a moment to add them to his library."—*Fed. Gazette.*

"This excellent work continues to increase in public favor, and to receive fresh accessions of force to its corps

LARDNER'S
CABINET CYCLOPÆDIA.

"IT IS NOT EASY TO DEVISE A CURE FOR SUCH A STATE OF THINGS (THE DECLINING TASTE FOR SCIENCE;) BUT THE MOST OBVIOUS REMEDY IS TO PROVIDE THE EDU-CATED CLASSES WITH A SERIES OF WORKS ON POPULAR AND PRACTICAL SCIENCE, FREED FROM MATHEMATICAL SYMBOLS AND TECHNICAL TERMS, WRITTEN IN SIMPLE AND PERSPICUOUS LANGUAGE, AND ILLUSTRATED BY FACTS AND EXPERIMENTS, WHICH ARE LEVEL TO THE CAPACITY OF ORDINARY MINDS."—*Quarterly Review.*

PRELIMINARY DISCOURSE ON THE OB-JECTS, ADVANTAGES, AND PLEAS-URES OF THE STUDY OF NATURAL PHILOSOPHY. By J. T. W. Herschel, A. M. late Fellow of St. John's College, Cambridge.

"Without disparaging any other of the many interest-ing and instructive volumes issued in the form of cabinet and family libraries, it is, perhaps, not too much to place at the head of the list, for extent and variety of condensed information, Mr. Herschel's discourse of Natural Philoso-phy in Dr. Lardner's Cyclopædia."—*Christian Observer.*

"The finest work of philosophical genius which this age has seen."—*Mackintosh's England.*

"By far the most delightful book to which the existing competition between literary rivals of great talent and enterprise has given rise."—*Monthly Review.*

"Mr. Herschel's delightful volume. * * * We find scattered through the work instances of vivid and happy illustration, where the fancy is usefully called into action, so as sometimes to remind us of the splendid pictures which crowd upon us in the style of Bacon."—*Quarterly Review.*

"It is the most exciting volume of the kind we ever met with."—*Monthly Magazine.*

"One of the most instructive and delightful books we have ever perused."—*U. S. Journal.*

A TREATISE ON MECHANICS. By Capt. Kater, and the Rev. Dionysius Lardner. With numerous engravings.

"A work which contains an uncommon amount of useful information, exhibited in a plain and very intelli-gible form."—*Olmsted's Nat. Philosophy.*

"This volume has been lately published in England, as a part of Dr. Lardner's Cabinet Cyclopædia, and has re-ceived the unsolicited approbation of the most eminent men of science, and the most discriminating journals and reviews, in the British metropolis.—It is written in a popular and intelligible style, entirely free from mathe-matical symbols, and disencumbered as far as possible of technical phrases."—*Boston Traveller.*

"Admirable in development and clear in principles, and especially felicitous in illustration from familiar sub-jects."—*Monthly Mag.*

"Though replete with philosophical information of the highest order in mechanics, adapted to ordinary capaci-ties in a way to render it at once intelligible and popu-lar."—*Lit. Gazette.*

"A work of great merit, full of valuable information, not only to the practical mechanic, but to the man of sci-ence."—*N. Y. Courier and Enquirer.*

A TREATISE ON HYDROSTATICS AND PNEUMATICS. By the Rev. D. Lardner. With numerous engravings.

"It fully sustains the favorable opinion we have already expressed as to this valuable compendium of modern sci-ence."—*Lit. Gazette.*

"Dr. Lardner has made a good use of his acquaintance with the familiar facts which illustrate the principles of science."—*Monthly Magazine.*

"It is written with a full knowledge of the subject,

LARDNER'S
CABINET CYCLOPÆDIA.

HISTORY OF THE RISE, PROGRESS, AND PRESENT STATE OF THE SILK MANUFACTURE; with numerous En-gravings.

"It contains abundant information in every depart-ment of this interesting branch of human industry—in the history, culture, and manufacture of silk."—*Monthly Magazine.*

"There is a great deal of curious information in this little volume."—*Literary Gazette.*

HISTORY OF THE ITALIAN REPUBLICS; being a View of the Rise, Progress, and Fall of Italian Freedom. By J. C. L. DE SISMONDI.

"The excellencies, defects, and fortunes of the gov-ernments of the Italian commonwealths, form a body of the most valuable materials for political philosophy. It is time that they should be accessible to the American people, as they are about to be rendered in Sismondi's masterly abridgment. He has done for his large work, what Irving accomplished so well for his Life of Colum-bus."—*National Gazette.*

HISTORY OF THE RISE, PROGRESS, AND PRESENT STATE OF THE MANUFAC-TURES OF PORCELAIN AND GLASS. With numerous Wood Cuts.

"In the design and execution of the work, the author has displayed considerable judgment and skill, and has so disposed of his valuable materials as to render the book attractive and instructive to the general class of readers."—*Sat. Ev. Post.*

"The author has, by a popular treatment, made it one of the most interesting books that has been issued of this series. There are, we believe, few of the useful arts less generally understood than those of porcelain and glass making. These are completely illustrated by Dr. Lardner, and the various processes of forming differ-ently fashioned utensils, are fully described."

HISTORY OF THE RISE, PROGRESS, AND PRESENT STATE OF THE IRON AND STEEL MANUFACTURE. (In press.)

"This volume appears to contain all useful informa-tion on the subject of which it treats."—*Lit. Gazette.*

THE HISTORY OF SPAIN AND PORTU-GAL. In 5 vols.

"A general History of the Spanish and Portuguese Peninsula, is a great desideratum in our language, and we are glad to see it begun under such favorable aus-pices. We have seldom met with a narrative which fixes attention more steadily, and bears the reader's mind along more pleasantly."

"In the volumes before us, there is unquestionable evidence of capacity for the task, and research in the execution."—*U. S. Journal.*

HISTORY OF SWITZERLAND.

"Like the preceding historical numbers of this valu-able publication, it abounds with interesting details, illustrative of the habits, character, and political com-plexion of the people and country it describes; and af-

TRAVELS, ANNUALS, &c.

NOTES on ITALY, during the years 1829-30. By REMBRANDT PEALE. In 1 vol. 8vo.

"This artist will gratify all reasonable expectation; he is neither ostentatious, nor dogmatical, nor too minute; he is not a partisan nor a carper; he admires without servility, he criticises without malevolence; his frankness and good humor give an agreeable color and effect to all his decisions, and the object of them; his book leaves a useful general idea of the names, works, and deserts, of the great masters; it is an instructive and entertaining index."—*Nat. Gaz.*

"We have made a copious extract in preceding columns from this interesting work of our countryman, Rembrandt Peale, recently published. It has received high commendation from respectable sources, which is justified by the portions we have seen extracted."—*Commercial Advertiser.*

"Mr. Peale must be allowed the credit of candor and entire freedom from affectation in the judgments he has passed. At the same time, we should not omit to notice the variety, extent, and minuteness of his examinations. No church, gallery, or collection, was passed by, and most of the individual pictures are separately and carefully noticed."—*Am. Quarterly Review.*

FRAGMENTS OF VOYAGES AND TRAVELS, INCLUDING ANECDOTES OF NAVAL LIFE; intended chiefly for the Use of Young Persons. By BASIL HALL, Capt. R. N. In 2 vols. royal 18mo.

"His volumes consist of a *melange* of autobiography, naval anecdotes, and sketches of a somewhat discursive nature, which we have felt much pleasure in perusing."

"The title page to these volumes indicates their being chiefly intended for young persons, but we are much mistaken if the race of gray-beards will be among the least numerous of the readers of 'midshipmen's pranks and the humors of the green room.'"—*Lit. Gazette.*

A TOUR IN AMERICA. By BASIL HALL, Capt. R. N. In 2 vols. 12mo.

SKETCHES OF CHINA, with Illustrations from Original Drawings. By W. W. WOOD. In 1 vol. 12mo.

"The residence of the author in China, during the years 1826-7-8 and 9, has enabled him to collect much very curious information relative to this singular people, which he has embodied in his work; and will serve to gratify the curiosity of many whose time or dispositions do not allow them to seek, in the voluminous writings of the Jesuits and early travellers, the information contained in the present work. The recent discussion relative to the renewal of the East India Company's Charter, has excited much interest; and among ourselves, the desire to be further acquainted with the subjects of 'the Celestial Empire,' has been considerably augmented."

EXPEDITION TO THE SOURCES OF THE MISSISSIPPI, Executed by order of the Government of the United States. By MAJOR S. H. LONG. In 2 vols. 8vo. With Plates.

HISTORICAL, CHRONOLOGICAL, GEOGRAPHICAL, AND STATISTICAL ATLAS OF NORTH AND SOUTH AMERICA, AND THE WEST INDIES, with all their Divisions into States, Kingdoms, &c. on the Plan of Le Sage, and intended as a companion to Lavoisne's Atlas. In 1 vol. folio, containing 54 Maps. Third Edition, improved and enlarged.

ATLANTIC SOUVENIR, FOR 1832.

This volume is superbly bound in embossed leather and ornamented with numerous plates

to render it worthy of the purpose for which it is intended.

EMBELLISHMENTS.—1. The Hungarian Princess, engraved by Illman and Pillbrow, from a picture by Holmes.—2. The Bower of Paphos, engraved by Ellis, from a picture by Martin.—3. The Duchess and Sancho, engraved by Durand, from a picture by Leslie.—4. Richard and Saladin, engraved by Ellis, from a picture by Cooper.—5. The Rocky Mountains, engraved by Hatch and Smilie, from a picture by Doughty.—6. Lord Byron in Early Youth, engraved by Ellis, from a picture by Saunders.—7. Tiger Island, engraved by Neagle, from a picture by Stanfield.—8. The Blacksmith, engraved by Kelly, from a picture by Neagle.—9. The Tight Shoe, engraved by Kelly, from a picture by Richter.—10. Isadore, engraved by Illman and Pillbrow, from a picture by Jackson.—11. The Dutch Maiden, engraved by Neagle, from a picture by Newton.—12. The Mother's Grave, engraved by Neagle, from a picture by Schaffer.

ATLANTIC SOUVENIR FOR 1831.

EMBELLISHMENTS.—1. Frontispiece. The Shipwrecked Family, engraved by Ellis, from a picture by Burnet.—2. Shipwreck off Fort Rouge, Calais, engraved by Ellis, from a picture by Stanfield.—3. Infancy, engraved by Kelly, from a picture by Sir Thomas Lawrence.—4. Lady Jane Grey, engraved by Kelly, from a picture by Leslie.—5. Three Score and Ten, engraved by Kearny, from a picture by Burnet.—6. The Hour of Rest, engraved by Kelly, from a picture by Burnet.—7. The Minstrel, engraved by Ellis, from a picture by Leslie.—8. Arcadia, engraved by Kearny, from a picture by Cockerell.—9. The Fisherman's Return, engraved by Neagle, from a picture by Collins.—10. The Marchioness of Carmarthen, granddaughter of Charles Carroll of Carrollton, engraved by Illman and Pillbrow, from a picture by Mrs. Mee.—11. Morning among the Hills, engraved by Hatch, from a picture by Doughty.—12. Los Musicos, engraved by Ellis, from a picture by Watteau.

A few copies of the ATLANTIC SOUVENIR, for 1830, are still for sale.

THE BOOK OF THE SEASONS. By WILLIAM HOWITT.

"Since the publication of the Journal of a Naturalist, no work at once so interesting and instructive as the Book of the Seasons has been submitted to the public. Whether in reference to the utility of its design, or the grace and beauty of its execution, it will amply merit the popularity it is certain to obtain. It is, indeed, cheering and refreshing to meet with such a delightful volume, so full of nature and truth—in which reflection and experience derive aid from imagination—in which we are taught much; but in such a manner as to make it doubtful whether we have not been amusing ourselves all the time we have been reading."—*New Monthly Magazine.*

PRIVATE MEMOIRS OF NAPOLEON BONAPARTE, from the French of M. FAUVELET DE BOURRIENNE, Private Secretary to the Emperor. SECOND AMERICAN EDITION, complete in one volume.

** This edition contains almost a fourth more matter than the previous one, as in order to render it as perfect as possible, extracts have been given from the Memoirs from St. Helena, Official Reports, &c. &c. in all cases where they differ from the statements of M. de Bourrienne.

" This English translation, which has been very faithfully rendered, is still more valuable than the original work, as upon all points where any obliquity from other published recitals occurs, the translator has given several accounts, and thus, in the form of notes, we are presented with the statements obtained from Napoleon's own dictation at St. Helena, from the Memoirs of the Duke of Rovigo, of General Rapp, of Constant, from the writings of the Marquis of Londonderry, &c·."—*U. Ser. Jour.*

"Those who desire to form a correct estimate of the character of one of the most extraordinary men " that ever lived in the tide of time," will scarcely be without it. The present edition possesses peculiar advantages.

The peculiar advantages of position in regard to his present subject, solely enjoyed by M. de Bourrienne, his literary accomplishments and moral qualifications, have already obtained for these memoirs the first rank in contemporary and authentic history. In France, where they had been for years expected with anxiety, and where, since the revolution, no work connected with that period or its consequent events has created so great a sensation, the volumes of Bourrienne have, from the first, been accepted as the only trustworthy exhibition of the private life and political principles of Napoleon.

" We know from the best political authority now living in England, that the writer's accounts are perfectly corroborated by facts."—*Lit. Gaz.*

" The only authentic Life of Napoleon extant."—*Courier.*

"This splendid publication that literally leaves nothing to be desired."—*Atlas.*

"These volumes may be read with all the interest of a romance."—*Courier.*

" No person who is desirous rightly to appreciate the character of Bonaparte, will neglect the perusal of this work; whoever wishes to know, not merely the General or the Emperor, but what the man really was, will find him well pictured here."—*Times.*

" The completest personal recollections of Napoleon that have appeared."—*Morn. Post.*

" As a part of the history of the most extraordinary man, and the most extraordinary times that ever invited elucidation, these memoirs must continue to the latest ages to be

THE BRAVO, by the author of the "Spy," " Pilot," " Red Rover," &c. In 2 vols. 12mo.

" Let us honestly avow in conclusion, that in addition to the charm of an interesting fiction to be found in these pages, there is more mental power in them, more matter that sets people thinking, more of that quality that is accelerating the onward movement of the world, than in all the Scotch novels that have so deservedly won our admiration."—*New Monthly Magazine.*

"This new novel from the pen of our countryman, Cooper, will win new laurels for him. It is full of dramatic interest—" hair-breadth escapes"—animated and bustling scenes on the canals, in the prisons, on the Rialto, in the Adriatic, and in the streets of Venice."—*N. Y. Courier & Enquirer.*

" Of the whole work, we may confidently say that it is very able—a performance of genius and power."—*Nat. Gazette.*

" The Bravo will, we think, tend much to exalt and extend the fame of its author. We have hurried through its pages with an avidity which must find its apology in the interesting character of the incidents and the very vivid and graphic style in which they are described."

By the same author.

THE HEIDEN-MAUER, or PAGAN CAMP. In 2 vols.

SALMONIA; or, Days of Fly Fishing; by SIR HUMPHRY DAVY.

"One of the most delightful labors of leisure ever seen; not a few of the most beautiful phenomena of nature are here lucidly explained."—*Gentleman's Magazine.*

NATURAL HISTORY OF SELBORNE AND ITS INHABITANTS. By the Rev. GILBERT WHITE. 18mo.

THE MECHANISM OF THE HEAVENS, by MRS. SOMERVILLE. In 18mo.

" We possess already innumerable discourses on Astronomy, in which the wonders of the heavens and their laws are treated of; but we can say most conscientiously that we are acquainted with none—not even La Place's own beautiful *exposé* in his *System du Monde,* —in which all that is essentially interesting in the motions and laws of the celestial bodies, or which is capable of popular enunciation, is so admirably, so graphically, or we may add, so unaffectedly and simply placed before us. * * * Is it asking too much of Mrs. Somerville to express a hope that she will allow this beautiful preliminary Dissertation to be printed separately, for the delight and instruction of thousands of readers, young and old, who cannot understand, or are too indolent to apply themselves to the more elaborate parts of the work? If she will do this, we hereby promise to exert our best endeavors to make its merits

MISCELLANEOUS.

A MEMOIR OF SEBASTIAN CABOT, with a Review of the History of Maritime Discovery. Illustrated by Documents from the Rolls, now first published.

"Put forth in the most unpretending manner. and without a name, this work is of paramount importance to the subjects of which it treats."—*Literary Gazette.* "The author has corrected many grave errors, and in general given us a clearer insight into transactions of considerable national interest."—*Ib.* "Will it not," says the author, with just astonishment, "be deemed almost incredible, that the very instrument in the Records of England, which recites the Great Discovery, and plainly contemplates a scheme of Colonization, should, up to this moment, have been treated by her own writers as that which first gave permission to go forth and explore?"—*Ib.* "We must return to investigate several collateral matters which we think deserving of more space than we can this week bestow. Meanwhile we recommend the work as one of great value and interest."—*Ib.*

"The general reader, as well as the navigator and the curious, will derive pleasure and information from this well-written production."—*Courier.*

"A specimen of honest inquiry. It is quite frightful to think of the number of the inaccuracies it exposes: we shall cease to have confidence in books." "The investigation of truth is not the fashion of these times. But every sincere inquirer after historical accuracy ought to purchase the book as a curiosity: more false assertions and inaccurate statements were never exposed in the same compass. It has given us a lesson we shall never forget, and hope to profit by."—*Spectator.*

HISTORY OF THE NORTHMEN, OR NORMANS AND DANES; from the earliest times to the Conquest of England by William of Normandy. By Henry Wheaton, Member of the Scandinavian and Icelandic Literary Societies of Copenhagen.

This work embraces the great leading features of Scandinavian history. commencing with the heroic age, and advancing from the earliest dawn of civilization to the introduction of Christianity into the North—its long and bloody strife with Paganism—the discovery and colonization of Iceland, Greenland, and North America, by the Norwegian navigators, before the time of Columbus—the military and maritime expeditions of the Northmen—their early intercourse of commerce and war with Constantinople and the Eastern empire—the establishment of a Norman state in France, under Rollo. and the subjugation of England, first by the Danes, under Canute the Great, and subsequently by the Normans, under Duke William. the founder of the English monarchy. It also contains an account of the mythology and literature of the ancient North—the Icelandic language prevailing all over the Scandinavian countries until the formation of the present living tongues of Sweden and Denmark—an analysis of the Eddas, Sagas, and various chronicles and songs relating to the Northern deities and heroes, constituting the original materials from which the work has been principally composed. It is intended to illustrate the history of France and England during the middle ages, and at the same time to serve as an introduction to the modern history of Denmark, Norway, and Sweden.

LETTERS TO A YOUNG NATURALIST, on the Study of Nature, and Natural Theology. By JAMES L. DRUMMOND, M. D. &c. With numerous engravings.

"We know of no work, compressed within the same limits, which seems so happily calculated to generate in a young mind, and to renovate in the old, an ardent love of nature in all her forms."—*Monthly Review.*

"We cannot but eulogize, in the warmest manner, the endeavor, and we must say the successful endeavor, of a man of science, like Dr. Drummond, to bring down so

---

PRIVATE MEMOIRS OF NAPOLEON BONAPARTE, from the French of M. FAUVELET DE BOURRIENNE, Private Secretary to the Emperor.

The peculiar advantages of position in regard to his present subject, solely enjoyed by M. de Bourrienne, his literary accomplishments and moral qualifications, have already obtained for these memoirs the first rank in contemporary and authentic history. In France, where they had been for years expected with anxiety, and where, since the revolution, no work connected with that period or its consequent events has created so great a sensation, the volumes of Bourrienne have, from the first, been accepted as the only trustworthy exhibition of the private life and political principles of Napoleon.

"We know from the best political authority now living in England, that the writer's accounts are perfectly corroborated by facts."—*Lit. Gaz.*

ANNALS OF THE PENINSULAR CAMPAIGNS. By the Author of CYRIL THORNTON. In 3 vols. 12mo. with plates.

THE HISTORY OF LOUISIANA, particularly the Cession of that Colony to the United States of North America; with an Introductory Essay on the Constitution and Government of the United States, by M. DE MARBOIS, Peer of France, translated from the French by an American Citizen. In 1 vol. 8vo.

THE PERSIAN ADVENTURER. By the Author of the KUZZILBASH. In 2 vols. 12mo.

"It is full of glowing descriptions of Eastern life."—*Courier.*

MORALS OF PLEASURE, Illustrated by Stories designed for Young Persons, in 1 vol. 12mo.

"The style of the stories is no less remarkable for its ease and gracefulness, than for the delicacy of its humor, and its beautiful and at times affecting simplicity. A lady must have written it—for it is from the bosom of woman alone, that such tenderness of feeling and such delicacy of sentiment—such sweet lessons of morality—such deep and pure streams of virtue and piety, gush forth to cleanse the juvenile mind from the grosser impurities of our nature. and prepare the young for lives of usefulness here, and happiness hereafter."—*N. Y. Com. Advertiser.*

CLARENCE; a Tale of our own Times. By the Author of REDWOOD, HOPE LESLIE, &c. In 2 vols.

AMERICAN QUARTERLY REVIEW, published on the first of March, June, September, and December. Price $5 per ann.

*** A few complete Sets of the Work are still for sale.**

CONSIDERATIONS ON THE CURRENCY AND BANKING SYSTEM OF THE UNITED STATES. By ALBERT GALLATIN.

THE

NATIONAL SCHOOL MANUAL:

A

REGULAR AND CONNECTED COURSE OF ELEMENTARY STUDIES,

EMBRACING

THE NECESSARY AND USEFUL BRANCHES OF A COMMON EDUCATION.

IN FOUR PARTS, WITH A QUARTO ATLAS.

COMPILED FROM THE LATEST AND MOST APPROVED AUTHORS,

BY M. R. BARTLETT.

The plan of this work was the suggestion of the late Governor CLINTON, whose zeal and efforts in the cause of our Public Schools, will be cherished with grateful remembrance to the latest posterity; and this work, so far as it had advanced, up to the time of his lamented death, received his favorable regard and patronage.

The object of the NATIONAL SCHOOL MANUAL, is to furnish a *System* of instruction, for a thorough English education, in a plain, practical, and progressive Series of Lessons, collaterally arranged.

It is believed that the plan of this work is sufficiently wide and comprehensive for all the purposes of a good English Education, and that it is capable of advancing the pupil much faster in his studies, and to much higher attainments in the useful sciences, than is possible in the present mode, with the help of the best teachers.

The practical results of a general adoption of the National School Manual will be:

1st. To introduce system, uniformity and order into our Schools. 2d. To define and regulate the duties of teachers, and give them the means of being more thorough, precise, and useful. 3d. To present to the opening minds of pupils, the various subjects of human science, in a clear and lucid manner, and with all the advantages of natural order, and philosophical arrangement, adapted to the progress of knowledge: and, 4th. To Parents and Guardians, exemption from the vexation and expense of changing the whole *catalogue of School Books*, and the whole course of studies, with every change of School or Teacher—a thing of very frequent occurrence in our Country Schools. As to the saving of expense in the article of School Books, the entire cost of the Common School Manual, embracing the Primer and the Four Parts, of upwards of 1500 pages, for the whole course of a good English education, and an Atlas of 20 maps, is between three and four dollars.

From the Teachers of Public Schools in the city of New-York.

We have examined the National School Manual, and are pleased with the plan. From our knowledge of the various systems pursued in the country schools, many of which, upon the change of teachers, serve rather to retard, than advance, the pupil, we do not hesitate to recommend the Manual, as having not only a tendency to uniformity and order, but also to save expense, the complaint of which is without parallel.

LOYD D. WINDSOR,
Teacher of Public School, No. 1.
JOSEPH BELDEN,
Teacher of Public School, No. 11.
A. DE MONTFREDY,
February 8, 1830.   Teacher of Public School, No. 10.

From the Rev. James Carnahan, President of Princeton College.

Having examined the general plan of the 1st, 2d, and 3d parts of the "NATIONAL SCHOOL MANUAL," and having also taken a cursory view of some of the details, I am satisfied that it is a work of no common merit.

The evils which this work proposes to remedy are great and generally felt by parents and instructors. The expense of books, according to the course heretofore pursued, is a very serious inconvenience; and the loss of time and labor arising from the want of a connected series of instruction adapted to the capacities of children and youth, is a consideration of vast moment.

Comparatively few instructors are competent to select, from the great number of books now used in common schools, those adapted to the improving capacities of their pupils. If a book, which he cannot understand, be put into the hands of a pupil, he will lose his time, and what is worse, he will probably contract a disgust for learning. The great art of teaching consists in beginning with the simplest elements, and advancing gradually to things more difficult as the capacity of acquiring knowledge expands, presenting something new to arrest the attention and to exercise the ingenuity of the pupil. To answer these ends, the work of Mr. Bartlett seems to me well suited. If these small volumes be thoroughly studied, I am persuaded that the pupil will be better prepared to transact the business of life, and by his own exertions to improve himself after he leaves school, than if he had spent twice the time under an ill-arranged system of instruction.

It will, doubtless, be difficult to introduce a uniform system of instruction into our common schools; yet the object is so desirable, that it deserves a vigorous and persevering effort; and I indulge the hope that the day is not far distant, when the "National School Manual," improved and enlarged by its able and experienced author, will be very generally adopted.

JAMES CARNAHAN.
Nassau Hall, April 27, 1832.

From the Rev. Charles S. Stewart, Chaplain in the United States Navy—Author of a Journal of Voyages to the Pacific, &c. &c.

I have examined with much care, and great satisfaction, the "NATIONAL SCHOOL MANUAL," compiled by M. R. Bartlett. The opinion I have formed of its merits, is of little importance, after the numerous and highly respectable testimonials to its value already in your possession.

A work of this kind has long been a *desideratum* in the economy of our public schools, and I am persuaded that the advantages which this compilation is calculated to secure to *pupils, teachers,* and *parents,* need only to be appreciated to secure its introduction throughout our country. It will be found on trial, I think, greatly to aid the instructor in his arduous service, while the pupil cannot fail, in the use of it, if I am not mistaken, to make a more rapid and understanding progress than by the method now generally pursued. To teacher and scholar the importance and value of the system, I doubt not, would be fully shown after a very brief trial, while the parent and guardian would soon learn its advantage in an exemption from the heavy tax now imposed on them by a constant change of books.

I should be happy to see the Manual in every common school in the Union, from the conviction that the best interests of education would be promoted by it.

(Signed)   CHAS. SAML. STEWART,
Chaplain U. S. Navy.
New-York, March 30, 1832.

I have examined with care and a high degree of interest the work called the "NATIONAL SCHOOL MANUAL," by Mr. M. R. Bartlett, and am so well satisfied with its merits, and that it will eventually be adopted in all our common schools, to the exclusion of every other work of the kind now in use, that I feel authorized to exert my influence to have the work introduced forthwith into my school.

JAS. W. FAIRCHILD,
Principal of the Hudson Academy.
Hudson, Jan. 23, 1832.

The Publishers have similar letters from fifty or sixty Teachers of the highest respectability.

NATIONAL SCHOOL MANUAL—IN FOUR PARTS.

BRANCHES OF STUDY.

ALPHABETS of the English Language.
SPELLING, 1, 2, 3 and 4 syllables.
READING, easy exercises and familiar stories. (Collaterally arranged.)
COUNTING numbers.

ELEMENTS of the Language, combined. Key to vowel sounds.
SPELLING, 1 to 4 syllables.
READING, interesting stories, in prose and verse
COUNTING, and elements of Arithmetic.
APPENDIX OF TABLES, &c.

SPELLING, 1 to 4 syllables, with pronunciation.
READING, conversations, and Poetry.
ARITHMETIC, as far as Interest.
GRAMMAR, Prosody, and Syntax.
GEOGRAPHY. APPENDIX, with Maps.

SPELLING.
READING.
ARITHMETIC.
GRAMMAR. Exercises in false Syntax, &c.
RHETORIC, &c.
MENSURATION.
TRIGONOMETRY.
BOOK-KEEPING.
APPENDIX.

GEOGRAPHY.
HISTORY.
NATURAL SCIENCES.

PRIMER.
48 pages, 18mo.

FIRST PART.
108 pages, 12mo. All the exercises collaterally arranged.

SECOND PART.
302 pages, 12mo. Pronunciation after Walker. Arithmetic from various sources. Grammar after L. Murray. Reading, Elements of Elocution. Appendix, 30 or 40 pages, elements of Geography, with Maps.

THIRD PART.
380 pages, 12mo. Words of three and more syllables, pronunciation after Walker. Biography, Conversations on Governments, &c. County and Town Officers of the State, Select Poetry, &c. Higher branches—Mensuration, Elements of Geometry, &c. with practical exercises, confined principally to Federal currency. 1. Book-Keeping in three forms—the Farmer's the Mechanic's and the Merchant's. 2. Forms of mercantile and negotiable papers, with notes illustrating their nature, &c. 3. Declaration of Independence, and signers' names. The Constitution of the United States and of New-York, with critical questions.

FOURTH PART.
674 pages 12mo. and Atlas 20 Maps 4to. This part embraces General Geography, General History from the Deluge, alternately arranged with Geography, and referring to the same Maps. Natural Sciences in the form of an Appendix, presenting some general principles of the most useful branches of Natural Philosophy.

NOTES.

Lessons brief, simple, and interesting. Three exercises for each half day, preparatory to the First Part of the System. Embellished with Cuts, &c.

This part exhibits a series of first lessons adapted to the use of children between six and eight years of age. The Arithmetical exercises managed by proper signs.

An Appendix with Arithmetical Tables.

In this part the scholar has four recitations for each half day, all brief, but gradually increasing, and suited to pupils between nine and twelve years.

The Geographical exercises are designed as a premium for prompt recitations, in his daily exercises.

This part is designed for pupils of fourteen or fifteen years of age. It closes the studies opened in the First and Second Parts, and furnishes good common education without the aid of the Fourth Part. As the lessons are arranged collaterally, the pupil will be obliged to apply to the spelling exercises through the whole course. The Appendix is devoted to those branches of study which could not be collaterally arranged.

As this part will offer but three exercises, the pupil will revise his studies, Book-Keeping, &c.

MEDICINE.

THE PRACTICE OF PHYSIC. By W. P. DEWEES, M. D. Adjunct Professor of Midwifery, in the University of Pennsylvania, 2d edition, complete in 1 vol. 8vo.

"We have no hesitation in recommending it as decidedly one of the best systems of medicine extant. The tenor of the work in general reflects the highest honor on Dr. Dewees's talents, industry, and capacity for the execution of the arduous task which he had undertaken. It is one of the most able and satisfactory works which modern times have produced, and will be a standard authority."—*London Med. and Surg. Journal, Aug.* 1830.

DEWEES ON THE DISEASES OF CHILDREN. 4th ed. In 8vo.

The objects of this work are, 1st, to teach those who have the charge of children, either as parent or guardian, the most approved methods of securing and improving their physical powers. This is attempted by pointing out the duties which the parent or the guardian owes for this purpose, to this interesting, but helpless class of beings, and the manner by which their duties shall be fulfilled. And 2d, to render available a long experience to these objects of our affection when they become diseased. In attempting this, the author has avoided as much as possible, "technicality;" and has given, if he does not flatter himself too much, to each disease of which he treats, its appropriate and designating characters, with a fidelity that will prevent any two being confounded together, with the best mode of treating them, that either his own experience or that of others has suggested.

DEWEES ON THE DISEASES OF FEMALES. 4th edition, with Additions. In 8vo.

A COMPENDIOUS SYSTEM OF MIDWIFERY; chiefly designed to facilitate the Inquiries of those who may be pursuing this Branch of Study. In 8vo. with 13 Plates. 6th edition, corrected and enlarged. By W. P. DEWEES, M. D.

THE ELEMENTS OF THERAPEUTICS AND MATERIA MEDICA. By N. CHAPMAN, M. D. 2 vols. 8vo. 5th edition, corrected and revised.

MANUAL OF PATHOLOGY: containing the Symptoms, Diagnosis, and Morbid Character of Diseases, &c. By L. MARTINET. Translated, with Notes and Additions, by JONES QUAIN. Second American Edition, 12mo.

"We strongly recommend M. Martinet's Manual to the profession, and especially to students; if the latter wish to study diseases to advantage, they should always have it at hand, both when at the bedside of the patient, and when making post mortem examinations."—*American Journal of the Medical Sciences, No. I.*

CLINICAL ILLUSTRATIONS OF FEVER, comprising a Report of the Cases treated at the London Fever Hospital in 1828-29, by Alexander Tweedie, M. D., Member of the Royal College of Physicians of London, &c. 1 vol. 8vo.

"In short, the present work, concise, unostentatious as it is, would have led us to think that Dr. Tweedie was a man of clear judgment, unfettered by attachment to any fashionable hypothesis, that he was an energetic but judicious practitioner, and that, if he did not dazzle his readers with the brilliancy of theoretical speculations, he would command their assent to the solidity of his didactic precepts."—*Med. Chir. Journal.*

THE ANATOMY, PHYSIOLOGY, AND DISEASES OF THE TEETH. By THOMAS BELL, F.R.S., F.L.S. &c. In 1 vol. 8vo. With Plates.

"Mr. Bell has evidently endeavored to construct a work of reference for the practitioner, and a text-book for the student, containing a 'plain and practical digest of the information at present possessed on the subject, and results of the author's own investigations and experience.'" * * * "We must now take leave of Mr. Bell, whose work we have no doubt will become a class-book on the important subject of dental surgery."—*Medico-Chirurgical Review.*

"We have no hesitation in pronouncing it to be the best treatise in the English language."—*North American Medical and Surgical Journal, No.* 19.

AMERICAN DISPENSATORY. Ninth Edition, improved and greatly enlarged. By JOHN REDMAN COXE, M. D. Professor of Materia Medica and Pharmacy in the University of Pennsylvania. In 1 vol. 8vo.

* This new edition has been arranged with special reference to the recent Pharmacopœias, published in Philadelphia and New-York.

ELLIS' MEDICAL FORMULARY. The Medical Formulary, being a collection of prescriptions derived from the writings and practice of many of the most eminent Physicians in America and Europe. By BENJAMIN ELLIS, M. D. 3d. edition. With Additions.

"We would especially recommend it to our brethren in distant parts of the country, whose insulated situations may prevent them from having access to the many authorities which have been consulted in arranging the materials for this work."—*Phil. Med. and Phys. Journal.*

MANUAL OF MATERIA MEDICA AND PHARMACY. By H. M. EDWARDS, M. D. and P. VAVASSEUR, M. D. comprising a concise Description of the Articles used in Medicine; their Physical and Chemical Properties; the Botanical Characters of the Medicinal Plants; the Formulæ for the Principal Officinal Preparations of the American, Parisian, Dublin, &c. Pharmacopœias; with Observations on the proper Mode of combining and administering Remedies. Translated from the French, with numerous Additions and Corrections, and adapted to the Practice of Medicine and to the Art of Pharmacy in the United States. By JOSEPH TOGNO, M. D. Member of the Philadelphia Medical Society, and E. DURAND, Member of the Philadelphia College of Pharmacy.

"It contains all the pharmaceutical information that the physician can desire, and in addition, a larger mass of information, in relation to the properties, &c. of the different articles and preparations employed in medicine, than any of the dispensatories, and we think will entirely supersede all these publications in the library of the physician."—*Am. Journ. of the Medical Sciences.*

MEMOIR ON THE TREATMENT OF VENEREAL DISEASES WITHOUT MERCURY, employed at the Military Hospital of the Val-de-Grace. Translated from the French of H. M. J. Desruelles, M. D. &c. To which are added, Observations by G. J. Guthrie, Esq. and various documents, showing the results of this Mode of Treatment, in Great Britain, France, Germany, and America. 1 vol. 8vo.

MEDICINE AND SURGERY.

A TREATISE on FEVER. By SOUTHWOOD SMITH, M. D., Physician to the London Fever Hospital.

"No work has been more lauded by the Reviews than the Treatise on Fevers, by Southwood Smith. Dr. Johnson, the editor of the Medico-Chirurgical Review, says, 'It is the best we have ever perused on the subject of fever, and in our conscience, we believe it the best that ever flowed from the pen of physician in any age or in any country.'"—*Am. Med. Journ.*

AN ESSAY on REMITTENT AND INTERMITTENT DISEASES, including generically Marsh Fever and Neuralgia—comprising under the former, various Anomalies, Obscurities, and Consequences, and under a new systematic View of the latter, treating of Tic Douloureux, Sciatica, Headache, Ophthalmia, Toothache, Palsy, and many other Modes and Consequences of this generic Disease; by JOHN MACCULLOCH, M. D., F. R. S. &c. &c.

"In rendering Dr. Macculloch's work more accessible to the profession, we are conscious that we are doing the state some service."—*Med. Chir. Review.*

"We most strongly recommend Dr. Macculloch's treatise to the attention of our medical brethren, as presenting a most valuable mass of information, on a most important subject."—*N. A. Med. and Surg. Journal.*

A PRACTICAL SYNOPSIS OF CUTANEOUS DISEASES, from the most celebrated Authors, and particularly from Documents afforded by the Clinical Lectures of Dr. Biett, Physician to the Hospital of St. Louis, Paris. By A. CAZENAVE, M. D. and H. E. SCHEDEL, M. D. Second edition.

"We can safely recommend this work to the attention of practitioners as containing much practical information, not only on the treatment, but also on the causes of cutaneous affections, as being in fact the best treatise on diseases of the skin that has ever appeared."—*American Journal of the Medical Sciences, No. 5.*

SURGICAL MEMOIRS OF THE RUSSIAN CAMPAIGN. Translated from the French of Baron LARREY.

LECTURES ON INFLAMMATION, exhibiting a view of the General Doctrines, Pathological and Practical, of Medical Surgery. By JOHN THOMPSON, M. D., F. R. S. E. Second American edition.

THE INSTITUTES AND PRACTICE OF SURGERY; being the Outlines of a Course of Lectures. By W. GIBSON, M. D. Professor of Surgery in the University of Pennsylvania. 3d edition, revised, corrected, and enlarged. In 2 vols. 8vo.

PRINCIPLES OF MILITARY SURGERY, comprising Observations on the Arrangements, Police, and Practice of Hospitals, and on the History, Treatment, and Anomalies of Variola and Syphilis; illustrated with cases and dissections. By JOHN HENNEN, M. D., F. R. S. E. Inspector of Military Hospitals—first American from the third London edition, with the Life of the Author, by his son, DR. JOHN HENNEN.

"The value of Dr. Hennen's work is too well appreciated to need any praise of ours. We were only required then, to bring the third edition before the notice of our readers; and having done this, we shall merely add, that

AMERICAN JOURNAL OF THE MEDICAL SCIENCES.

Published Quarterly.

And supported by the most distinguished Physicians in the United States, among which are Professors Bigelow, Channing, Chapman, Coxe, De Butts, Dewees, Dickson, Dudley, Francis, Gibson, Hare, Henderson, Horner, Hosack, Jackson, Macneven, Mott, Mussey, Physick, Potter, Sewall, Warren, and Worthington; Drs. Daniell, Drake, Emerson, Fearn, Geddings, Griffith, Hale, Hays, Hayward, Ives, Jackson, Moultrie, Ware, and Wright. It is published *punctually* on the first of November, February, May, and August. Each No. contains about 280 large 8vo. pages, and one or more plates —being a greater amount of matter than is furnished by any other Medical Journal in the United States. Price $5 per annum.

The following Extracts show the estimation in which this Journal is held in Europe:—

"Several of the American Journals are before us. * * * Of these the American Journal of the Medical Sciences is by far the better periodical; it is, indeed, the best of the trans-atlantic medical publications; and, to make a comparison nearer home, is in most respects superior to the great majority of European works of the same description."—*The Lancet, Jan.* 1831.

"We need scarcely refer our esteemed and highly eminent cotemporary, [*The American Journal of the Medical Sciences,*] from whom we quote, to our critical remarks on the opinions of our own countrymen, or to the principles which influence us in the discharge of our editorial duties." "Our copious extracts from his unequalled publication, unnoticing multitudes of others which come before us, are the best proof of the esteem which we entertain for his talents and abilities."—*London Medical and Surgical Journal, March,* 1830.

"The American Journal of the Medical Sciences is one of the most complete and best edited of the numerous periodical publications of the United States."—*Bulletin des Sciences Medicales, Tom. XIV.*

PATHOLOGICAL AND PRACTICAL RESEARCHES on DISEASES of THE BRAIN AND SPINAL CORD. By JOHN ABERCROMBIE, M. D.

"We have here a work of authority, and one which does credit to the author and his country."—*North Amer. Med. and Surg. Journal.*

By the same Author.

PATHOLOGICAL AND PRACTICAL RESEARCHES on DISEASES of THE STOMACH, THE INTESTINAL CANAL, THE LIVER, AND OTHER VISCERA OF THE ABDOMEN.

"We have now closed a very long review of a very valuable work, and although we have endeavored to condense into our pages a great mass of important matter, we feel that our author has not yet received justice."—*Medico-Chirurgical Review.*

A RATIONAL EXPOSITION OF THE PHYSICAL SIGNS OF DISEASES OF THE LUNGS AND PLEURA; Illustrating their Pathology and facilitating their Diagnosis. By CHARLES J. WILLIAMS, M. D. In 8vo. with plates.

"If we are not greatly mistaken, it will lend to a better understanding, and a more correct estimate of the value of auscultation, than any thing that has yet appeared."—*Am. Med. Journal.*

MANUAL OF THE PHYSIOLOGY OF MAN; or a concise Description of the Phenomena of his Organization. By P. HUTIN. Translated from the French, with Notes by J.

THE PEOPLE'S LIBRARY.

"The editors and publishers should receive the thanks of the present generation, and the gratitude of posterity, for being the first to prepare in this language what deserves to be entitled not the ENCYCLO-PÆDIA AMERICANA, but the PEOPLE'S LIBRARY."—*N. Y. Courier and Enquirer.*

Just Published, by Carey, Lea, & Blanchard,

And sold in Philadelphia by *E. L. Carey & A. Hart*; in New York by *G. & C. & H. Carvill*; in Boston by *Carter & Hendee*; in Baltimore by *E. J. Coale. & W. & J. Neal*; in Washington by *Thompson & Homans*; in Richmond by *J. H. Nash*; in Savannah by *W. T. Williams*; in Charleston by *W. H. Berrett*; in New-Orleans by *W. M'Kean*; in Mobile by *Odiorne & Smith*; and by the principal booksellers throughout the Union,

THE

ENCYCLOPÆDIA AMERICANA:

A
POPULAR DICTIONARY

OF

ARTS, SCIENCES, LITERATURE, HISTORY, AND POLITICS,

BROUGHT DOWN TO THE PRESENT TIME, AND INCLUDING A COPIOUS COLLECTION OF ORIGINAL ARTICLES IN

AMERICAN BIOGRAPHY:

On the basis of the Seventh Edition of the German

CONVERSATIONS-LEXICON.

EDITED BY FRANCIS LIEBER,

ASSISTED BY

EDWARD WIGGLESWORTH AND T. G. BRADFORD, ESQRS.

IN THIRTEEN LARGE VOLUMES, OCTAVO, PRICE TO SUBSCRIBERS, BOUND IN CLOTH, TWO DOLLARS AND A HALF EACH.

EACH VOLUME CONTAINS BETWEEN 600 AND 700 PAGES.

"THE WORLD-RENOWNED CONVERSATIONS-LEXICON."—*Edinburgh Review.*

"To supersede cumbrous Encyclopædias, and put within the reach of the poorest man, a *complete library*, equal to about forty or fifty good-sized octavos, embracing every possible subject of interest to the number of 20,000 in all—provided he can spare either from his earnings or his extravagancies, *twenty cents* a week, for three years, a library so contrived, as to be equally suited to the learned and the unlearned,—the mechanic—the merchant, and the professional man."—*N. Y. Courier and Inquirer.*

"The reputation of this valuable work has augmented with each volume; and if the unanimous opinion of the press, uttered from all quarters, be true, which in this instance happens to be the case, it is indeed one of the best of publications. It should be in the possession of every intelligent man, as it is a library in itself, comprising an immense mass of lore upon almost every possible subject, and in the cheapest possible form."—*N. Y. Mirror.*

"Witnesses from every part of the country concurred in declaring that the Encyclopædia Americana was in a fair way to degrade the dignity of learning, and especially the learning of Encyclopædias, by making it *too cheap*—that the multitudes of all classes were infatuated with it in saying in so many words from the highest to the lowest, 'the more we see of the work the better we like it.'"—*N. Y. Courier and Inquirer.*

"The articles in the present volume appear to us to evince the same ability and research which gained so favorable a reception for the work at its commencement. The *Appendix* to the volume now before us, containing an account of the *Indian Languages of America*, must prove highly interesting to the reader in this country; and it is at once remarkable as a specimen of history and philology. The work altogether, we may again be permitted to observe, reflects distinguished credit upon the literary and scientific character, as well as the scholarship of our country."—*Charleston Courier.*

"The copious information which this work affords on American subjects, fully justifies its title of an American Dictionary; while at the same time the extent, variety, and felicitous disposition of its topics, make it the most convenient and satisfactory Encyclopædia that we have ever seen."—*National Journal.*

"If the succeeding volumes shall equal in merit the one before us, we may confidently anticipate for the work a reputation and usefulness which ought to secure for it the most flattering encouragement and patronage."—*Federal Gazette.*

"A compendious library, and invaluable book of refer-

"The variety of topics is of course vast, and they are treated in a manner which is at once so full of information and so interesting, that the work, instead of being merely referred to, might be regularly perused with as much pleasure as profit."—*Baltimore American.*

"We view it as a publication worthy of the age and of the country, and cannot but believe the discrimination of our countrymen will sustain the publishers, and well reward them for this contribution to American Literature."—*Baltimore Patriot.*

"It reflects the greatest credit on those who have been concerned in its production, and promises, in a variety of respects, to be the best as well as the most compendious dictionary of the arts, sciences, history, politics, biography, &c. which has yet been compiled. The style of the portion we have read is terse and perspicuous; and it is really curious how so much scientific and other information could have been so satisfactorily communicated in such brief limits."—*N. Y. Evening Post.*

"Those who can, by any honest modes of economy, reserve the sum of two dollars and fifty cents quarterly, from their family expenses, may pay for this work as fast as it is published; and we confidently believe that they will find at the end that they never purchased so much general, practical, useful information at so cheap a rate."—*Journal of Education.*

"If the encouragement to the publishers should correspond with the testimony in favor of their enterprise, and the beautiful and faithful style of its execution, the hazard of the undertaking, bold as it was, will be well compensated; and our libraries will be enriched by the most generally useful encyclopedic dictionary that has been offered to the readers of the English language. Full enough for the general scholar, and plain enough for every capacity, it is far more convenient, in every view and form, than its more expensive and ponderous predecessors."—*American Farmer.*

"The high reputation of the contributors to this work, will not fail to insure it a favorable reception, and its own merits will do the rest."—*Silliman's Journ.*

"The Encyclopædia Americana is a prodigious improvement upon all that has gone before it; a thing for our country, as well as the country that gave it birth, to be proud of; an inexhaustible treasury of useful, pleasant, and familiar learning on every possible subject, so arranged as to be speedily and safely referred to on emergency, as well as on deliberate inquiry; and better still, adapted to the understanding, and put within the reach of the multitude. * * * The Encyclopædia Americana is a work without which no library worthy of the name can here-

ENCYCLOPÆDIA AMERICANA.

" The work will be a valuable possession to every family or individual that can afford to purchase it ; and we take pleasure, therefore, in extending the knowledge of its merits."—*National Intelligencer.*

" This work appears to improve as it issues from the press. The number of able writers, who contribute original matter in all the departments of literature and science is amply sufficient to give it celebrity and high character. To men engaged in the active pursuits of life—whose time is precious—this popular dictionary is a most valuable and ready mode of reference. It embraces brief views and sketches of all the late discoveries in science—and the present condition of literature, politics, &c. &c. Every merchant's counting-room—every lawyer's library —every mechanic—every farmer ought to possess a copy of this useful and valuable work."—*Courier.*

" From the specimen which has already been given, we have no hesitation in saying, that in regard to intelligence, skill, and faithful diligence, it is a work of the very highest order. We know of no similar publication that can bear any comparison with it for the rich variety of valuable information, which it condenses within so small a compass. It is free from all the narrowness of English prejudice, it contains many important and interesting details which can be found in no English production, and is a work which could be written by none but German scholars, more than two hundred of whom were employed in the original compilation."—*Boston Observer.*

" This cannot but prove a valuable addition to the literature of the age."—*Mer. Advertiser.*

" The vast circulation this work has had in Europe, where it has already been reprinted in four or five languages, not to speak of the numerous German editions, of which SEVEN have been published, speaks loudly in favor of its intrinsic merit, without which such a celebrity could never have been attained. To every man engaged in public business, who needs a correct and ample book of reference on various topics of science and letters, the Encyclopædia Americana will be almost invaluable. To individuals obliged to go to situations where books are neither numerous nor easily procured, the rich contents of these twelve volumes will prove a mine which will amply repay its purchaser, and be with difficulty exhausted ; and we recommend it to their patronage in the full conviction of its worth. Indeed, it is difficult to say to what class of readers such a book would not prove useful, nay, almost indispensable, since it combines a great amount of valuable matter in small compass, and at moderate expense, and is in every respect well suited to augment the reader's stock of ideas, and powers of conversation, without severely taxing time or fatiguing attention."—*Am. Daily Advertiser.*

" The department of American Biography, a subject of which it should be disgraceful to be ignorant, to the degree that many are, is, in this work, a prominent feature, and has received the attention of one of the most indefatigable writers in this department of literature, which the present age can furnish."—*Boston Courier.*

" According to the plan of Dr. Lieber, a desideratum will be supplied ; the substance of contemporary knowledge will be brought within a small compass ;—and the character and uses of a manual will be imparted to a kind of publication heretofore reserved, on strong shelves, for occasional reference. By those who understand the German language, the *Conversation Lexicon* is consulted ten times for one application to any English Encyclopædia."—*National Gazette.*

" The volume now published is not only highly honorable to the taste, ability, and industry of its editors and publishers, but furnishes a proud sample of the accuracy and elegance with which the most elaborate and important literary enterprises may now be accomplished in our country. Of the manner in which the editors have thus far completed their task, it is impossible, in the course of a brief newspaper article, to speak with adequate justice."—*Boston Bulletin.*

" It continues to be particularly rich in the departments of Biography and Natural History. When we look at the large mass of miscellaneous knowledge spread before the reader, in a form which has never been equalled for its condensation, and conveyed in a style that cannot be surpassed for propriety and perspicuity, we cannot but think that the American Encyclopædia deserves a place in every collection, in which works of reference form a portion."—*Southern Patriot.*

" By far the best work of the kind ever offered for sale

NEARLY all of the volumes of this work are now before the public, and the reception they have met with is the best evidence that the publishers have fulfilled the promises made at its outset. They have now only to promise, for the editors and themselves, that no exertion shall be spared to render the remaining volumes equal to those already published, and thus sustain the reputation it has acquired. The subscription is large, and increasing ; and in those quarters where its circulation is greatest, and where it is best known, there is a constantly increasing demand. The publishers invite the attention of those who may not already have possessed themselves of it, or may not have had an opportunity to become acquainted with its merits, to the following account of the original work, upon which it is based, and which is termed by the Edinburgh Review—

THE WORLD-RENOWNED LEIPZIG CONVERSATIONS-LEXICON.

It was intended to supply a want occasioned by the character of the age, in which the sciences, arts, trades, and the various forms of knowledge and of active life, had become so much extended and diversified, that no individual engaged in business could become well acquainted with all subjects of general interest ; while the wide diffusion of information rendered such knowledge essential to the character of an accomplished man. This want, no existing works were adequate to supply. Books treating of particular branches, such as gazetteers, &c. were too confined in character ; while voluminous Encyclopædias were too learned, scientific, and cumbrous, being usually elaborate treatises, requiring much study or previous acquaintance with the subject discussed. The conductors of the CONVERSATION LEXICON endeavored to select from every branch of knowledge what was necessary to a well-informed mind, and to give popular views of the more abstruse branches of learning and science ; that their readers might not be incommoded, and deprived of pleasure or improvement, by ignorance of facts or expressions used in books or conversation. Such a work must obviously be of great utility to every class of readers. It has been found so much so in Germany, that it is met with everywhere, among the learned, the lawyers, the military, artists, merchants, mechanics, and men of all stations. The reader may judge how well it is adapted to its object, from the circumstance, that though it now consists of twelve volumes, seven editions, comprising about ONE HUNDRED THOUSAND COPIES, have been printed in less than fifteen years. It has been translated into the Swedish, Danish and Dutch languages, and a French translation is now preparing in Paris.

In the preparation of the American edition, no expense has been spared to secure the ablest assistance, and the editors have been aided by many gentlemen of distinguished ability.

The American Biography, which is very extensive, has been furnished by MR. WALSH, who has long paid particular attention to that branch of our literature, and from materials in the collection of which he has been engaged for some years. For obvious reasons, the notices of distinguished Americans are confined to deceased individuals : the European biography contains notices of all distinguished living characters, as well as those of past times.

The articles on Zoology and the various branches of Natural Science, and those on Chemistry and Mineralogy, have been prepared expressly for this work by gentlemen distinguished in the several departments.

In relation to the Fine Arts, the work is exceedingly rich. Great attention was given to this in the German work, and the Editors have been anxious to render it, by the necessary additions, as perfect as possible.

To gentlemen of the Bar, the work will be peculiarly valuable, as in cases where legal subjects are treated, an account is given of English, French, German and American Law.

MISCELLANEOUS.

THE COMPLETE POETICAL WORKS OF JOANNA BAILLIE. 1 vol. 8vo.

This edition corresponds with the Library Editions of Byron, Scott, Moore, &c.

"Miss Baillie's Plays on the Passions have been long known as among the best in the language. No one who reads them can entertain a doubt of the character of the writer's affections. Such works could never have been dictated by a cold heart."—*Christian Examiner.*

"We are among the most earnest admirers of her genius, her literary attainments and skill, her diction, her success, her moral designs, and her personal worth. Some of her tragedies have deservedly passed into the stock of the principal British and American theatres. They are express developments and delineations of the passions, marked by a deep insight into human nature, great dramatic power of treatment, a fertile spirit of poetry, and the loftiest and purest moral sentiment."—*National Gazette.*

TREATISE ON CLOCK AND WATCH-MAKING, Theoretical and Practical. By THOMAS REID, Edinburgh, Honorary Member of the Worshipful Company of Clock-Makers, London. Royal 8vo. Illustrated by numerous Plates.

GEOLOGICAL MANUAL. By H. T. DE LA BECHE. In 8vo. with numerous wood-cuts.

"A work of first-rate importance in the science to which it relates, and which must henceforth take its place in the library of every student in Geology."—*Phil. Magazine.*

"Mr. De la Beche's Geological Manual is the first and best work of the kind, and he has performed his task with a perfect knowledge of all that has been ascertained in Geology, and with considerable judgment and taste in the manner of doing it. So much geological science was never before compressed in so small a space."—*Spectator.*

MEDICINE, &c.

MANUAL OF GENERAL, DESCRIPTIVE, AND PATHOLOGICAL ANATOMY. By J. F. MECKEL, Professor of Anatomy at Halle, &c. &c. Translated from the French, with Notes, by A. SIDNEY DOANE, A. M. M. D. 3 vols. 8vo.

"It is among the most classical, learned, and authoritative treatises on Anatomy."—*American Journal of Med. Science.*

SURGICAL MEMOIRS OF THE CAMPAIGNS OF RUSSIA, GERMANY, AND FRANCE. Translated from the French of BARON LARREY. In 8vo. with Plates.

A MANUAL OF MEDICAL JURISPRUDENCE, compiled from the best Medical and Legal Works; comprising an account of—I. The Ethics of the Medical Profession; II. Charters and Laws relative to the Faculty; and III. All Medico-legal Questions, with the latest Decisions: being an Analysis of a course of Lectures on Forensic Medicine. By MICHAEL RYAN, M. D., Member of the Royal College of Physicians in London, &c. First American edition, with Additions, by R. EGLESFIELD GRIFFITH, M. D. In 8vo.

"There is not a fact of importance or value connected with the science of which it treats, that is not to be found in its pages. The style is unambitious but clear and strong, and such as becomes a philosophic theme."—*Monthly Review.*

"It is invaluable to medical practitioners, and may be consulted safely by the legal profession."—*Weekly Dispatch.*

MEDICINE, &c.

CHOLERA, as it recently appeared in the towns of Newcastle and Gateshead, including cases illustrative of its Physiology and Pathology, with a view to the establishment of sound principles of Practice. By T. M. GREENHOW, of Newcastle-upon-Tyne, Member of the Royal College of Surgeons in London, &c. &c. &c. In 1 vol. 8vo.

DIRECTIONS FOR MAKING ANATOMICAL PREPARATIONS, formed on the basis of Pole, Marjolin, and Breschet, and including the new method of Mr. Swan. By USHER PARSONS, M. D., Professor of Anatomy and Surgery. 1 vol. 8vo. with Plates.

"It is compiled and prepared with judgment, and is the best and most economical companion the student can possess to aid him in the pursuit of this delightful department of his labors."—*Bost. Med. & Surg. Jour.*

"This is unquestionably one of the most useful works on the preparation of Anatomical Specimens ever published. It should be in the hands of every lover of anatomy; and as attention now is more directed to the formation of museums, it will be found a very valuable book. Nothing is omitted that is important, and many new formulæ are introduced, derived from the author's experience, and from rare books, which he has had the industry to collect."—*N. Y. Med. Journal, Aug. 1831.*

A PRACTICAL GUIDE TO OPERATIONS ON THE TEETH. By JAMES SNELL, Dentist. In 1 vol. 8vo. with Plates.

"Those of our readers who practise in the department of Surgery, on which Mr. Snell's essay treats, will find some useful instructions on the mode of extracting teeth."—*Med. Gazette.*

"This is an excellent practical work, and will be found generally useful."—*Athenæum.*

"This is the best practical manual for the dentist we have seen in the English language."—*Gaz. of Health.*

PRINCIPLES OF PHYSIOLOGICAL MEDICINE, including Physiology, Pathology, and Therapeutics, in the form of Propositions, and commentaries on those relating to Pathology, by F. J. V. BROUSSAIS, &c.; translated by ISAAC HAYS, M. D. and R. E. GRIFFITH, M. D. In 8vo.

"The present work will form an indispensable addition to the library of every physician. It is a very important and necessary companion to the Treatise on Physiology as applied to Pathology, by the same author."—*American Journal of Med. Science.*

PRINCIPLES OF SURGERY. By JOHN SYME, Professor of Surgery in the University of Edinburgh. In 8vo.

HUMAN PHYSIOLOGY, illustrated by numerous Engravings; by ROBLEY DUNGLISON, M. D., Professor of Physiology, Pathology, &c. in the University of Virginia, Member of the American Philosophical Society, &c. 2 vols. 8vo.

"It is the most complete and satisfactory system of Physiology in the English language. It will add to the already high reputation of the author."—*American Journal of Med. Science.*

A TREATISE ON THE DISEASES OF THE EYE. By WILLIAM LAWRENCE, M. D. 1 vol. 8vo. *In the press.*

"It is almost unnecessary to say, that it contains marks of vast erudition and exact judgment, and that experience has dictated the principles that are comprised in them, experience drawn from a hospital devoted solely to the treatment of diseases of the Eye."—*Billaud.*

A TREATISE ON DISEASES OF THE HEART AND GREAT VESSELS. By J. R. BERTIN. Edited by G. BOUILLAUD. Translated from the French. 8vo.

FAMILY CABINET ATLAS.

The FAMILY CABINET ATLAS, constructed upon an original plan: Being
a Companion to the Encyclopædia Americana, Cabinet Cyclopædia, Family Library,
Cabinet Library, &c.

This Atlas comprises, in a volume of the Family Library
size, nearly 100 Maps and Tables, which present equal
to *Fifty Thousand Names of Places*; a body of information three times as extensive as that supplied by the
generality of *Quarto Atlases.*

Opinions of the Public Journals.

"This beautiful and most useful little volume," says
the Literary Gazette, "is a perfect picture of elegance,
containing a vast sum of geographical information. A
more instructive little present, or a gift better calculated
to be long preserved and often referred to, could not be
offered to favored youth of either sex. Its cheapness, we
must add, is another recommendation; for, although this
elegant publication contains 100 beautiful engravings
it is issued at a price that can be no obstacle to its being
procured by every parent and friend to youth."

"This Atlas far surpasses any thing of the kind which
we have seen, and is made to suit the popular libraries
which Dr. Lardner and Mr. Murray are now sending into
every family in the empire."—*Monthly Review.*

"Its very ingenious method of arrangement secures to
the geographical student the information for which hitherto he has been obliged to resort to works of the largest
dimensions."—*Athenæum.*

"This miniature and beautiful Atlas is likely to supersede, for general purposes, maps of a more expensive and
elaborate character. It appears to us to answer the
double purpose of exercising the attention while it im-
prints all that is important in Geography on the memory."—*Atlas.*

"The workmanship is among the best of the kind we
have ever witnessed."—*Examiner.*

"It contains all the information to be derived from the
most expensive and unwieldy Atlas."—*York Courant.*

"By a moment's reference, the exact situation of any
place may be found."—*Birmingham Journal.*

"An excellent little work, engraved with a clearness
and correctness which is quite surprising: when complete, travellers will have a system of Geography and a
complete Atlas, which they may carry in their pocket."—
Spectator.

"This is the most perfect gem of an Atlas which has
ever been published."—*Bristol Journal.*

"It corresponds in size with those popular publications
to which it will form so useful an addition—namely,
'The Family Library,' 'The Classical Library,' and
'Cabinet Cyclopædia."—*Court Journal.*

"Nothing could be devised better calculated to impress
upon the mind a knowledge of the general principles of
geography, than the plan of this publication."—*The
Warder.*

"It will be a crying shame in this age of intellect, if
this able and beautiful work be not extensively patron-
ized; but we cannot doubt the success which we feel
assured its intrinsic merits must secure to it."—*Intelligencer.*

"It is scarcely in the nature of things, that a work of
so much public service should fail in meeting with that
extensive patronage which can alone remunerate the
projectors."—*Leeds Intelligencer.*

"The plates are beautifully executed; and the geographical student may obtain in this little work, such is
the excellence of its arrangement, as much information
as he could gain by wading through several books of far
greater bulk."—*Weekly Dispatch.*

"We have seldom seen a work so perfect in its arrangement, and so elegant in its execution."—*York Courant.*

"For the accuracy of its delineation, and the extent
of the information which it conveys, it stands without
a rival in English topography."—*Freeman's Journal.*

"The plan of this useful and elegant work may, in-
deed, be called original. The style and execution of the
Maps are of the first character."—*Woolmer's Exeter and
Plymouth Gazette.*

"This work is one of the most useful publications
which has yet issued from the press; it will be an unique
and brilliant accession to the library, and a very useful
work to the student in geography."—*Reading Mercury
and Oxford Gazette.*

"Its qualifications will render it one of the most popular, highly interesting, and useful publications of the
day."—*Liverpool Courier.*

MISCELLANEOUS.

MEMOIRS of the LIFE of SIR WALTER
RALEGH, with some account of the Period
in which he lived. By Mrs. A. T. Thomson,
With a portrait.

"Such is the outline of a life, which, in Mrs. Thomson's hands, is a mine of interest; from the first page
to the last the attention is roused and sustained, and
while we approve the manner, we still more applaud
the spirit in which it is executed."—*Literary Gazette.*

"In all respects a most appropriate volume for the
Cabinet Library. We shall take an opportunity in
another notice, to give some of the many interesting
passages in the volume that offer themselves for
quotation."—*N. Y. American.*

"Mrs. Thomson has written a very interesting book.
It takes what we are inclined to think, a just, and at
the same time, favorable view of Ralegh, and is occupied beside with many entertaining and illustrative
anecdotes."—*Craftsman.*

"Presents in a concise but succinct style the variety
of incidents connected with the life of the distinguished subject of the memoir."—*National Journal.*

"The book is unquestionably the best Life of Ralegh that has ever been written."—*Album.*

"This is a piece of biography which combines the
fascinations of romance with the deeper interest that
attaches to historical narrative."—*Southern Patriot.*

ELEGANT LIBRARY EDITIONS

OF THE FOLLOWING WORKS.

WORKS OF JOANNA BAILLIE.

COMPLETE IN ONE VOLUME, 8vo.

WORKS OF HENRY FIELDING.

IN TWO VOLUMES 8vo., WITH A PORTRAIT.

WORKS OF TOBIAS SMOLLETT.

IN TWO VOLUMES 8vo., WITH A PORTRAIT.

SELECT SPEECHES

OF THE

RIGHT HONORABLE GEORGE CANNING.

EDITED BY ROBERT WALSH, ESQ.

WITH A BIOGRAPHICAL AND CRITICAL INTRODUCTION,

BY THE EDITOR.

IN ONE VOLUME 8vo.

In the press.

SELECT SPEECHES

OF THE

RIGHT HONORABLE WILLIAM HUSKISSON,

AND OF THE

RIGHT HONORABLE WILLIAM WINDHAM.

EDITED BY ROBERT WALSH, ESQ.

WITH A BIOGRAPHICAL AND CRITICAL INTRODUCTION,

BY THE EDITOR.

IN ONE VOLUME 8vo.

In the press.

SCOTT, COOPER, AND WASHINGTON IRVING.

BY SIR WALTER SCOTT.

COUNT ROBERT OF PARIS, a Tale of the Lower Empire. By the Author of Waverley. In 3 vols.

"The reader will at once perceive that the subject, the characters and the scenes of action, could not have been better selected for the display of the various and unequalled powers of the author. All that is glorious in arts and splendid in arms—the glitter of armor, the pomp of war, and the splendor of chivalry—the gorgeous scenery of the Bosphorus—the ruins of Byzantium—the magnificence of the Grecian capital, and the richness and voluptuousness of the imperial court, will rise before the reader in a succession of beautiful and dazzling images."—*Commercial Advertiser.*

AUTOBIOGRAPHY OF SIR WALTER SCOTT. With a Portrait.

"This is a delightful volume, which cannot fail to satisfy every reader, and of which the contents ought to be known to all those who would be deemed conversant with the literature of our era."—*National Gazette.*

HISTORY OF SCOTLAND. In 2 vols.

"The History of Scotland, by Sir Walter Scott, we do not hesitate to declare, will be, if possible, more extensively read, than the most popular work of fiction, by the same prolific author, and for this obvious reason: it combines much of the brilliant coloring of the Ivanhoe pictures of by-gone manners, and all the graceful facility of style and picturesqueness of description of his other charming romances, with a minute fidelity to the facts of history, and a searching scrutiny into their authenticity and relative value, which might put to the blush Mr. Hume and other professed historians. Such is the magic charm of Sir Walter Scott's pen, it has only to touch the simplest incident of every-day life, and it starts up invested with all the interest of a scene of romance; and yet such is his fidelity to the text of nature, that the knights, and serfs, and collared fools with whom his inventive genius has peopled so many volumes, are regarded by us as not mere creations of fancy, but as real flesh and blood existences, with all the virtues, feelings and errors of common-place humanity."—*Lit. Gazette.*

TALES OF A GRANDFATHER, being a series from French History. By the Author of WAVERLEY.

BY MR. COOPER.

THE BRAVO. By the Author of the SPY, PILOT, &c. In 2 vols.

THE WATER-WITCH, OR THE SKIMMER OF THE SEAS. In 2 vols.

"We have no hesitation in classing this among the most powerful of the romances of our countryman."—*U. States Gazette.*

THE HEIDENMAUER; or, THE BENEDICTINES. 2 vols.

New Editions of the following Works by the same Author.

NOTIONS OF THE AMERICANS, by a Travelling Bachelor, 2 vols. 12mo.

THE WEPT OF WISH-TON-WISH, 2 vols. 12mo.

THE RED ROVER, 2 vols. 12mo.

THE SPY, 2 vols. 12mo.

THE PIONEERS, 2 vols. 12mo.

LIONEL LINCOLN, OR THE LEAGUER OF BOSTON, 2 vols.

THE LAST OF THE MOHICANS, 2 vols. 12mo.

THE PRAIRIE, 2 vols. 12mo.

BY WASHINGTON IRVING.

VOYAGES AND ADVENTURES OF THE COMPANIONS OF COLUMBUS. By WASHINGTON IRVING, Author of the Life of Columbus, &c. 1 vol. 8vo.

"Of the main work we may repeat that it possesses the value of important history and the magnetism of romantic adventure. It sustains in every respect the reputation of Irving." "We may hope that the gifted author will treat in like manner the enterprises and exploits of Pizarro and Cortes; and thus complete a series of elegant recitals, which will contribute to the especial gratification of Americans, and form an imperishable fund of delightful instruction for all ages and countries."—*Nat. Gazette.*

"As he leads us from one savage tribe to another, as he paints successive scenes of heroism, perseverance and self-denial, as he wanders among the magnificent scenes of nature, as he relates with scrupulous fidelity the errors, and the crimes, even of those whose lives are for the most part marked with traits to command admiration, and perhaps esteem—everywhere we find him the same undeviating, but beautiful moralist, gathering from every incident some lesson to present in striking language to the reason and the heart."—*Am. Quarterly Review.*

"This is a delightful volume; for the preface truly says that the expeditions narrated and springing out of the voyages of Columbus may be compared with attempts of adventurous knights-errant to achieve the enterprise left unfinished by some illustrious predecessors. Washington Irving's name is a pledge how well their stories will be told: and we only regret that we must of necessity defer our extracts for a week."—*London Lit. Gazette.*

A CHRONICLE OF THE CONQUEST OF GRENADA. By WASHINGTON IRVING, Esq. In 2 vols.

"On the whole, this work will sustain the high fame of Washington Irving. It fills a blank in the historical library which ought not to have remained so long a blank. The language throughout is at once chaste and animated; and the narrative may be said, like Spenser's Fairy Queen, to present one long gallery of splendid pictures."—*Lond. Lit. Gazette.*

"Collecting his materials from various historians, and adopting in some degree the tone and manner of a monkish chronicler, he has embodied them in a narrative which in manner reminds us of the rich and storied pages of Froissart. He dwells on the feats of chivalry performed by the Christian Knights, with all the ardor which might be expected from a priest, who mixed, according to the usage of the times, not only in the palaces of courtly nobles, and their gay festivals, as an honored and welcome guest, but who was their companion in the camp, and their spiritual and indeed bodily comforter and assistant in the field of battle.—*Am. Quarterly Review.*

New Editions of the following Works by the same Author.

THE SKETCH BOOK, 2 vols. 12mo.

KNICKERBOCKER'S HISTORY OF NEW YORK, revised and corrected. 2 vols.

BRACEBRIDGE HALL, OR THE HUMORISTS, 2 vols. 12mo.

CLASSICAL LITERATURE.

INTRODUCTION TO THE STUDY OF THE GREEK CLASSIC POETS, for the use of Young Persons at School or College.

    Contents.—General Introduction; Homeric Questions; Life of Homer; Iliad; Odyssey; Margites; Batrachomyomachia; Hymns; Hesiod. By Henry Nelson Coleridge.

"We have been highly pleased with this little volume. This work supplies a want which we have often painfully felt, and affords a manual which we should gladly see placed in the hands of every embryo under-graduate. We look forward to the next portion of this work with very eager and impatient expectation."—*British Critic.*

"Mr. Coleridge's work not only deserves the praise of clear, eloquent and scholar-like exposition of the preliminary matter, which is necessary in order to understand and enter into the character of the great Poet of antiquity; but it has likewise the more rare merit of being admirably adapted for its acknowledged purpose. It is written in that fresh and ardent spirit, which to the congenial mind of youth, will convey instruction in the most effective manner, by awakening the desire of it; and by enlisting the lively and buoyant feelings in the cause of useful and improving study; while, by its pregnant brevity, it is more likely to stimulate than to supersede more profound and extensive research. If then, as it is avowedly intended for the use of the younger readers of Homer, and, as it is impossible not to discover, with a more particular view to the great school to which the author owes his education, we shall be much mistaken if it does not become as popular as it will be useful in that celebrated establishment."—*Quarterly Review.*

"We sincerely hope that Mr. Coleridge will favor us with a continuation of his work, which he promises."—*Gent. Mag.*

"The author of this elegant volume has collected a vast mass of valuable information. To the higher classes of the public schools, and young men of universities, this volume will be especially valuable; as it will afford an agreeable relief of light reading to more grave studies, at once instructive and entertaining."—*Wesleyan Methodist Magazine.*

ATLAS OF ANCIENT GEOGRAPHY, consisting of 21 Colored Maps, with a complete Accentuated Index. By Samuel Butler, D. D., F. R. S. &c. Archdeacon of Derby.

By the same Author.

GEOGRAPHIA CLASSICA: a Sketch of Ancient Geography, for the Use of Schools. In 8vo.

Extract of a Letter from Professor Stuart of Andover.

"I have used Butler's Atlas Classica for 12 or 14 years, and prefer it on the score of convenience and correctness to any atlas within the compass of my knowledge. It is evidently a work of much care and taste, and most happily adapted to classical readers and indeed all others, who consult the history of past ages. I have long cherished a strong desire to see the work brought forward in this country, and I am exceedingly gratified that you have carried it through this undertaking. The beautiful manner in which the specimen is executed that you have sent me does great credit to engravers and publishers. It cannot be that our schools and colleges will fail to adopt this work, and bring it into very general circulation. I know of none which in all respects would supply its place."

"The abridged but classical and excellent work of Butler, on Ancient Geography, which you are printing as an accompaniment to the maps, I consider one of the most

MECHANICS, MANUFACTURES, &c.

A PRACTICAL TREATISE ON RAIL-ROADS, AND INTERIOR COMMUNICATION IN GENERAL—containing an account of the performances of the different Locomotive Engines at, and subsequent to, the Liverpool Contest; upwards of two hundred and sixty Experiments with Tables of the comparative value of Canals and Railroads, and the power of the present Locomotive Engines. By Nicholas Wood, Colliery Viewer, Member of the Institution of Civil Engineers, &c. 8vo. with plates.

"In this, the able author has brought up his treatise to the date of the latest improvements in this nationally important plan. We consider the volume to be one of great general interest."—*Lit. Gaz.*

"We must, in justice, refer the reader to the work itself, strongly assuring him that, whether he be a man of science, or one totally unacquainted with its technical difficulties, he will here receive instruction and pleasure, in a degree which we have seldom seen united before."—*Monthly Rev.*

REPORTS ON LOCOMOTIVE AND FIXED ENGINES. By J. Stephenson and J. Walker, Civil Engineers. With an Account of the Liverpool and Manchester Railroad, by H. Booth. In 8vo. with plates.

MILLWRIGHT AND MILLER'S GUIDE. By Oliver Evans. New Edition, with additions and corrections, by the Professor of Mechanics in the Franklin Institute of Pennsylvania, and a description of an improved Merchant Flour-Mill, with engravings, by C. & O. Evans, Engineers.

THE NATURE AND PROPERTIES OF THE SUGAR CANE, with Practical Directions for its Culture, and the Manufacture of its various Products; detailing the improved Methods of Extracting, Boiling, Refining, and Distilling; also Descriptions of the Best Machinery, and useful Directions for the general Management of Estates. By George Richardson Porter.

"This volume contains a valuable mass of scientific and practical information, and is, indeed, a compendium of everything interesting relative to colonial agriculture and manufacture."—*Intelligencer.*

"We can altogether recommend this volume as a most valuable addition to the library of the home West India merchant, as well as that of the resident planter."—*Lit. Gazette.*

"This work may be considered one of the most valuable books that has yet issued from the press connected with colonial interests; indeed, we know of no greater service we could render West India proprietors, than in recommending the study of Mr. Porter's volume."—*Spectator.*

"The work before us contains such valuable, scientific, and practical information, that we have no doubt it will find a place in the library of every planter and person connected with our sugar colonies."—*Monthly Magazine.*

A TREATISE ON MECHANICS. By James Renwick, Esq. Professor of Natural and

LARDNER'S CABINET CYCLOPÆDIA.

HISTORY OF ENGLAND. By Sir James Mackintosh. In 8 Vols. III Vols. pub-lished.

"In the first volume of Sir James Mackintosh's History of England, we find enough to warrant the anticipations of the public, that a calm and luminous philosophy will diffuse itself over the long narrative of our British History."—*Edinburgh Review.*

"In this volume Sir James Mackintosh fully developes
those great powers, for the possession of which the public
have long given him credit. The result is the ablest com-
mentary that has yet appeared in our language upon some
of the most important circumstances of English History."
—*Atlas.*

"Worthy in the method, style, and reflections, of the
author's high reputation. We were particularly pleased
with his high vein of philosophical sentiment, and his
occasional survey of contemporary annals."—*National
Gazette.*

"If talents of the highest order, long experience in politics, and years of application to the study of history
and the collection of information, can command superiority in a historian, Sir James Mackintosh may, without
reading this work, be said to have produced the best history of this country. A perusal of the work will prove
that those who anticipated a superior production, have
not reckoned in vain on the high qualifications of the
author."—*Courier.*

"Our anticipations of this volume were certainly very
highly raised, and unlike such anticipations in general,
they have not been disappointed. A philosophical spirit,
a nervous style, and a full knowledge of the subject, acquired by considerable research into the works of preceding chroniclers and historians, eminently distinguish
this popular abridgment, and cannot fail to recommend it
to universal approbation. In continuing his work as he
has begun, Sir James Mackintosh will confer a great benefit on his country."—*Lond. Lit. Gazette.*

"Of its general merits, and its permanent value, it is
impossible to speak, without the highest commendation,
and after a careful and attentive perusal of the two volumes which have been published, we are enabled to declare that, so far, Sir James Mackintosh has performed
the duty to which he was assigned, with all the ability
that was to be expected from his great previous attainments, his laborious industry in investigation, his excellent judgment, his superior talents, and his honorable
principles."—*Inquirer.*

"We shall probably extract the whole of his view of
the reformation, merely to show how that important topic
has been handled by so able and philosophical a writer,
professing Protestantism.—*National Gazette.*

"The talents of Sir James Mackintosh are so justly and
deeply respected, that a strong interest is necessarily excited with regard to any work which such a distinguished
writer may think fit to undertake. In the present instance,
as in all others, our expectations are fully gratified."—
Gentleman's Magazine.

"The second volume of the History of England, forming the sixth of Carey & Lea's Cabinet Cyclopædia, has
been sent abroad, and entirely sustains the reputation of
its predecessors. The various factions and dissensions,
the important trials and battles, which render this period
so conspicuous in the page of history, are all related with
great clearness and masterly power."—*Boston Traveller.*

BIOGRAPHY OF BRITISH STATESMEN; containing the Lives of Sir Thomas More, Cardinal Wolsey, Archbishop Cranmer, and Lord Burleigh.

"A very delightful volume, and on a subject likely to

HISTORY OF SCOTLAND. By Sir Walter Scott. In 2 Vols.

"The History of Scotland, by Sir Walter Scott, we do
not hesitate to declare, will be, if possible, more extensively read, than the most popular work of fiction, by the
same prolific author, and for this obvious reason: it combines much of the brilliant coloring of the Ivanhoe pictures of by-gone manners, and all the graceful facility of
style and picturesqueness of description of his other
charming romances, with a minute fidelity to the facts
of history, and a searching scrutiny into their authenticity and relative value, which might put to the blush
Mr. Hume and other professed historians. Such is the
magic charm of Sir Walter Scott's pen, it has only to
touch the simplest incident of every-day life, and it starts
up invested with all the interest of a scene of romance;
and yet such is his fidelity to the text of nature, that the
knights, and serfs, and collared fools with whom his inventive genius has peopled so many volumes, are regarded
by us as not mere creations of fancy, but as real flesh and
blood existences, with all the virtues, feelings and errors
of common-place humanity."—*Lit. Gazette.*

HISTORY OF FRANCE. By Eyre Evans Crowe. In 3 vols.

HISTORY OF FRANCE, from the Restora-tion of the Bourbons, to the Revolution of 1830. By T. B. Macaulay, Esq. M. P. Nearly ready.

"The style is concise and clear; and events are sum-
med up with much vigor and originality."—*Lit. Gazette.*

"His history of France is worthy to figure with the
works of his associates, the best of their day, Scott and
Mackintosh."—*Monthly Mag.*

"For such a task Mr. Crowe is eminently qualified.
At a glance, as it were, his eye takes in the theatre of
centuries. His style is neat, clear, and pithy; and his
power of condensation enables him to say much, and
effectively, in a few words, to present a distinct and
perfect picture in a narrowly circumscribed space."—*La
Belle Assemblee.*

"The style is neat and condensed; the thoughts and
conclusions sound and just. The necessary conciseness
of the narrative is unaccompanied by any baldness; on
the contrary, it is spirited and engaging."—*Balt. American.*

"To compress the history of a great nation, during a
period of thirteen hundred years, into three volumes, and
to preserve sufficient distinctness as well as interest in
the narrative, to enable and induce the reader to possess
himself clearly of all the leading incidents, is a task by
no means easily executed. It has, nevertheless, been well
accomplished in this instance."—*N. Y. American.*

"Written with spirit and taste."—*U. S. Gazette.*

"Could we but persuade our young friends to give
these volumes a careful perusal, we should feel assured
of their grateful acknowledgments of profit and pleasure."—*N. Y. Mirror.*

"At once concise and entertaining."—*Saturday Bulletin.*

THE HISTORY OF THE NETHERLANDS, to the Battle of Waterloo. By T. C. Grat-tan.

"It is but justice to Mr. Grattan to say that he has
executed his laborious task with much industry and proportionate effect. Undisfigured by pompous nothingness,
and without any of the affectation of philosophical pro-
fundity, his style is simple, light, and fresh—perspicuous,
smooth, and harmonious."—*La Belle Assemblee.*

"Never did work appear at a more fortunate period.
The volume before us is a compressed but clear and im-
partial narrative."—*Lit. Gaz.*

"A long residence in the country, and a ready access to
libraries and archives, have furnished Mr. Grattan with
materials which he has arranged with skill and out of

CABINET LIBRARY.

No. 1.—NARRATIVE OF THE LATE WAR IN GERMANY AND FRANCE. By the MARQUESS OF LONDONDERRY. With a Map.

No. 2.—JOURNAL OF A NATURALIST, with plates.

No. 3.—AUTOBIOGRAPHY OF SIR WALTER SCOTT. With a portrait.

No. 4.—MEMOIRS OF SIR WALTER RALEGH. By Mrs. A. T. THOMSON. With a portrait.

No. 5.—LIFE OF BELISARIUS. By Lord MAHON.

No. 6.—MILITARY MEMOIRS OF THE DUKE OF WELLINGTON. By Capt. MOYLE SHERER. With a portrait.

No. 7.—LETTERS TO A YOUNG NATURALIST ON THE STUDY OF NATURE AND NATURAL THEOLOGY. By J. L. DRUMMOND, M. D. With numerous engravings.

IN PREPARATION.

LIFE OF PETRARCH. By THOMAS MOORE.

GLEANINGS IN NATURAL HISTORY, being a Companion to the Journal of a Naturalist.

"The Cabinet Library bids fair to be a series of great value, and is recommended to public and private libraries, to professional men, and miscellaneous readers generally. It is beautifully printed, and furnished at a price which will place it within the reach of all classes of society."—*American Traveller.*

"The series of instructive, and, in their original form, expensive works, which these enterprising publishers are now issuing under the title of the "Cabinet Library," is a fountain of useful, and almost universal knowledge; the advantages of which, in forming the opinions, tastes, and manners of that portion of society, to which this varied information is yet new, cannot be too highly estimated."—*National Journal.*

"Messrs. Carey and Lea have commenced a series of publications under the above title, which are to appear monthly, and which seem likely, from the specimen before us, to acquire a high degree of popularity, and to afford a mass of various information and rich entertainment, at once eminently useful and strongly attractive. The mechanical execution is fine, the paper and typography excellent."—*Nashville Banner.*

MEMOIRS OF THE LIFE OF SIR WALTER RALEGH, with some Account of the Period in which he lived. By MRS. A. T. THOMSON. With a Portrait.

"Such is the outline of a life, which, in Mrs. Thomson's hands, is a mine of interest; from the first page to the last the attention is roused and sustained, and while we approve the manner, we still more applaud the spirit in which it is executed."—*Literary Gazette.*

JOURNAL OF A NATURALIST. With Plates.

————Plants, trees, and stones we note; Birds, insects, beasts, and rural things.

and more particularly of our country readers. It will induce them, we are sure, to examine more closely than they have been accustomed to do, into the objects of animated nature, and such examination will prove one of the most innocent, and the most satisfactory sources of gratification and amusement. It is a book that ought to find its way into every rural drawing-room in the kingdom, and one that may safely be placed in every lady's boudoir, be her rank and station in life what they may."—*Quarterly Review, No. LXXVIII.*

"We think that there are few readers who will not be delighted (we are certain all will be instructed) by the 'Journal of a Naturalist.'"—*Monthly Review.*

"This is a most delightful book on the most delightful of all studies. We are acquainted with no previous work which bears any resemblance to this, except 'White's History of Selborne,' the most fascinating piece of rural writing and sound English philosophy that ever issued from the press."—*Athenæum.*

"The author of the volume now before us, has produced one of the most charming volumes we remember to have seen for a long time."—*New Monthly Magazine, June, 1829.*

"A delightful volume—perhaps the most so—nor less instructive and amusing—given to Natural History since White's Selborne."—*Blackwood's Magazine.*

"The Journal of a Naturalist, being the second number of Carey and Lea's beautiful edition of the Cabinet Library, is the best treatise on subjects connected with this train of thought, that we have for a long time perused, and we are not at all surprised that it should have received so high and flattering encomiums from the English press generally."—*Boston Traveller.*

"Furnishing an interesting and familiar account of the various objects of animated nature, but calculated to afford both instruction and entertainment."—*Nashville Banner.*

"One of the most agreeable works of its kind in the language."—*Courier de la Louisiane.*

"It abounds with numerous and curious facts, pleasing illustrations of the secret operations and economy of nature, and satisfactory displays of the power, wisdom and goodness, of the great Creator."—*Philad. Album.*

THE MARQUESS OF LONDONDERRY'S NARRATIVE OF THE LATE WAR IN GERMANY AND FRANCE. With a Map.

"No history of the events to which it relates can be correct without reference to its statements."—*Literary Gazette.*

"The events detailed in this volume cannot fail to excite an intense interest."—*Dublin Literary Gazette.*

"The only connected and well authenticated account we have of the spirit-stirring scenes which preceded the fall of Napoleon. It introduces us into the cabinets and presence of the allied monarchs. We observe the secret policy of each individual: we see the course pursued by the wily Bernadotte, the temporizing Metternich, and the ambitious Alexander. The work deserves a place in every historical library."—*Globe.*

"We hail with pleasure the appearance of the first volume of the Cabinet Library." "The author had singular facilities for obtaining the materials of his work, and he has introduced us to the movements and measures of cabinets which have hitherto been hidden from the world."—*American Traveller.*

"It may be regarded as the most authentic of all the publications which profess to detail the events of the important campaigns, terminating with that which secured the capture of the French metropolis."—*Nat. Journal.*

"It is in fact the only authentic account of the memorable events to which it refers."—*Nashville Banner.*

Chemistry, Natural History, and Philosophy.

THE CHEMISTRY OF THE ARTS, on the basis of Gray's Operative Chemist, being an Exhibition of the Arts and Manufactures dependent on Chemical Principles, with numerous Engravings, by ARTHUR L. PORTER, M. D. late Professor of Chemistry, &c. in the University of Vermont. In 8vo. With numerous Plates.

The popular and valuable English work of Mr. Gray, which forms the groundwork of the present volume, was published in London in 1829, and designed to exhibit a systematic and practical view of the numerous Arts and Manufactures which involve the application of Chemical Science. The author himself, a skilful, manufacturing, as well as an able, scientific chemist, enjoying the multiplied advantages afforded by the metropolis of the greatest manufacturing nation on earth, was eminently qualified for so arduous an undertaking, and the popularity of the work in England, as well as its intrinsic merits, attest the fidelity and success with which it has been executed. In the work now offered to the American public, the practical character of the Operative Chemist has been preserved, and much extended by the addition of a great variety of original matter, by numerous corrections of the original text, and the adaptation of the whole to the state and wants of the Arts and Manufactures of the United States. Among the most considerable additions will be found full and extended treatises on the Bleaching of Cotton and Linen, on the various branches of Calico Printing, on the Manufacture of the Chloride of Lime, or Bleaching Powder, and numerous Staple Articles used in the Arts of Dying, Calico Printing, and various other processes of Manufacture, such as the Salts of Tin, Lead, Manganese, and Antimony; the most recent Improvements on the Manufacture of the Muriatic, Nitric, and Sulphuric Acids, the Chromates of Potash, the latest information on the comparative Value of Different Varieties of Fuel, on the Construction of Stoves, Fire-Places, and Stoving Rooms, on the Ventilation of Apartments, &c. &c. The leading object has been to improve and extend the *practical* character of the Operative Chemist, and to supply, as the publishers flatter themselves, a deficiency which is felt by every artist and manufacturer, whose processes involve the principles of chemical science, the want of a Systematic Work which should embody the most recent improvements in the chemical arts and manufactures, whether derived from the researches of scientific men, or the experiments and observations of the operative manufacturer and artisans themselves.

CHEMICAL MANIPULATION. Instruction to Students on the Methods of performing Experiments of Demonstration or Research, with accuracy and success. By MICHAEL FARADAY, F. R. S. First American, from the second London edition, with Additions by J. K. MITCHELL, M. D.

"After a very careful perusal of this work, we strenuously recommend it, as containing the most complete and excellent instructions for conducting chemical experiments. There are few persons, however great their experience, who may not gain information in many important particulars; and for ourselves, we beg most unequivocally to acknowledge that we have acquired many new and important hints on subjects of even every-day occurrence."—*Philosophical Mag.*

"A work hitherto exceedingly wanted in the laboratory, equally useful to the proficient and to the student, and eminently creditable to the industry and skill of the author, and to the school whence it emanates."—*Journal of Science and Arts.*

GEOLOGICAL MANUAL, by H. T. De la Beche, F. R. S., F. G. S., Mem. Geol. Soc. of France. In 8vo. With 104 Wood Cuts.

ELEMENTS OF PHYSICS, OR NATURAL PHILOSOPHY, GENERAL AND MEDICAL, explained independently of TECHNICAL MATHEMATICS, and containing New Disquisitions and Practical Suggestions. By NEILL ARNOTT, M. D. Second American from the fourth London edition, with Additions by ISAAC HAYS, M. D.

"Dr. Arnott's work has done for Physics as much as Locke's Essay did for the science of mind."—*London University Magazine.*

"We may venture to predict that it will not be surpassed."—*Times.*

"Dr. A. has not done less for Physics than Blackstone did for the Law."—*Morning Herald.*

"Dr. A. has made Natural Philosophy as attractive as Buffon made Natural History."—*French Critic.*

"A work of the highest class among the productions of mind."—*Courier.*

"We regard the style and manner as quite admirable."—*Morning Chronicle.*

"As interesting as novel-reading."—*Athenæum.*

"Never did philosophic hand wield a pen more calculated to win men to be wise and good."—*Edinburgh Observer.*

"Of this valuable, or we might say, invaluable work, a second edition has been speedily demanded by the public voice."—*Lit. Gaz.*

A FLORA OF NORTH AMERICA, with 108 colored Plates. By W. P. C. BARTON, M. D. In 3 vols. 4to.

ARNOTT'S ELEMENTS OF PHYSICS. Vol. II. Part I. Containing Light and Heat.

"Dr. Arnott's previous volume has been so well received, that it has almost banished all the flimsy productions called popular, which falsely pretend to strip science of its mysterious and repulsive aspect, and to exhibit a holy-day apparel. The success of such a work shows most clearly that it is plain, but sound knowledge which the public want."—*Monthly Review.*

AMERICAN ORNITHOLOGY, OR NATURAL HISTORY OF BIRDS, INHABITING THE UNITED STATES, by CHARLES LUCIEN BONAPARTE; designed as a continuation of Wilson's Ornithology, Vols. I. II. and III.

⁎ Gentlemen who possess Wilson, and are desirous of rendering the work complete, are informed that the edition of this work is very small, and that but a very limited number of copies remain unsold. Vol. IV. in the Press.

A DISCOURSE ON THE REVOLUTIONS OF THE SURFACE OF THE GLOBE AND THE CHANGES THEREBY PRODUCED IN THE ANIMAL KINGDOM. By BARON G. CUVIER. Translated from the French, with Illustrations and a Glossary. In 12mo. With Plates.

' One of the most scientific and important, yet plain and lucid works, which adorn the age ———— Here is vast aid to the reader interested in the study of nature, and the lights which reason and investigation have thrown upon the formation of the universe."—*New Monthly Magazine.*

PHYSIOLOGICAL MEDICINE AND ANATOMY.

HISTORY OF CHRONIC PHLEGMASIÆ, OR INFLAMMATIONS, founded on Clinical Experience and Pathological Anatomy, exhibiting a View of the different Varieties and Complications of these Diseases, with their various Methods of Treatment. By F. J. V. BROUSSAIS, M. D. Translated from the French of the fourth edition, by ISAAC HAYS, M. D. and R. EGLESFELD GRIFFITH, M. D. Members of the American Philosophical Society, of the Academy of Natural Science, Honorary Members of the Philadelphia Medical Society, &c. &c. In 2 vols. 8vo.

EXAMINATION OF MEDICAL DOCTRINES AND SYSTEMS OF NOSOLOGY, preceded by Propositions containing the Substance of Physiological Medicine, by F. J. V. BROUSSAIS, Officer of the Royal Order of the Legion of Honor; Chief Physician and First Professor in the Military Hospital for Instruction at Paris, &c. Third edition. Translated from the French, by ISAAC HAYS, M. D. and R. E. GRIFFITH, M. D. In 2 vols. 8vo. *In the press.*

A TREATISE ON PHYSIOLOGY, Applied to PATHOLOGY. By F. J. V. BROUSSAIS, M. D. Translated from the French, by Drs. BELL and LA ROCHE. 8vo. Third American edition, with additions.

"We cannot too strongly recommend the present work to the attention of our readers, and indeed of all those who wish to study physiology as it ought to be studied, in its application to the science of disease." "We may safely say that he has accomplished his task in a most masterly manner, and thus established his reputation as a most excellent physiologist and profound pathologist." —*North American Med. and Surg. Journ. Jan.* 1827.

THE PRINCIPLES AND PRACTICE OF MEDICINE. By SAMUEL JACKSON, M. D. Adjunct Professor of the Institutes and Practice of Medicine in the University of Pennsylvania. 8vo.

THE PRACTICE OF MEDICINE, upon the Principles of the Physiological Doctrine. By J. G. COSTER, M. D. Translated from the French.

AN EPITOME OF THE PHYSIOLOGY, GENERAL ANATOMY, AND PATHOLOGY OF BICHAT. By THOMAS HENDERSON, M. D. Professor of the Theory and Practice of Medicine in Columbia College, Washington City. 8vo.

PHYSIOLOGICAL PYRETOLOGY; or, A TREATISE ON FEVERS, according to the Principles of the New Medical Doctrine. By F. G. BOISSEAU, Doctor in Medicine of the Faculty of Paris, &c. &c. From the fourth French edition. Translated by J. R. KNOX, M. D. 1 vol. 8vo.

"Boisseau's Pyretology is not merely the most remarkable performance that has as yet appeared among the disciples of Broussais, but is really the ablest and most satisfactory exposition of the pathology of Fevers with which we are acquainted."—*American Journal of Medical Sciences, No. XIV.*

DIRECTIONS FOR MAKING ANATOMICAL PREPARATIONS, formed on the basis of Pole, Marjolin and Breschet, and including the new method of Mr. Swan, by USHER PARSONS, M. D. Professor of Anatomy and Surgery. In 1 Vol. 8vo. with plates.

A TREATISE ON PATHOLOGICAL ANATOMY. By WILLIAM E. HORNER, M. D. Adj. Prof. of Anatomy in the University of Pennsylvania.

"We can conscientiously commend it to the members of the profession, as a satisfactory, interesting, and instructive view of the subjects discussed, and as well adapted to aid them in forming a correct appreciation of the diseased conditions they are called on to relieve."—*American Journal of the Medical Sciences, No. 9.*

By the same Author.

A TREATISE ON SPECIAL AND GENERAL ANATOMY. Third edition, revised and corrected, in 2 Vols. 8vo.

LESSONS IN PRACTICAL ANATOMY, for the use of Dissectors. 2d edition, in 1 Vol. 8vo.

SYSTEM OF ANATOMY, for the use of Students of Medicine. By CASPAR WISTAR. Fifth edition, revised and corrected, by W. E. HORNER, Adjunct Professor of Anatomy in the University of Pennsylvania. In 2 Vols. 8vo.

ELEMENTS OF GENERAL ANATOMY, or a description of the Organs comprising the Human Body. By P. A. BECLARD, Professor of Anatomy to the Faculty of Medicine at Paris. Translated by J. TOGNO.

TREATISE ON SURGICAL ANATOMY. By ABRAHAM COLLES, Professor of Anatomy and Surgery, in the Royal College of Surgeons in Ireland, &c. Second American edition, with notes by J. P. HOPKINSON, Demonstrator of Anatomy in the University of Pennsylvania, &c. &c.

A TREATISE ON PATHOLOGICAL ANATOMY. By E. GEDDINGS, M. D. Professor of Anatomy in the Medical College of South Carolina. In 2 vols. 8vo. (In the press.)

ELEMENTS OF MYOLOGY. By E. GEDDINGS, M. D. illustrated by a series of beautiful Engravings of the Muscles of the Human Body, on a plan heretofore unknown in this country. *In the press.*

This work, in addition to an ample and accurate description of the general and special anatomy of the muscular system, will comprise illustrations of the subject from comparative anatomy and physiology, with an account of the irregularities, variations and anomalies, observed by the various ancient and modern anatomists, down to the present time.

EDUCATION.

A New Abridgement of AINSWORTH'S DICTIONARY, English and Latin, for the use of Grammar Schools. By JOHN DYMOCK, LL. D., with Notes, by CHARLES ANTHON. 1 vol. 18mo.

In this edition are introduced several alterations and improvements, for the special purpose of facilitating the labor and increasing the knowledge of the young scholar.

GREEK AND ENGLISH LEXICON. By D. DONNEGAN. Abridged for the use of Schools. In 1 vol. royal 18mo., containing above 800 pages.

This work is printed on a handsome distinct type, and contains as much matter as many of the larger lexicons; but owing to the form in which it is printed, it is sold at such price as to be within the reach of all students. It offers more advantages to the young student than any other lexicon now in use. The vocabulary is more extensive and complete—comprising not only words found in the classics, but also such as are found in the writings of Hippocrates and the Greek physicians. The meanings attached to words by the several writers are also given.

Words are given in alphabetical order in every poetical and dialectic variety.

The conjugation of verbs and flection of nouns are more complete than in other lexicons;—the meanings of words fuller and more correct—there being first a primary and then a secondary meaning, each distinguished from the metaphorical and idiomatical. Phrases are also given when they note any peculiarity in signification. The etymology of words is only omitted where it is confused or disputed. There is nothing left out which the young student would find necessary in studying the classics, and which would enable him to understand the true meaning of a word. In short, in this work the essential advantages of a good Dictionary are combined with those of a good Grammar—advantages not found in any Greek and English lexicon now used.

ELEMENTS OF MECHANICS. By JAMES RENWICK, Esq., Professor of Natural and Experimental Philosophy, Columbia College, N. Y. In 8vo. with numerous Engravings.

"We think this decidedly the best treatise on Mechanics, which has issued from the American press, that we have seen; one, too, that is alike creditable to the writer, and to the state of science in this country."—American Quarterly Review.

ELEMENTS OF OPTICS. By DAVID BREWSTER. First American edition, with Notes and Additions, by A. D. BACHE, Professor of Natural Philosophy and Chemistry in the University of Pennsylvania. 18mo.

"The author has given proof of his well-known industry, and extensive acquaintance with the results of science in every part of Europe."—Monthly Mag.
"The subject is, as might be expected, ably treated, and clearly illustrated."—U. S. Jour.

A TREATISE ON HYDROSTATICS AND PNEUMATICS. By the Rev. DIONYSIUS LARDNER, LL. D. F. R. S. &c. First American from the first London edition, with Notes by BENJAMIN F. JOSLIN, M. D., Professor of Natural Philosophy in Union College.

"It fully sustains the favorable opinion we have already expressed as to this valuable compendium of modern science."—Lit. Gaz.
"Dr. Lardner has made a good use of his acquaintance with the familiar facts which illustrate the principles of science."—Monthly Mag.
"It is written with a full knowledge of the subject, and in a popular style, abounding in practical illustrations of the abstruse operations of these important

AN ESSAY ON MORAL CULTURE, addressed to Parents and Teachers. By M. M. CARLL. 18mo.

AN ELEMENTARY TREATISE ON ALGEBRA, Theoretical and Practical; with attempts to simplify some of the more difficult parts of the science, particularly the demonstration of the Binomial Theorem, in its most general form; the Solution of Equations of the higher orders; the Summation of Infinite Series, &c. By J. R. YOUNG. First American edition, with Additions and Improvements, by SAMUEL WARD, Jun. 8vo.

"A new and ingenious general method of solving Equations has been recently discovered by Messrs. H. Atkinson, Holdred, and Horner, independently of each other. For the best practical view of this new method and its applications, consult the Elementary Treatise on Algebra, by Mr. J. R. Young, a work which deserves our cordial recommendation."—Dr. Gregory's edition of Hutton's Mathematics.
"For the summation of Infinite Series the author gives a new and ingenious method, which is very easy and extensive in its application."—Newcastle Mag.

By the same Author.

ELEMENTS OF GEOMETRY; containing a new and universal Treatise on the Doctrine of Proportions, together with Notes, in which are pointed out and connected several important errors that have hitherto remained unnoticed in the writings of Geometers. Also, an Examination of the various Theories of Parallel Lines that have been proposed by Legendre, Bertrand, Ivory, Leslie, and others.

"His observations on the theory of parallel lines, the labor he has bestowed on the doctrines of proportion, as well as his corrections of many errors of preceding Geometers, and supplying their defects, together with his minute attention to accuracy throughout, may be justly considered as rendering his performance valuable, especially to the learner."—Philosophical Magazine.
"We have never seen a work so free from pretension and of such great merit. Various fallacies latent in the reasoning of some celebrated mathematicians, both of ancient and modern date, are pointed out and discussed in a tone of calm moderation, which we regret to say is not always employed in the scientific world."—Monthly Magazine.
"This is a work of valuable information, the conception of a most enlightened mind, and executed with a simplicity which cannot but carry the important truth it speaks of, home to the conviction of every understanding."—Weekly Times.

THE ELEMENTS OF ANALYTICAL GEOMETRY; comprehending the Doctrine of the Conic Sections, and the General Theory of Curves and Surfaces of the second order, with a variety of local Problems on Lines and Surfaces. Intended for the use of Mathematical Students in Schools and Universities.

"If works like the present be introduced generally into our schools and colleges, the continent will not long boast of its immense superiority over the country of Newton, in every branch of modern analytical science."—Atlas.

ELEMENTS OF PLANE AND SPHERICAL TRIGONOMETRY, comprehending the Theory of Navigation and of Nautical Astronomy.

ELEMENTS OF MECHANICS, comprehend-

EDUCATION.

LESSONS on THINGS, intended to improve Children in the Practice of Observation, Reflection and Description, on the System of Pestalozzi, edited by John Frost, A. M.

The publishers request the attention of teachers, school committees, and all who are desirous of improving the methods of instruction, to this work, which is on a plan hitherto unattempted by any school-book in this country, and which has been attended with extraordinary success in England.

The following remarks on the work are extracted from the "Quarterly Journal of Education."

"This little volume is a 'corrected and re-corrected' edition of lessons actually given to children, and, therefore, possesses a value to which no book made in the closet can lay claim, being the result of actual experiment. The work consists of a number of lessons, divided into five series; beginning with subjects the most easy and elementary, it gradually increases in difficulty, each successive step being adapted to the mind of the child as it acquires fresh stores of knowledge.

"Every part of these lessons is interesting to the child, both on account of the active operation into which his own mind is necessarily called by the *manner* in which the lessons are given; and also by the attractive nature of many of the *materials* which form the subject of the lessons. In the first and most elementary series, the pupil is *simply taught* to make a right use of his organs of sense, and to exercise his judgment so far only as relates to the objects about him; and accordingly the matter brought before him at this stage, is such that its obvious properties can be discovered and described by a child who has acquired a tolerable knowledge of his mother tongue."

OUTLINES of HISTORY, from the Earliest Records to the Present Time. Prepared for the Use of Schools, with Questions, by John Frost, A. M.

"The main object of the work is, by giving a selection of interesting and striking facts from more elaborate histories, properly and carefully arranged, with chronological tables, to render the study of general history less dry and repulsive than it has been heretofore. This, we think is fully accomplished. Very great care appears to have been bestowed on the selections, and in arranging the chronological tables, as well as in the classification of the historical matter into parts and chapters. The work will sufficiently recommend itself to all who examine it."—*Sat. Evening Post.*

"To concentrate in one comparatively small volume, a complete epitome of the entire history of the world, ancient and modern, so treated as to present a correct image of it, would seem to be an object to be wished for, rather than expected; the 'Outlines of History,' however, realize this object."—*Asiatic Journal.*

"We consider that Mr. F. has done a service to schools, by the time and labor which he has bestowed upon this work; the marginal dates will be found of great service, but the chapters of questions upon the text, and upon the maps, to illustrate the geography of the history, will especially recommend the work to the attention of teachers."—*U. S. Gazette.*

Philadelphia, July 10th, 1831.
"The 'Outlines of History,' I consider an excellent class-book of general history for the use of schools. The questions added by Mr. Frost, are a most valuable auxiliary for the teacher as well as the pupil. I shall use the 'Outlines' in my school, and cordially recommend it to parents and teachers.   S. C. WALKER."

Philadelphia, April 30th, 1831.
"Dear Sir,—I have just received a copy of your edition of the 'Outlines of History.' From a cursory perusal, I am disposed to give it a high rank as a school-book. So well satisfied am I with the arrangement and execution of the work, that I intend to put it immediately into the hands of a class in my own school.

FRENCH.

BY A. BOLMAR.

A COLLECTION of COLLOQUIAL PHRASES on every Topic necessary to maintain Conversation, arranged under different heads, with numerous remarks on the peculiar pronunciation and use of various words—the whole so disposed as considerably to facilitate the acquisition of a correct pronunciation of the French. By A. Bolmar. One vol. 18mo.

A SELECTION of ONE HUNDRED PERRIN'S FABLES, accompanied by a Key; containing the text, a literal and free translation, arranged in such a manner as to point out the difference between the French and the English idiom, also a figured pronunciation of the French, according to the best French work extant on the subject; the whole preceded by a short treatise on the sounds of the French language, compared with those of the English.

LES AVENTURES DE TELEMAQUE PAR FENELON, accompanied by a Key to the first eight books; containing like the Fables—the Text—a Literal—and Free Translation; intended as a Sequel to the Fables.

The expression 'figured pronunciation,' is above employed to express that the words in the Key to the French Fables are spelt and divided as they are pronounced. It is what WALKER *has done in his Critical Pronouncing Dictionary; for instance, he indicates the pronunciation of the word* enough, *by dividing and spelling it thus,* e-nuf. *In the same manner I indicate the pronunciation of the word* comptaient *thus,* kon-tè. *As the understanding of the figured pronunciation of* WALKER *requires the student to be acquainted with the primitive sounds of the English vowels, he must likewise, before he can understand the figured pronunciation of the French, make himself acquainted with the 20 primitive sounds of the French vowels. This any intelligent person can get from a native, or from anybody who reads French well, in a few hours.*

A COMPLETE TREATISE on the GENDERS of FRENCH NOUNS; in a small pamphlet of fourteen pages.

This little work, which is the most complete of the kind, is the fruit of great labor, and will prove of immense service to every learner.

ALL THE FRENCH VERBS, both REGULAR and IRREGULAR, in a small volume.

The verbs *être* to be, *avoir* to have, *parler* to speak, *finir* to finish, *recevoir* to receive, *vendre* to sell, *se lever* to rise, *se bien porter* to be well, *s'en aller* to go away, are here all conjugated through—*affirmatively*—*negatively*—*interrogatively*—and *negatively* and *interrogatively*—an arrangement which will greatly facilitate the scholar in his learning the French verbs and which will save the master the trouble of explaining over and over again what may be much more easily learned from books, thus leaving him more time to give his pupil, during the lesson, that instruction which cannot be found in books, but which must be learned from a master.

NEUMAN'S SPANISH and ENGLISH DICTIONARY. New Edition, in one vol.

∎

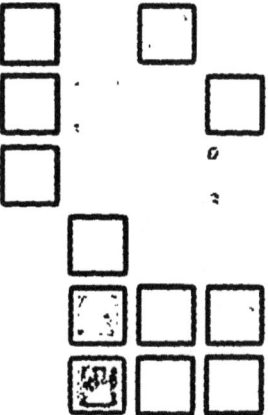

CPSIA information can be obtained
at www.ICGtesting.com
Printed in the USA
LVHW041454270323
742704LV00011B/974